Mozart's Music of Friends

In 1829 Goethe famously described the string quartet as "a conversation among four intelligent people." Inspired by this metaphor, Edward Klorman's study draws on a wide variety of documentary and iconographic sources to explore Mozart's chamber works as "the music of friends." Illuminating the meanings and historical foundations of comparisons between chamber music and social interplay, Klorman infuses the analysis of sonata form and phrase rhythm with a performer's sensibility. He develops a new analytical method called multiple agency that interprets the various players within an ensemble as participants in stylized social intercourse – characters capable of surprising, seducing, outwitting, and even deceiving one another musically. This book is accompanied by online resources that include original recordings performed by the author and other musicians, as well as video analyses that invite the reader to experience the interplay in time, as if from within the ensemble.

EDWARD KLORMAN is Assistant Professor of Music Theory and Viola at Queens College and The Graduate Center, City University of New York (CUNY). He also teaches graduate analysis seminars and chamber music performance at The Juilliard School, where he was founding chair of the Music Theory and Analysis department. Committed to intersections between musical scholarship and performance, he currently serves as co-chair of the Performance and Analysis Interest Group of the Society for Music Theory. He has performed as guest artist with the Borromeo, Orion, and Ying Quartets and the Lysander Trio, and he is featured on two albums of chamber music from Albany Records. He has published and presented widely on topics in the performance of eighteenth-century chamber music.

Frontispiece: Artist unknown, *String Quartet Playing under a Bust of Mozart*, nineteenth century. Lithograph, likely based on a painting (whereabouts unknown). Czech Museum of Music, National Museum, Prague.

Mozart's Music of Friends

Social Interplay in the Chamber Works

———

EDWARD KLORMAN

Foreword by Patrick McCreless

CAMBRIDGE
UNIVERSITY PRESS

CAMBRIDGE
UNIVERSITY PRESS

University Printing House, Cambridge CB2 8BS, United Kingdom

One Liberty Plaza, 20th Floor, New York, NY 10006, USA

477 Williamstown Road, Port Melbourne, VIC 3207, Australia

4843/24, 2nd Floor, Ansari Road, Daryaganj, Delhi - 110002, India

79 Anson Road, #06-04/06, Singapore 079906

Cambridge University Press is part of the University of Cambridge.

It furthers the University's mission by disseminating knowledge in the pursuit of education, learning and research at the highest international levels of excellence.

www.cambridge.org
Information on this title: www.cambridge.org/9781107474666

First published 2016
First paperback edition 2017

A catalogue record for this publication is available from the British Library

Library of Congress Cataloging in Publication data
Names: Klorman, Edward, 1982–
Title: Mozart's music of friends : social interplay in the chamber
works / Edward Klorman ; foreword by Patrick McCreless.
Description: Cambridge : Cambridge University Press, 2016. | Includes
bibliographical references and index.
Identifiers: LCCN 2015035033 | ISBN 9781107093652 (Hardback : alk. paper)
Subjects: LCSH: Mozart, Wolfgang Amadeus, 1756–1791–Criticism and
interpretation. | Chamber music–18th century–History and criticism.
Classification: LCC ML410.M9 K78 2016 | DDC 785.0092–dc23 LC record
available at http://lccn.loc.gov/2015035033

ISBN 978-1-107-09365-2 Hardback
ISBN 978-1-107-47466-6 Paperback

Additional resources for this publication at www.cambridge.org/9781107474666

In memoriam
CHARLES ROSEN
1927–2012

Classic textures have strong mimetic values. Individual voices or parts in [a chamber] ensemble can move with or against each other much as actors or dancers do on the stage. Their musical figures are like gestures, taking on bold relief in the free and varied interplay of classic part-writing. The typical sound of classic instrumental music – transparent, with neat and uncluttered layouts and luminous, balanced sonorities – promotes this "little theater."

– Leonard G. Ratner, *Classic Music: Expression, Form and Style* (New York: Schirmer, 1980), 118

Contents

Figures

Frontispiece: Artist unknown, *String Quartet Playing under a Bust of Mozart*, nineteenth century. Lithograph, likely based on a painting (whereabouts unknown). Czech Museum of Music, National Museum, Prague. [*page* ii]

1.1 Heliogravure by Franz Hanfstaengl, 1907, after Julius Schmid, *Haydn Quartet*, c. 1905–6 (painting now lost). Vienna City Museum. Reproduced by permission. [5]

1.2 String quartet table (*Quartetttisch*), late-eighteenth century. Kunsthistorisches Museum, Vienna. Reproduced by permission of the KHM-Museumsverband. [7]

1.3 Detail from title page of Haydn, Piano Trio, Hob. XV:10. Vienna: Artaria, 1798. Reproduced by the permission of the Jean Gray Hargrove Music Library, University of California, Berkeley. [8]

1.4 Gabriel Jacques de Saint-Aubin, *The Musical Duo*, c. 1772. Watercolor, gouache, brown and black ink, and graphite. The Fine Arts Museums of San Francisco. Reproduced by permission. [8]

1.5 Nicolaes Aartman, *Interior with a Musical Gathering*, c. 1723–60. Graphite and watercolor. Rijksmuseum, Amsterdam. Reproduced by permission. [9]

2.1 Title page of Haydn, String Quartets, op. 1, nos. 1–4. Paris: La Chevardière, [1764]. Reproduced by the permission of the Jean Gray Hargrove Music Library, University of California, Berkeley. [31]

2.2 Jeremy Ballard, caricature of Amadeus Quartet first violinist Norbert Brainin (left) and violist Peter Schidlof (right) performing the Mozart *Sinfonia concertante*. Reproduced by permission of Kay Ballard. [40]

3.1 Johann Ernst Mansfeld, *Private Concert during Court Mourning*. Engraving published in Joseph Richter, *Bildergalerie weltlicher Misbräuche: ein Gegenstück zur Bildergalerie katholischer und klösterlicher* (Frankfurt and Leipzig, 1785), 38. Reproduced by permission of the Burke Library, Union Theological Seminary. [93]

Music examples

Foreword

Patrick McCreless
Yale University

What Edward Klorman brings to Mozart's chamber music is not a single perspective, but a combination of three: performance, theory and analysis, and history. The strength of his book inheres in the skill with which he brings these perspectives to bear on Mozart's chamber music, and in the imagination with which he combines them into an original synthesis. In his own experience, performance came first. Trained as a violist, he has learned over many years what it feels like, and sounds like, to be in a chamber ensemble – especially in the middle of such an ensemble, where violists invariably find themselves. Through his experience in performance he developed an interest in music theory and analysis, which he then pursued through graduate school. His living with the chamber music repertoire as both performer and analyst accordingly inspired a curiosity about its history, especially that of Mozart's chamber works – and hence, the book you are about to read.

But what about history? In our current culture of Western art music, chamber music is regarded as the most rarified and elitist of genres – musicians' music *par excellence*. At a string quartet concert one expects to find educated and knowledgeable listeners – listeners who can follow, and who indeed delight in, the musical arguments set before them. Nor is much of the chamber repertoire easy to play. Beethoven's middle and late string quartets, Schubert's quartets and piano trios, all Brahms's chamber music, and the quartets and other chamber pieces of canonic twentieth-century composers such as Bartók, Shostakovich, and Carter: These works, and many, many more, demand professional musicians of the highest caliber – even well-rehearsed professional musicians of the highest caliber. Pushing back against this hyper-refined concept of chamber music, Klorman draws our attention to what we have known for a long time, but which has generally been lost in the public consciousness: Chamber music was born, in the second half of the eighteenth century, not in the concert hall (the concert hall itself was just in the process of being born then), but in the aristocratic salon. Not only was such music not intended for professional performers; it was not even intended for "listeners," if by listeners we mean those who listen to professionally prepared chamber works in formal concert situations. Rather, string quartets and piano trios, and sonatas for piano and violin, to name the most popular genres, were fashioned for capable amateurs to play *a prima vista* – at first sight – at aristocratic social gatherings, for their own enjoyment and that of those present who chose to listen for a while rather than participate in conversation.

This is where Klorman begins, with the late-eighteenth-century's favorite metaphor for chamber music in general, and the string quartet in particular – *conversation*. It is surely no accident that the string quartet and other chamber genres developed simultaneously in the eighteenth century with a growing interest in conversation, and with the publication of many how-to manuals and countless journal articles about it. From a recent collection of essays on the topic we read:

Conversation, as concept and practice, arrived at a pivotal, and unprecedented, stage in its development during the historical period that has come to be known as the long eighteenth century. The eighteenth century's attention to, and production of, conversational forms manifests itself in the period's plethora of texts and images that address themselves to the description and conceptualization of conversation across a range of disciplines and genres. (Halsey and Slinn, eds., *The Concept and Practice of Conversation in the Long Eighteenth Century, 1688–1848*, 2008, ix)[1]

To consider chamber works such as string quartets and piano trios as conversations was a natural step to take. Unlike the symphony, which was viewed as a formal, public statement governed by rhetoric, chamber works were experienced as conversations among individuals, and were governed by different values and different rules. The late-eighteenth-century theorist Heinrich Christoph Koch expressed the difference succinctly: "Since the melody of a sonata [of which the quartet was an exemplar] portrays the sentiments of individual people, it must be exquisitely cultivated and seem to represent the subtlest nuances of the sentiments. In contrast, the melody of the symphony must distinguish itself not through such subtleties of expression but through power and force" (Koch, *Versuch einer Anleitung zur Composition*, vol. 3, 1793, 315–16).

The telling phrase here is "individual people." If the individual instruments of a chamber ensemble each express the thoughts and sentiments of

---

[1] Since my short essay is only a foreword, I will exempt myself from the scholarly obligation of citing each source in full detail the first time it is mentioned, on the assumption that the reader can easily find all the sources in the text of the book, its bibliography, and its index.

a single person, then the interaction of the parts becomes a conversation, and the individual players become agents who enact musical ideas with regard for one another. It is from this notion that Klorman derives the concept that drives the book, *multiple agency* – an idea that has its roots in both performance and music analysis, and that is also grounded historically, as he shows in abundance in the three chapters that comprise his Part I – "Historical perspectives." These chapters ably document the social history of the genre into which Mozart's chamber music fits, establishing through both citation of many primary sources and the ample work of music historians that this music was/is indeed "the music of friends," that its practice involved sight-reading rather than rehearsing, and that the textural freedom of its ensembles enabled both changes of musical topic within a single movement and easy interchange of voices back and forth, with one voice after another claiming primary agency in the temporal unfolding of the music.

Klorman has done his homework: He builds carefully on important work of others, as his numerous references to scholars past and present make clear. He is up to date, for example, on the work of those who have contributed to our understanding of the history of the string quartet in the eighteenth century through studies of sources, style, and social contexts – scholars such as Cliff Eisen, Ludwig Finscher, Floyd and Margaret Grave, Mary Hunter, Simon Keefe, Elisabeth Le Guin, Nancy November, Elaine Sisman, W. Dean Sutcliffe, and Gretchen Wheelock. One older source that is of particular relevance to Klorman's project, since it is of analytical more than historical character, is Charles Rosen's eye-opening (for me, at least, in 1971) discussion, in *The Classical Style*, of how a single voice in Haydn's quartets can morph imperceptibly from tune to lively rhythmic accompaniment before our very ears (Rosen, *The Classical Style* 1971/1997, 141–42).

What he adds to such a point of view is the consistent perspective of a player from *inside* the music – from the musical experience of a violist, whose roles have surely included putting up with a first violin's penchant for being the star, providing harmonic and rhythmic support for themes stated by other instruments, playing the crucial sharp that turns a sonata exposition from the tonic to the dominant, and occasionally interrupting the other players to play his own theme in the sunlight. Such a player can also imagine the experience of his/her colleagues – what it feels like to "lay back" while another instrument plays a theme, to come suddenly together in a homophonic passage, to react to a dramatic surprise introduced by another player, or to coordinate with "friends" in a taut fugato in a development section. We have all read descriptions or analyses of chamber works that discuss the music in such terms, but I know of no one who does so so explicitly from the perspective of the players, and so systematically through entire movements – or, as is the case with Klorman's Chapter 7, on Mozart's "Kegelstatt" trio, even through a whole multi-movement work.

And what shines through in his analytical chapters (Chapters 4–7) is not just the perspective of the player – a perspective that at least at times, is that of an imagined musician playing and experiencing the music for the first time, *a prima vista*, in a late-eighteenth-century salon. What also emerges is a point of view that is enriched by, and seasoned by, scholarship in modern music theory and analysis. To be sure, the modern discipline of music theory (from, say, the 1970s) is in some respects vulnerable to critique on the grounds of formalism and presentism. But, I would argue, it also offers a number of elements that, used sensitively, can bring us closer to, rather than taking us farther from, historical and musical understanding. It is precisely some of these features that Klorman adopts in his book.

Having noted above some of the musicological perspectives that inform Klorman's book, I outline here some of the musical theories that are in his interpretive arsenal and that undergird his whole project. Since he generally does not introduce these systematically or place them in their larger disciplinary context, a brief overview of some of these may be useful. I should also note that he is admirably eclectic in what he brings to the table: Even though American music scholarship is divided into music theory, on the one hand, and musicology, on the other, as presumably separate disciplines, he is comfortable with both, paying little attention to such disciplinary distinctions, but rather appropriating freely whatever he finds useful. Here are some of the analytical points of view that inform his work, in some cases along with comments on the issues that they raise both in the book, and beyond.

Schenkerian theory: It might seem odd to list Schenker, whose major publications appeared between 1906 and 1935, as a recent theorist. Yet no theorist of tonal music has had a more powerful impact on Anglo-American music theory than has the Austrian Heinrich Schenker (1868–1935). In the 1970s and 1980s Schenkerian theory was essentially synonymous with tonal theory. Schenker's aesthetic – which dictated absolute devotion to the concept of the musical work, to the masterpiece as the product of (almost exclusively) German genius, and the obligation of the performer faithfully to reproduce the work in the spirit of the composer – sits uneasily with Klorman's historical tale of aristocratic amateurs sight-reading string quartets as a diversion (albeit a sophisticated and rewarding one) at dinner parties. But many of the *musical* aspects of Schenker's approach are central to Klorman's work: the centrality of harmonic and contrapuntal goal-directedness to cadences; the notion of musical levels, such that even in texturally adventurous chamber works the surface of the music is guided by an underlying simple counterpoint; and the tendency of melodic lines to move by step (especially by ascending step to points of melodic climax, and by descending step to cadential goals) – a concept that he called *melodic fluency* (*fliessender Gesang*). These concepts are foundational, and we encounter them throughout the analytical chapters of the book.

The New *Formenlehre*: *Formenlehre* is the German theory of musical form (as it functions in [mostly] German instrumental works), as developed in the nineteenth century by Adolph Bernhard Marx (1795–1866) and numerous theorists of later generations. In the eyes of some, it also reaches back to the approaches to form in the theoretical thinking of earlier generations – e.g., the work of Koch (1749–1816), whose ideas are more relevant to Mozart's chamber music than are those of Marx, who addressed himself primarily to the works of Beethoven. What makes the New *Formenlehre* "new" is that it involves the reinvigoration of an aspect of music theory that had fallen out of favor for many years, roughly from the 1960s through the 1990s. Schenker dismissed most earlier theories of form, proposing instead his own (though never fully worked-out) approach. In the decades when his influence held sway, the theory of form in tonal music became more or less moribund. Still, Edward T. Cone (*Musical Form and Musical Performance*, 1968), and Charles Rosen (*The Classical Style*, 1971/1997; *Sonata Forms*, 1982/1998) published important work on form during this period, and more recently William Caplin's *Classical Form* (1998) initiated a dramatic resurgence of interest in formal studies. Caplin's book and James Hepokoski and Warren Darcy's *Elements of Sonata Theory* (2006) constitute the two central texts of the New *Formenlehre*, which has to some degree supplanted Schenkerian theory within the world of Anglophone music theory as the industry that preserves and illuminates the Western canon of instrumental music. (Nonetheless, both theories interact with Schenkerian theory in intriguing ways, and most tonal theorists maintain competence in both Schenkerian and *Formenlehre* analysis.) In the analytical chapters of *Mozart's Music of Friends*, one encounters the New *Formenlehre* constantly, in Caplin's classification of theme-types as periods, sentences, or hybrids, and in

Hepokoski and Darcy's concept of teleology and goal-directedness toward important cadences in sonata form.

Performance and analysis: The discipline of music theory, as it has developed over the past few decades, has witnessed an ever-increasing interest in the relation of musical analysis to musical performance. Earlier studies were often glibly unidirectional – in the most one-sided endeavors, the analyst simply explained musical structure to the performer, who was then expected gratefully to incorporate these insights into his or her performance. More recent studies typically place the analyst and the performer on equal footing, with the idea that the instincts of performers are held to be as likely to offer insights to analysts as the observations of analysts are thought to be valuable for performers. Klorman, who has one foot firmly planted in each camp, is a committed proponent of the latter point of view, and an entertaining and informative aspect of his book is experiencing how his musician's sense of multiple agency – how individual musical parts/players pass around themes, interchange leading and accompanying functions, and compete, jostle, and joke with one another – squares with his analytical insights.

The body and musical gesture: From the 1960s through much of the 1980s the enterprises of historical musicology and music theory were predominantly positivist and formalist – musicologists focusing on the study of historical documents, theorists on theory-based music analysis. But the late 1980s and 1990s saw a sea change, thanks in part to Joseph Kerman's *Contemplating Music* (1985), which took both disciplines to task and called for a newly humanistic music criticism. A propitious response on both sides of the aisle was the awakening of an interest in the musical body: a response evident in musicology in the 1990s feminist work of Susan McClary and Suzanne Cusick, and in the more recent performance studies of Elisabeth Le Guin; and in music theory in studies of musical gesture by Robert Hatten, Arnie Cox, and others. Klorman's concept of multiple agency resonates nicely with this work, since the act of making live musical sound requires bodily gestures by individual musicians, and such gestures are as open to observation, analysis, and interpretation as the notes in a musical score. Study of physical and musical gestures has the advantage of directing attention away from the object that is the score to the enactment of music in real time – a change of direction very much in keeping with the broadening interests of current musical scholarship.

Theories of musical rhythm and meter: Western music theory has generally focused primarily on aspects of musical pitch and harmony, but the past thirty years have seen a rapidly increasing interest in rhythm and meter. I need not address this issue in detail here, because Chapter 6 of *Mozart's Music of Friends* is entirely dedicated to the analysis and interpretation of musical meter in some of the chamber works, in the context of multiple agency. Of the seven chapters of the book, this is easily the one most explicitly based on specific theories, and Klorman explains their particulars and historical context adequately in the text, so that discussion here is unnecessary. Recent theories of meter show how it is established perceptually, and how it functions not only on the measure-to-measure level but also on the level of three- and four-measure units and beyond. As is eminently evident in Chapter 6, such theories afford rich insights into Mozart's chamber works, showing how their frequent asymmetry and unpredictability have important ramifications for performers, listeners, and analysts.

Musical topics: A wonderful and frequently noted feature of Mozart's music, both instrumental and vocal (and especially operatic), is its capability of moving, whether smoothly or abruptly, from one expressive state or register to another: from military march, to gentle and lyrical melody, to show of virtuosity. The historian Leonard Ratner called attention to this aspect of mid- to late-eighteenth-century music in his *Classic Music: Expression, Form, and Style* (1980), and his students Wye Jamison Allanbrook and Kofi Agawu helped to bring the idea of such musical "topics," as they are called, into the musical mainstream. Further work by Robert Hatten and Raymond Monelle, both of whom have brought the perspective of semiotics into music scholarship, has been especially influential in the ongoing loosening of the grasp of formalism on music theory, and the recent *Oxford Handbook of Topic Theory*, edited by Danuta Mirka (2014), synthesizes a variety of historical and analytical perspectives within a single, comprehensive volume. This is yet another thread that enriches Klorman's account of Mozart's chamber music.

Music as play: Finally, an appealing aspect of Klorman's book is its willingness to *play*: to indulge in fantasy and language that mimic how musicians, whether of the eighteenth century or the twenty-first, might speak with one another about what they are doing. Without compromising the insightfulness or sophistication of his work, he is able to write cheerily about instrumental personas being chummy, coquettish, suave, and much more – far beyond what we're used to reading in analytical music theory, but refreshing, perceptive, and invariably assuring us that we are in the company of a sensitive and knowledgeable musician.

Preface

According to an oft-recounted founding myth, Haydn's first forays into quartet writing were motivated by a social occasion:

The following purely chance circumstances had led him to try his luck at the composition of quartets. A Baron Fürnberg had a place in Weinzierl, several stages from Vienna [about 50 miles], and he invited from time to time his pastor, his manager, Haydn, and Albrechtsberger (a brother of the celebrated contrapuntist, who played the violoncello) in order to have a little music. Fürnberg requested Haydn to compose something that could be performed by these four amateurs. Haydn, then eighteen years old, took up this proposal, and so originated his first quartet [see Ex. 0.1], which immediately appeared, received such great approval that Haydn took courage to work further in this form.[1]

Ex. 0.1 Haydn, String Quartet in B♭ Major ("La chasse"), op. 1, no. 1, Presto (i)

While this charming story is hardly a factual history of the string quartet's birth,[2] it does exemplify an intertwining of sociability and chamber music prevalent in late-eighteenth- and early-nineteenth-century thought. At the time, the typical setting for playing sonatas and ensemble chamber music was the drawing room, a space that also served as the venue for gatherings

---

[1] Georg August Griesinger, *Biographische Notizen über Joseph Haydn* (Leipzig, 1810), 15–16 (Web Doc. #7). English translation from Vernon Gotwals, trans., *Haydn: Two Contemporary Portraits*, by Georg August Griesinger and Albert Christoph Dies (Madison: University of Wisconsin Press, 1968), 13. On the capacity of string quartets to forge bonds of friendship, compare Griesinger's remarks to an essay, also published in 1810, by Johann Conrad Wilhelm Petiscus (quoted in the epigraph to Chapter 1).

[2] See David P. Schroeder's appraisal of Griesinger's account in "The Art of Conversation: From Haydn to Beethoven's Early String Quartets," *Studies in Music from University of Western Ontario* 19–20 (2000–1): 377–8. See also James Webster and George Feder, *The New Grove Haydn* (New York: Macmillan, 2002), 8–9; Floyd K. Grave and Margaret Grave, *The String Quartets of Joseph Haydn* (Oxford University Press, 2006), 9–10; Mary Hunter, "The Quartets," in *The Cambridge Companion to Haydn*, ed. Caryl Clark (Cambridge University Press, 2005), 112–13; and David Wyn Jones, "The Origins of the Quartet," in *The Cambridge Companion to the String Quartet*, ed. Robin Stowell (Cambridge University Press, 2003), 177–78.

with witty, artful conversation and conviviality among friends. Could it be that social elements, manifest in the conception and playing of chamber music, *were also composed into musical scores?*

This book examines stylized social intercourse as it is encoded in Mozart's chamber music and animated by the musicians who play it. I was initially drawn to this subject by a dissonance I perceived between my education as a music theorist and my experience performing chamber music as a violist. Inspired by ideas I encountered as a student during coachings with eminent interpreters of Mozart's chamber music – including Robert Levin, Pamela Frank, and members of the Borromeo, Brentano, Emerson, Juilliard, Orion, and Takács Quartets – I was eager to capture in my analytical writing the moment-to-moment interchanges and "conversations" among instrumental parts that make this music so enjoyable to play. Yet I struggled to forge this connection between scholarly inquiry and performance experience using existing analytical methods. This book is the fruit of my effort to resolve that dissonance and to unite the two halves of my musical life.

The argument proceeds in two phases, the first historical and the second analytical. The historical survey in Part I begins with accounts of Mozart's own domestic music-making (Chapter 1) followed by a study of the eighteenth- and early-nineteenth-century sources that describe chamber music as a metaphorical conversation or social interaction among the instruments (Chapter 2). Whereas the comparison of the string quartet to conversation was most famously articulated by Johann Wolfgang von Goethe, his remark is but one in a long tradition that originates in the 1770s and continues to this day. Chapter 3 examines aspects of private music-making that engendered a temporal, of-the-moment quality. Specifically, the evidently common practice of playing at sight and from individual parts (since scores were rarely available, even for chamber music with piano) suggests an experience of moment-to-moment musical discovery that shares affinities with improvisation and that departs from today's public performances, which are carefully prepared in advance.

Part II develops a concept I call *multiple agency*, which refers to the capacity for independent action on the part of musical characters enacted by the various instrumentalists. This perspective, a refinement to traditional metaphors of conversation, offers a new vantage point for analyzing form and phrase rhythm as the interplay among these performer-personas. Instead of framing an analysis in terms of "what happens" in a musical work, one might conceive of a violin character seeking a cadence while a cello character evades it, or of clarinet and piano characters who exchange a melodic motive but disagree about its proper hypermetrical context. Multiple agency becomes a vocabulary for and theoretical model of how chamber music players conceive of their musical actions and agency as they play. It furthermore underscores their authority as creative agents in their own performances, as opposed to more conventional discourses that ascribe agency to "the work" or "the composer." While this analytical perspective is a thoroughly modern invention, it is nevertheless inspired by the historical ideas surveyed in Part I as well as by my own experience playing this music.

The Epilogue examines more closely the relationship of the historical and analytical parts of the book. I also address what multiple agency may offer chamber musicians performing today and situate it relative to current scholarship on musical performance. Suffice it to say, I do not intend an oversimple, one-to-one correspondence between how "they" played in Mozart's time and how "we" should analyze or perform today. Nor is "they" even a useful construct, since chamber music practices varied widely from Vienna to Paris to London, between amateurs and professionals, and in salon settings compared to more public spaces.

In recent decades, the analysis of musical "works" has come under scrutiny by some musicologists on a variety of grounds: (1) that musical analysis so defined tends to privilege composers and scores over the people who played and listened to them; (2) that it tends to essentialize a post-1800 concept of musical workhood; and (3) that it tends toward anachronism by inventing concepts and terminology foreign to the music's original context. As it is my aim within these pages to bring historical, analytical, and performance perspectives closer together, I am mindful of these critiques. In fact, the concept of multiple agency is inspired by them: Whereas some passages of chamber music may seem to express the agency of a single, unified persona ("the work" or "the composer"), the examples I have chosen for analysis are those in which distinct "characters" demonstrate their capacity to act independently, at times even in opposition to one another. This focus draws attention to the role musicians play in enacting the social interplay for which the score is but a script. Mozart may have chosen the notes, but the players compose the musical dialogue as they find meaning in their musical utterances, gestures, and interactions, in time, as they play. Listeners, when they are present, are then drawn into the social discourse through mimetic engagement. Although the medium of the scholarly monograph necessarily uses annotated scores to present analytical interpretations, the truest form of multiple-agency analysis, perhaps, is that conducted tacitly by musicians as they play together from their individual parts. The analytical videos provided among the Web Resources (about which more soon) are my best effort to simulate this experience, and I encourage readers to watch them while reading the analyses.

This book does not offer anything like a comprehensive survey of Mozart's chamber music output, nor does it endeavor to survey the diverse landscape of composers and performers active during this period; other existing volumes present excellent style criticism along these lines. Rather, my principal aim is to develop an original analytical method, explore its historical and conceptual underpinnings, and test it through a series of analyses ranging from short passages to whole movements to one complete composition (Mozart's "Kegelstatt" trio, K. 498).

Although this book focuses almost exclusively on Mozart, the multiple agency concept surely has something to offer other repertoires – beyond the late-eighteenth century, beyond instrumental chamber music, beyond Western music. I welcome future contributions from other scholars who may wish to pursue these ideas further and in new contexts.

Advice to readers

I have endeavored to compose this book for a diverse readership, which may include historical musicologists, music theorists, performers, and Mozart enthusiasts of all stripes. For readers principally interested in my analytical method, the theoretical exposition commences in Part II, which may be read as a standalone study. But as the historical voices examined in Part I provide a richer context for the analyses, I recommend reading it first and believe it will reward the time spent.

For readers unfamiliar with recent theories of musical agency, sonata form, and meter: Although Part II involves some amount of technical language, jargon is kept to a minimum and terminology is explained along the way. Additional background and clarification are available through the supplemental Web Resources. Some readers may prefer to bypass Chapters 4–6 to begin with, proceeding directly to the discussion of Mozart's "Kegelstatt" trio, K. 498, in Chapter 7, and only then circling back for some more rigorous analyses and a discussion of their theoretical foundations.

Notes on the text

On the use of third-person pronouns: I refer to musical participants as "he" or "she" somewhat in accordance with the gendered realities of the late-eighteenth century, when performance on string and wind instruments was reserved for men, while women enjoyed more equal treatment as keyboard players and, of course, as listeners. I will largely follow this convention both for real-world instrumentalists and their fictional personas, a distinction I introduce in Chapter 4. For any readers – especially Italian speakers – who are troubled by the masculine pronoun "he" in reference to the grammatically feminine "viola," I beg forgiveness for this dissonance.

All translations are my own unless otherwise indicated. Citations stating "English translation *from* ..." indicate that the quoted text is from the cited translation, whereas citations stating "see English translation in ..." or "see also English translation in ..." merely cross-reference a published translation to supplement my own. For short passages, the original, foreign-language text is generally provided in a footnote. More extended original texts appear online (as explained below).

Harmonies are indicated with uppercase Roman numerals only, regardless of chord quality. Scale degrees are designated as $\hat{1}$, $\hat{2}$, $\hat{3}$, etc. Pitches (and pitch classes) are generally designated simply as uppercase letter names. When more clarity about a precise register is required, I have adopted the following Helmholtz-like system: CC, C, c, c^1, c^2, c^3, where middle C is c^1. I have occasionally added the indication "great octave" to clarify in cases when a capital letter refers to the specific register as opposed to the pitch class. Captions for musical examples use lowercase Roman numerals to indicate the number of a given movement within a large-scale composition.

The abbreviation PAC, for "perfect authentic cadence" (introduced in Chapter 4), refers approximately to what many European scholars (following Rameau) call a "perfect cadence" (from root-position V to root-position I), except that it furthermore requires the melody to close on the tonic note. If the melody instead closes on $\hat{3}$, it is deemed an "imperfect authentic cadence," which is considered to be a weaker cadence. The distinction between these two types of authentic cadence accords with compositional theories contemporaneous to Mozart (see the references to Heinrich Christoph Koch in Chapter 5) and is an important consideration in the analysis of sonata form. A cadence that comes to rest on a root-position V harmony – sometimes called an "imperfect cadence" or "semicadence" – will be designated a "half cadence" (HC). For more information about the categories of cadence observed in this book, readers may consult the two publications by William E. Caplin listed in the bibliography.

Though style manuals advise authors to avoid lengthy footnotes, I confess that I have not heeded this wise guideline within these pages. As a part-time historian, trained primarily in music analysis and performance, some of my greatest joys in writing this book have been encountering compelling historical anecdotes and connections that, although not strictly essential to my central argument, provide colorful sidelights along the way. Since some of these documents will not be known to many readers and can be difficult to access, I have erred on the side of inclusion, quoting rather than paraphrasing historical documents and, where possible, citing them in both original and modern editions. But to avoid a meandering main text, I have relegated some sources to footnotes. Readers whose curiosity is piqued by historical details are invited to peruse the footnotes, but those who prefer a more streamlined reading can rest assured that the main text is self-sufficient and presents the complete argument.

Edward Klorman
New York, spring 2015

Acknowledgments

Chamber music is a collaborative art in which musical ideas blossom through an animated interchange; each person makes a distinctive, essential contribution. This book developed in much the same way, and I wish to acknowledge the many people who have shaped its development. First and foremost, I thank William Rothstein (who supervised the dissertation on which this book is based and whom I am honored to count among my colleagues at the Aaron Copland School of Music, Queens College, CUNY) for his enthusiastic engagement with this project over the course of several years. The integration of historical, analytical, and performance perspectives in his research and teaching, along with the imposing example set by his scholarly discipline, has shaped my own perspective. I am also enormously grateful to L. Poundie Burstein and Joseph Straus for their generous support, advice, and encouragement from the earliest stages of my work on this book.

I have also been fortunate to discuss aspects of this research with Kofi Agawu, Ellen Bakulina, Tom Beghin, Zachary Bernstein, William E. Caplin, Norman Carey, Nicholas Cook, Roger Graybill, L. Michael Griffel, Robert Hatten, James Hepokoski, Richard Kramer, Joseph Kraus, Joel Lester, Warwick Lister, Simon McVeigh, Danuta Mirka, Seth Monahan, Fabio Morabito, Markus Neuwirth, Nancy November, John Rink, Carl Schachter, Liza Stepanova, W. Dean Sutcliffe, Roger Tapping, and Channan Willner, as well as with dozens of students who have participated in my seminars on Mozart's chamber music or in ensembles I have coached at The Juilliard School. All of these conversations have stimulated many ideas that appear within these pages.

Special thanks are due to William Rothstein and Liza Stepanova for their consultations regarding translations from German, and to Rafael Klorman for his assistance with those from French. Their many fine suggestions helped to render sometimes-unwieldy historical texts into clear, English prose. Markus Neuwirth and Alexandra Moellmann kindly assisted with interpreting a number of regional or antiquated German words found in Mozart's letters.

David Bynog graciously read an early draft and has been an uncommonly forthcoming consultant on a wide variety of matters; his sound advice and meticulous attention to detail have influenced this book for the better. Patrick McCreless, Rowland Moseley, and Nathan Pell reviewed the final manuscript, and for their expert suggestions and extraordinary generosity, I am deeply grateful. Two anonymous readers offered vital feedback that helped this book take shape in its current form. I thank my commissioning editors from Cambridge University Press: Vicki Cooper, who guided me through the initial proposal process, and Katharina Brett, who took over for the final stages after Vicki's retirement. Fleur Jones, assistant editor at CUP, deserves particular recognition for coordinating every aspect of the process with such remarkable virtuosity. Thanks are due to my production editor Sarah Starkey for her time and expertise, and to my copy-editor Andrew Dawes, who turned the final review of the manuscript into a particularly rewarding collaboration. Any errors that remain in this book are my own.

The Aaron Copland School of Music provided generous subvention funding and afforded me release time to complete this book. Additional subvention funding was provided by a grant from the Society for Music Theory. John A. Rice was a valuable and generous consultant, especially in matters of musical iconography. I also thank Kim de Beaumont (Hunter College and Pace University), Albert Rice (independent scholar), and Nicholas Wise (Frick Collection) for sharing their expertise about artwork that appears in this book. Rex Isenberg expertly typeset the musical examples, and Samantha Schaefer oversaw graphic design work for musical examples and figures.

The following museums, libraries, and publishing houses generously furnished materials reproduced in this book: Burke Library, Union Theological Seminary, Columbia University; Czech Museum of Music, National Museum, Prague; Fine Arts Museums of San Francisco; Jean Gray Hargrove Music Library, University of California, Berkeley; Kunsthistorisches Museum, Vienna; Metropolitan Museum of Art, New York; MIT Press; Nederlands Muziek Instituut, The Hague; Oxford University Press; Rijksmuseum, Amsterdam; Vienna City Museum; and Universal Edition.

Kay Ballard kindly provided permission to reproduce the cartoon by her late husband, Jeremy Ballard, that appears as Fig. 2.2. I am grateful to Bernard Zaslav (former violist of the Kohon, Composers, Fine Arts, Vermeer, and Stanford String Quartets) for bringing this drawing to my attention, and to Michael Dennison for providing information about the artist. The musical comedy duo Igudesman & Joo granted permission to include their video "Endless Coda" (arranged and adapted from the Finale of "Colonel Bogey Variations" by Dudley Moore) among the Web

Resources. I thank all copyright holders for permission to reproduce these materials; all copyrights belong to their respective owners.

I dedicate this work to my family, whose constant love and support over many years have made me who I am; and to my major viola teachers, Heidi Castleman and Libba Seka, whose wisdom and guidance have shaped my musical sensibilities. And above all, I thank my partner, Heath, whose love, companionship, and support throughout this project have seen me through the best and worst of times.

About the web resources

www.mozartsmusicoffriends.com
The web resources comprise a variety of supplemental materials designed to enhance the reading experience. Although the print volume is self-sufficient, the online materials are recommended. They are divided into the following sections:

Chapter resources

Throughout the book, the symbol ▶ next to a musical example or section heading indicates that a corresponding recording and analytical video are available online. These videos present a recorded performance of a given excerpt timed to a scrolling score with animated annotations, thus allowing the analyses to be experienced more viscerally. Some readers may opt to watch the videos first for an overview and to return to the prose discussion after for a more detailed presentation. These recordings and videos are organized by chapter and are generally numbered to correspond to the printed examples to which they pertain. Thus, Video 4.2 corresponds to Ex. 4.2 in the book and is filed online under resources for Chapter 4. (In a few cases, videos are given descriptive names rather than numbers, since they either pertain to multiple examples or to music not included as an example in the book.)

For two extended musical examples too lengthy to include in the text, PDF scores are provided online among the resources for the relevant chapter: J. J. de Momigny's analysis/arrangement of Mozart's String Quartet in D Minor, K. 421 (Chapter 2) and Mozart's "Kegelstatt" trio, K. 498 (Chapter 7).

The video "Endless Coda" by the musical comedy duo Igudesman & Joo – referenced in Chapter 4 – is included among that chapter's resources.

Also provided are brief primers entitled "Notes on Sonata Form" and "Notes on Metrical Theory," which offer background information about theories that inform Chapters 5 and 6; some readers may find these helpful.

Web documents

This section provides original, untranslated texts for extended quotations presented in English translation in the book. References in the form of "Web Doc. #x" refer readers to this online resource, in which sources are ordered alphabetically by author, or by title for anonymous sources. Excerpts from Mozart's letters are excluded because their original texts are easily accessible in Bauer and Deutsch's complete edition, which also appears online at http://dme.mozarteum.at.

Illustrations

This section provides color images for paintings that are reproduced in grayscale in the book. Likewise, for figures in the text representing details from larger images, the complete versions are provided online. For ease of cross-reference, these illustrations are assigned figure numbers identical to the corresponding material in the book.

A variety of supplemental illustrations that do not appear in the text are also provided, which readers may enjoy perusing. Most of these pertain to eighteenth-century domestic music-making but a handful relate to the game skittles (*Kegelspiel*), the sport for which Mozart's "Kegelstatt" trio was named (as explained in Chapter 7). To facilitate browsing, the illustrations are divided into categories, within which they are ordered alphabetically by artist's surname or by title when the artist is unknown.

Musician biographies

For the musical recordings, in which I feature as violist, it was my very good fortune to perform together with such fine musicians, many of them faculty colleagues, former students, or former classmates from The Juilliard School: Charles Neidich, clarinetist; Laura Strickling, soprano; Matthew Patrick Morris, baritone; Liza Stepanova, pianist; Siwoo Kim and Emily Daggett Smith, violinists; and Alice Yoo, cellist. Their artistry and generosity enhance this book enormously, making the connection between musical scholarship and performance all the more tangible. Brief biographies of each musician are provided online.

I wish in particular to recognize Laura Strickling for her enthusiasm taking on the staggering role of Dido in J. J. de Momigny's adaptation of Mozart's String Quartet in D Minor, K. 421, in what is in all likelihood its first performance. What Momigny has achieved in musical notation and prose, Laura has acccomplished in sound, transforming Mozart's idiomatic violin music into a coloratura aria. I also thank Ryan Streber of Oktaven Audio for producing the recordings so beautifully.

PART I

Historical perspectives

1 | The music of friends

From the Tagus to the Neva, our quartets are played. Not only in larger cities everywhere [but] also in smaller ones [and] even in some villages, wherever there are friends of music [*Musikfreunde*] who play string instruments, they get together to play quartets. The magic of music makes everyone equal and binds together in friendship those whom rank and conditions would otherwise have kept eternally apart . . . Those who ever drank together became friends; [but] the quartet table [*Quartetttisch*] will soon replace the pub table [*Schenktisch*]. A person cannot hate anyone with whom he has ever made music in earnest. Those who throughout a winter have united on their own initiative to play quartets will remain good friends for life.

–Johann Conrad Wilhelm Petiscus, "Ueber Quartettmusik" (1810)[1]

The environment in which a musical genre developed is often deeply intertwined with that genre's history and style. A study of Bach's cantatas, for instance, is greatly enhanced by awareness of their original liturgical context in Lutheran practice, just as a full account of the history of Italian opera surely considers the ethos of the opera house, along with the singers, impresarios, and audiences who inhabited it. Scholarship on the "place" for which a work was conceived can examine not only a cultural setting and social context but also the physical performance space. For example, the layout of St. Mark's Basilica was vital in the development of the antiphonal style of the Venetian school, just as the design of Wagner's theater at Bayreuth was essential for the realization of his concept of music drama as *Gesamtkunstwerk*.

---

[1] [Johann Conrad Wilhelm] P[etiscus], "Ueber Quartettmusik," *Allgemeine musikalische Zeitung (Leipzig)* 12, no. 33 (May 16, 1810): col. 514 (Web Doc. #23). Although the article is simply signed "P.," the writer is identified as Petiscus, a Lutheran theologian, in Nancy November, "Haydn's Vocality and the Ideal of 'True' Quartets" (Ph.D. diss., Cornell University, 2003), 129. Two insightful discussions of Petiscus's essay appear in Mary Hunter, "'The Most Interesting Genre of Music': Performance, Sociability and Meaning in the Classical String Quartet, 1800–1830," *Nineteenth-Century Music Review* 9 (2012): 55–59 and *passim*; and Nancy November, *Beethoven's Theatrical Quartets: Opp. 59, 74, and 95* (Cambridge University Press, 2014), 11–13 and *passim*.

In the case of late-eighteenth-century chamber music – a designation that overtly references the music's venue – the culture of the drawing room is an integral part of the music's spirit.[2] Christina Bashford, in her brief account of the string quartet's social history, defines late-eighteenth-century chamber music as "music to be performed for its own sake and the enjoyment of its players, in private residences (usually in rooms of limited size), perhaps in the presence of a few listeners, perhaps not."[3] In referring to musicians with the neutral word "players," Bashford nicely avoids the more customary term "performers"; the latter locution tends to unduly (and anachronistically) suggest a more formal, public spectacle undertaken mainly for the enjoyment of an audience of strangers. Bashford's historically sensitive definition positions chamber music as a type of *Gebrauchsmusik*, serving a function by providing friends and family a way to engage together socially through music, either as players, listeners, or both. Richard Henry Walthew, the British pianist and prolific composer of chamber music, beautifully captured the tradition of *Hausmusik* in a lecture that dubbed chamber music "the music of friends."[4]

The painting *Haydn Quartet* by Julius Schmid (Fig. 1.1) is an early-twentieth-century image depicting an (imagined) late-eighteenth-century domestic musical scene.[5] With music strewn about the floor and a violin

---

[2] I will generally use the term "chamber music" in the modern sense, to indicate duets (including sonatas for keyboard and violin), trios, quartets, etc. In the eighteenth century, such works were all designated as types of "sonata" (see discussion of sonatas in Chapter 2). In Mozart's lifetime, the term *Kammermusik* retained an older meaning, referring broadly to any instrumental music for the aristocratic chamber, as opposed to church or theater; this included concerti just as well as sonatas. See Johann Philipp Kirnberger's entry "Cammermusik" in Johann Georg Sulzer, ed., *Allgemeine Theorie der schönen Künste*, vol. 1 (Leipzig, 1771), 440–41 (Web Doc. #33); and Heinrich Christoph Koch, *Musikalisches Lexikon* (Frankfurt am Main, 1802), s.v. "Kammermusik," cols. 820–21 (Web Doc. #10). Cliff Eisen discusses the changing meaning of *Kammermusik* in "Mozart's Chamber Music," in *The Cambridge Companion to Mozart*, ed. Simon P. Keefe (Cambridge University Press, 2003), 105–17.
  On the multiple authorship of Sulzer's *Allgemeine Theorie der schönen Künste*, see *Aesthetics and the Art of Musical Composition: Selected Writings of Johann Georg Sulzer and Heinrich Christoph Koch*, ed. Nancy Baker and Thomas Christensen (Cambridge University Press, 1996), 14 n. 22.

[3] Christina Bashford, "The String Quartet and Society," in *The Cambridge Companion to the String Quartet*, 3. As a precedent to the string quartet, Bashford cites the madrigal as an important genre for domestic musical recreation.

[4] Richard Henry Walthew, *The Development of Chamber Music* (London: Boosey and Hawkes, 1909), 42. This publication is based on three lectures that Walthew delivered at the South Place Institute in London in 1909. The phrase "music of friends" is probably his original coinage, but the idea is an old one (cf. the Petiscus passage quoted in the epigraph to this chapter).

[5] Authentic, eighteenth-century paintings depicting string quartet playing are rare (but see a c. 1785 silhouette of Wallerstein court musicians included among the Web Resources). As a much later depiction of an eighteenth-century musical gathering, Fig. 1.1 is but an evocative

Fig. 1.1 Heliogravure by Franz Hanfstaengl, 1907, after Julius Schmid, *Haydn Quartet*, c. 1905–6 (painting now lost). Vienna City Museum.

case leaning precariously against a bench, it seems these players hope to sight-read a good deal of music at this gathering (cf. Fig. 1.3 below and the unknown painting on the cover of this book).[6] No scores are in sight; string

product of its creator's fantasy and should in no way be taken as direct evidence of Haydn's period. Yet *other* documentary and iconographic evidence I will examine below suggests that the scene it depicts cuts to the heart of *Hausmusik* practices that Haydn and Mozart would have recognized, namely, the notion that this music was often (if not usually) played primarily for the enjoyment of the players themselves. A variety of authentic, eighteenth-century images depicting domestic music-making are provided among the Web Resources, as are color versions of several illustrations in this chapter. An insightful analysis of nineteenth-century depictions of string quartet playing and their relation to French and German conceptions of the genre is Nancy November, "Theater Piece and *Cabinetstück*: Nineteenth-Century Visual Ideologies of the String Quartet," *Music in Art* 29, nos. 1–2 (Spring–Fall 2004): 134–50.

[6] Regarding the dating of the unknown painting reproduced on the cover, which is preserved in a nineteenth-century lithograph: Although Ludwig Finscher considers it to be an eighteenth-century work, November is more likely correct that it dates from the nineteenth century. The central position of the bust of Mozart, the watchful eye of the master composer dominating over the music-making, reflects nineteenth-century values (cf. Josef Danhauser's *Liszt at the Piano* [1840]). Moreover, the depiction of musicians in the eighteenth-century playing underneath a bust of Mozart is likely an anachronism, since it is doubtful anyone would have owned such a bust until some years after the composer's death in 1791. See Ludwig Finscher, "Streichquartett,"

quartets were available only in parts at the time. Haydn, leaning in toward his colleagues and with raised bow, seems poised to speak. Perhaps the players stumbled during a tricky passage, requiring him to offer instructions or even to conduct.

Several other people are in attendance: a lady (one of the players' wives?) stands on the right, with a boy and his governess; a gentleman watches from behind the ensemble, perhaps to follow one of the players' parts (if he too is a dilettante musician); and in the rear, a late arrival is shown in by a domestic servant, pausing in the doorway until he can enter without disturbing the music. This is not a conventional "concert" or "performance," at least not as those words are generally used today. Rather, quartet playing is depicted as an activity undertaken by the players largely for their own enjoyment within their enclosed circle. The others, for whom no seating is provided, listen in as spectators rather than as a concert audience.

This sense of chamber music playing being directed inward, emphasizing intercourse *among* the players, is borne out in several earlier images and artifacts datable to Mozart's lifetime or shortly thereafter. The late-eighteenth-century quartet table (*Quartetttisch*) in Fig. 1.2 is designed such that musicians could play to one another within their circle. The images in Figs. 1.3 and 1.4 show chamber music with keyboard instruments, with small music stands placed on their lids to support the string players' music. This arrangement, commonly seen in such depictions, would seem to foster an intimately circumscribed locus of musical activity.[7] The watercolor *Interior with a Musical Gathering* (Fig. 1.5) depicts a private concert in a salon, possibly a performance of a concerto or chamber piece featuring the lady at the keyboard, accompanied by the male string and wind players seated around the adjacent table, led by the first violinist conducting.[8] Although

---

in *Die Musik in Geschichte und Gegenwart*, ed. Ludwig Finscher, vol. 8 (Kassel: Bärenreiter, 1998), col. 1936; and November, "Haydn's Vocality," 15.

[7] The complete Artaria title page from which Fig. 1.3 is extracted is provided among the Web Resources. For an account of Susan Burney sight-reading this piece, see below, 94. On the likely attribution of Fig. 1.4 to Gabriel Jacques de Saint-Aubin (rather than his brother Augustin, to whom it was formerly attributed), see Phyllis Hattis, *Four Centuries of French Drawings in the Fine Arts Museums of San Francisco* (San Francisco: Fine Arts Museums of San Francisco, 1977), 156, catalog item #119.

[8] My suggestion that the keyboard player seems to play a concerto or other keyboard-centric chamber piece is based on the premise that an avocational lady pianist is unlikely to be realizing a continuo part in a symphony or concerto grosso, especially considering the distance between her and the cellist. However, the focus of the composition on the musicians around the table, rather than on the keyboard player, may speak against this interpretation. The drawing is undated, but Aartman's working dates are often given as 1723–60. Robert-Jan te Rijdt, curator of eighteenth- and nineteenth-century drawings at the Rijksmuseum, speculates that the artist may

Fig. 1.2 String quartet table (*Quartetttisch*), late eighteenth century. Kunsthistorisches Museum, Vienna.

the keyboard player would be featured in such an ensemble, neither she nor any other individual figure is the center of visual interest. Rather, the composition makes a focal point of the musicians as a group and draws attention to the drawing room as a site for both *social* music-making and *musical* socializing. Instead of directing their playing outward, the musicians seem to draw the surrounding company into their circle. The listeners appear to be engaged with the music but are not strictly silent; note the

have been active later, since a drawing exists dated 1779 that may be by Aartman (personal communication). The drawing in question is signed "A: 1779" (similarly to *Interior with a Musical Gathering*) but was sold with attribution to Aert Schouman (Sotheby's, Amsterdam, November 21, 1989, lot 183).

Fig. 1.3 Detail from title page of Haydn, Piano Trio, Hob. XV:10. Vienna: Artaria, 1798.

Fig. 1.4 Gabriel Jacques de Saint-Aubin, *The Musical Duo*, c. 1772. Watercolor, gouache, brown and black ink, and graphite. The Fine Arts Museums of San Francisco.

chatting figures in the rear right and foreground left. Such depictions and artifacts of domestic music-making in Figs. 1.2–1.5 contrast sharply with the formal performances heard in today's public concert halls.[9]

---

[9] Finscher ("Streichquartett," 8: col. 1936) emphasizes the contrast between the circular quartet formation, characteristic of private settings and mirroring salon conversation, with the semi-circular formations associated with public performance, which he states emerged only around the 1870s. At John Ella's Musical Union concerts (established in London in 1845),

Fig. 1.5 Nicolaes Aartman, *Interior with a Musical Gathering*, c. 1723–60. Graphite and watercolor. Rijksmuseum, Amsterdam.

Mozart as chamber musician

It is a challenge to piece together a detailed historical record of late-eighteenth-century *Hausmusik* practices.[10] Bashford notes that "the essentially private nature of quartet-playing renders documentation scanty, suggesting a less extensive activity than was almost certainly the case; but occasional accounts in diaries, letters and the like enable some glimpses to be caught."[11] Although such terse "glimpses" cannot illustrate the extent of

performers were positioned in the center of the hall, with the audience seated in the round, in order to simulate the private quartet concerts Ella had attended in Vienna at the palace of Prince Czartoryski. John Ella, *Musical Sketches: Abroad and at Home*, 3rd ed., rev. and ed. John Belcher (London, 1878), 349. See also a related picture of a string quartet performance at Ella's Musical Union, reproduced in Tully Potter, "From Chamber to Concert Hall," in *The Cambridge Companion to the String Quartet*, 43. I will return to adaptations of chamber music for semi-public and public performance in Chapter 3.

[10] A historical sketch of string quartet performance during this period in Vienna appears in Horst Walter, "Zum Wiener Streichquartett der Jahre 1780 bis 1800," *Haydn-Studien* 7, nos. 3–4 (February 1998): 289–314. See also Mary Sue Morrow, *Concert Life in Haydn's Vienna: Aspects of a Developing Musical and Social Institution* (Stuyvesant, NY: Pendragon Press, 1989), esp. 1–33 on private concerts and musical activities.

[11] Bashford, "The String Quartet and Society," 4. To Bashford's list of text-based sources, I would add iconographic evidence as well. See, for example, Richard Leppert, *Music and Image: Domesticity, Ideology, and Socio-Cultural Formation in Eighteenth-Century England* (Cambridge University Press, 1988), which focuses on domestic music in general, not the string

domestic musical activity during this period, they nevertheless provide an enticing picture of its character.

Two of the most vivid accounts of Mozart's domestic music-making come from the memoirs of Michael Kelly, the Irish tenor who sang in the first production of *Le nozze di Figaro*:

I went one evening to a concert of the celebrated [Leopold] Kozeluch's, a great composer for the piano-forte, as well as a fine performer on that instrument. I saw there the composers Vanhall [*sic*] and Baron Dittersdorf; and, what was to me one of the greatest gratifications of my musical life was there introduced to that prodigy of genius – Mozart. He favoured the company by performing fantasias and capriccios on the piano-forte. His feeling, the rapidity of his fingers, the great execution and strength of his left hand particularly, and the apparent inspiration of his modulations astounded me. After his splendid performance we sat down to supper and I had the pleasure to be placed at the table between him and his wife, Madame Constance Weber, a German lady, of whom he was passionately fond, and by whom he had three children. He conversed with me a good deal about Thomas Linley, the first Mrs. [Elizabeth Ann] Sheridan's brother, with whom he was intimate at Florence, and spoke of him with great affection. He said that Linley was a true genius; and he felt that, had he lived, he would have been one of the greatest ornaments of the musical world. After supper the young branches of our host had a dance, and Mozart joined them. Madame Mozart told me, that great as his genius was, he was an enthusiast in dancing, and often said that his taste lay in that art, rather than in music.

He was a remarkably small man, very thin and pale, with a profusion of fine fair hair, of which he was rather vain. He gave me a cordial invitation to his house, of which I availed myself, and passed a great part of my time there. He always received me with kindness and hospitality. – He was remarkably fond of punch, of which beverage I have seen him take copious draughts. He was also fond of billiards, and had an excellent billiard table in his house. Many and many a game have I played with him, but always came off second best. He gave Sunday concerts, at which I never was missing. He was kind-hearted, and always ready to oblige; but so very particular, when he played, that if the slightest noise were made, he instantly left off.[12]

quartet in particular. Leppert's remarks (pp. 3–8 and *passim*) about iconography as evidence of an ideology, and not necessarily of actual practices, are especially illuminating.

[12] Michael Kelly, *Reminiscences of Michael Kelly, of the King's Theatre, and Theatre Royal Drury Lane* (London, 1826), 1:225–26. These memoirs were prepared for publication by Theodore Edward Hook based on materials furnished by Kelly. Kelly's (or Hook's) penchants for name-dropping and for dramatic rhetorical effects make for highly engaging prose, but readers should beware of some probable exaggerations within his memoir.

Extraordinary as this gathering of musical celebrities at Kozeluch's home was,[13] several aspects of Kelly's narrative are illuminating for domestic musical activity in general. Although Kelly refers to the event as a "concert," his account describes something more like a musical dinner party, and his description of socializing eclipses that of the music. To be sure, Kelly provides precious few details about the music, such as which pieces (or kinds of pieces) were played or whether anyone besides Kozeluch and Mozart played. Perhaps these particulars were lost to memory after several decades, but Kelly managed to describe people, conversations, and even beverages in considerable detail.[14]

Understanding Kozeluch's "concert" as a social event implies an atmosphere and etiquette entirely different from modern concerts. Especially revealing are Kelly's remarks about Mozart's Sunday concerts, which seem to have been rather more formal affairs than the gathering at Kozeluch's. By describing Mozart as a generous host and eager performer "*but* [emphasis added] so very particular" in insisting on absolute silence while he played, Kelly indicates that such strict concert protocols were not standard practice even for relatively formal house concerts.[15]

---

[13] More representative portraits of the impressive private musical activities of Vienna's nobility and upper middle classes are found in Johann Ferdinand von Schönfeld, *Jahrbuch der Tonkunst von Wien und Prag* (Vienna, 1796); partially trans. Kathrine Talbot as "A Yearbook of Music in Vienna and Prague, 1796," in *Haydn and His World*, ed. Elaine Sisman (Princeton University Press, 1997), 289–320. See also the diaries of Count Karl Zinzendorf, discussed in Dorothea Link, "Vienna's Private Theatrical and Musical Life, 1783–92, as Reported by Count Karl Zinzendorf," *Journal of the Royal Musical Association* 122, no. 2 (1997): 205–57. Link divides musical events mentioned by Zinzendorf into several categories, including domestic music-making (with the guests playing or singing), social dinners with hired professional musicians, and concerts whose main purpose was the serious enjoyment of music. A similar categorization of private musical activities appears in Morrow, *Concert Life in Haydn's Vienna*, 1–33.

[14] For a fascinating history of punch as the quintessential social beverage, see David Wondrich, *Punch: The Delights (and Dangers) of the Flowing Bowl* (New York: Perigree Trade, 2010).

[15] Contemporary accounts of Baron Gottfried van Swieten similarly comment on his unusual insistence on silence and serious attention during the music at gatherings of the *Gesellschaft der Associierten*, anticipating modern concert etiquette. See Tia DeNora, *Beethoven and the Construction of Genius: Musical Politics in Vienna, 1792–1803* (Berkeley: University of California Press, 1995), 26–27. For a broad overview of this issue, including an eloquent defense of eighteenth-century listening habits, see William Weber's article "Did People Listen in the 18th Century?," *Early Music* 25, no. 4 (November 1997): 678–91.

An imaginative take on conversations among guests in salon-concert settings appears in Elisabeth Le Guin, "A Visit to the Salon Parnasse," in *Haydn and the Performance of Rhetoric*, ed. Tom Beghin and Sander M. Goldberg (University of Chicago Press, 2007), 14–35. This whimsical yet amply documented publication takes the form of a fictional conversation between the author and a cadre of celebrated eighteenth-century *philosophes* and aesthetes. While musicians play a Haydn trio, the guests discuss the nature of chamber music as a form of conversation, contrasting eighteenth- and twenty-first-century perspectives and using the

Kelly's reference to Mozart's "capriccios and fantasias" suggests that Mozart's playing at Kozeluch's concert was improvised. Tellingly, Kelly's commentary makes no distinction between praise for Mozart's pianistic technique ("the rapidity of his fingers, the great execution and strength of his left hand particularly") and for his compositional or improvisational skill ("his feeling ... and the apparent inspiration of his modulations"). This entangling of instrumental and compositional command reflects characteristically eighteenth-century sensibilities, similar to how one today might describe a concert by a jazz (rather than classical) pianist. A premium on improvisational prowess effaces the now-conventional separation between musical invention and execution; these were understood to be overlapping competencies.[16]

This image of Mozart astonishing an intimate company with his remarkable improvisation is consistent with the following anecdote, drawn from Vincent and Mary Novello's report of an interview with Abbé Maximilian Stadler (no relation to the famed clarinetist Anton Stadler, discussed below):

On enquiring what were the most favourite pieces with Mozart when he was in private amongst his intimate friends, The Abbé said he usually played *extemporaneously*, but that his imagination was so inexhaustible and at the same time his ideas were so symmetrical and regularly treated that Albrechtsberger could not be persuaded but what they were regular pieces that had been studied beforehand – One evening when Mozart, the Abbé Stadler and Albrechtsberger were together, the latter asked Mozart to sit down to the Instrument and play something. Mozart directly complied, but instead of taking a subject of his own, he told Albrechtsberger to give him a theme. Albrechtsberger accordingly invented a subject on the spot, and which he was quite certain that Mozart could not possibly have heard before; he also selected the most trivial features he could think of in order to put Mozart's ingenuity, invention and creative powers to the severest test.

---

ensuing performance to provide examples. At one point, Le Guin depicts the musicians as stopping after a cadence in order to participate in the conversation, thus reversing the more obvious question of whether the "audience" was quiet enough to listen to the "performance." Le Guin defends this fluid exchange between music and discourse: "I doubt that eighteenth-century drawing-room listening precluded speech. In my view, the varieties of attentional possibility in a social situation far exceed any simple duality of listening *or* talking" (ibid., 23 n. 17).

[16] On the idea of "musicking" as an activity (as opposed to "music" as a noun), see Christopher Small, *Musicking* (Middletown, CT: Wesleyan University Press, 1998). Small's English-language neologism is similar to the time-honored German verb "musizieren" (spelled "musicieren" in historical texts), although Small significantly broadens its traditional usage to encompass not only performing but also any form of musical participation, such as listening, dancing, composing, or rehearsing.

This extraordinary Genius immediately took the theme that had been given him thus unexpectedly, and played for upwards of an hour upon it, treating it in all possible variety of form – fugue, Canon, and from the most simple to the most elaborate Counterpoint – until Albrechtsberger could hold out no longer, but exclaimed in transport, "I am now perfectly convinced that your extemporaneous playing is really the thought of the moment and that you fully deserve all the fame you have acquired from this wonderful talent."[17]

This 1829 conversation between the elderly Stadler and the Novellos is emblematic of a generational shift in thinking between eighteenth- and nineteenth-century ideas about the musical work.[18] The wording of the Novellos' question indicates that they expected Stadler to list specific compositions that Mozart frequently played among friends.[19] The emphatic italics on the word "extemporaneously" may suggest their astonishment at Stadler's reply. Furthermore, lavish detail in the anecdote about Albrechtsberger betrays not only Stadler's veneration for Mozart's impressive improvisational gifts but perhaps also some nostalgia for an art of improvisation that was vibrant during Mozart's lifetime but was less widely practiced by 1829.

Turning now from accounts of Mozart's solo-keyboard improvisations to descriptions of parties with ensemble chamber music, Kelly offers the following report of a gathering in 1784:

[Stephen] Storace gave a quartett [*sic*] party to his friends. The players were tolerable; not one of them excelled on the instrument he played, but there was a little science among them, which I dare say will be acknowledged when I name them:

The First Violin	. . . .	HAYDN.
" Second Violin	. . .	BARON DITTERSDORF.
" Violoncello	. . . .	VANHALL [*sic*].
" Tenor	. . . . . .	MOZART.

---

[17] Vincent and Mary Novello, *A Mozart Pilgrimage: Being the Travel Diaries of Vincent & Mary Novello in the Year 1829*, ed. Rosemary Hughes (London: Eulenburg Books, 1975), 167–68.

[18] See Lydia Goehr, *The Imaginary Museum of Musical Works: An Essay in the Philosophy of Music* (Oxford University Press, 1994). Vincent Novello played an active role in the nineteenth-century project of canon formation, as a choirmaster (who introduced the choral music of Haydn and Mozart in England), as a founder of the Philharmonic Society, and perhaps most famously as founder of the Novello & Co. publishing house.

[19] Many eighteenth-century reports of domestic music fail to mention specific compositions, the composer, or even the type of composition that was played. Descriptions of solo keyboard performances – such as Kelly's – frequently blur the boundary between improvised playing and the performances of set compositions, and Abbé Stadler's anecdote about Albrechtsberger reveals that this ambiguity existed at the events themselves and not only in their written descriptions. I will return to the role of improvisation in Mozart's musical activities in Chapter 3.

The poet [Giovanni Battista] Casti and [Giovanni] Paesiello [*sic*] formed part of the audience. I was there, and a greater treat, or a more remarkable one, cannot be imagined.

On the particular evening to which I am now specially referring, after the musical feast was over, we sat down to an excellent supper, and became joyous and lively in the extreme.[20]

Like his report of the performance at Kozeluch's, Kelly's description of this gathering unites social and musical aspects by referring to a "quartett party" *given* by Storace "to his friends" as a "musical feast." Though Kelly provides little information about what music was played (presumably quartets by some or all of the players), his account mentions some prominent attendees and effusively captures the festive mood of the occasion.

Whereas Kelly's and Abbé Stadler's accounts of Mozart's solo-keyboard performances revel in describing his extraordinary virtuosity, here Kelly almost makes a virtue out of the unpolished, impromptu nature of the quartet playing. The quartet musicians were likely sight-reading, playing more for their own enjoyment than for any audience; in this context, it would be misleading to refer to their playing as a "performance" or "concert."[21] But for Kelly, any shortcomings in the instrumentalists' technique were no hindrance to the extraordinary opportunity to socialize through music and to be intimate with esteemed composers. Elisabeth Le Guin addresses a related point in a fictional dialogue between herself and Diderot:

HIM. When we listen to music at home, or at the house of close friends, we're all together in the same room, and we, or our sons and daughters, are the performers.

ME. Pardon my asking, but doesn't that condemn you to hearing a great many clumsy performances?

HIM. The truth is, when you are that close to the making of the music you don't judge the result in at all the same way you would at the *concert spirituel.*

ME. All the same, I think it might be painful to hear a good sonata blundered through by my neighbors and relations.

HIM. I am not sure what you mean; how can a sonata ever be better than its performance?

---

[20] Kelly, *Reminiscences*, 1:237–38. In Kelly's usage, the word "science" is a synonym for "knowledge."

[21] I return to evidence of sight-reading in eighteenth-century "concerts" in Chapter 3.

ME. Well, that very question does imply quite a shift. We tend nowadays to esteem the work independently of its execution; and we judge the execution according to the ethics of production and perfection that entered European society with the Industrial Revolution. But I'm sorry: that's after your day.[22]

For Le Guin's "Diderot," as for Kelly, the enjoyment of making music with or hearing music played by friends and family is central to the experience of the music. To judge a performance's technical excellence is beside the point, in the same way that family and friends can enjoy playing games or recreational sports together even when participants are of mixed ability levels. The double meaning of the verb *spielen* (to play a game or to play music) is instructive in this respect, since either a game or a piece of chamber music serves as a diverting vehicle for familiars to socialize together. The eighteenth-century tradition of musical dice games (*musikalische Würfelspiele*) exemplifies this connection between music and other forms of divertissement.[23] Another contemporaneous source that compares

---

[22] Le Guin, "A Visit to the Salon Parnasse," 15–16. Le Guin's point is intriguing but overstated, since several influential eighteenth-century authors explicitly discuss poor performances of good compositions. For instance, in the final chapter of his violin treatise, Leopold Mozart asks rhetorically: "[T]o whom … is it not known that the best composition is often played so wretchedly that the composer himself has great difficulty in recognizing his own work?" Leopold Mozart, *Versuch einer gründlichen Violinschule* (Augsburg, 1756), 252. English translation from *A Treatise on the Fundamental Principles of Violin Playing*, 2nd ed., trans. Editha Knocker (Oxford University Press, 1951), 215. Decades later, he made a similar point in a letter to his son, whose symphonies he described as written with such discernment and so unconventionally that they suffer when played by mediocre orchestras. L. Mozart to W. A. Mozart, Salzburg, December 4, 1780, in Mozart, *Briefe und Aufzeichnungen: Gesamtausgabe*, ed. Wilhelm A. Bauer and Otto Erich Deutsch, vol. 3, *1780–86* (Kassel: Bärenreiter, 1962), 45. A similar distinction between the quality of a composition and its performance appears in Johann Joachim Quantz's flute treatise, the final chapter of which is entitled: "How a Musician and a Musical Composition Are to Be Judged" (*Wie ein Musikus und eine Musik zu beurtheilen sey*). Johann Joachim Quantz, *Versuch einer Anweisung die Flöte traversiere zu spielen* (Berlin, 1752), 275–334. See English translation in *On Playing the Flute*, trans. Edward R. Reilly (London: Faber and Faber, 1985), 295–342.

The treatises by L. Mozart and Quantz are addressed to students engaged in serious training, whereas Le Guin's point may apply primarily to avocational music-making, either by dilettantes or even by professionals when playing socially for their own enjoyment. Yet even dilettantes are not spared from this type of criticism; see, for example, the comments of an anonymous critic in the *Journal des Luxus und der Moden* quoted below, 97–98.

[23] Hideo Noguchi's remarkable explanation of Mozart's Musical Game in C, K. Anh. 294d (now cataloged as K. 516f) appears in his article "Mozart: Musical Game in C, K. 516f," *Mitteilungen der Internationalen Stiftung Mozarteum* 38 (1990): 89–101; I thank Robert Levin for bringing Noguchi's article to my attention. Unlike other musical games attributed to Mozart (e.g., K. Ang. 30.01), K. Anh. 294d/516f can be positively attributed since it survives in an autograph manuscript. For an overview of Enlightenment-era musical dice games, see Leonard G. Ratner, "*Ars combinatoria*: Chance and Choice in Eighteenth-Century Music," in *Studies in 18th-Century Music: A Tribute to Karl Geiringer on His Seventieth Birthday*, ed. H. C. Robbins

music and card games is an essay attributed to Giuseppe Maria Cambini, which complains of the casual, light-hearted way in which musicians commonly sight-read quartets: "It causes me grief and I must shrug my shoulders helplessly, when I hear musicians say, 'Come, let's play quartets!' just as lightly as one says in society, 'Come, let's play [the card game] Reversis!'"[24]

Mozart as composer

For a composer such as Mozart, the social aspect of chamber music often began well before the first performance of a new piece, probably in the earliest stages of the creative process. Many of his compositions were conceived with a specific musician in mind – if not himself, then a dedicatee, friend, student, colleague, mentor (in the case of Haydn), or some combination of these – and so elements of that person's playing, musical taste, and perhaps even personality must have inspired Mozart's imagination early in the genesis of these works. Part of the enjoyment of composing surely included the anticipation of hearing the completed piece come to life in that musician's hands.[25] But in the case of chamber music, a

Landon and Roger E. Chapman (Oxford University Press, 1970), 343–63; and Stephen A. Hedges, "Dice Music in the Eighteenth Century," *Music and Letters* 59, no. 2 (April 1978): 180–87.

Mozart's penchant for playing card games is discussed in Günther G. Bauer, "'... mit der Tarockkarten Tarockkarten gespielt': die Kartenspiele des Wolfgang Amadeus Mozart," *Das Blatt: Schriftenreihe der Deutschen Spielkartengesellschaft* 19 (October 1999): 17–63. For a broader portrait of Mozart as game player, see also Günther G. Bauer, "Mozart: Spiele ohne Musik. Mozarts dokumentierte Gesellschaftsspiele, 1768–1791," *Musik und Spiel: Homo Ludens – Der spielende Mensch* 10 (2000): 135–86.

[24] [Giuseppe Maria] Cambini (?), "Ausführung der Instrumentalquartetten," *Allgemeine musikalische Zeitung (Leipzig)* 6, no. 47 (August 22, 1804): col. 783 (Web Doc. #2). I quote the complete document in translation and discuss its disputed authorship below, 80–86. On card-playing and gambling at public and private concerts in Vienna, see Morrow, *Concert Life in Haydn's Vienna*, 4, 22, and 53–54; and Dexter Edge, review of ibid., *Haydn Yearbook* 17 (1992): 115. See also Pietro Longhi's painting *The Concert* (1741), reproduced on the cover of Danuta Mirka, *Metric Manipulations in Haydn and Mozart: Chamber Music for Strings, 1781–1791* (Oxford University Press, 2009).

[25] For Mozart, this was especially true of opera composition, as evidenced by his *Verzeichnüss aller meiner Werke*, in which he listed the names of the original singers alongside several arias. Mozart's correspondence betrays his delight in tailoring his aria to match a specific singer's voice. He writes (in a letter to L. Mozart, Mannheim, February 28, 1778) of custom-tailoring an aria he had written for the tenor Anton Raaff, who was past his prime and could no longer sustain long notes: "I assured him that I would arrange the aria in such a way that it would give him pleasure to sing it. For I like an aria to fit a singer as perfectly as a well-made suit of clothes." Mozart, *Briefe und Aufzeichnungen: Gesamtausgabe*, ed. Wilhelm A. Bauer and Otto Erich Deutsch, vol. 2, *1777–79* (Kassel: Bärenreiter, 1962), 304. English translation from Ian

still greater delight was the anticipation of playing the composition with others and thus animating the witty intercourse among the parts.

Even for a non-musician dedicatee or patron, who would enjoy a new work by listening to it in a private salon rather than playing it, the genesis of a composition involved social elements. Mozart's correspondence with Michael von Puchberg, a wealthy Viennese textile merchant and fellow Freemason who also became his creditor, is revealing. Mozart appended the following postscript to a 1788 letter to Puchberg: "P.S.: When are we going to make a little music at your house again? I have written a new trio!"[26] Almost a year later, Mozart wrote to Puchberg to inform him of a performance of the trio: "Tomorrow, Friday, Count Hadik has invited me to perform for him [Anton] Stadler's quintet and the trio I composed for you."[27] In the first letter, Mozart implicitly offers the trio to Puchberg as a gift, connected with a specific (proposed) social gathering and no doubt to Mozart's ongoing requests for Puchberg's financial support around this time. The later letter cements the connection with a reference pairing "Stadler's quintet" (i.e., the Clarinet Quintet, K. 581) and "the trio I composed for you"; in conception, the quintet was thus firmly linked to a particular clarinettist, just as the trio carried a permanent association with its would-be dedicatee.[28]

Where Mozart's chamber music output is concerned, his most influential musical friendship was surely with Haydn, whose op. 33 quartets

Woodfield, "Mozart's Compositional Methods: Writing for His Singers," in *The Cambridge Companion to Mozart*, 35. Mozart made a similar comment later that year (letter to L. Mozart, Mannheim, December 3, 1778) when he sent his father a copy of an aria written for Aloysia Weber, then his love interest. The accompanying letter provided instructions not to give the aria to anyone since "it was written solely for her and fits her like a garment that was tailored just for her" (ibid., 517). English translation from *Mozart's Letters, Mozart's Life*, trans. Robert Spaethling (New York: W. W. Norton, 2000), 197–98.

[26] W. A. Mozart to Michael Puchberg, Vienna, June 17, 1788, in Mozart, *Briefe und Aufzeichnungen: Gesamtausgabe*, ed. Wilhelm A. Bauer and Otto Erich Deutsch, vol. 4, *1787–1857* (Kassel: Bärenreiter, 1963), 67. Most scholars have assumed that the piece in question is the Divertimento in E♭ Major for String Trio, K. 563, but others have suggested that it could be the Piano Trio in G Major, K. 542. Contrasting views emerge in the prefaces to the respective volumes of the *Neue Mozart-Ausgabe*; see Dietrich Berke and Marius Flothius's preface to VIII/21 (including the string trio), and Wolfgang Plath and Wolfgang Rehm's preface to VIII/22 (the piano trios). See also Dietrich Berke, "Nochmals zum Fragment eines Streichtrio-Satzes in G-Dur KV Anh. 66 (562e)," *Acta Mozartiana* 29, no. 2 (1982): 42–47.

[27] W. A. Mozart to Michael Puchberg, Vienna, April 8, 1790, in Mozart, *Briefe*, 4:105. Mozart mentioned the "Puchberg trio" in an earlier letter to Constanze, Dresden, April 16, 1789 (ibid., 4:83). The latter letter is also discussed below, 101–2.

[28] Alfred Einstein hears a "fraternal rivalry" among the parts within the clarinet quintet, a description that evokes other aspects of Mozart's relationship with his Masonic "brother" Stadler. Einstein, *Mozart: His Character, His Work* (Oxford University Press, 1945), 194.

inspired Mozart to return to quartet writing after a nine-year hiatus with a renewed energy and deeper commitment to the genre.[29] Mozart's lavish dedication of the six "Haydn" quartets and Haydn's flattering response (as recounted by Leopold Mozart) are well known.[30] It is uncertain whether Haydn himself played together with Mozart and the Barons Anton and Bartholomäus Tinti at the first documented readings of the quartets (at Mozart's home on January 15 and February 12, 1785), but Haydn was in any event celebrated as the dedicatee and guest of honor.[31] Whereas Kelly's report of Storace's party recounts the one documented occasion when Mozart and Haydn played chamber music together, Abbé Stadler's testimony to the Novellos asserts that this was a regular activity. The Novellos' report states: "Mozart and Haydn frequently played together with Stadler in Mozart's Quintettos; [Stadler] particularly mentioned the 5th in D major,

[29] Mozart's first forays into quartet writing, about a decade earlier, may have been inspired by Haydn's quartets opp. 17 and 20. See, for example, Ernst Fritz Schmid, "Mozart and Haydn," *Musical Quarterly* 42, no. 2 (April 1956): 145–61. Schmid's article mentions specific Viennese homes in which Haydn and Mozart may have been frequent guests for social musical gatherings in the 1780s (ibid., 156–58). Eisen qualifies this traditional view of Haydn's influence on Mozart's early quartets, arguing that Mozart "adopted a generalized local style of which Haydn's are perhaps the finest examples." Eisen, "Mozart's Chamber Music," 108.
See also Webster and Feder's brief account of Haydn and Mozart's friendship, which offers a corrective against the traditional, romanticized view of their relationship. Webster and Feder, *The New Grove Haydn*, 28–29. Another concise overview is David Wyn Jones, "Haydn and His Fellow Composers," in *The Cambridge Companion to Haydn*, 49–52.

[30] Mark Evan Bonds provides a sophisticated evaluation of the Mozart/Haydn relationship in a pair of articles about Mozart's "Haydn" quartets: "The Sincerest Form of Flattery? Mozart's 'Haydn' Quartets and the Question of Influence," *Studi Musicali* 22 (Spring 1991): 365–409; and "Replacing Haydn: Mozart's 'Pleyel' Quartets," *Music and Letters* 88, no. 2 (May 2007): 201–25. For an intriguing reading of Mozart's letter of dedication, see David P. Schroeder, *Mozart in Revolt: Strategies of Resistance, Mischief and Deception* (Bath Press, 1999), 189–91.

[31] Although these gatherings are documented in two letters by L. Mozart dated January 22 and February 16, 1785 (in Mozart, *Briefe*, 3:367–68 and 3:372–74), his penchant for the passive voice leaves some ambiguities about who the players were. At the second gathering, at Mozart's residence in Vienna, L. Mozart was present, as were the Barons Tinti and, of course, Haydn himself. Otto Erich Deutsch speculates that Leopold played the quartets, along with W. A. Mozart (on viola) plus the Barons, a view echoed recently by Ludwig Finscher. But H. C. Robbins Landon, who argues that Leopold, at his advanced age, would have preferred to listen rather than sight-read such challenging new works, suggests that Haydn himself was the quartet's fourth member (possibly on viola). To these hypotheses, I add yet another possibility: perhaps all of the musicians present took turns playing, possibly even exchanging parts, as is still customary at chamber music parties to this day. See Otto Erich Deutsch, ed., *Mozart: A Documentary Biography*, trans. Eric Blom, Peter Branscombe, and Jeremy Noble (Stanford University Press, 1965), 236; Ludwig Finscher, preface to *Neue Mozart-Ausgabe* VIII/20, pt. 1/2 *Streichquartette* (Kassel: Bärenreiter, 1962), ix; and H. C. Robbins Landon, *Haydn: Chronicle and Works*, vol. 2 (Bloomington: Indiana University Press, 1978), 509 n. 1.

singing the Bass part."[32] Vincent Novello's notes from this conversation add the following tantalizingly terse detail: "Quintets of Mozart – 1st Violin Schmidt, 2nd Stock, 1st Viola either Haydn or Mozart in turn, 2nd Viola Abbé Stadler – Bass he could not recollect."[33] This image of Haydn and Mozart taking turns at playing the first viola part is indeed touching.[34] Despite a twenty-four-year age difference, these two musicians reportedly addressed each other with the familiar *du*,[35] and their warm relationship is emblematic of chamber music's role as "the music of friends."

---

[32] Novello and Novello, *A Mozart Pilgrimage*, 170.   [33] Ibid., 347 n. 123.

[34] Mozart's growing preference for playing viola in chamber music may itself reflect his penchant for "the social" in chamber music. That is, the viola's supporting position places it in a dynamic interplay, frequently interacting and exchanging roles with the other parts. Moreover, unlike a violinist encumbered with sight-reading a virtuosic first-violin part, the violist's comparatively lesser technical demands tend to free the player to devote more attention to engaging with colleagues.

Mozart's fondness for the viola is mentioned in Vincent Novello's notes from an interview with the Viennese banker Joseph Henickstein, who had visited Mozart often during the composition of *Don Giovanni* and who was a prominent musical patron and gifted amateur performer. Novello writes: "Mozart played the Violin [*sic*] very well and the viola still better, he [Henickstein] often heard him play that part in pieces of his own writing." Novello and Novello, *A Mozart Pilgrimage*, 144. Mozart's penchant for viola playing was shared with a number of other prominent chamber music composers and contrapuntists, among them J. S. Bach, Beethoven, Schubert (in his own early quartets, playing with his father and brothers), Mendelssohn (who in his later years preferred to play viola, especially in private performances of his Octet), Dvořák, Britten, and Hindemith. On Schubert's viola playing, see Maurice J. E. Brown, *The New Grove Schubert* (New York: Macmillan, 1983), 5. On Mendelssohn's, see Clive Brown, *A Portrait of Mendelssohn* (New Haven: Yale University Press, 2003), 236–7; and Franz Krautwurst, "Felix Mendelssohn Bartholdy als Bratschist," in *Gedenkschrift Hermann Beck*, ed. Hermann Dechant and Wolfgang Sieber (Laaber: Laaber-Verlag, 1982), 151–60.

[35] Otto Jahn, *W. A. Mozart*, vol. 3 (Leipzig, 1858), 315.

2 | Chamber music and the metaphor of conversation

If I were in Berlin, I would rarely miss the quartet evenings at [Karl] Möser's. This form of exhibition has always been, to me, the most comprehensible type of music: one hears four intelligent people conversing among themselves [and] believes one might learn something from their discourse and [might] get to know the special characteristics of their instruments.

–Johann Wolfgang von Goethe, letter to Carl Friedrich Zelter (November 9, 1829)[1]

It is . . . a true string quartet in which everyone has something to say; an oftentimes really beautiful, [but] oftentimes strange and abstrusely woven conversation among four people.

–Robert Schumann, "Erster Quartettmorgen" (1838)[2]

Perhaps it is the intertwining of social and musical elements in eighteenth-century domestic music-making that has led so many commentators to invoke metaphors of social intercourse in discussions of the repertoire. The comparison of chamber music (especially string quartets) to conversation among cultured individuals has been repeated so often by scholars,

---

[1] "Wäre ich in Berlin, so würde ich die Möserschen Quartettabende selten versäumen. Dieser Art Exhibitionen waren mir von jeher von der Instrumentalmusik das Verständliche: man hört vier vernünftige Leute sich untereinander unterhalten, glaubt ihren Diskursen etwas abzugewinnen und die Eigentümlichkeiten der Instrumente kennen zu lernen." J. W. von Goethe to C. F. Zelter, Weimar, November 9, 1828, in *Briefwechsel zwischen Goethe und Zelter in den Jahren 1796 bis 1832*, ed. Friedrich Wilhelm Riemer (Berlin, 1834), 5:20. See discussion in Jürgen Mainka, "Haydns Streichquartette: 'Man hört vier vernünftige Leute sich untereinander unterhalten,'" *Musik und Gesellschaft* 32 (1982): 146–50. Goethe's famous characterization of sophisticated musical ambiance at Möser's quartet evenings arises in context as a foil to his disparaging account of a concert he had attended by Niccolò Paganini. In an apparent allusion to the Book of Exodus, he described the latter as a senseless "pillar of flames and clouds [*Flammen- und Wolkensäule*]" (Mir fehlte zu dem was man Genuss nennt und was bey mir immer zwischen Sinnlichkeit und Verstand schwebt, eine Basis zu dieser Flammen- und Wolkensäule).

[2] "Es ist, im Gegensatz dem beschriebenen Spohrschen [Louis Spohr's *Quatuor brillant* in A Major, op. 97] ein wahres Quartett wo jeder etwas zu sagen hat, ein oft wirklich schön, oft sonderbar und unklarer verwobenes Gespräch von vier Menschen." Robert Schumann, "Erster Quartettmorgen," in *Gesammelte Schriften über Musik und Musiker*, 5th ed., ed. Martin Kreisig (Leipzig: Breitkopf & Härtel, 1914), 1:335.

performers, composers, and audiences alike that it has become rather a cliché. Although this idea was most famously expressed by Goethe in his 1829 letter (see above), his oft-quoted remark is but one in a long tradition dating back to the 1770s, around the date Haydn composed his quartets opp. 17 and 20.

The present chapter traces this thread with representative historical sources that either compare chamber music to artful conversation or describe the individual parts as representing distinct characters engaged in intercourse. The survey proceeds roughly chronologically and partly geographically, contrasting German and Franco-Italian perspectives.[3] For the present chapter, I will discuss these sources primarily in their own terms, saving critiques, refinements, and extensions of the "conversation" concept for Chapter 4.[4]

Music as utterance: classical rhetoric versus Enlightenment sociability

Whereas comparisons between music and rhetorical speech have a long history, dating back to antiquity and flourishing in the Baroque, innovations in musical thought after around 1770 stimulated a new focus on the interaction or communication *among* the parts *within* small ensembles, reflecting Enlightenment-era currents promoting the virtue of sociability in general and artful conversation in particular.[5] One of the strongest pronouncements distinguishing the deliberate musical rhetoric of the Baroque from the lighter discourse associated with the Galant style comes from one of the latter's detractors:

We are now divided into parties for the old and the new Music, in which there is undoubtedly a great diversity of Style and Attention to Different Effects . . .

As for *Haydn* and *Boccherini*, who merit a first place among the Moderns for *invention*, they are sometimes so desultory and unaccountable in their way of

---

[3] A related survey is found in Ludwig Finscher, *Studien zur Geschichte des Streichquartetts* (Kassel: Bärenreiter, 1974), 1:279–301.

[4] Specifically, some historical authors hear a musical dialogue only in the *melodic* statements within the texture. This problematic notion will be addressed in Chapter 4, in connection with recent critiques by Gretchen Wheelock and W. Dean Sutcliffe of the quartet-as-conversation model.

[5] On late-eighteenth-century music as a "sociable art," see W. Dean Sutcliffe, "The Shapes of Sociability in the Instrumental Music of the Later Eighteenth Century," *Journal of the Royal Musical Association* 138, no. 1 (2013): 1–45.

treating a Subject, that they must be reckoned among the wild warblers of the wood: And they seem to differ from some pieces of *Handel*, as the Talk of the Tea-table (where, perhaps, neither Wit nor Invention are wanting) differs from the Oratory of the Bar and the Pulpit.[6]

To Rev. William Jones's taste, "modern" composers such as Haydn and Boccherini have a gift for melodic invention (*inventio*) but evidently, in his view, fall short of Handel's standard for the rigorous treatment of their subjects (*dispositio* and *elocutio*). Over two centuries later, however, Gretchen A. Wheelock would take Jones to task for unduly applying the standards of public address to the domestic sphere:

A partisan of the music of the "Ancients," Jones apparently considered conversations at tea to be frivolous titters in comparison with the (manly) speeches of the judiciary and the church; Handel could be counted on to deliver more substantial messages than those purveyed by the wit and invention of the flighty "Moderns." In marking his preference for this stirring rhetoric of public address, however, Jones sets inappropriate terms for instrumental music in the chamber. The informal amusements of witty exchange among familiars presumed a more intimate discourse.[7]

---

[6] William Jones, *A Treatise on the Art of Music* (Colchester, 1784), iii and 49; cited in Leonard G. Ratner, *Classic Music: Expression, Form and Style* (New York: Schirmer, 1980), 27. See also W. Dean Sutcliffe's discussion in "The Shapes of Sociability," 3. A similarly dismissive appraisal of Galant instrumental music (also mentioning Haydn) appeared in 1792 in a provincial newspaper published in Flensburg. "Pure instrumental music [i.e., without text] can certainly make, in and of itself, a very lively impression: a beautifully performed Haydn sonata can do a lot. But in this type of music always lies a great deal that is vague, ambiguous, uncertain – and you have to have a certain amount of musical training to get true pleasure from it. *Such things . . . are like an agreeable, entertaining conversation that one hears with relish, but without interest. They are more sleight-of-hand than nourishment for the heart* [emphasis added]." *Flensburgisches Wochenblat*, February 21, 1799; cited in Mary Sue Morrow, *German Music Criticism in the Late Eighteenth Century: Aesthetic Issues in Instrumental Music* (Cambridge University Press, 1997), 11–12.

[7] Gretchen A. Wheelock, *Haydn's Ingenious Jesting with Art: Contexts of Musical Wit and Humor* (New York: Schirmer, 1992), 90. This gendered binary that Wheelock reads into Jones's remarks – opposing serious, manly, public affairs with the entertaining but frivolous repartee of the domestic sphere – is stated in more overtly paternalistic language in Lord Chesterfield's *Letters to His Son on the Art of Becoming a Man of the World and a Gentleman* (posthumously published in 1774): "Women, then, are only children of a larger growth; they have an entertaining tattle, and sometimes wit; but for solid reasoning, good sense, I never knew in my life one that had it, or who reasoned or acted consequentially for four-and-twenty hours together . . . A man of sense only trifles with them, plays with them, humors and flatters them, as he does with a sprightly forward child; but he neither consults them about, nor trusts them with serious matters; though he often makes them believe that he does both; which is the thing in the world that they are proud of; for they love mightily to be dabbling in business (which by the way they always spoil)." Cited in Leppert, *Music and Image*, 36.

At the crux of Jones's criticism and Wheelock's defense is a distinction between an older aesthetic of musical rhetoric as a formal, public proclamation on a serious subject and with a specified aim (persuasion), and a newly emerging mode of expression that celebrates the more impromptu – but no less artful – private discourse of the drawing room.

Following that distinction, I wish to disentangle notions such as musical "discourse" or "conversation" from the more traditional "rhetoric," which denotes a style of formal, public address that is foreign to drawing-room conversation among familiars. Many authors, beginning with Cicero, explicitly distinguish between the arts of rhetoric and conversation, underscoring their vastly differing functions, rules, and styles of delivery.[8] For example, whereas an oration is delivered by a single speaker addressing a faceless public, a conversation takes place among a circle of friends, all of whom participate. The rhetorical tradition (according to Cicero and Quintilian) furthermore outlines a process of preparation (*inventio, dispositio, elocutio,* and *memoria*) prior to the delivery of the address in performance (*pronunciato* or *actio*). Indeed, while an oration is not performed word-for-word, as if from a script, it is nevertheless understood to have taken shape prior to its delivery, thus prompting scholars to observe "a rudimentary notion of the [oration as a] 'work.'"[9] One could hardly make the same claim of conversation, since even the most artful conversations are inherently ephemeral, created in the moment, requiring no specific preparation beyond the ongoing cultivation of a cultured disposition, keen intellect, and sharp sense of wit.

In contradistinction to "the Oratory of the Bar and the Pulpit," worthy subjects for the rhetorical arts, many treatises on artful conversation specifically recommend adhering to lighter fare, endorsing the still-familiar rule proscribing politics and religion as subject matter.[10] A defining

---

[8] Cicero's treatment of ordinary talk (*sermo communis*) appears not in his writings on rhetoric but in his treatise on social duties, *De officiis*. Cicero's discussion begins with the observation that the rules of rhetoric have been codified but those of conversation have not (ibid., 1.37). Although Cicero's influence (through Quintilian) on the tradition of classical rhetoric is well known, his lasting impact on the art of conversation has only recently been recognized by Peter Burke, who describes early-modern conversation treatises as essentially "a series of footnotes to Cicero." Peter Burke, *The Art of Conversation* (Ithaca: Cornell University Press, 1993), 96. One influential seventeenth-century treatise justifies a prohibition on garrulousness by paraphrasing Cicero's distinction between conversation and oration: "Conversation is not like making speeches [*harangues*]. Everyone should listen and speak in turn." Joachim Trotti de la Chetardye, *Instructions pour un jeune seigneur* (Paris, 1683), 1:53. English translation from Burke, *The Art of Conversation*, 106.

[9] Patrick McCreless, "Music and Rhetoric," in *The Cambridge History of Western Music Theory*, ed. Thomas Christensen (Cambridge University Press, 2002), 847.

[10] On appropriate topics for conversation, see Burke, *The Art of Conversation*, 107–8.

characteristic of conversation, as opposed to public forms of address, is that it is done for its own sake. Writing of Dr. Johnson's style of conversation, Hester Lynch Piozzi (also known as Hester Thrale) opines that "talk beyond that which is necessary to the purposes of actual business is a kind of game."[11] The venerable hostess Madame de Staël likewise emphasizes that the essence of conversation lies solely in the vivacity of its repartee, whose intoxicating effects she compares to music (among other delights). Its ostensible subject is all but irrelevant; whereas seriousness of purpose is required for oration or debate, it is the enemy of delightful conversation:

The necessity of conversation is felt by all classes of people in France: speech is not there, as elsewhere, merely the means of communicating from one to another ideas, sentiments, and transactions; but it is an instrument on which they are fond of playing, and which animates the spirits, like music among some people, and strong liquors among others.

That sort of pleasure, which is produced by an animated conversation, does not precisely depend on the nature of that conversation; the ideas and knowledge which it develops do not form its principal interest; it is a certain manner of acting upon one another, of giving mutual and instantaneous delight, of speaking the moment one thinks, of acquiring immediate self-enjoyment, of receiving applause without labor, of displaying the understanding in all its shades by accent, gesture, look; of eliciting, in short, at will, the electric sparks, which relieve some of the excess of their vivacity, and serve to awaken others out of a state of painful apathy.

Nothing is more foreign to this talent than the character and disposition of the German intellect; they require in all things a serious result. Bacon has said, *that conversation is not the road leading to the house, but a by-path where people walk with pleasure.* The Germans give the necessary time to all things, but what is necessary to conversation is amusement; if men pass this line, they fall into discussion, into serious argument, which is rather a useful occupation than an agreeable art.[12]

---

[11] This quotation is often attributed directly to Johnson (as in ibid., 91), but the actual source is Piozzi, *Anecdotes of the Late Samuel Johnson* (Dublin, 1786), 44–48. On Dr. Johnson as conversationalist, see also *Dr. Johnson's Table Talk, or Conversations of the late Samuel Johnson* (London, 1785), a volume compiled by Stephen Jones and containing Johnson's observations on "a variety of useful and entertaining subjects" arranged in alphabetical order.

[12] Anne-Louise-Germaine de Staël, "L'esprit de conversation," in *De l'Allemagne*, vol. 1 (Paris, 1813), 96–97 (Web Doc. #31). English translation from *Germany*, trans. O. W. Wight (New York, 1861), 1:77–78. De Staël's paraphrase of Francis Bacon probably refers to his essay "Of Discourse," included in *Essays or Counsels, Civil and Moral* (London, 1625); also published in *Francis Bacon: The Major Works*, ed. Brian Vickers (Oxford University Press, 1996), 406.

To her list of shortcomings of German conversation, De Staël later adds the structure of the language itself, whereby "the sense is usually not understood until the end of the sentence. Thus the pleasure of interrupting, which, in France, gives so much animation to discussion, and forces one to utter so quickly all that is of importance to be heard . . . cannot exist in Germany."

This is not to say that such a conversation is entirely unrhetorical; to be sure, the Enlightenment aesthetic of wit might be described as the art of performing *elocutio* extemporaneously,[13] and some Enlightenment-era writers of conversation manuals cite ancient texts on classical rhetoric to justify their work.[14] Yet, whatever these two modes of artful speech may share, there is nevertheless a fundamental conceptual difference between classical rhetoric, in which the style of the language is elevated to enhance the orator's point, and that of witty conversation, in which the style *is* the point.[15]

While the Enlightenment did not invent private conversation and social engagement, it did elevate the art of the social to new heights as a subject worthy of meticulous cultivation, serious philosophical inquiry, and imitation in literature and music.[16] In his discerning discussion of Haydn's quartets, Charles Rosen identifies the flexible, seemingly spontaneous interchange of roles – an essential component of any graceful social interaction – as a defining element of (what he calls) the "Classical style"; such a free exchange, Rosen writes, lends Haydn's quartets their "most striking innovation," namely, their "air of conversation."[17] David

---

De Staël, "De la langue allemande dans ses rapports avec l'esprit de conversation," in *De l'Allemagne*, 1:117. English translation from *Germany*, ibid., 90.

[13] For an engaging and well-documented survey of eighteenth-century perspectives on wit, see Wheelock, *Haydn's Ingenious Jesting*, 19–32.

[14] Abbé André Morellet's essay "De la conversation" cites treatises on rhetoric by Cicero and Quintilian, maintaining that "this art [i.e., conversation, just as well as rhetoric] can be taught up to a point." But Morellet's comment is telling, because he refers to rhetoric and conversation as separate areas of study. To note that they are both teachable is not to claim that they are one and the same. Morellet, "De la conversation," *Éloges de Madame Geoffrin . . . par MM. Morellet, Thomas, d'Alembert; suivis de lettres de Madame Geoffrin et à Madame Geoffrin et d'un essai sur la conversation . . . par M. Morellet* (Paris, 1812), 168. English translation from Barbara R. Hanning, "Conversation and Musical Style in the Late Eighteenth-Century Parisian Salon," *Eighteenth-Century Studies* 22, no. 4 (Summer 1989): 515.

[15] A given musical genre, composition, or performance can incorporate elements suggestive of both rhetoric and conversation. Certainly the string quartet literature, frequently compared to conversation, is replete with passages resembling rhetoric (e.g., the stylized recitative in the slow movement of Haydn's op. 17, no. 5). I merely assert that conversation and rhetoric are distinct concepts. On the relationship between classical theories of rhetoric and Enlightenment salon conversation, see Le Guin, "A Visit to the Salon Parnasse," 17–22. Another insightful discussion integrating conversation and rhetorical gestures is Gretchen Wheelock, "The 'Rhetorical Pause' and Metaphors of Conversation in Haydn's Quartets," in *Haydn und das Streichquartett*, Eisenstädter Haydn-Berichte 2, ed. Georg Feder and Walter Reicher (Tutzing: Hans Schneider, 2003), 71.

[16] For an illuminating overview on artful conversation, see Burke's essay "The Art of Conversation in Early Modern Europe" in his volume *The Art of Conversation*, 89–122. Another brief introduction appears in Stephanie D. Vial, *The Art of Musical Phrasing in the Eighteenth Century* (University of Rochester Press, 2008), 51–56.

[17] Charles Rosen, *The Classical Style: Haydn, Mozart, Beethoven*, expanded ed. (New York: W. W. Norton, 1997), 141. On the fluid exchange of roles within the string quartet's texture, see also 116–17. On the problematic implications of the term "Classical" as applied to musical style in the late-eighteenth century, see James Webster, *Haydn's "Farewell" Symphony and the Idea of*

P. Schroeder hears the flexible interchange of roles within Haydn's quartets as "a realization of one of the highest goals of the Enlightenment. With accompaniments that can be transformed into melodies and vice versa, there is an apparent recognition of a higher social truth, which is that differences do not preclude equality."[18]

Characterization in the chamber music salon: Sulzer and Koch

In his *Allgemeine Theorie der schönen Künste*, Johann Georg Sulzer invokes the metaphor of conversation to address matters of *Empfindsamkeit* in an article entitled "Sonate," a term that was defined broadly in eighteenth-century parlance:

The sonata is an instrumental work consisting of two, three, or four consecutive movements of different character, and one or more instrumental parts that are not doubled. Depending upon the number of principal concerting instruments performing, it will be called *sonata a solo, a due, a tre*, etc.

There is no form of instrumental music that is more capable of depicting wordless sentiments than the sonata. The symphony and overture have a somewhat more fixed character, while the form of a concerto seems suited more for providing a skilled performer the opportunity to be heard and accompanied by many instruments than for the depiction of passions. Other than these (and dances which also have their own character), no form other than the sonata may assume any character and every expression. In a sonata, the composer might want to express through the music a monologue marked by sadness, misery, pain, or of tenderness, pleasure and joy; *using a more animated kind of music, he might want to depict a passionate conversation between similar or complementary characters* [emphasis added]; or he might wish to depict emotions that are impassioned, stormy, or contrasting, or ones that are light, delicate, flowing, and delightful. To be sure, only a few composers will have such intentions in mind when composing a sonata, and still fewer of the Italians and their imitators . . .

The possibility of endowing sonatas with character and expression is shown in a number of easy and challenging harpsichord sonatas written by our Hamburg Bach. The majority of these are so eloquent that one almost believes oneself to be

Classical Style: Through-Composition and Cyclic Integration in His Instrumental Music (Cambridge University Press, 1991); and James Webster, "The Eighteenth Century as a Music-Historical Period?," *Eighteenth-Century Music* 1, no. 1 (March 2004): 47–60.

[18] David P. Schroeder, *Haydn and the Enlightenment: The Late Symphonies and Their Audience* (Oxford: Clarendon Press, 1990), 62. See also Schroeder's article "The Art of Conversation: From Haydn to Beethoven's Early String Quartets."

hearing not a series of musical tones, but a comprehensible speech that moves and engages our imagination and emotion. It cannot be denied that the composition of such sonatas requires genius, knowledge, and above all, a refined lyrical and delicate sensibility. Such pieces also demand a kind of expressive performance that no German-Italian is in a position to deliver, although sometimes children are, at least those who have over time been exposed to such sonatas.

The sonatas of C. P. E. Bach for two concerted instruments accompanied by a bass are truly passionate conversations in tone. Those who do not believe they can either feel or hear this would do well to consider whether they have heard them performed as well as they should be. Among these sonatas, there is one that stands out as so excellent and so full of invention and character, that it can be considered a masterpiece of good instrumental music: the conversation between a certain *Melancholicus* and *Sanguineus* [the Trio in C Minor, H. 579] published in Nuremberg. Any aspiring composer who wishes to compose a sonata would do well to take the music of Bach and other similar pieces as his model.[19]

In contrast with the more fixed characters of such public instrumental genres as the symphony, overture, or concerto, Sulzer describes the capacity of "sonatas" (i.e., any type of chamber music) to communicate a limitless range of characters and sentiments. Pursuing the traditional equation of music and speech, he observes that music can wordlessly evoke either a monologue expressing a single primary affect or, alternatively, a conversation among similar or contrasting characters. Thus, Sulzer's notion of conversation seems to arise in connection with a central issue in music criticism around the third quarter of the eighteenth century, namely, the problem of intra-movement contrasts of theme and character. If the quintessential Baroque forms (fugue, ritornello, and *da capo* aria) broadly adhere to one primary topic or idea (like an oration) and therefore also to a single primary affect, how are listeners to interpret the meaning of contrasting themes and sentiments?[20] Sulzer's imagined

---

[19] Sulzer, *Allgemeine Theorie*, vol. 4 (Leipzig, 1774), s.v. "Sonate," 4:424–26 (Web Doc. #34). English translation from Sulzer and Koch, *Aesthetics and the Art of Musical Composition*, 103–4. This passage was probably written by J. A. Peter Schulz (see ibid., 14 n. 22). Sulzer is by no means the first author to discuss a composition's individual parts as portraying characters engaged in conversation. For earlier sources, see Finscher, *Studien zur Geschichte des Streichquartetts*, 285ff. Definitions of "dialogue" from several eighteenth-century music dictionaries are quoted in Simon P. Keefe, *Mozart's Piano Concertos: Dramatic Dialogue in the Age of Enlightenment* (Woodbridge: Boydell Press, 2001), 26–27.

[20] Charles Burney discusses the emergence of intra-movement contrasts as a novel stylistic development, writing that J. C. Bach was "the first composer who observed the law of *contrast*, as a *principle*. Before his time, contrast there frequently was, in the works of others; but it seems to have been accidental." Charles Burney, *A General History of Music*, vol. 4 (London, 1789), 483.

"passionate conversation between similar or complementary characters" provides an explanatory context for a sequence of contrasting musical ideas, topics, and affects.

In his enthusiastic praise for Emanuel Bach's sonata H. 579, Sulzer singles out a rare example in which the principal players are cast in distinct roles – as Melancholicus and Sanguineus, respectively – much as actors portray individual characters in a play.[21] The sonata's close alternation of contrasting sentiments is easily understood as an interaction between these two allegorical personas, each represented by one violinist, an interpretation that is facilitated by Bach's evocative title and elaborate explanatory preface in the score.[22] For Sulzer, H. 579 is not an isolated example but an extreme instance of a broadly applicable metaphor, since he describes all of Bach's trio sonatas as being "truly passionate conversations in tone." It bears mentioning that, in Sulzer's hearing of Bach's trio sonatas, the notion of conversation is limited to the melodic, upper voices; the bass retains its traditional accompanimental or functional role, more a part of the scenery than one of the characters.[23]

Gotthold Ephraim Lessing frames the issue bluntly in the twenty-seventh essay of his *Hamburgische Dramaturgie* (July 31, 1767): "Now we are melting with woefulness, and all of a sudden we are supposed to rage. How so? Why? Against whom? Against the very one for whom our soul was just full of sympathy? Or against another? All these things music cannot specify; it leaves us in uncertainty and confusion; we have feelings, but without perceiving them in a correct sequence; we feel as in a dream; and all these disorderly feelings are more exhausting than delightful." In *G. E. Lessings gesammelte Werke*, ed. Wolfgang Stammler, vol. 2 (Munich: Carl Hanser Verlag, 1959), 444 (Web Doc. #18). English translation from Bellamy Hosler, *Changing Aesthetic Views of Instrumental Music in 18th-Century Germany* (Ann Arbor: UMI Research Press, 1981), 5.

[21] A similar depiction of an exchange between two characters is Haydn's divertimento for four-hand keyboard duet known as "Il maestro e lo scolare," Hob. XVIIa:1, in which the *secondo* player represents a music teacher and the primo player his student. See Tom Beghin, *The Virtual Haydn: Paradox of a Twenty-First Century Keyboardist* (University of Chicago Press, 2015), 121–24.

[22] For a discussion of H. 579 and other depictions of "confrontational" musical conversations, see Richard Will, "When God Met the Sinner, and Other Dramatic Confrontations in Eighteenth-Century Instrumental Music," *Music and Letters* 78, no. 2 (May 1997): 176–209.

[23] This aspect of Sulzer's commentary, arguably out of date by the 1770s, is consistent with Johann Joachim Quantz's earlier definition of a quartet (n.b., not a *string* quartet) as a sonata with three concertante instruments and a bass. Quantz thus regards the basso continuo part as being different in kind from the more melodic (concertante) upper voices, and he reinforces the basso continuo's distinct role throughout his discussion. Among his requirements for "a good quartet," he lists "a fundamental part with a true bass quality." Quantz also requires that "each part, after it has rested, must re-enter not as a middle part, but as a principal part, with a pleasing melody; *but this applies only to the three concertante parts, not to the bass*" (emphasis added). Quantz's only nod to a melodic role for the basso continuo part is a requirement that "if a fugue appears, it must be carried out *by all four parts* [emphasis added] in a masterful yet

Writing about a generation later, Heinrich Christoph Koch's article on sonatas in his *Musikalisches Lexikon* borrows liberally from Sulzer, echoing his praise of Bach's sonatas and additionally praising those of Haydn and Mozart. Whereas Sulzer wrote that a sonata might be construed as either a monologue or dialogue, Koch adds a significant clarification by introducing explicit criteria for distinguishing between these two paradigms:

In the two-voiced sonata in which a main part [*Hauptstimme*] is accompanied by a bass part [*Grundstimme*] – that is, in which only a [single] main part exists – only the passions [*Empfindungen*] of a single person are conveyed. But in the two-, three- or four-voiced sonata in which two, three, or four main voices exist, the passions of exactly that many individual people are conveyed ...

The sonata comprehends various categories – designated by the terms solo, duet, trio, quartet, and so on – according to the number of different parts and the diverse manner of handling these parts, in so far as they assert themselves as main parts [*Hauptstimmen*]. Each of these categories is treated [in the *Musikalisches Lexikon*] in its own article.[24]

Refining and expanding on Sulzer's treatment, Koch describes how a chamber work can represent any number of individuals, exactly equal to the number of main parts (*Hauptstimmen*).[25] Sulzer's conception of the H. 579

tasteful fashion, in accordance with all the rules." Quantz, *Versuch*, 302 (Web Doc. #25). English translation from *On Playing the Flute*, 316–17. Quantz recommends Telemann's six quartets (mostly for flute, oboe, violin, and basso continuo) as examples. For a further analysis of Quantz's comments, see Janet M. Levy, "The *Quatuor Concertant* in Paris in the Latter Half of the Eighteenth Century" (Ph.D. diss., Stanford University, 1971), 46–7.

[24] Koch, *Musikalisches Lexikon*, s.v. "Sonate," cols. 1415 n. and 1417 (Web Doc. #12). An early version of Koch's "Sonate" discussion appears in his *Versuch einer Anleitung zur Composition*, vol. 3 (Leipzig, 1793), 315–16 (Web Doc. #14). See also the English translation published in Sulzer and Koch, *Aesthetics and the Art of Musical Composition*, 103–5. Augustus Frederic Christopher Kollmann (whose writings are strongly influenced by Koch) draws an equivalent distinction between (1) sonatas for a single *principal* part, with the others designated as *accompaniments*, and what he calls (2) "regular or proper Duos, Trios, Quatuors, Quintetts, &c.," which consist of "concerting" instruments only. Kollmann, *Essay on Practical Musical Composition* (London, 1799), 12–14. The term "concerting" (along with its cognates *concertirend* and *concertant*) is discussed below, 36–40.

 The word "Hauptstimme" frequently appears (in both singular and plural forms) in Sulzer's and Koch's writings. It has a broad meaning, referring not to a single main melody (*Hauptmelodie*) but to up to four melodic voices that are not overtly accompanimental filler (e.g., sustained chords in orchestral wind parts). See, for instance, Koch's separate articles for "Hauptstimme," "Nebenstimmen," and "Füllstimme" in his *Musikalisches Lexikon*. The "Hauptstimme" entry is quoted as Web Doc. #9.

[25] It should be noted that Koch's notion of musical dialogue is not limited to small instrumental ensembles, since he discusses the concerto as "a passionate dialogue" (*leidenschaftliche Unterhaltung*) between soloist and orchestra (*Versuch*, 3:332). Yet, earlier in the same passage, he also describes the concerto soloist's expression as a "Monolog in leidenschaftlichen Tönen"

trio sonata as a conversation between only *two* personas reflects his older perspective, whereby the number of musical personas equals the number of parts *other than the bass line*, which will automatically be regarded as a mere *Grundstimme*. This difference between Sulzer's and Koch's conceptions betrays a shift in musical style regarding the bass at the twilight of the thoroughbass era.[26] By the time of Koch's writing in 1802, the bass part had emerged from its former accompanimental role and had been honored as a legitimate *obbligato* voice; no longer made to dine with the servants, the sonata's bass instrument was now invited to join the party and mingle with the other guests.

The string quartet: Koch's theory of textural roles

Since its infancy, the string quartet has been compared so often to conversation that, even by the end of the eighteenth century, the genre had all but monopolized the idea of musical conversation.[27] The designation "quatuors dialogués" appeared on the very first edition of Haydn's quartets, which dates from 1764 (see title page, Fig. 2.1).[28] One of the earliest critical

(ibid., 3:331). See discussion in Keefe, *Mozart's Piano Concertos*, 1–23. See also William Benjamin, "Mozart: Piano Concerto No. 17 in G Major, K. 453, Movement I," in *Analytical Studies in World Music*, ed. Michael Tenzer (Oxford University Press, 2006), 337 n. 11.

[26] See James Webster's series of studies of the evolving role of the cello/bass part in Haydn's music: "Towards a History of Viennese Chamber Music in the Early Classical Period," *Journal of the American Musicological Society* 27 (1974): 212–47; "Violoncello and Double Bass in the Chamber Music of Haydn and His Viennese Contemporaries, 1750–1780," *Journal of the American Musicological Society* 29, no. 3 (Autumn 1976): 413–38; and "The Bass Part in Haydn's Early String Quartets," *Musical Quarterly* 63, no. 3 (July 1977): 390–424.

[27] Finscher, *Studien zur Geschichte des Streichquartetts*, 285–89. See also Mara Parker, *The String Quartet, 1750–1797: Four Types of Conversation* (Burlington: Ashgate, 2002), 49–52. Whereas "conversational" aspects of eighteenth-century quartets are by necessity highly stylized, by the twentieth century it was possible to enact musical conversations far more literally, as in Charles Ives's famous depiction of an argument in his Second String Quartet (c. 1913–15). A generation later, Elliott Carter likewise described his Second String Quartet (1959) in terms of an interaction among four characters each represented by one of the instruments.

[28] Le Chevardière's 1764 edition (see Fig. 2.1) included the quartets now catalogued as op. 1 nos. 1–4 along with two flute quartets that are actually by Toeschi. The term "dialogué" became a common designation for quartets and other chamber music published in Paris after around 1770 and was often used interchangeably with "concertant." See discussion of *quatuors concertants* below, 47–8. Paul Griffiths has criticized references to Haydn's op. 1 as evoking dialogue, arguing that true musical conversation emerges only in op. 9. Griffiths, *The String Quartet* (New York: Thames and Hudson, 1983), 11 and 22. For a defense of op. 1 as conversation, see Daniel Heartz, *Haydn, Mozart, and the Viennese School: 1740–1780* (New

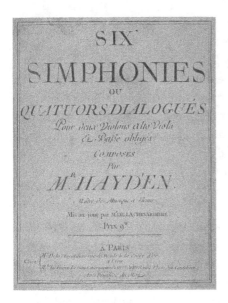

Fig. 2.1 Title page of Haydn, String Quartets, op. 1, nos. 1–4. Paris: La Chevardière, [1764].

statements to invoke this metaphor appears in the preface to Johann Friedrich Reichardt's *Vermischte Musikalien*:

In the quartet, I was guided by the idea of a conversation among four characters. When I attempted to apply this idea to the quintet, I realized that the precept which Horace gave to dramatists – "nec quarta loqui persona laboret" – is perfectly apt here as well. The fifth character is irrelevant both to the variety of the conversation and to the completeness of the harmony, merely causing confusion in the former and blurring the piece as a whole.[29]

York: W. W. Norton, 1995), 250; and Elaine Sisman's chapter "Haydn's Career and the Multiple Audience," in *The Cambridge Companion to Haydn*, 5.

[29] Joseph Friedrich Reichardt, *Vermischte Musikalien* (Riga, 1773); also published in *Joh. Friedrich Reichardt: Sein Leben und seine Werke*, ed. Hans Michel Schletterer (Augsburg, 1865), 204 (Web Doc. #27). Reichardt alludes to the so-called rule of three actors from Horace's *Ars poetica*, usually interpreted to mean that only three actors should participate in dialogue at once; others appearing on stage should be mute.

A similar swipe at the quintet comes from Haydn, who nevertheless reportedly enjoyed playing quintets with Mozart. Explaining why he had never composed a quintet himself, he told Ferdinand Ries that "he had always had enough with four voices" and even declined a commission for three quintets because "he could not find the fifth voice." Franz Gerhard Wegeler and Ferdinand Ries, *Biographische Notizen über Ludwig van Beethoven*, ed. Alfred Christlieb Kalischer (Berlin: Schuster & Loeffler, 1906), 103. Tchaikovsky made much the same point while working on his sextet, *Souvenir de Florence*, op. 70: "One needs six independent but at the same time homogeneous voices. This is frightfully difficult. Haydn never managed to conquer this problem and never wrote anything but quartets for *Kammermusik*." Piotr Ilyich Tchaikovsky to Modest Tchaikovsky, Frolovskoie, June 15/27, 1890. Tchaikovsky, *Letters to His*

What is it about the string quartet that has drawn so many authors to make this comparison? Perhaps timbral homogeneity is suggestive of four human voices,[30] but other timbrally homogeneous genres (such as Renaissance consort music) are rarely described in conversational terms. An important consideration is the historical moment of the quartet's rise to prominence during the final quarter of the eighteenth century, a period of intense interest in the art of conversation. The origin of the "art" quartet in simpler, more functional genres used as background music at social events is also relevant. That string chamber music often served as accompaniment for conversation may partly explain why it has so often been construed as an imitation of it.

But the most fundamental factor, discussed by numerous authors both historical and modern, is the frequent textural renewal, suggestive of a spontaneous interchange among the parts. Their dynamic interaction and constant role exchange – to come forward and to recede, to assert and to riposte – mimics the spirited exchanges of artful conversation and fosters an appealing variety of vibrant instrumental combinations and textures, reflecting Galant aesthetics. These considerations form the central thread in Koch's discussion of "Quatuor" in the third volume of his *Versuch einer Anleitung zur Composition*:

The quartet, currently the favorite of intimate musical society, has been intensively cultivated by recent composers.

If it is truly to consist of four *obbligato* voices, of which none can claim the privilege [*Vorrecht*] of being the [sole] main part [*Hauptstimme*], then it can only be treated in the manner of a fugue.

But since the modern quartet is written in the Galant style, one must content oneself with there being four main parts of a particular kind that exchange being dominant [*vier solchen Hauptstimmen, die wechselweise herrschend sind*] and of which now one, now another takes the customary Galant-style bass.

While one of these voices is busy playing the main melody [*Hauptmelodie*], the two others [those not playing the main melody or bass] must play accessory melodies

Family: An Autobiography, trans. Galina von Meck (New York: Stein and Day, 1981), 462–63. On the history of the quintet's reception as a derivative (or inferior) genre, see Sarah J. Adams, "'Mixed' Chamber Music of the Classical Period and the Reception of Genre," in *Music, Libraries, and the Academy: Essays in Honor of Lenore Coral*, ed. James P. Cassaro (Middleton: A-R Editions, 2007), 3–20.

[30] J. C. W. Petiscus emphasizes the homogeneity of an all-string ensemble, stating that the effect would be ruined if a wind instrument were substituted for one of the parts. P[etiscus], "Ueber Quartettmusik," 520–21 (Web Doc. #23).

[*zusammen hängenden Melodien*] that enhance the expression without obscuring the main melody. From this, it is evident that the quartet is one of the most difficult types of compositions. It should be ventured only by a composer who is both fully trained and experienced in many musical textures [*Ausarbeitungen*].

Among recent composers in this genre of sonatas, *Haydn*, *Pleyl* [*sic*], and *Hofmeister* [*sic*] have provided the public with the greatest riches. But among all the modern four-part sonatas, the six quartets for two violins, viola, and cello by the late *Mozard* [*sic*], published in Vienna with a dedication to *Haydn*, best embody the idea of a true quartet. They are unique in their special mixture of strict and free style and in their treatment of harmony.[31]

In focusing so intently on matters of texture, Koch addresses an unspoken tension that loomed over the Viennese quartet as the genre rose to its first maturity: How is a composer to reconcile the Enlightenment ideal of *egalité* among four independent voices, all asserting themselves as main parts (*Hauptstimmen*), with the Galant style's preference for transparent textures? Does the division of the ensemble into melodic and accompanying roles transgress against the tenets of refined discourse, which implore conversationalists to take turns and to avoid dominating?[32]

In positing that a truly egalitarian quartet ought to be fugal, Koch suggests a style that would enact a literal (if rather formal) musical exchange, with all instruments taking turns with entries of the subject and thus dividing melodic opportunities more or less equitably.[33]

---

[31] Koch, *Versuch*, 3:325–27 (Web Doc. #15). See also the English translation published in *Introductory Essay on Composition*, trans. Nancy Kovaleff Baker (New Haven: Yale University Press, 1983), 207. Koch may be responding to Jean-Jacques Rousseau, who defined "quatuor" as follows: "This is the name given to pieces of vocal or instrumental music that are executed by four parts (see *Parts*). There are no true *Quartets*, or [if there are] they are worthless. It is necessary in a good *Quartet* that the parts are nearly always alternating, because in each chord there are at most two parts that are melodic [*fassent Chant*] and that the ear can distinguish at the same time; the other two are nothing but filler [*remplissage*], and one must never put filler in a [true] quartet." Jean-Jacques Rousseau, *Dictionnaire de musique* (Paris, 1768), s.v. "quatuor" (Web Doc. #30).

[32] See, for example, Adolph Knigge, *Über den Umgang mit Menschen* (Hannover, 1788). Haydn owned a copy of this treatise. See the catalog of Haydn's library listed in the appendix to Sisman, *Haydn and His World*, 462.

[33] Although Koch does not refer to any specific pieces (other than Mozart's "Haydn" quartets), it is likely he had Haydn's op. 20 quartets in mind in connection with the fugal style. Kollmann's discussion of quartets (which is essentially a gloss on Koch's) singles out one set by Haydn "which contains the finest simple and double fugues," a clear reference to op. 20. Kollmann, *Essay on Practical Composition*, 14. On fugue in string chamber music, see Warren Kirkendale, *Fugue and Fugato in Rococo and Classical Chamber Music* (Durham, NC: Duke University Press, 1979); and William Drabkin, *A Reader's Guide to Haydn's Early String Quartets* (Westport, CT: Greenwood Press, 2000), 51–68.

However, recognizing the incompatibility of strict fugal treatment with Galant aesthetics, Koch settles for a non-fugal texture but, significantly, one in which all four parts are designated as *Hauptstimmen*. Koch clarifies that his usage departs from the singular *Hauptstimme* (as in a two-voiced sonata for a melody instrument and continuo), in which one melodic part asserts its ancestral privilege to dominate (*das Vorrecht der Hauptstimme*). Instead, Koch describes a more egalitarian arrangement in which four co-*Hauptstimmen* are each endowed with certain natural rights to exchange roles (*vier solchen Hauptstimmen, die wechselweise herrschend sind*).[34] For Koch, status as a *Hauptstimme* is an earned rather than conferred honor. His discussion of sonatas (of which quartets are a sub-category) clarifies that these rights (*Rechte als Hauptstimmen*) belong only to parts that establish themselves as sufficiently independent; this is the distinction between a *bona fide* duet for two *Hauptstimmen* and a two-voiced sonata for one *Hauptstimme* with accompanying bass line (*begleitende Grund-stimme*).[35] Moreover, Koch's notion that *Hauptstimmen* are those parts that "portray the sentiments of individual people"[36] explicitly equates

---

Paul Griffiths describes Haydn's op. 20 as "an astounding achievement away from the main route of the string quartet's development, most spectacularly and mercilessly bizarre in its fugues, since fugue, in its ordained responses, its direct imitation and its lack of characterization in the voices, is the very antithesis of dialogue." Griffiths, *The String Quartet*, 29. See also W. Dean Sutcliffe's response, which notes that each of these fugal finales has between two and four subjects, resulting in a lively interchange among the parts. W. Dean Sutcliffe, *Haydn String Quartets Op. 50* (Cambridge University Press, 1992), 15–16. For a summary of critical responses to Haydn's fugal finales (including their relationship to the emancipation of the cello part), see Parker, *The String Quartet*, 263–64.

[34] Koch's language evokes overtones suggestive of Enlightenment political thought. The term "Vorrecht" (rather than the more neutral "Recht") may invoke ancestral or feudal rights such as the *droit du seigneur*. The word "herrschend" (from the root "Herr," meaning "Lord") could also be translated as "reigning" or "ruling."

[35] Koch, *Versuch*, 3:292 (Web Doc. #13).

[36] Koch writes: "Because in the execution of sonatas the main parts [*Hauptstimmen*] are scored with only one on a part [*einfach besezt*], the melody of a sonata must relate to that of a symphony like the melody of an aria compared to that of a chorus; that is, since the melody of a sonata portrays the sentiments of individual people, it must be exquisitely cultivated and seem to represent the subtlest nuances of the sentiments. In contrast, the melody of the symphony must distinguish itself not through such subtleties of expression but through power and force [*Kraft und Nachdruck*]" (ibid., 3:315–16) (Web Doc. #14).

Koch is yet more explicit in the entry for "Hauptstimme" in his *Musikalisches Lexikon*, which distinguishes homophonic (*homophonisch*) and polyphonic (*polyphonisch*) compositions on the basis of the number of *Hauptstimmen*. "Homophonic" denotes a composition "in which the individual sentiment of a single person [*individuelle Empfindungsart eines einzigen Menschen*] is expressed by means of a single main part [*Hauptstimme*]," whereas "polyphonic" indicates one "in which the composer expresses the sentiment[s] of various people [*die Empfindung*

Hauptstimme status with personhood, adumbrating a rudimentary concept of a musical persona or agent.[37]

Within a string quartet, Koch regards the four *Hauptstimmen* as constantly exchanging the three paradigmatic textural roles: (1) the primary melody (*Hauptmelodie*), (2) the Galant-style bass line, and (3) the accessory melodies (*zusammen hängenden Melodien*, literally "connected" melodies) of the two remaining parts, which must enhance the expression without obscuring the *Hauptmelodie*.[38] Koch thus distinguishes decisively between the *instrumental parts* (violin I, violin II, viola, and cello, all *Hauptstimmen*) and *textural roles* (*Hauptmelodie*, bass, and accessory melodies), positing no fixed or normative relationship between them. Although the most common arrangement is surely for the first violin to act as *Hauptmelodie*, inner parts as accessory melodies, and cello as bass line, Koch does not even so much as imply this.[39] Instead, he emphasizes the constant exchange of roles, noting that even the bass role is traded among the parts.[40] It is also significant that Koch avoids referring to any of the roles as accompanimental or of secondary importance. Even the accessory melodies are nevertheless described as melodies, different in kind from, but no less essential than, the *Hauptmelodie*. The only restriction on their behavior is that they not obscure the *Hauptmelodie*, a principle of cooperation or fairness rather than subordination.[41]

verschiedener Menschen] through multiple main parts [*Hauptstimmen*]." Koch, *Musikalisches Lexikon*, s.v. "Hauptstimme," col. 749 (Web Doc. #9).

[37] I will return to theories of musical agency in Chapter 4.

[38] An alternative translation of "zusammen hängenden Melodien" is "complementary melodic material" (adopted in Hunter, "The Quartets," 120). Koch's distinction between *Hauptmelodie* and *zusammen hängenden Melodien* anticipates Schoenberg's use of the markings for *Hauptstimme* and *Nebenstimme*. One difference, however, is that Koch designates as accessory melodies any musical material within a quartet other than *Hauptmelodie* and bass, whereas Schoenberg restricts the marking *Nebenstimme* more narrowly to figures that are motivic (and often expressive, similar to the hairpin marking in Brahms's music).

[39] Moreover, Koch does not proscribe any unlikely combinations (such as first violin as bass supporting cello as melody), nor does he address unison textures or combinations that may arise when one or more parts rest.

[40] The emancipation of the cello from an exclusively bass-line role calls to mind Mozart's "Prussian" quartets (K. 575, 589, and 590), dedicated (according to Mozart's private thematic catalog) to Friedrich Wilhelm II, King of Prussia and an avid cellist. Certain Haydn quartets, such as the Quartet in C Major, op. 20, no. 2, likewise feature the cello prominently as a melodic instrument. The extensive use of the cello as *Hauptmelodie* results in a theretofore-unprecedented richness of role exchange among the other voices.

[41] The respect Koch confers on the accessory melodies contrasts sharply with Quantz's earlier commentary, which states that a good quartet requires "ideas that can be exchanged with one another, so that the composer can build both above and below them, and *middle parts that are at least passable and not unpleasant* [emphasis added]." Quantz, *Versuch*, 302 (Web Doc. #25),

In sum, Koch has described a dynamic relationship within the quartet texture, one that reconciles the ideal of overall textural clarity with the need for each *Hauptstimme* to have its own integrity and to express a variety of roles, including melodic ones. In praising Mozart's "Haydn" quartets for their mix of free and fugal styles, Koch may have been thinking especially of the finale to K. 387, which alternates fugal and *opera-buffa*-type sections (see analysis below, 118–22).[42] But, to interpret Koch's praise more broadly, these six quartets are prime examples of Mozart's virtuosic command of textural variety. From the players' perspective, the experience of sight-reading these quartets involves the constant search for new partners with each change of textural roles – a shared rhythm with one instrument here, a contrapuntal interchange with another there, and now a passage with all four parts in unison – that resembles a spirited social exchange.

Koch adds a small but noteworthy detail in a later version of the same discussion about quartets included in the *Musikalisches Lexikon*. Whereas the earlier *Versuch* article describes the quartet as consisting of four principal parts, here Koch adds the modifier "concerting" (*vier concertirende Hauptstimmen*).[43] The term "concerting" (an English-language cognate of the German *concertirend* or French *concertant*) is partly synonymous with "obbligato," designating a part that is essential (as opposed to an *ad libitum* accompanimental part) and that is played by a

---

discussed above, 28 n. 23. It bears repeating, however, that Quantz's discussion pertains to quartets for three concertante instruments plus continuo, not to string quartets.

[42] The mixture of homophonic and fugal styles was not universally praised. Carl Friedrich Zelter observed that "Haydn, in one of his newest and finest symphonies in C major, has a fugue as a final movement [Hob. I: 95, actually in C minor but with a finale in C major]; Mozart did this, too, in his tremendous Symphony in C major [K. 551], in which, as we all know, he pushed things a little too far" (Haydn brachte in einer seiner neuern und schönsten Symfonieen aus C, in den Schlusssaz [*sic*] eine Fuge; *Mozart* hat das auch in seiner furchtbaren Symfonie aus C dur, worin er's bekanntlich ein wenig arg macht). Z[elter], "Bescheidene Anfragen an die modernsten Komponisten und Virtuosen," *Allgemeine musikalische Zeitung (Leipzig)* 1, no. 10 (December 5, 1798): col. 153. English translation from Neal Zaslaw, "The Breitkopf Firm's Relations with Leopold and Wolfgang Mozart," in *Bach Perspectives 2: J. S. Bach, the Breitkopfs, and the Eighteenth-Century Music Trade*, ed. George B. Stauffer (Lincoln: University of Nebraska Press, 1996), 89. The finale to the "Jupiter" Symphony bears some resemblance to that of K. 387. For a nuanced discussion comparing the "rhetoric of the learned style" in these two finales, see Elaine Sisman, *Mozart: The Jupiter Symphony* (Cambridge University Press, 1993), 68–79.

[43] Koch, *Musikalisches Lexikon*, col. 1209 (Web Doc. #11). Another minor difference is that, in this later version in the *Musikalisches Lexikon*, Koch praises all of Mozart's "four-voiced sonatas" (*vierstimmigen Sonaten*, i.e., quartets) without specifically highlighting the six quartets dedicated to Haydn. Additionally, though Koch repeats and bolsters his praise of Haydn, the references to Pleyel and Hoffmeister are removed, presumably indicating a change in Koch's appraisal of their stature in the ensuing decade. Ludwig Finscher notes that the broad transmission of Koch's ideas helped establish Haydn and Mozart as the quintessential exemplars (*Gattungsnorm*) for the string quartet (Finscher, *Studien zur Geschichte des Streichquartetts*, 291).

single player.[44] Koch defines the term in a separate entry in the *Musika-lisches Lexikon*:

Concertirend (*concertando, concertato*) indicates those voices of a composition that alternate carrying the melody [*Melodie*] with the given main voice [*Hauptstimme*], or that are heard with solo phrases [*Solosätzen*] between the phrases [*Sätzen*] of the main voice, in order to compete [*wettstreiten*], so to speak, either among themselves or with the main voice, as indicated by the word's root, *concertare*.[45]

Koch's intended meaning of "concertirend" as it applies to quartets remains somewhat vague, since the two examples he provides – a symphony with a pair of concerting violins and an aria with concerting oboe – both pertain to orchestral music. In these contexts, when Koch refers to an alternation between the concerting instrument and the *Hauptstimme*, the latter term designates whichever part would normally carry the melody (i.e., the *ripieno* first violins in the symphony and the vocal soloist in the aria). This usage of "Hauptstimme" is thus slightly different from that of the "Quatuor" article, in which all four parts were designated as *Hauptstimmen*. In these orchestral contexts, the term *Hauptstimme* refers both to a specific *part* (the *ripieno* violins or the aria's soloist) and to the fixed *role* played by that part (the primary melody, or *Hauptmelodie*).[46]

Since the *Hauptstimme* reasonably expects to be the most prominent part, the *concertirend* instrument could be understood as a kind of interloper encroaching on the *Hauptstimme*'s domain. Koch provocatively describes a contest between the *concertirend* instrument and the *Hauptstimme*, referring to the former's motivations in less than innocent terms; the verb "wettstreiten" literally means "to dispute," and the noun form "Wettstreit" denotes a "contest," "challenge," or "rivalry."[47] This sense of musical one-upmanship is palpable in passages from the finales of *sinfonie*

---

[44] Janet Levy's critical survey of "concertirend" and "concertant" in eighteenth-century writings meticulously documents four primary meanings: (1) a setting with one player per part, (2) a style resembling dialogue, in which all parts are alternately or mutually important, (3) a soloistic, sometimes virtuosic style; and (4) an opposition, struggle, or competition of unequal forces, from the root "concertare." Levy, "The *Quatuor Concertant* in Paris," 45–59. Her survey corrects the tendency of modern scholars to interpret the term as necessarily denoting virtuoso display, as in a concerto.

[45] Koch, *Musikalisches Lexikon*, s.v. "Concertirend," cols. 355–56 (see Web Doc. #8).

[46] In contrast, Koch's view of the quartet designates all four parts as *Hauptstimmen*, none of which can legitimately expect to be the exclusive, primary melodic voice since the role of *Hauptmelodie* is constantly exchanged.

[47] A similar connotation for "concertiren" is expressed by Sulzer: "A true trio has three main parts [*Hauptstimmen*] that concert against one another [*die gegen einander concertiren*], and have, as it were, a conversation in tones." Sulzer, *Allgemeine Theorie*, s.v. "Trio," 4:599 (Web Doc. #35). This article was probably written by Schulz. Koch's notion of *Wettstreit* resembles the kind of musical confrontations discussed in Will, "When God Met the Sinner, and Other Dramatic Confrontations in Eighteenth-Century Instrumental Music."

Ex. 2.1 Haydn, *Sinfonia concertante* in B♭ Major, Hob. I:105, Allegro con spirito (iii), final soli

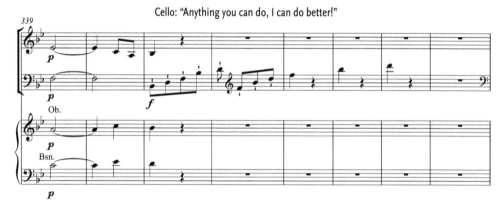

concertanti by Haydn and Mozart (shown in Exx. 2.1 and 2.2, respectively). In the Haydn excerpt, the cellist's final solo soars to an unbelievably, almost comically stratospheric note (d^3), seemingly so as not to let the violinist outdo him.

Ex. 2.2 Mozart, *Sinfonia concertante* in E♭ Major, K. 364, Presto (iii), final soli

Fig. 2.2 Jeremy Ballard, caricature of Amadeus Quartet first violinist Norbert Brainin (left) and violist Peter Schidlof (right) performing the Mozart *Sinfonia concertante*.

In a comparable passage, Mozart's viola soloist reaches up to a range far beyond his characteristic tessitura – his last hurrah, as it were – before the violin imitates an octave higher.

This spirit of friendly rivalry is captured in Fig. 2.2, a caricature of the Amadeus Quartet's first violinist Norbert Brainin (left) and violist Peter Schidlof (right) performing Mozart's *Sinfonia concertante*. But a more intensely *wettstreitend* exchange is that between Madame Herz and Mademoiselle Silberklang, the two prima donnas who vie for supremacy in "Ich bin die erste Sängerin" from Mozart's *Der Schauspieldirektor*, K. 486.

Unlike a concerting oboe alternating statements with an aria's soloist, Koch's notion of a string quartet containing four concerting *Hauptstimmen* is more complex, since it suggests that all four vie for prominence on an ongoing basis. Might this element of gamesmanship and competition among the quartet's members be a motivating factor behind the constant exchanging of roles, like a subtle rivalry among friends beneath a veneer of polite decorum?[48]

---

[48] A similar element of one-upmanship is frequently mentioned in discussions of artful conversation in conduct manuals. One seventeenth-century French author, seemingly the first

The string quartet as conversation: Italian and French perspectives

The quartet-as-conversation trope came into its own in the early nine-teenth century, with some sources offering such fanciful descriptions and characterizations that they overshadow any discussion of the music's technical features. One particularly colorful example comes from Giuseppe Carpani's early biography of Haydn:

A friend of mine imagined, in listening to a quartet of Haydn, that he was witnessing a conversation of four amiable people. I always liked this idea, as it very much resembles the truth. It seemed to him that he recognized in the first violin a man of spirit and affability, middle aged, a good speaker [*parlatore*], who sustained the major part of the discourse, which he himself initiated and animated. In the second violin he recognized a friend of the first, who sought in every way to make him shine [*farlo comparire*], rarely taking turns for himself [*occupandosi rare volte di se stesso*], and intent on sustaining the conversation more by agreeing to what he heard from the other [violin] than with his own ideas. The *Bass* [*basso*, i.e., cello] was a solid man, learned, and sententious. Bit by bit he went along supporting the discourse of the first violin with laconic but confident statements [*sicure sentenze*], and occasion-ally – as a prophet, a man well experienced in the knowledge of things – predicted what the principal speaker [*l'oratore principale*] would have said and gave strength and direction [*norma*] to what was said. The viola, then, seemed to him a somewhat loquacious matron, who actually did not have very important things to say but nonetheless wanted to intrude [*intromettersi*] into the discourse and seasoned the conversation with her grace and sometimes with delightful chatterings [*cicalate*] that gave the others a chance to take a breath; in the rest [of the time], she was more the friend of the *Bass* than of all the other interlocutors.[49]

of many to compare conversation specifically to racquet sports, emphasizes the importance of maintaining an underlying spirit of friendly competition: "Just as it is useless in handball [*au jeu de la Paulme*] to strike the ball hard if it is not returned to you, so conversation cannot be pleasant if repartee is lacking." François la Mothe le Vayer, *Opuscules, ou petits traictez* (Paris, 1644), 2:228. English translation from Burke, *The Art of Conversation*, 91.

A more overtly aggressive style is advocated by sixteenth-century Italian authors, who recommend that language be witty (*motteggievole*) and biting (*mordace*) in conversation. It may seem a touch Orwellian that Giovanni della Casa refers to the "sweetness of victory" (*la dolcezza di vincere*) in conversation in a book ostensibly about manners and courtesy. Della Casa, *Il Galateo* (Venice, 1558), Ch. 18; summarized in Burke, *The Art of Conversation*, 98–99. The tension between cooperation and competition is a throughline in Burke's discussion of early-modern conversation manuals (ibid., 89–122).

49   Giuseppe Carpani, *Le Haydine, ovvero Lettere sulla vita e opere del célèbre maestro Giuseppe Haydn* (Milan, 1812), 91–92 n. (Web Doc. #4). English translation adapted from Fabio Morabito, "Authorship, Performance and Musical Identity in Restoration Paris" (Ph.D. diss.,

Carpani's "friend" describes himself as being present while four figurative friends converse. Like Koch, Carpani outlines various roles within the string quartet: as "l'oratore principale," the intelligent first violin animates the discussion by introducing ideas, which the second violin supports and approves (without introducing new ones of his own), while the solid cello delivers his laconic pronouncements, and the viola contributes her feminine grace.[50]

To speak in broad terms (and at risk of turning Carpani's remarks into a kind of analytical method), his discussion could inspire a reasonably good account of the four parts in the opening of Haydn's Quartet in G Major, op. 77 no. 1 (shown in Ex. 2.3a). As the piece begins, the first violin introduces the first thematic idea, supported by *leggiero* chords from the others and the occasional "approving" commentary figure from the second violin (m. 4 and m. 8), who endorses the first violin's statements without adding anything original. The cello introduces certain salient accidentals throughout the excerpt, notably the A♯ shared with the viola in m. 12, which fleetingly implies a possible swerve toward E minor (as in Ex. 2.3b).

King's College, University of London, in progress). A paginated version of Morabito's dissertation was not available at the time of writing; all citations are from his Chapter 2.

Carpani's discussion has subsequently become known in a plagiarized French-language adaptation by Stendhal (Marie-Henri Beyle), intended as an improvement on and translation of Carpani's *Le Haydine* (but without any reference to him as the original author) and with added material about Mozart and Metastasio. The corresponding passage about Haydn's quartets appears in Stendhal, *Lettres écrites de Vienne en Autriche, sur le célèbre compositeur Jh. Haydn* (Paris, 1814), 61–62 (Web Doc. #32). Trans. Richard N. Coe as *Lives of Haydn, Mozart and Metastasio* (London: Calder & Boyars, 1972), 35–36. Stendhal curiously inverts two of Carpani's characterizations, describing the viola as "un homme solide, savant, et sentencieux" who delivers "maximes laconiques, mais frappantes de vérité," and the cello as a "bonne femme un peu bavarde" possessing a "penchant secret" for the viola. The Carpani and Stendhal passages are frequently cited in studies of quartets. See, for example, Elaine Sisman, "Rhetorical Truth in Haydn's Chamber Music," in *Haydn and the Performance of Rhetoric*, 301–2.

[50] Carpani's gendered characterizations of the instruments' discourse is striking. The violins and cello are described with words borrowed from rhetoric or regular speech (e.g. *parlatore, oratore, interlocutori*), whereas the viola character is described as chattering (*cicalate*, literally, denotes the sound of a cicada) and as pushing her way (*intromettersi*) into a predominantly male exchange, to which she offers nothing of substance.

Carpani's treatment of the viola as female is puzzling since, at the time, bowed string instruments were played almost exclusively by men. Schönfeld's *Jahrbuch der Tonkunst von Wien und Prague*, which lists sixty-some string players active in Vienna around 1796, includes but two women (both violinists); see Schönfeld, "A Yearbook of Music in Vienna and Prague, 1796," 289–320. It is, of course, possible for a male player to enact a female musical persona; I will return to the distinction between player and persona in Chapter 4. However, there may be a simpler explanation for Carpani's description, namely, the genders of "il violino," "il violoncello," and "la viola" in his native language.

Ex. 2.3 Haydn, String Quartet in G Major, op. 77, no. 1, Allegro moderato (i), opening

a. Score

Ex. 2.3 (*cont.*)

Violins exchange triplets, viola
emphasizes syncopated slurs

Cello comes to fore ...

... leading to new key dominant pedal

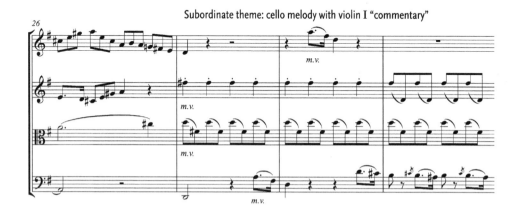

Subordinate theme: cello melody with violin I "commentary"

b. Recomposition of mm. 11–14

He had previously suggested this same key in m. 10, perhaps commenting subtly on the first violin's part in m. 3.

After the opening returns in m. 14, significant accidentals are introduced in m. 16 by the second violin (C♯) and viola (B♭), revealing that this seeming repetition of the primary theme is proving to be the transition. In harmonic terms, these accidentals have the effect of turning the cello's tonic pedal into a dissonance – exerting pressure on him to resolve down to F♯ – and ushering in the necessary modulation to the dominant. As the modulation gets underway, with the two violins exchanging their triplet figures (mm. 19ff., with the second violin still imitating his more inspired colleague), the cello responds by coming to the fore in m. 21. With his descending minor-scale figure, the most sustained material in the quartet so far, he leads to the new-key dominant pedal (mm. 24–26), thus preparing for the subordinate theme. Like "a prophet or a man well-experienced in the knowledge of things," he has anticipated where the exchange was headed and offered "strength and direction" to establish the new key, thereby earning the right to introduce the subordinate theme (mm. 27ff.), a D-major statement of the opening thematic idea that comments on the first violin's original presentation. As for the poor viola: she has not yet had occasion to reveal her chatterbox character – her most independent figures so far, the syncopated slurs in mm. 19–20 and 24–25, having been largely overshadowed by the parts above and below her – but then, the quartet has only just begun.

Beyond the obvious differences in tone and intent between Carpani's caricatures and Koch's technical comments, what sets their notions of the string quartet apart is Carpani's vision of a clearer hierarchy in which the four instruments' relative roles are fixed as opposed to Koch's emphasis on role exchange. For instance, Carpani's second violin "rarely took turns [i.e., the *Hauptmelodie*] for himself," content to play Dr. Watson to the first violin's Holmes. In a sense, this acknowledgment of inequality is to

Carpani's credit, since he arguably describes the generic, relative prominence of each part more accurately than does Koch.

While Koch overstates his case about the quartet's supposed egalitarianism (surely more an ideal than a literal reality), he nevertheless shows a refined sensitivity to texture and concurrent activity within the ensemble.[51] Whereas Koch painstakingly describes how the *Hauptmelodie*, Galant bass, and accessory melodies interact simultaneously to create the complete quartet texture, Carpani seems to hear only melodic statements as representing conversational speech.[52] His description of the viola's role is a case in point: her principal activity – what Koch would call "accessory melodies that enhance the expression" – constitutes for Carpani "not hav[ing] very important things to say"; and on those rare occasions when she has the melody, the others (who presumably take up the "accessory melodies") are, for Carpani, merely "tak[ing] a breath." In short, Carpani falls into the common trap of acknowledging only melodic utterance as part of the quartet's conversation.[53]

Such focus on melodic utterance is, in fact, a trend among Franco-Italian musicians.[54] One source with an unprecedented focus on melody is the *Traité de mélodie* by the Czech-born French composer Anton Reicha. Reicha provides the following instructions about how a composer may "dialogue" (*dialoguer*) a melody:

Writing a melody in the form of a dialogue involves the distribution of the phrases, members, ideas, and periods among two or more voices or instruments, or even

---

[51] Koch's overstatement of the instruments' equality of rank represents a privileging of the ideology of egalitarianism over the actual practice in the repertoire. Koch may also be mistaking a trend toward a more equitable interchange with the actual attainment of equality.

[52] Indeed, my neo-Carpanian analysis of Ex. 2.3 goes beyond Carpani's original purview since it incorporates salient accidentals and harmonies as influenced by accompanimental parts. This broadened purview allowed for an analysis involving all four parts to a greater degree than would be possible in an analysis focused exclusively on the exchange of melodic motives.

[53] Indeed, the opposite extreme – regarding every utterance simultaneously declaimed as part of a (rather cacophonous) conversation – is equally problematic. See the discussion by W. Dean Sutcliffe, quoted below, 116–18.

[54] Cf. Berlioz's anecdote about his earliest attempts at composition, which included two quintets for flute and strings written at the age of twelve. His father (who had provided elementary musical instruction) was unimpressed with the first of these, but Berlioz recounts how he evaluated the second one: "My father was like *many people who think they can judge a quartet by hearing the first violin part* [emphasis added], and asked me to play him over the flute part beforehand. I did so, and at a particular passage he called out, 'Bravo! that *is* music!'" Berlioz was fortunate to receive his father's praise based on the melody only, since the subsequent read-through of the quintet with amateur string players who "blundered about most hopelessly" would have made a less favorable impression. See *Memoirs of Hector Berlioz*, trans. Ernest Newman (New York: Alfred A. Knopf, 1932), 12.

between an instrument and a voice. In practicing this, one first makes a succession of well-connected periods, while observing the following.

There are only four ways to write a melody in the form of a dialogue: (1) by alternately performing entire periods, (2) by distributing the phrases, or members of periods, between the different voices which must perform the melody, (3) by creating a dialogue with the figures, that is, through small imitations, (4) by beginning a phrase in one voice, and concluding it in another.

The former is the easiest, where one period is given to one part, and another to a second part, etc.; however, one must be careful to create only short periods, without which the dialogue would become sluggish. In all other aspects, the periods follow the same principles as those written for a single voice.

The dialogue between phrases is more intense and more interesting. In terms of the rhythm, it should proceed in the following way:

The First part.	The Second part.
First four-measure phrase;	Second four-measure phrase;
Third four-measure phrase;	Fourth four-measure phrase;
Fifth three-measure phrase;	Sixth three-measure phrase;
Seventh eight-measure phrase, etc.	Eighth eight-measure phrase, etc.[55]

Reicha's notion of dialogue, then, is an egalitarian alternation whereby several voices or instruments share successively in the melodic action of a piece. Although Reicha's treatise addresses vocal melody primarily, his evenhanded melodic exchange might well describe the *style dialogué* of the Parisian *quatuor concertant*.[56] This now-neglected genre, represented by several thousand compositions by over two hundred composers published between c. 1770 and 1800, appealed to amateur players in Parisian salons because it was often easier to execute compared to Viennese quartets, and perhaps also, as Barbara R. Hanning has suggested, because it mimicked the spirit of artful conversation that was so vital to Parisian salon culture. Many sets of quartets were published in Paris with titles

---

[55] Anton Reicha, *Traité de mélodie* (Paris, 1814), 89–90 (Web Doc. #26). English translation from *Treatise on Melody*, trans. Peter M. Landey (Hillsdale, NY: Pendragon Press, 2000), 88. I have emended Landey's translation, which erroneously states "four-measure phrase" on all four lines. See also Keefe's discussion of Reicha's notion of dialogue in *Mozart's Piano Concertos*, 24–41.

[56] The foundational study of this genre is Levy, "The *Quatuor Concertant* in Paris." On the application of Reicha's musical dialogue to *quatuors concertants*, see pp. 178–81. On the *symphonie concertante*, a related genre, see also Barry S. Brook, "The *Symphonie Concertante*: An Interim Report," *Musical Quarterly* 47, no. 4 (October 1961): 493–516; and Barry S. Brook, "The *Symphonie Concertante*: Its Musicological and Sociological Bases," *International Review of the Aesthetics and Sociology of Music* 25, nos. 1–2 (June–December 1994): 131–48.

similar to *Six Quatuors Concertants et Dialogués*; the most appealing specimens were commonly praised as "bien dialogués."[57]

The locution "style dialogué" suggests close parallels between the arts of music and conversation as understood by French Enlightenment authors.[58] Many suggestions about conversation in etiquette manuals resemble musical ideas discussed above, such as the notion that participants in a conversation have roles that are both complementary and exchangeable. De Staël observes that conversation demands participants who "alternate [being] hearers and admirers," and "excel in the art of knowing where to speak and where to be silent."[59] Implicit in her remarks is that artful conversationalists know how to draw their companions into the discourse, an idea that resembles Koch's emphasis on reciprocal role exchange. A first violinist might cede the *Hauptmelodie* role to the second violinist, whom the former then supports with accessory melodies that enhance the expression but do not compete for prominence. By providing such accessory melodies, the first violin enables the second violin to sound his best, just as the act of asking a thoughtful question and then listening intently helps to elicit an entertaining or interesting reply. However, conversation also includes roles that are not so easily exchanged. Abbé André Morellet, for instance, outlines distinct roles for women and men in mixed company and particularly emphasizes the hostess's special responsibility to facilitate the give and take.[60] Like Carpani's conception of the viola persona, the hostess's role is fixed (and, for that matter, gendered). She is expected to contribute not so much through speaking but by establishing an atmosphere that enables the (mostly male) conversationalists to bring their best contributions to the discourse.

If Carpani offers a listener's perspective, and Reicha a composer's, the esteemed French violinist Pierre Baillot writes as a performer in his *L'art du violon: nouvelle méthode*.[61] It is in Baillot's discussion that the

---

[57] Hanning, "Conversation and Musical Style," 520. Regarding "concertant" and "dialogué" as quasi-synonyms: Nicolas Etienne Framery's definition of "concertant" explicitly entails a notion of motives "dialogued" between two or more instruments ("On appelle symphonie *concertante* celle ou le motif est dialogué entre deux ou plusieurs instrumens"). Nicolas Etienne Framery, "Concertant," in *Encyclopédie méthodique: Musique*, vol. 1 (Paris, 1791), 298–99. See also Levy, "The *Quatuor Concertant* in Paris," 49 and *passim*.

[58] These affinities are examined in Hanning, "Conversation and Musical Style."

[59] De Staël, "L'esprit de conversation," in *De l'Allemagne*, 1:95–96 (Web Doc. #31). English translation from *Germany*, 1:81.

[60] Morellet, "De la conversation," 225; cited in Hanning, "Conversation and Musical Style," 517.

[61] An illuminating study of Baillot focusing on his ideology and aesthetics as quartet performer – and offering an alternative reading of the same documents I examine here – is Morabito, "Authorship, Performance and Musical Identity."

Franco-Italian focus on the melody (and therefore the first violin part) finds its strongest expression. Describing the violinist's performing style for quartets, as opposed to sonatas or concerti, Baillot writes:

In the quartet, [the performer] sacrifices all the riches of his instrument to the general effect; he enters into the spirit of this other type of composition, whose charming dialogue seems to be a conversation among friends, who convey to each other their feelings, their sentiments, their mutual affections; their sometimes different opinions give rise to an animated discussion to which each gives his own development; they soon take pleasure in following the stimulus given by their leader, whose ascendancy carries them along, an ascendancy which he makes felt only by the power of thought that he displays, and which he owes less to the brilliance of his playing than to the persuasive sweetness of his expression.[62]

If Baillot's remarks seem to be centered squarely on the first violinist, the nature of his treatise – an encyclopedic manual of virtuoso violin playing – explains why. The first violinist's technical prowess, which Baillot imagines will far surpass that of the other players, becomes an important focus in this passage. In advising the violinist to "sacrifice all the riches of his instrument to the general effect," Baillot directs the player to forgo those virtuoso techniques that, left unchecked, would unduly draw attention to his part at the expense of the overall ensemble. Indeed, that is Baillot's main point, namely, that the (first) violin should take pains not to dominate a quartet the same way he would in a sonata or concerto.[63] It is this desire not to overshadow the others that draws him into a conversational exchange.

Addressing a readership of violinists (presumably aspiring first violinists), Baillot scarcely mentions the roles of the other instruments except to note that they interact as friends whose interchange conveys "their mutual affections." Only in those special passages in which disagreement leads to "animated discussion" does each part make its own contribution, according to Baillot. In such instances, it is the duty of the first violinist,

---

[62] Pierre-Marie-François de Sales Baillot, *L'art du violon: nouvelle méthode* (Paris, 1834), 266–67. English translation from Robin Stowell, *Violin Technique and Performance Practice in the Late Eighteenth and Early Nineteenth Centuries* (Cambridge University Press, 1985), 276–77. Web Doc. #1 quotes Baillot's complete discussion, including the discussion of sonatas and concerti as well as quartets.

[63] Cf. Baillot's discussion of sonatas: "The *sonata*, a kind of concerto divested of its accompaniments, gives him [the violinist] the means of displaying his powers, of developing a part of his resources, of letting himself be heard alone, without pomp, without pause and without any support other than an accompanying bass; left entirely to himself, he draws his nuances and his contrasts from his own resources, and by the variety of his intentions restores the effects in which this type of music may be lacking." Baillot, *L'art du violon*, 266 (Web Doc. #1). English translation from Stowell, *Violin Technique*, 276.

through "the power of [his] thought" and "persuasive sweetness of his expression" (rather than through brilliant, technical display), to guide his friends back into agreement. By discharging this responsibility, he establishes himself as the quartet's leader.[64]

---

[64] While the term "leader" for a quartet's first violinist is common in British usage, no equivalent term is used in French or German. The isolated German reference of which I am aware is Theodor Helm's assertion that the finale of Beethoven's third "Razumovsky" quartet demands a "brilliant leader [*Leitung eines genialer Führers*]." Theodor Helm, *Beethoven's Streichquartette: Versuch einer technischen Analyse dieser Werke im Zusammenhange mit ihrem geistigen Gehalt* (Leipzig, 1885), 117. Nevertheless, a privileged status of the first violinist is suggested by the tradition of naming quartets after him (as in the Schuppanzigh, Baillot, Joachim, and Rosé Quartets, among many others well into the twentieth century).

The following anecdote about the Parisian premiere of Beethoven's op. 131 speaks to Baillot's conception of the first violin as the quartet's leader. The story appears in the memoirs of Eugène Sauzay, who was Baillot's prize student and later his quartet-mate and son-in-law (Eugène Sauzay and Brigitte François-Sappey, "La vie musicale à Paris à travers les *Mémoires* d'Eugène Sauzay [1809–1901]," *Revue de Musicologie* 60, nos. 1–2 [1974]: 159–210). Sauzay describes himself as one among a group of "young revolutionaries" (p. 175) during his studies at the Conservatoire who had tired of Haydn's and Mozart's quartets and were eager to explore Beethoven's late quartets, then just a few years old. When Baillot informally read through op. 131 with them, he was reportedly moved to tears by the piece (p. 169). But when the Baillot Quartet performed it at a *séance* on May 24, 1829 as an experiment in avant-garde music, it thoroughly confounded the audience and prompted letters from Baillot's friends counseling him to give up performing this style of new music or the Séance series would fail. Sauzay attributes the audience's negative reaction to the unusual equality of voices and demands on each instrumental part in op. 131, which he thought incomprehensible to an audience accustomed to the clearer hierarchy dominated by the first violin, as in Haydn, Mozart, and early Beethoven ("cette musique à quatre voix *également importantes*, qui exige quatre exécutants de même talent, ne fut pas du tout comprise par l'auditoire des séances habitué aux formes hiérarchiques, claires et consacrées de Haydn, de Mozart et du premier Beethoven, où la voix du premier violon est prépondérante" [p. 195]). This story is paraphrased more fully in Ora Frishberg Saloman, *Listening Well: On Beethoven, Berlioz, and Other Music Criticism in Paris, Boston, and New York, 1764–1890* (New York: Peter Lang, 2009), 56–57. For Berlioz's impressions of the Baillot Quartet's performance of op. 131, which moved him profoundly, see ibid., 58–59. Note that Sauzay regards the first violin as dominating in quartets by Haydn and Mozart, the very pieces in which Koch had emphasized the equality of exchange.

Beethoven himself (reportedly) also weighed in on the novel interplay among the parts in his late quartets. Karl Holz, the second violinist of the Schuppanzigh quartet since 1823, transmits the following conversation: "When he [Beethoven] had finished composing the Quartet in B♭ [op. 130], I said I thought it was indeed the best of the set comprising opp. 127, 130 and 132. He replied: 'Each in its own way! Art does not permit us to stand still' (he often used the royal 'we' jokingly). 'You will notice a new type of part-writing [*Stimmführung*]' (by this he meant the distribution of tasks among the instruments [*hiermit ist die Instrumentirung, die Vertheilung der Rollen gemeint*]) 'and there is no less imagination than ever before, thank God.'" Wilhelm von Lenz, *Beethoven: Eine Kunst-Studie*, vol. 5 (Hamburg, 1860), 5 (Web Doc. #17). English translation from William Drabkin, "The Cello Part in Beethoven's Late Quartets," in *Beethoven Forum 7*, ed. Mark Evan Bonds, Lewis Lockwood, Christopher Reynolds, and Elaine R. Sisman (Lincoln: University of Nebraska Press, 1999), 45–46.

Baillot's exalted view of the first violinist's role was reflected is in his own performances with the Baillot Quartet at his Parisian Soirées ou Séances de Quatuors et de Quintettes. Although evidence is unclear whether (as is often reported) he indeed performed in a standing position while his colleagues remained seated,[65] it is true that he was regarded as the "headliner" or main performer of these concerts, which typically included four or five chamber works by Haydn, Mozart, Boccherini, or Beethoven, but invariably closed the evening with a virtuoso violin showpiece.[66] It is therefore not entirely surprising to read a review of one performance written by none other than the famed theorist François-Joseph Fétis that lavishly praises Baillot's gifts as a chamber musician ("passionate musician, prodigious violinist, he took on any key [*ton*] or style with an incredible flexibility, and never did his bow fail to render the exaltation that inspires him") but mentions the other musicians only as an afterthought, stating only that it was an honor for them to accompany such a prodigy![67] (Three of these musicians were regular members of the Baillot Quartet.)

Baillot's concept of the (first) violin as glorified leader within the quartet is further evinced by a poem he composed in 1839:

"Characters of the Various Musical Instruments"
Under a new scepter, leading his republic
Limiting himself to playing [*toucher*] as the only policy,
The violin appears: this king, this happy soldier,
Father of his subjects, friend of the wretched,
[He] commands, [while] obeying the passions he expresses,
His voice, through such obedience, his voice becomes sublime;
If he persuades and disarms or dominates [as] victor,
It is because he has been able to find the true way of the heart!

---

[65] The assertion that Baillot stood to perform while the others were seated stems from Joël-Marie Fauquet, who cites the eyewitness testimony of one Guillaume de Lenz, who Fauquet states attended the performance of op. 131 cited above, 50 n. 64. Joël-Marie Fauquet, *Les sociétés de musique de chambre à Paris de la Restauration à 1870* (Paris: Aux amateurs de livres, 1986), 48. However, as Morabito points out, Fauquet's statement is difficult to evaluate since no citation or other evidence of Lenz's testimony is provided (Morabito, "Authorship, Performance and Musical Identity").

[66] Bashford, "The String Quartet and Society," 10. Baillot's series is discussed extensively in Morabito, "Authorship, Performance and Musical Identity." A list of its concert programs is available from the Fonds Baillot website, www.bruzanemediabase.com/Fonds-d-archives/Fonds-Baillot/Programmes-des-seances-de-musique-de-chambre-Pierre-Baillot (accessed May 1, 2015).

[67] François-Joseph Fétis, review of Soirées musicales de Quatuors et de Quintetti, données par M. Baillot, *Revue Musicale (Paris)* (February 1827): 37–39 (Web Doc. #5).

When the modest *viola* joins his voice to the violin's
So that in a quartet interest is sustained,
The cello, to this concert admitted,
Becomes the controller of this group of friends,
And mingling his accents [i.e., expression] with those he favors,
His grave melody fraternizes with them.[68]

His poem betrays a pronounced influence of Carpani's (or, more likely, Stendhal's) characterization of the instruments' roles within a quartet.[69] Baillot significantly downplays the social elements present in both Carpani's and Stendhal's passages and foregrounds images of regal or executive power. For Baillot, the instruments may be a group of friends who fraternize in a "republic," but the (first) violin is "king," the others his "subjects." The paradoxical metaphor of a republic ruled by a king encapsulates the tension between hierarchy and equality in Baillot's conception of the quartet. An enlightened ruler who wields a scepter (his bow), he obeys only his own passions, which, in leading him on the way of the heart, empower him to use his sublimely expressive musical voice to persuade, disarm, and conquer. This vision stands decidedly at odds with Koch's proscription on any one instrument asserting an ancestral right to dominate over the others (*Vorrecht der Hauptstimme*). For Baillot, it would seem, "le quatuor, c'est moi."

Out of the salon and into the opera house: Jérôme-Joseph de Momigny ▶

An intriguingly idiosyncratic view of the quartet's hierarchy emerges in Jérôme-Joseph de Momigny's celebrated analysis of the first movement of

---

[68] "Sous un Sceptre nouveau tenant Sa république/ Se bornant à toucher, pour toute politique,/ paraît *le Violon*: ce Roi, Soldat heureux,/ père de Ses Sujets, Ami des malheureux,/ Commande, Obéissant aux passions qu'il exprime,/ Sa Voix, Soumise ainsi, sa Voix devient Sublime;/ S'il persuade et désarme ou Subjugue en Vainqueur,/ C'est qu'il a Su trouver le Vrai chemin du Cœur!/ Quand le modeste *Alto* Joint sa Voix à la Sienne/ pour qu'en un Quatuor l'intérêt se Soutienne,/ *Le Violoncel-basse*, à ce Concert admis,/ devient régulateur de ce groupe d'amis,/ et mêlant Ses Accens à Ceux qu'il favorise,/ Sa grave Mélodie avec eux fraternise." Baillot, "Caractère des divers instrumens de Musique," unpublished manuscript dated August 11, 1839, Bibliothèque national de France (F-Pn, Fond Madeleine Panzera-Baillot, Souvenir II), 2–3. To my knowledge, this excerpt of Baillot's poem was first published in Ella, *Musical Sketches*, 402.

[69] I thank Fabio Morabito for this observation and for drawing my attention to the poem. The complete poem appears in Morabito, "Authorship, Performance and Musical Identity," Appendix 1.

Mozart's Quartet in D Minor, K. 421, in his *Cours complet d'harmonie et de composition*.[70] Although the tradition of comparing *quatuors concertants* to salon conversation was firmly established in Paris by this time, Momigny ignores that metaphor, opting instead to transform Mozart's movement into an operatic aria by supplying the first-violin part with his own French verse.[71] (Ex. 2.4a reproduces the first page of Momigny's example; his complete example and a recording of it are available among the Web Resources.) He describes the inspiration for his analysis as follows:

> The style of this *Allegro Moderato* is noble and pathetic. I decided that the best way to have my readers recognize its true expression was to add words to it. But since these verses, if one can call them that, were improvised, as it were, they ought not to be judged in any other regard than that of their agreement with the sense of the music.

> I thought I perceived that the feelings expressed by the composer were those of a lover who is on the point of being abandoned by the hero she adores: *Dido*, who had had a similar misfortune to complain of, came immediately to mind. Her noble rank, the intensity of her love, the renown of her misfortune – all this convinced me to make her the heroine of this piece. She should be made to speak in a manner worthy of herself, but this is the task of a great lyric poet. It is sufficient to my task that the feelings of this unhappy queen be recounted and carefully set to music that renders them faithfully.[72]

A Parisian precedent associating string quartets with opera can be found in the *quatuor concertant* repertoire, since operatic idioms, arrangements, and medleys (known as *quatuors d'airs connus*) permeate this repertoire.[73] However, Momigny's more immediate inspiration came from the composer André Grétry, who not long before had posed the question: "Why shouldn't

---

[70] Jérôme-Joseph de Momigny, *Cours complet d'harmonie et de composition* (Paris, 1806); Momigny's prose commentary spans pp. 371–403 (vols. 1–2), and his massive (ten-staff) musical example spans 3:109–56. Momigny's discussion of K. 421 thus represents a substantial portion of his overall treatise. An extended excerpt of this material appears in Wye Jamison Allanbrook's English translation in Leo Treitler, ed., *Strunk's Source Readings in Music History*, rev. ed. (New York: W. W. Norton, 1998), 826–48.

[71] A similar method of adding text – coincidentally also about Dido – to an existing instrumental work appears in Elisabeth Le Guin's discussion of Boccherini's Cello Sonata in C Major, G. 17. Elisabeth Le Guin, *Boccherini's Body: An Essay in Carnal Musicology* (Berkeley: University of California Press, 2005), 112–17.

[72] Momigny, *Cours complet*, 1:371. English translation from Treitler, ed., *Strunk's Source Readings*, 827.

[73] Levy discusses several examples that sound virtually like transcriptions of arias or even complete operatic scenes ("The *Quatuor Concertant* in Paris," 298–306). See also Bashford, "The String Quartet and Society," 6.

Ex. 2.4 Momigny, arrangement of Mozart, String Quartet in D Minor, K. 421, Allegro moderato (i) (from *Cours complet d'harmonie et de composition* [Paris, 1806], Plate #30) ▶

a. Facsimile of first page

b. "Commentary" by Aeneas (Enée)

[instrumental] music be supplied with words, just as one has long set words to music?"[74] Grétry and Momigny were, in fact, in close contact, meeting on a daily basis for three weeks in 1803 – the same year that the serial publication of the *Cours complet* commenced – because the elder composer had engaged his fellow Liègois to assist with orchestrating his opera *Delphis et Mopsa*.[75] Further evidence connecting Grétry to Momigny's discussion of

[74] André Grétry, *Mémoires, ou essai sur la musique*, vol. 1 (Paris, 1789), 414. Grétry mentions that, when listening to Haydn's symphonies, he often imagined the words that the music seemed to ask for.

[75] Albert Palm, *Jérôme-Joseph de Momigny: Leben und Werk* (Cologne: Arno Volk Verlag, 1969), 36–37. Momigny's own writings (which effusively praise Grétry's operas) attest to their close relationship: "I loved Grétry because he was truly kind and because, [since] he was born in the bishopric of Liège, I was nearly one of his compatriots. A further reason for my attachment is that I saw in him some of the ways and habits I had cherished in my father." (J'aimois Grétry, parce qu'il étoit vraiment aimable & que, né comme lui dans l'évêché de Liège, jétois presque l'un de ses compatriotes. Un motif qui m'y attachoit encore, c'est que je retroavois en lui quelques unes des habitudes & des manières que j'avois chéries dans mon père.) Momigny, "Opéra," in Framery et al., eds., *Encyclopédie méthodique: Musique*, vol. 2 (Paris, 1818), 231. See also Momigny's article "Opéra comique," in ibid., 241–44.

Ex. 2.4 (*cont.*)

c. Statements by the Chorus

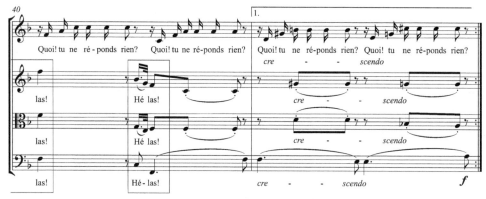

the Mozart quartet is a passing reference to Grétry's blind nephew, André-Joseph, praising his exceptional facility as a *parodiste* who could "aptly and effortlessly" add words to existing instrumental pieces.[76]

Momigny's arrangement renders Mozart's quartet as an *aria con pertichino*, that is, an affecting soliloquy by Dido (portrayed by the first violin) with a momentary appearance by Aeneas (portrayed by the cello, in mm. 19–21 only, as shown in Ex. 2.4b).[77] There is also a brief passage with

[76] Momigny, *Cours complet*, 1:372. See also Ian Bent, ed., *Music Analysis in the Nineteenth Century*, vol. 2, *Hermeneutic Approaches* (Cambridge University Press, 1994), 128.

[77] On this point, I part company with Palm, whose (otherwise excellent) discussion misrepresents Momigny's text as a "Dialog zwischen Dido und Äneas." In fact, Aeneas's speaking role is extremely circumscribed, comprising just the two statements shown in Ex. 2.4b ("que je suis malheureux" and "fatal devoir"). Bent describes the text as a "monologue of Dido addressing her departing lover Aeneas," without even mentioning Aeneas's small speaking role. Although the cello (as Aeneas) is the only "official" *pertichino* shown in Momigny's musical example, his prose commentary implies additional *pertichini* in the development section, as I will discuss

d. Coda

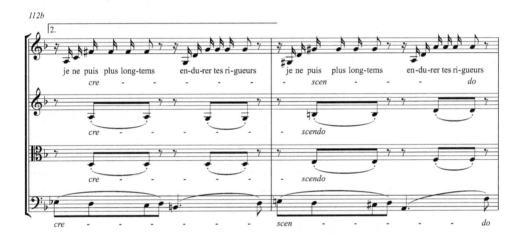

Ex. 2.4 (*cont.*)

... instrumental coda (no added text)

chorus (portrayed by the lower three instruments), which makes two lamenting statements of "hélas" at the end of the exposition, mm. 39–40 (see Ex. 2.4c).[78] Save for these fleeting statements by Aeneas and the chorus (both in the exposition), Momigny's added verse is limited to the first violin part alone, which is texted throughout. Only the final two measures of the first violin part are left without added text; after Dido's dying statement ("je le sens; je meurs"), a final "orchestral" *tutti* seems appropriate (see Ex. 2.4d).

In casting the first violin as the spurned Queen of Carthage (cf. Baillot's violin as king) and treating it as the only part consistently outfitted with verse, Momigny establishes the first violin as the unequivocal protagonist, implicitly relegating the others to the orchestra pit (except for the cello's fleeting stint as Aeneas and the brief choral statements). The notation of Momigny's example (Ex. 2.4a) underscores the categorical difference between the first violin and the other parts; in the systems labeled "Chant et Accompagnement de PIANO," the first violin part is rewritten in vocal notation (with underlaid text and syllabic beaming), while the other instruments are absorbed into the homogeneous piano accompaniment, relinquishing their integrity as individual parts.[79] Thus, Momigny would

below. See Albert Palm, "Mozarts Streichquartett D-moll, KV 421, in der Interpretation Momignys," *Mozart-Jahrbuch* (1962/63): 269; and Bent, ed., *Music Analysis in the Nineteenth Century*, 2:128.

[78] Since only the development and recapitulation are excerpted in Treitler, ed., *Strunk's Source Readings*, the statements by Aeneas and the chorus are not shown in that volume.

[79] Indeed, although Momigny's example seems more an "analytical fiction" intended to instruct composers rather than a transcription intended to be sung, his notation of a vocal part with piano accompaniment and the registral adjustments he (inconsistently) makes in the vocal part point to a potentially performable arrangement, if a supremely vocally taxing one. The term "analytical fiction" was coined in Marion A. Guck, "Analytical Fictions," *Music Theory Spectrum* 16, no. 2 (Autumn 1994): 217–30.

appear to have set up a strongly fixed, bifurcated division – with the first violin as a character on stage and the remaining parts collectively making up the accompaniment – that contrasts sharply with the principle of role exchange acknowledged by all of the sources surveyed above.[80] Simply put, the presence of (essentially) just one speaking character precludes the possibility of a musical conversation and departs sharply from Koch's egalitarian ethics of the quartet.

Momigny's hierarchy is justified, to an extent, by the unusual prominence of the first violin in the first movement of K. 421 (especially during the exposition and recapitulation), compared to the other nine of Mozart's celebrated quartets. This stylistic feature may relate in part to the movement's grave character, which indeed evokes not the spontaneous exchange of the salon but the more formal world of *opera seria*.[81] In discussing this movement as a *seria* aria, Momigny seems to be responding to the unusually solemn style of K. 421, which is one of a handful of Mozart chamber works in a minor key,[82] rather than making a broad statement about the string quartet as a genre.[83]

---

[80] Even Carpani's and Baillot's first-violin-centered views of the quartet nevertheless characterize the exchange as a conversation; Carpani may downplay the importance of the viola's contributions, but he does not dispute that the viola is capable of speech. On the other hand, Momigny effaces the individuality of the lower three parts and conflates them into the piano accompaniment. This choice evinces his view of their secondary status. Cf. Koch's equation of personhood with *Hauptstimme* status and, implicitly, non-personhood with exclusively accompanimental parts (see above, 34 n. 36, and Web Doc. #14).

[81] Gretchen Wheelock sensitively addresses the impact of both serious and comic opera on Haydn's quartets, comparing the slow movements of op. 17, no. 5 and op. 20, no. 2 to "*seria* characters [who] moved the spectator from a distance in grand solo numbers of reflection, and rarely in polyphonic ensembles." Wheelock, *Haydn's Ingenious Jesting*, 92. By contrast, the quintessential spirit of *opera buffa* is found in its ensemble numbers, which "staged more immediate conversations in diverse voices and gestures paced for intrigue and dramatic action more wide-ranging than in its serious counterpart" (ibid., 92–93). For Mozart's own views on serious and comic opera, which emerge in letters to his father from September and October 1781 (during the composition of *Die Entführung aus dem Serail*), see David P. Schroeder, "Mozart and Late Eighteenth-Century Aesthetics," in *The Cambridge Companion to Mozart*, 55–58.

[82] Wheelock warns against "the automatic tendency to regard works in the minor mode as deeply solemn." Wheelock, *Haydn's Ingenious Jesting*, 106. In the case of K. 421, several features beyond the mode evoke the high style of *opera seria*, including the movement's deliberate pacing, lack of abrupt textural contrasts, relative lack of emphasis on interaction within the ensemble, and generally smooth melodic declamation.

[83] Momigny defines the term "quatuor" briefly in the *Dictionnaire* appended to the *Cours complet*. Directly rebutting Rousseau (quoted above, 33 n. 31, and in Web Doc. #30), Momigny writes: "A piece for four parts of which two or three are nothing but filler-parts [*Parties de remplissage*] is not a true quartet but simply a piece for four voices or four instruments" (Un morceau à quatre Parties dont deux ou trois ne sont que des Parties de remplissage, n'est pas un vrai

In fact, Momigny reveals (understandable) discomfort with the rigid division between the first violin and the other instruments that his operatic recasting implies. Early in his discussion of K. 421, in a fascinating passage labeled "Petite digression sur les Accompagnemens," he expresses ambivalence about the status of the lower three parts:

Each party in the accompaniment can, by turns, play the role of interlocutor; but, more often, the accompanying parts [*accompagnemens*][84] are nothing but the diverse parts of the same individual of which the vocal part [*chant*] is the face [*figure*].[85] What this face (which should never be insignificant) cannot say all by itself, even with the very powerful aid of words, the accompanying instruments assist in expressing. Sometimes they trace in their own way the setting of the scene; finally, they bring back under the eyes of the listener, or, less figuratively, they recall to his mind, by means of the ear, anything that can make him take a greater interest in what is presented to him. Above all, they depict the state where the actor[86] finds himself, his calm, his agitation, his outbursts, his pain, his pleasures, his sadness, his joy, his indifference, his love or his hatred. On occasion, they seem to form the retinue of a great personage, a hero's entourage. Based on this, one cannot doubt that a good opera will make a greater impression than a tragedy of equal strength that is only spoken, assuming however that the listeners are equally capable of understanding both of them.[87]

Quatuor, mais simplement un Morceau à quatre voix ou à quatre instrumens). Momigny, *Cours complet*, 2:694. Momigny's remarks recall Kollmann's designation of "regular or proper" for a duet, trio, etc., consisting of "concerting" instruments only, as opposed to one for solo instrument plus accompaniment (discussed above, 29 n. 24). Also cf. Koch's discussion of *Hauptstimme* status vs. other, subordinate statuses.

However, in a later and more expansive discussion, Momigny acknowledges that, relative to the first violin, the other parts play a subordinate role: "Although a quartet requires that the four parts be obbligato, there nevertheless should be one principal player who is the main object of interest" (Malgré que le quatuor exige que les quatre parties soient obligées, il y faut cependant un acteur principal, sur lequel l'intérêt se porte de préférence). Momigny, "Quatuor," in Framery et al., *Encyclopédie méthodique: Musique*, 2:298–99.

[84] The plural term "les accompagnemens" refers not to "the accompaniment" as a corporate entity but to the individual *parts* that comprise the accompaniment (in this case the violin II, viola, and cello). This usage is similar to the common, eighteenth-century designation for a trio for piano and strings as a "sonate pour le piano avec accompagnemens d'un violon et d'un violoncelle." See also Kollmann's discussion of "sonatas for one or more principal instruments, with some others as accompaniments." Kollmann, *Essay on Practical Musical Composition*, 12.

[85] In this context, the word "chant" refers not only to the act of singing but specifically to the melodic voice (as in the *chant donné* in species counterpoint). Momigny's plate (reproduced as Ex. 2.4a) labels the vocal part (which is identical to the first violin part) as "chant."

[86] [Momigny's footnote:] The word "actor" is not used here to mean he who represents in a theater something that supposedly takes place elsewhere; rather, it signifies he who takes action.

[87] Momigny, *Cours complet*, 1:374 (see Web Doc. #19). I am grateful to Nicolas Meeùs for his insights regarding the translation of this passage.

Momigny's discussion anticipates some challenging narratological questions that would be taken up nearly two centuries later by Edward T. Cone.[88] Within the brief aside, Momigny wanders in circles, vacillating between two conflicting notions: (1) that the accompanying instruments are part of the vocal persona (i.e., the *chant*, played by the first violin), or (2) that the accompanying instruments are themselves individual personas, capable of independent action and utterance (endowed with what Koch would call *Rechte als Hauptstimmen*). Momigny contradicts himself even within the first sentence, which begins by positing the *accompagnemens* as the protagonist's interlocutors but curiously concludes instead that they more typically are parts of the protagonist's own body. The latter formulation conjures an evocative metaphor: the *chant* is the protagonist's face (the locus of expression and the only part of the body that is capable of speech or song), yet a face requires a body below it (*les accompagnemens*) to support basic life functions and, furthermore, to enhance its expression through gesture and body language.[89]

Momigny's wavering explanation recognizes a value in maintaining flexibility to interpret the *accompagnemens* sometimes as (1) depicting or enhancing the expression of the vocal part (similar to Koch's accessory melodies) and other times as (2) members of the vocal part's entourage (as separate characters from the *chant* but sworn to its faithful service). It is significant that Momigny regards only the vocal persona as a genuine *acteur*, a term that (according to his footnote) is roughly equivalent to Cone's "agent."[90] Momigny's statement that the *accompagnemens* "trace in their own way the setting of the scene [*tracent à leur manière le lieu de la scène*]" probably means that they can depict the setting of the scene ("tracer" means "to trace" or "to draw"), as if to provide a backdrop and scenery that appeal to the (mind's) eye of the listener. However, since

---

[88] Edward T. Cone, *The Composer's Voice* (Berkeley: University of California Press, 1974). I will return to narratological theories of agency and persona in Chapter 4.

[89] Mary Hunter (evidently independently) introduces related similes, comparing Koch's accessory melodies to "the body language of an interlocutor, subtly shaping the main speaker's utterance." Hunter, "The Quartets," 120.

[90] One significant difference, however, is that Cone specifically points out that the concept of "agent" should not be limited to melodic parts only (*The Composer's Voice*, 99). Incidentally, Momigny's footnote notwithstanding, his use of "acteur" in this quasi-theatrical context anticipates his future comments in the *Encyclopédie méthodique: Musique* (1818). He praises the violinist Alexandre-Jean Boucher as an "acteur parfait" (ibid., s.v. "Quatuor," 2:299) and Pierre Baillot as an "acteur consommé sur le violon" (ibid., s.v. "Soirées ou Séances Musicales," 2:374). On a French tradition evoking metaphors of theater for violin performance, see Morabito, "Authorship, Performance and Musical Identity"; and November, "Theater Piece and *Cabinetstück*."

"tracer" also means "to trace one's way," an alternative translation might suggest the possibility that an accompanying part can occasionally "find its way, in its own way, to the place of the scene," crossing the border from the orchestra pit onto the stage, so to speak, temporarily becoming an honorary *pertichino* (as in the cello's brief appearance as Aeneas). Like Leporello's yearning to rise above his station, this evocative image reflects the potential (and desire?) of an accompanying part to strive for opportunities to become melodic or to engage the *prima donna* in musical discourse – a prospect that is especially germane in a quartet *qua* pit orchestra (compared to a "real" pit orchestra, where such ambitions would hardly be tolerated).

Does this mean that Momigny recognizes some give and take among the instruments' roles after all? It depends whether one consults his musical example or his prose commentary. As noted above, the notation of Momigny's score enforces a rigid separation of the first violin from the rest of the ensemble, since the aria paradigm fixes the first violin's primary role, regardless of musical events that might warrant a temporary reassessment of the parts' relative prominence. If Momigny's example truly acknowledged the exchangeability of roles, it could have indicated when one of the *accompagnemens* comes to the fore by providing it with text, beyond the paltry statements given to the cello as Aeneas. Moreover, in those rare passages wherein the first violin recedes in prominence or joins his colleagues in the orchestral accompaniment, Momigny might have stripped the violin of text. But instead, he dutifully (or stubbornly?) sets words to the entire first violin part, even when another part is of equal or greater importance in the musical texture.[91] The rigidity of Momigny's roles as depicted in his example's notation calls to mind the home video of an elementary-school play as recorded by a stage mother who focuses so steadfastly on her own child (who plays the lead role) that she blithely leaves other characters out of the frame, even when they are speaking.

Momigny's prose commentary, however, reflects subtle exchanges of roles not shown in the musical example, most notably in the development section, which he calls the "première partie de la seconde Reprise" (see extended excerpt in Ex. 2.4e). Compared to the exposition and

---

[91] By comparison, the cello seems to represent Aeneas only when specifically marked (Ex. 2.4b), and otherwise it resumes its normal place among the *accompagnemens.* The character of Aeneas seems to remain on stage, so to speak, since Dido addresses and regards him directly, but the cello ceases to portray him. In contrast, the first violin never sheds the role of Dido, except for the "orchestral" *tutti* in the movement's final two measures (Ex. 2.4d).

Ex. 2.4 (*cont.*)

e. Development

Ex. 2.4 (*cont.*)

recapitulation, the development is more contrapuntal and contains more frequent changes of musical texture, topic, and instrumental roles. Throughout his discussion, Momigny lavishly praises Mozart's masterful counterpoint, marveling at its intricate details and admiring the seamless transitions between free and imitative styles.[92] To accommodate these features in his operatic paradigm, Momigny resorts to some creative solutions. Mozart's development, for instance, begins with the first violin reprising the main theme, which quickly dissolves into fragmentation and contrapuntal treatment that seems more instrumental than operatic (mm. 46–49). Momigny describes the passage thus:

Mozart, who composed almost all his first reprise in the free style, begins to make use of a subject here, after the first two measures of the second reprise.

This subject is furnished by the second measure of the beginning: *E♭ d e♭ e♭ e♭* [m. 43].

---

[92] Cf. Koch, who also praised the masterful mixture of free and contrapuntal styles in Mozart's quartets; see above, 32–36, and Web Docs. #11 and #15.

After the first violin has played the subject twice, the cello takes hold of it [m. 46], sounding it three times in its turn, but in A minor. The viola becomes the echo of the cello at the distance of a half-measure, repeating the same motive in *broken imitation* at the octave. It continues with the same subject, but shortens it and climbs diatonically, *f♯ e f♯ f♯, g♯ f♯ g♯ g♯.*

Over this cello and viola, which present only a subordinate subject, the second violin plays no. 1, the principal motive, *a g♯ c b e* [mm. 46–48], imitated at the second and *alla stretta*, that is to say, in rhythmic compression, by the first violin: no. 2 *b♮ a d c f.* This is true skill. For all its merit, it is not coldly calculated, but has a somber and genuine expression that penetrates to the depths of the soul. This should be attributed equally to the rhythm, the movement, and the intonations of the passage.[93]

Whereas the first violin had held forth as *Hauptmelodie* (like an aria's soloist) for nearly the entire exposition, here it seems to take a wrong turn, accidentally leaving the set for *Dido and Aeneas* and wandering into a *fugato* environment.[94] To be sure, it would be a rare aria in which the soprano's melody is fragmented and subjected to rigorous contrapuntal treatment among the lower voices of the orchestra, since imitative counterpoint is typically understood to take place among voices belonging to the same ontological category (i.e., the sections of a choir or orchestra, the instruments of a quartet, or characters of an opera). Similarly, the close, canonic writing between the two violins (mm. 46–49) weaves these parts together with suspensions and voice crossings that exploit their timbral homogeneity; while this interplay could be natural between a pair of voices in an operatic duet (or, of course, the pair of violins in Mozart's original quartet), it is far less convincing to imagine Momigny's Dido in such close counterpoint with the orchestral violins.

Momigny implicitly acknowledges the difficult fit between this contrapuntal passage and the operatic scenario, since his discussion of this section resorts to the language of abstract counterpoint, without mentioning

---

[93] Momigny, *Cours complet*, 2:391–92. English translation from Treitler, ed., *Strunk's Source Readings*, 829–30. I have retained Momigny's capitalization for note names, which does not correspond with the system of octave designation adopted elsewhere in this book.

[94] This image of the first violin inadvertently drifting from the shores of Carthage into an abstract fugue accords nicely with Momigny's description of the enharmonic reinterpretation in m. 45 (E♭ = D♯ in the first violin), which he colorfully compares to "a kind of marvelous flying bridge by means of which one passes, almost magically, from one climate into another far distant." Momigny, *Cours complet*, 2:391. English translation from Treitler, ed., *Strunk's Source Readings*, 830. Momigny's commentary refers to the sudden modulation from E♭ major to A minor (ushered in by the enharmonic reinterpretation), but this juncture (m. 46) coincides with a change of topic as the main theme trails off and the fugal or imitative material takes over.

the Dido narrative. The next reference to Dido coincides with the brief return to a homophonic texture ("the free style") around m. 51:

With the words *voilà le prix de tant d'amour!* Mozart resumes the free style exclusively until the fifth verse.

How the anger of the queen of Carthage bursts out in the music of the third musical verse [mm. 50ff.]! and how the last syllable of the word *amour* is felicitously placed on the *bb* [m. 51], in order to express the grief that Dido feels at having rashly abandoned herself to this passion for a perjurer! The second time she repeats this word she cannot finish it [upbeat to m. 53], because she is choked by the grief that overwhelms her. It is here that the viola part, which represents her sister or confidante, takes up the word to address the Trojan the reproaches that Dido no longer has the strength to make herself.[95]

Momigny's observations about the word "amour" highlight an arresting rhetorical moment; if m. 50 seems to point toward a perfect authentic cadence in A minor, this expectation is shattered on the downbeat of m. 51 when the first violin resolves irregularly and the lower voices drop out. As Momigny notes, the first violin's "false melodic cadence" on Bb accords nicely with the textual reference to Aeneas's hollow professions of love.

The evasion of the expected cadence in m. 51 and the resumption of the cadential progression in the next bar (matched by Momigny's textual repetition) would seem to predict a completed cadence in m. 53 to close the period. However, both melody and bass trail off just as the cadence would be completed, resulting in the suppression of Dido's final syllable ("oui, voilà le prix de tant d'a[mour]"). Momigny interprets this melodic ellipsis as Dido "choked by the grief that overwhelms her," an explanation that is compelling dramaturgically yet unlikely to happen in any actual aria by Mozart, where every syllable would be declaimed. Momigny notates Dido's final syllable beneath a rest, more as *Augenmusik* for his reader than as a performable indication, demonstrating the extreme measures Momigny must take to maintain his aria paradigm at all costs.[96]

The elided cadence in m. 53 is concurrent with the beginning of the development's second period. Here, the viola initiates a stretto (a set of overlapping entrances) based on the head motive of the movement

---

[95] Momigny, *Cours complet*, 2:392. English translation from Treitler, ed., *Strunk's Source Readings*, 830.

[96] A similar texted rest occurs on the downbeat of m. 66 on the word "bonheur," where Momigny again describes Dido as breaking off before the final syllable. Note that this instance is not a textual repetition; the final syllable is simply never uttered, and the line is rendered as "rends la vie et le bon[heur]."

(from mm. 1–2) involving all four instruments. The viola's instigation of this passage (mm. 53ff.) provokes Momigny to expand his *dramatis personae*, interpreting the viola as "[Dido's] sister or confidante, who takes up the word to address the Trojan the reproaches that Dido no longer has the strength to make herself." This intriguing notion arguably raises more questions than it answers. Momigny's commentary describes the viola temporarily becoming a *pertichina* enacting the role of Dido's sister (in an odd cameo appearance in the middle of the aria, as if she had missed her call time), similarly to the cello's earlier portrayal of Aeneas. When the viola (as Dido's sister) "takes up the word" to address Aeneas in m. 53, why is her part not provided with text? Moreover, if the viola is indeed Dido's sister, what of the second violin in the following measure? Is this also the sister (curiously overlapping with herself), or some other member of Dido's train? And when the first violin returns in m. 55, how is the listener to know that this is Dido herself and not, for instance, yet another member of the entourage?

It is rather simpler, surely, to take this stretto passage for what it is: an instance of imitative counterpoint in which a motive is passed among all four parts. Indeed, whenever the music turns contrapuntal, Momigny's commentary downplays or drops the Dido story and begins to sound more like Koch, focusing on the intricacies of textural and motivic exchange. Describing this stretto passage (mm. 53ff.), he writes:

In the first period of this second reprise [mm. 42–52] he had taken for subject only one of the measures of his first motive – the second of these two measures. Here he takes two of them, the first and the second. *A A, a a, g♯ a, a a* [mm. 53–54].

After the first measure, an imitation in stretto at the second with this same subject is heard in the second violin. The cello enters one eighth note afterward, and plays a subordinate motive as accompaniment [m. 54]. This cello motive is an imitation, as regards rhythm, of the accompaniment that is found in the viola and in the second violin in the first measures of the second reprise.[97]

In the first three measures of the reprise *Mozart* could have put half notes in the second violin and viola just as he did in the cello. Probably he preferred to use an eighth-note rest and three eighth notes to keep the passage from becoming languid.

Dido, throwing an angry look at *Aeneas*, says to him: *Fuis, malheureux!* It is a shortened imitation of the passage in the second violin, at the second above, and *alla stretta*.

---

[97] This attention to subtleties of accompanimental figuration recalls Koch's careful consideration of accessory melodies (i.e., those parts other than the *Hauptmelodie* and bass line).

The cello, which during this time has kept to the subordinate motive, in its turn lays hold of the principal subject, and says: *D D, d d, c♯ d, d d* [mm. 56–57].

The subordinate motive in the cello then passes to the viola. The imitation in stretto at the second, or rather at the ninth above the principal subject in the cello, is reproduced in the second violin – *e♭ e♭, e♭ e♭, d e♭, e♭ e♭* – and then in the first violin one measure after – *f♯ f♯, f♯ g.*

Note the gradual rise of the subject of the fifth verse. This subject is successively carried on six consecutive degrees of the musical scale, moving from *a* up to *f♯* inclusively. The viola begins on *a*, the second violin on *b♭*, the first violin on *c♯*, the cello on *D*, the second violin on *e♭*, and the first on *f♯* [mm. 53–58].

A student would have put all these imitations of the same subject in the same part. Then we would no longer have heard anything but a kind of scale in place of this dialogue that is so compressed, so pressing, and so admirable.[98]

This excerpt foregrounds the underlying tension between Momigny's two concepts of the *accompagnemens* – namely, whether the lower three parts are consigned to a secondary, accompanimental role (as shown in his score) or whether they are capable of temporarily elevating their status to directly engage Dido in discourse (as described in his prose commentary). The issue reaches a breaking point when Momigny discusses the cello's entrance with the stretto figure (m. 56), stating that the cello *says* "*D D, d d, c♯ d, d d.*" But which is it? Does Momigny indeed conceive of the cello as a *bona fide* speaking role, that is, a *pertichino* who speaks or sings with words? Or is the cello merely an instrumental part, whose utterances consist of wordless notes that represent no identifiable character? To illustrate the almost risible incommensurability of these two perspectives, let us take Momigny at his word and imagine his libretto written thus:

Violin I (*as Dido*).	*Fuis, malheureux!*
Cello (*as Himself*).	*D D, d d, c♯ d, d d.*[99]

Evidently, Momigny's aria paradigm only works up to a point and, without explicitly saying so, he reverts to Koch-like commentary as needed when roles are exchanged in contrapuntal passages.

---

[98] Momigny, *Cours complet*, 2:393–94. English translation from Treitler, ed., *Strunk's Source Readings*, 831.

[99] By stating that the cello "says" the subject (D D, d d, etc.), Momigny suggests a temporary status as a *pertichino*, albeit one whose identity (Dido's butler or manservant?) is left undefined. Perhaps the term "subject" could be understood not only as a fugal term but as a rhetorical one. Since the viola's original statement in m. 53 is interpreted by Momigny as Dido's sister entreating Aeneas on Dido's behalf, the contrapuntal imitations by the second violin and cello

Momigny's fidelity to the aria idea results in further curiosities in his score. For instance, in mm. 59–60 and 61–62, Momigny's arrangement erases the equivalence of the two violins, effectively masking a would-be duet built on the exchange of motives. And in the same passage, Momigny's choice to add text on the sixteenth-note triplet figures ("Il paraît s'attendrir") forces Dido to demean herself with a pattering declamation ill-befitting the Queen of Carthage.[100] It would be more convincing musically to set the half-note entrances (marked with hairpins) as texted vocal statements and relegate the triplet figure to the untexted accompaniment alongside the viola. Another odd distortion concerns the movement's coda, when the cello finally comes to the fore (mm. 112ff., shown in Ex. 2.4d) to deliver one of Carpani's "laconic but confident statements." The cello's intervention lends the movement's close a dark, Neapolitan-tinged hue. Yet Momigny makes no mention of this event, and his score, once again, gives greatest prominence to Dido's chattering triplets.

For all its creativity and expressiveness, Momigny's operatic premise fails him in the development section. Its weakness stems from the rigidity of his characterizations (the first violin as Dido, the others as mere *accompagnemens*), which limits his ability to reflect shifting textural roles. The lesson of Momigny's experiment should have been obvious to him from the start, namely, that the roles within a chamber piece are enacted less literally and are less robust than those in an opera or a play.

Conclusions

The difficulty of characterizing the interaction among parts in a string quartet (and, by extension, any chamber ensemble) has attracted extensive critical attention essentially since the genre's birth. And it stands to reason,

could be heard as additional (unnamed) parties taking up the same message (i.e., subject). Nevertheless, it is curious that Momigny provides the viola no actual text and in addition neglects to comment on the identities of the second violin and cello as (presumed) *pertichini* in this passage. Furthermore, by providing text for only Dido's statements of the same subject, Momigny once again highlights a troublesome ontological distinction between that part and the other three, even as they are all engaged together in an imitative exchange.

[100] Momigny preemptively defends the text on this figure from criticism. Noting the change of motive and mood around m. 59, he writes: "In order to fit the words to this passage in a suitable manner, it was necessary to think the aside [i.e., the text for the triplet figure] out carefully. Since the preceding subject has no connection with the one to which these words are set, it could have seemed to be a shortcoming, whereas it is a genuine beauty." Momigny, *Cours complet*, 2:394. English translation from Treitler, ed., *Strunk's Source Readings*, 531–32.

since the degree of independence among an ensemble's parts relates directly to the level of difficulty for each player, a consideration salient to amateurs, professionals, composers, and publishers alike. The foregoing historical survey has followed several intertwining threads, interrogating chiefly: (1) under what circumstances authors interpret parts other than the main melody as representing distinct individuals; (2) whether the relationships among instrumental parts are characterized by hierarchy or egalitarianism, by fixed roles or exchangeable ones; and (3) how intercourse among the parts may be interpreted through human metaphors of social interaction or conversation.

To take up the last thread first: All of the authors surveyed above invoke to some degree anthropomorphic rationales to describe instrumental "behavior" – some to a great degree – including descriptions of instrumental personas endowed with such human attributes as consciousness, volition, emotion, and even hierarchical rank and gender. A tendency toward metaphors of human social relations stems from the notion that instruments are asserting autonomy from or even antagonizing one another (as in Koch's *Wettstreit*). Autonomy is demonstrated most strongly when the intercourse involves the exchange of roles, with "roles" construed either as strands within the musical texture or (more metaphorically) as personas of leader, follower, inventor of new musical ideas, bringer of direction, purveyor of grace, and so forth.

As a broad trend, the eighteenth-century German authors (including Sulzer, Koch, and Kollmann) adhere to technical, musical language and tend to give more careful attention to the simultaneous activity of all elements within a musical texture.[101] The early-nineteenth-century Franco-Italian authors, on the other hand, generally focus somewhat more on successive melodic utterance, probably a consequence of the elevated role of bravura and operatic traditions in those countries. These latter writers also entertain more colorful, wildly metaphorical descriptions (as in Carpani's and Stendhal's caricatures, Baillot's poem, and especially Momigny's operatic scene), anticipating the more elaborate modes of hermeneutical analysis that would become popular later in the nineteenth century.[102] Although many writers specifically introduce metaphors of conversation and dialogue to characterize the intercourse among the

---

[101] Although Kollmann's treatise is written in English and published in London, I count him among the Germans since he was born in Hannover and was heavily influenced by Sulzer and Koch.

[102] See, for example, the readings excerpted in vol. 2 of Bent, ed., *Music Analysis in the Nineteenth Century*, which is devoted to hermeneutic approaches.

instruments, few clues are offered for interpretation of the nature or meaning of particular dialogue in any given composition. Precisely what is being said remains an open question.

The language of these historical authors may seem quaint by the standards of modern music theory, but their writings nevertheless contain valuable insights. Koch, for example, offers a sophisticated theory of texture, a musical element that remains largely neglected in scholarship to this day.[103] In general, the language and metaphors used by historical authors supply potent imagery for interpreting the contemporaneous chamber music of Haydn, Mozart, and Beethoven, and nothing in this rich imagery is fundamentally at odds with the greater precision and rigor to which more modern analytical methodologies aspire. It would indeed be appealing to develop an analytical approach that infuses twenty-first-century methodologies with certain eighteenth-century attitudes. I take up the quest to marry these strange bedfellows in Chapter 4.

---

[103] Some notable exceptions include: (1) Charles Rosen, whose influential *The Classical Style* is highly sensitive to textural details; (2) Leonard Ratner, who (inspired by Koch) devotes several chapters in *Classic Music* to textures commonly used in various musical genres; and (3) Janet Levy, whose dissertation "The *Quatuor Concertant* in Paris" (supervised by Ratner) is likewise highly sensitive to textural considerations within Parisian quartets. A lucid survey of literature on texture in late-eighteenth-century chamber music is included in Olga (Ellen) Bakulina, "Polyphony as a Loosening Technique in Mozart's *Haydn* Quartets" (M.A. thesis, McGill University, 2010), 15–21. Bakulina illustrates the neglected state of texture in music scholarship by pointing to the meager two paragraphs it receives in *The New Grove Dictionary*, 2nd ed., compared to twelve pages on tonality, nineteen pages on harmony, and thirty-two pages on rhythm.

| Private, public, and playing in the present tense

> We only rehearse your quartets, not those of Haydn and Mozart, which
> work better without rehearsal.
>
> –Karl Holz (second violinist of the Schuppanzigh Quartet 1823–28)
> to Beethoven in a Conversation Book entry from 1825[1]

"The past is a foreign country," begins L. P. Hartley's nostalgic novel *The Go-Between*; "they do things differently there."[2] This memorable aphorism is a wise reminder for any scholar seeking to interpret historical evidence on its own terms without universalizing present-day practices and assumptions. With written documents, even the most familiar turns of phrase are fraught with potential for anachronistic interpretation. For instance, to understand the chamber music practices of Mozart's Vienna, two major assumptions of present-day practice must be dispelled: (1) that the activity of sight-reading or playing through a piece for no audience is necessarily a preparatory activity directed toward a subsequent performance event on a separate occasion; and (2) that an event described as a "concert" is necessarily a performance for an attentive audience that has been carefully rehearsed, its interpretive details finalized in advance.[3]

This chapter examines the in-time, of-the-moment qualities that characterized private and semi-public musical gatherings in Mozart's time. Such gatherings seem often to have been organized spontaneously, with little or no rehearsal, and, generally speaking, they were much more impromptu, open-ended affairs than today's public concerts. One way to

---

[1] *Ludwig van Beethovens Konversationshefte*, ed. Karl-Heinz Köhler, Grita Herre, et al., 11 vols. to date (Leipzig: VEB Deutscher Verlag für Musik, 1968–), 8: 259; cited in John M. Gingerich, "Ignaz Schuppanzigh and Beethoven's Late Quartets," *Musical Quarterly* 93, nos. 3–4 (2010): 466 n. 70.

[2] L. P. Hartley, *The Go-Between* (London: H. Hamilton, 1953), 3.

[3] I make no naïve case for "historical objectivity" – a goal that is as dubious as it is unattainable – but merely contend that scholars who invoke present-day notions to interpret past events should do so explicitly. The twin dangers of historicism and presentism in music theory are sensitively examined in Thomas Christensen, "Music Theory and Its Histories," in *Music Theory and the Exploration of the Past*, ed. Christopher Hatch and David W. Bernstein (University of Chicago Press, 1993), 9–39.

stage a recovery of these practices is to understand the historical moment
in which they became "past," by examining the roots of modern-day
conceptions of chamber music performance, many of which can be traced
to the early decades of the nineteenth century, when a public culture for
chamber music began to emerge. This chapter will proceed backwards,
beginning with developments during Beethoven's lifetime and then
returning to Mozart's.

From private to public

The gradual establishment of a public culture for chamber music, which by
no means signaled the end of private musical activites,[4] represents a
fundamental shift that affected every aspect of chamber music: how it
was conceptualized, composed, played, and listened to.[5] Before around
1800, chamber music was an essentially private art, enjoyed mainly by
those who could either play it themselves or who had the status to receive
invitations to salon concerts in private residences. Whereas string quartets
were occasionally performed publicly on London's stages,[6] they had no
place in Paris's public concert scene, which focused on orchestral, choral,

---

[4] That public events are understandably better documented should not be taken as evidence that
they supplanted domestic musical activities. Readers will recall J. C. W. Petiscus's enthusiastic, if
hyperbolic, remarks in 1810 about the widespread craze for quartet playing (see epigraph to
Chapter 1). My heading "from private to public" is not intended to suggest a simple teleology.

[5] Ludwig Finscher underscores the impact of these developments on the string quartet: "Between
about 1800 and 1810, with clear contours around 1820, a profound change took hold in the
social history of string quartets, which also influenced the genre's compositional history" (Etwa
zwischen 1800 und 1810, mit deutlichen Konturen um 1820, bahnt sich in der Sozialgeschichte
des Streichquartetts ein tiefgreifender Wandel an, der auch die Kompositionsgeschichte der
Gattung beeinflußt). Finscher, "Streichquartett," col. 1945. For overviews of the string quartet
during this period, see Bashford, "The String Quartet and Society," 7–12; Potter, "From
Chamber to Concert Hall," 41–59; and Parker, The String Quartet, 25–31.

[6] London's public concerts were divided into several "acts," each of which included music for
orchestra and for smaller forces; separate concerts of chamber music did not exist. Although
string quartets first appeared in London's public concerts as early as 1769, they were not
performed regularly until the 1790s. Haydn's famously extroverted op. 71 and 74 quartets,
presumed to have been composed for the 1794–95 season of Salomon's concerts in the Hanover
Square Rooms (see Grave and Grave, The String Quartets of Joseph Haydn, 282–84), may be
among the first quartets intended specifically for public performance. Yet despite these
developments, the string quartet was still viewed as an essentially domestic genre, and private
quartet gatherings remained common during this period. See Simon McVeigh, Concert Life in
London from Mozart to Haydn (Cambridge University Press, 1993); and Parker, The String
Quartet, 37–40.

and virtuoso solo instrumental music.[7] In Vienna, the extensive involvement of the aristocracy in music – as patrons, salon hosts, and in many
cases skilled players themselves – delayed the full development of a public
concert life comparable to that of London or Paris.[8] Public entertainment
in Vienna principally consisted of opera and theater. During this period in
Vienna, there were no public (or semi-public) performances of sonatas or
quartets outside of aristocratic residences.[9]

Against this backdrop, the establishment during the first decades of the
nineteenth century of public subscription concert series dedicated to
chamber music represented a significant change in thinking about what
constitutes appropriate "concert" music for public performances. The
violinist Ignaz Schuppanzigh, who had played in private, Friday-morning
quartet concerts at the apartments of Prince Lichnowsky in 1794–95, later
presented Vienna's first documented semi-public series of quartet concerts
at Count Razumovsky's palace beginning in the 1804–5 season, and it was
presumably under these auspices that the Schuppanzigh Quartet premiered
Beethoven's op. 59 quartets in early 1807.[10] In 1818, Vienna's newly

---

[7] Parker notes that not a single string quartet was performed at Paris's Concert Spirituel during
the whole of that institution's existence (1725–90), even as the *quatuor concertant* was all the
rage in Parisian salons. Parker, *The String Quartet*, 33 n. 48.

[8] For an overview of private and semi-private (*halböffentlich*) concerts during Mozart's time in
Vienna, see Otto Biba, "Grundzüge des Konzertwesens in Wien zu Mozarts Zeit," *Mozart-
Jahrbuch* (1978/79): 132–43; and Walter, "Zum wiener Streichquartett der Jahre 1780 bis 1800."
Contemporaneous accounts of amateur music-making appear in Schönfeld's *Jahrbuch der
Tonkunst von Wien und Prag* and in an anonymous report entitled "Neuer Versuch einer
Darstellung des gesammten Musikwesens in Wien" in *Allgemeine musikalische Zeitung
(Leipzig)* 3, no. 38 (June 17, 1801): cols. 638–43 (Web Doc. #22). The latter report is the
continuation of an article from the previous issue (cols. 622–27) about Vienna's public musical
events, chiefly opera.

[9] See Morrow, *Concert Life in Haydn's Vienna*, which includes appendices detailing all
documented concerts in Vienna from 1761 to 1810. However, Morrow's statement (p. 161) that
there were no public performances of quartets in Vienna during this period should be qualified.
Edge lists a small number of public Viennese chamber performances, including two
promotional events organized by the publisher Christoph Torricella connected to the
publication of quartets by Hoffmeister and Pleyel in 1783 and 1784, respectively, that must be
counted as public quartet performances (Edge, review of Morrow, *Concert Life in Haydn's
Vienna*, 129–30). See also Parker's overview of this period in *The String Quartet*, 41–45.
Although Mozart entertained the idea of mounting a series of subscription quartet concerts
("kleine quartett-suscriptions-Musiken [*sic*]") during Advent in 1790, as a way to earn income
during a difficult financial period, it is unclear whether these concerts ever occurred. W. A.
Mozart to Constanze Mozart, Frankfurt am Main, October 8, 1790, in Mozart, *Briefe*, 4:117.

[10] November, *Beethoven's Theatrical Quartets*, 29 and 52. The division between public and private
concerts is by no means hard and fast. Schuppanzigh's subscription series, as ticketed concerts
taking place in an aristocratic domicile, represents a kind of hybrid. For Morrow, these concerts
seem not to qualify as public performances; this opinion is implicit in her statement that no

established Gesellschaft der Musikfreunde inaugurated its *musikalische Abendunterhaltungen* (musical evening "conversations" or "entertainments"), a subscription series presenting chamber music in intimate settings.[11] Similar efforts arose around the same time in other European centers, including Karl Möser's quartet evenings in Berlin (founded 1813–14) and Baillot's evocatively named Séances de Quatuors et de Quintettes in Paris (founded in 1814).[12]

Many of these new series developed around a core repertoire of string quartets by Haydn, Mozart, and early-to-middle-period Beethoven (all of which came to be established as canonical), and sometimes Boccherini.[13]

string quartets were performed publicly in Vienna prior to 1810. Morrow, *Concert Life in Haydn's Vienna*, 161. Nevertheless, Eduard Hanslick emphasizes Schuppanzigh's "Quartettproductionen" as a pivotal turning point that introduced the string quartet to the Viennese public stage. Eduard Hanslick, *Geschichte des Concertwesens in Wien* (Vienna, 1869), 1:203.

    Evincing the quasi-public nature of these events is the fact that they garnered critical attention in the *Allgemeine musikalische Zeitung* (see, e.g., Web Docs. #21 and 40). Harold Love has described such reviews as "the main manifestation within the musical public of the critical rationality identified by [Jürgen] Habermas as the defining characteristic of the bourgeois public sphere." Love, "How Music Created a Public," *Criticism* 46 (2004): 265. On Habermas and the public sphere, see below, 125. For a nuanced critique of the traditional binaries of "private" vs. "public" compositional styles, see Mary Hunter, "Haydn's London Piano Trios and His Salomon String Quartets: Private vs. Public?," in *Haydn and His World*, 103–30.

[11] These *Abendunterhaltungen* are discussed in detail, and contrasted with Schuppanzigh's series, in John M. Gingerich, *Schubert's Beethoven Project* (Cambridge University Press, 2014), 59–84.

[12] For a more complete list, see Bashford, "The String Quartet and Society," 7–9. Bashford describes how the tension between the intimacy of the quartet and the grand performance spaces in which it was newly being presented was a catalyst for certain adaptations over the course of the nineteenth century, including: (1) a more extroverted playing style; (2) experimentation with seating formats (see above, 8 n. 9); and (3) a trend toward a more intensely dramatic style of quartet-writing.

    Along these lines, Joseph Kerman describes the decline of the quartet as intimate, musical "conversation" and the rise of a new "symphonic ideal" in Beethoven's "Razumovsky" quartets, which were conceived in the mighty wake of the "Eroica." Joseph Kerman, *The Beethoven Quartets* (New York: W. W. Norton, 1966), 151–52. In a subsequent publication, he makes this point more bluntly: "Think of the beginning of the first 'Razumovsky' and the end of the last one; there's not much conversation in evidence on either page. A better term might be determined ensemble shouting. At one time happy to converse, the string quartet has now acquired a new ambition: to project." Joseph Kerman, "Beethoven Quartet Audiences: Actual, Potential, Ideal," in *The Beethoven Quartet Companion*, ed. Robert Winter and Robert Martin (Berkeley: University of California Press, 1994), 15. The trend Kerman describes was not universally embraced. Schumann vehemently opposed the "symphonic furor" of incorporating orchestral textures in quartet writing; see John Daverio, *Robert Schumann: Herald of a "New Poetic Age"* (Oxford University Press, 1997), 255.

[13] On the formation of a string quartet canon during Beethoven's lifetime, see Lewis Lockwood and the Juilliard String Quartet, *Inside Beethoven's Quartets: History, Interpretation, Performance* (Cambridge, MA: Harvard University Press, 2008), 3–6; and November, *Beethoven's Theatrical Quartets*, 33–38. See also Gingerich's discussion of the term "Classical,"

Public chamber concerts with professional performers emerged during a period in which the technical and musical demands of many new compositions increasingly exceeded the reach of most amateur players; if this was not already true with Mozart's and Haydn's later quartets,[14] it certainly was from Beethoven's earliest ones.[15] Public concerts thus afforded connoisseurs the option of enjoying, from the safe vantage point of the audience, compositions that were beyond their own technical grasp.[16]

A generation earlier, the disparate technical demands among parts in many quartets (among other genres) enabled amateurs to play together with more accomplished musicians. Bashford notes that "wealthy and influential patrons [in the eighteenth century] could always buy their way out of difficulty" by hiring a professional first violinist to lead their quartet session.[17] However, this solution surely became less viable in the

as applied to Schuppanzigh's concerts by contemporaneous writers, in "Ignaz Schuppanzigh and Beethoven's Late Quartets," 452. On the reception and transmission of Boccherini's chamber works in Vienna, see Rupert Ridgewell, "Artaria's Music Shop and Boccherini's Music in Viennese Musical Life," *Early Music* 33, no. 2 (May 2005): 179–89. On Baillot's approach to programming his quartet and quintet Séances, see Morabito, "Authorship, Performance and Musical Identity."

[14] Mozart's chamber music was often criticized as suitable only for connoisseurs and too complex to be commercially viable for the amateur market. Carl Ditters von Dittersdorf articulates this point in a letter to Artaria offering his own recent quartets for publication: "I am sure that you will do better with mine than Mozart's (which according to my, as well as the great theorists', judgment are worthy of the highest praise but which, however, because of their unrelenting extreme artfulness are not everyone's purchase)" (August 18, 1788). Translated by Leo F. Balk and quoted in Robert O. Gjerdingen, *Music in the Galant Style* (Oxford University Press, 2007), 437. See also Eva Badura-Skoda, "Dittersdorf über Haydns und Mozarts Quartette," *Collectanea Mozartiana: herausgegeben zum 75järigen Bestehen der Mozartgemeinde Wien*, 41–50 (Tutzing: Hans Schneider, 1988). Dittersdorf's negative appraisal of Mozart's music as too complex is echoed in a passage from his autobiography: Dittersdorf recounts a conversation with Emperor Joseph II, who (he claims) agreed with his comparison of Mozart to the poet Friedrich Gottlieb Klopstock ("one must read Klopstock's works over and over again") and of Haydn to Christian Fürchtegott Gellert ("Gellert's merits are patent at the first glance"). Quoted in translated version in David Wyn Jones, "Haydn and His Fellow Composers," 50. On the accessibility of Mozart's music for amateur performance, a compilation of relevant source documents is provided in Zaslaw, "The Breitkopf Firm's Relations with Leopold and Wolfgang Mozart," 85–103. For a broader historical background, see DeNora, *Beethoven and the Construction of Genius*, 11–36.

[15] An early review of Beethoven's op. 18 quartets states that "they must be played frequently and well since they are very difficult to perform and are by no means popular" (Unter den neuen hier erscheinenden Werken zeichnen sich vortreffliche Arbeiten von *Beethoven* aus [bey *Mollo*]. Drey Quartetten geben einen vollgültigen Beweis für seine Kunst: doch müssen sie öfters und sehr gut gespielt werden, da sie sehr schwer auszuführen und keineswegs populair sind.) "Nachrichten. Wien," in *Allgemeine musikalische Zeitung* (Leipzig) 3, no. 48 (August 26, 1801): col. 800.

[16] Bashford points out that enthusiastic amateurs formed the core audience for many of the new subscription chamber music series in the nineteenth century ("The String Quartet and Society," 7.)

[17] Ibid., 6. See also Leppert, *Music and Image*, 11. Such practices blur the distinction between amateur and professional performance. Bashford sensitively cautions against such

nineteenth century as the technical demands of all four parts became more equal. Hanslick reports that Count Razumovsky himself initially played second violin together with Schuppanzigh, Franz Weiß, and J. Linke (all professionals) at private quartet gatherings at Lichnowsky's or his palaces but later gave up "this last bit of amateurish egoism (*dilettantischen Egoismus*)" and engaged a reconstituted, all-professional Schuppanzigh quartet with an unprecedented lifetime contract.[18] Thus Razumovsky and Schuppanzigh laid some of the first bricks in the "wall of separation" that came to divide amateur and professional chamber music.[19]

The establishment of public, professional chamber music performances led to a new, more official status for the audience: Whereas a quartet was previously viewed primarily as a conversation *among* the four players (which any listeners present essentially overhear), the new notion became that the players *performed* the piece specifically for a paying audience. Joseph Kerman nicely summarizes this evolution as follows: "Formed in 1804 for the express purpose of presenting concerts in Vienna, [the Schuppanzigh Quartet] ... was an obvious harbinger of the professional world of the string quartet as we know it. The genre today addresses principally not its own players but a concert audience; its aural field is no longer a closed circle but an open-ended cone."[20]

If Schuppanzigh's public performances transformed the practice of quartet playing, his immediate inspiration was Beethoven's compositions, which left an indelible mark on the genre. Beethoven's transformation of

---

simplistic binaries in "Historiography and Invisible Musics: Domestic Chamber Music in Nineteenth-Century Britain," *Journal of the American Musicological Society* 63, no. 2 (Summer 2010): 291–360.

[18] Hanslick, *Geschichte des Concertwesens in Wien*, 204. On Beethoven's relationship with the Schuppanzigh Quartet – his so-called "Leib-quartett" (personal quartet) – see November, *Beethoven's Theatrical Quartets*, 27–29.

[19] Concurrent with rising technical difficulty in "serious" chamber works during the final decades of the eighteenth century, a distinct body of *Hausmusik* emerged to cater to the needs of dilettantes. Written to be pleasing and sight-readable, this music is characterized by homophonic textures, simple or recognizable melodic materials, and clear layouts for easy reading. Finscher has suggested that the strong division between *Hausmusik* and more demanding chamber music was created largely by publishers; see "Hausmusik und Kammermusik," in *Geschichte und Geschichten: Ausgewählte Aufsätze zur Musikhistorie*, ed. Hermann Danuser (Mainz: Schott Musik, 2003), 79–88. See also Parker, *The String Quartet*, 26–30. Hanslick also mentions the popularity of arrangements of orchestral music for quartet or quintet, which filled a role equivalent to four-hand piano arrangements later in the nineteenth century – and, it should be added, to recordings in the twentieth. Hanslick, *Geschichte des Concertwesens in Wien*, 1: 202). On the *Journal für Quartetten Liebhaber* (Journal for Quartet Amateurs), of which twenty-four volumes appeared in the years 1807–10, see November, *Beethoven's Theatrical Quartets*, 34–35.

[20] Kerman, "Beethoven Quartet Audiences," 15.

the string quartet has been studied in depth fully elsewhere, and for present purposes it will suffice to underscore a few "firsts": (1) Beethoven's quartets were the first to demand nearly concerto-level virtuosity from all four players;[21] (2) Beethoven was the first composer to publish quartets simultaneously in score and parts (from op. 127 on), reflecting the exceptional amount of rehearsal and study demanded by these works, which surely could not be sight-read from parts alone;[22] (3) Beethoven was the first composer to declare a quartet unsuitable for public performance (the "Serioso" quartet, op. 95, in an 1816 letter to George Smart), signaling a remarkable shift in generic expectations only a decade after Vienna's first semi-public quartet concert series;[23] and (4) Beethoven's late quartets made extraordinary demands of the audience on account of their esoteric style – as evidenced, for instance, by a suggestion from Schuppanzigh Quartet second violinist Karl Holz that the premiere performance of op. 127 include two play-throughs of the piece[24] and by the need to substitute a new finale for op. 130 to replace the *Grosse Fuge*.[25]

---

[21] The famous anecdote in which Beethoven – responding to Schuppanzigh's complaints about the supremely demanding first violin part in op. 59, no. 1 – supposedly said "Do you think I care about your damn fiddle when the spirit moves me?" may not, in fact, be true. It is first transmitted (to my knowledge) in Adolf Bernhard Marx, *Ludwig van Beethoven: Leben und Schaffen* (Berlin, 1859); I examined the second edition (1863), where it appears in 2:39. This story has become cemented as a part of the legendary "Beethoven," but it cannot be traced convincingly to the historical Beethoven.

   Describing an "orchestral" style in the first movement of op. 59, no. 1, Marx makes a comparison to public address as opposed to private conversation: "At the forum, before the people, one speaks differently than at the green table [*Auf dem Forum, vor dem Volke redet man anders, als am grünen Tische*]" (ibid., 2:47). See commentary in November, *Beethoven's Theatrical Quartets*, 125.

[22] On the concurrent publication of score and parts (and the difficulty of serious rehearsal without scores), see Finscher, *Studien zur Geschichte des Streichquartetts*, 297–99. Pleyel published the *Collection complète des quatuors d'Haydn* in 1801 and pioneered the publication of miniature scores – suitable for use in rehearsal or for serious audiences to follow during concerts – with the *Bibliothèque musicale* series that commenced in 1802. See Cecil Hopkinson, "The Earliest Miniature Scores," *Music Review* 33 (1972): 138–44; Rita Benton, "Pleyel's *Bibliothèque musicale*," *Music Review* 35 (1975): 1–4; and Hans Lenneberg, "Revising the History of the Miniature Score," *Notes* 45, no. 2 (December 1988): 258–61.

[23] See David Wyn Jones, "Beethoven and the Viennese Legacy," in *The Cambridge Companion to the String Quartet*, 220.

[24] For a detailed study of the Beethoven/Schuppanzigh relationship and the unique difficulties posed by the late quartets, see Gingerich, "Ignaz Schuppanzigh and Beethoven's Late Quartets." An earlier study, which Gingerich partly criticizes for reliance on incomplete or unreliable sources, is Robert Adelson, "Beethoven's String Quartet in E Flat Op. 127: A Study of the First Performances," *Music and Letters* 79, no. 2 (1998): 219–43.

[25] On the relation of Beethoven's quartets to changing ideologies of the string quartet in the early decades of the nineteenth century, see November, *Beethoven's Theatrical Quartets*, 8–38.

It is astonishing how far the quartet genre evolved in such a short period, from its origins as a gentlemanly diversion in Haydn's generation to a vehicle for more intense, serious expression in the hands of Beethoven and his successors. Whether the change of venue from salon to concert hall was the catalyst for the stylistic development, or whether it was the other way around, is an unanswerable question. But what is clear is that the contrast between casual quartet gatherings among friends and public concerts by professional ensembles was as pronounced as that between the style of Haydn's op. 1 and Beethoven's op. 135.

A manifesto for quartet playing in the nineteenth century

The founding of public chamber concert series – many of them created with the explicit goal of preserving and promoting repertoire that had come to be regarded as canonical – can be situated within a broader narrative of shifting attitudes regarding the musical "work" and its relationship to performances, scores, and posterity.[26] A strong articulation of these evolving ideas and their implications for quartet performance is found in a fascinating 1804 essay entitled "On the Performance of Instrumental Quartets" ("Ausführung der Instrumentalquartetten") that appeared in Leipzig's *Allgemeine musikalische Zeitung* with an attribution to "Cambini in Paris":[27]

Whenever music does not excite or calm the emotions, it should at least attract our attention and thereby dispel the worries and cares of everyday life. In my opinion, instrumental music, without the support of poetry, has especially the latter purpose. But if it is to achieve this, then it must be *well* written and *well* executed [*ausgeführt*]. Haydn's symphonies, as we give [perform] them here, show the very

---

[26] See Goehr, *The Imaginary Museum of Musical Works*. On the rise of "serious music culture" in Vienna during this period, see also DeNora, *Beethoven and the Construction of Genius*, 11–36.

[27] The purported author is the violinist/composer Giuseppe Maria Cambini (1746? –1825?), who was Italian-born but Parisian-domiciled after around 1770. While in Paris, he was extraordinarily prolific, producing some 140 quartets (plus dozens of quartet arrangements), 150 quintets, 80 *symphonies concertantes*, and numerous stage works, to name only his most significant genres. For an insightful discussion of Cambini's astonishing productivity, as well as his alleged sabotaging of Mozart during the latter's visit to Paris in 1778, see Brook, "The *Symphonie Concertante*: An Interim Report," 500–502; also Robert D. Levin, *Who Wrote the Mozart Four-Wind Concertante?* (Hillsdale, NY: Pendragon Press, 1988), 5–15 and 26–27. Cambini's forenames are often incorrectly given as "Giovanni Giuseppe," an error that stems from François-Joseph Fétis, *Biographie universelle des musiciens* (Brussels, 1835–44); I examined vol. 2 of the second edition (Paris, 1867), 162.

matter that I am driving at with both requirements: no one hears them without being taken at least so far that he forgets his worries. The quartet, quintet, etc., can and should do the same, and further bestows the advantage that we can hear them if we are not in a large hall and do not have fifty musicians handy. But the perfect execution of this genre of music is as difficult as it is rare. Consistency of feeling and unity of expression, which are indispensable to the performers, are not achieved casually upon the first meeting [*treffen sich nicht zufällig und beym ersten Zusammenkommen*]. Someone who [sight-]reads very well is often very bad at expression; if one of the players is cold or careless, all of the charms that the composer set as truly, quasi-dialogued [*gleichsam dialogisirte*] quartets and that could and should have captured our attention will be destroyed.

My opinion is that in every place where there are men who truly love their art, and who have enough insight, practice, and feeling to be able to tell the real difference between a musician [*Tonkünstler*] and a mere player [*Musikant*] (perhaps even a very skillful and estimable player) – these men, I say, should definitely get themselves together, and study quartets and learn to execute them. Yes, yes, I say learn: for this will not come even to them by itself or instantly; I say study: for even they will not penetrate all the meaning in all the separate sections of such good works all at once. They must, working even more concordantly than do their instruments [*noch einstimmiger als ihre Instrumente*],[28] repeat often the foremost works in this genre, thus learning all of the nuances of the intended execution – how to apply more chiaroscuro here, more mezzotint there, here the accent [i.e., expression] should by and by become more pathetic, strong, grand, or naïve, or piercing, or weak; and how now, after such execution of the separate parts [*Ausführung des Einzelnen*], the sense of the whole (and consequently of the composer himself) arises. Meanwhile they must put their thoughts together, and their egos must thereby limit themselves, producing a beautiful painting together. The fruits of such studies will be the most perfect satisfaction for them, as well as the esteem of all connoisseurs. In my youth I spent six fortunate months in such study and such gratification. Three great masters – Manfredi, the foremost violinist in all Italy with respect to orchestral and quartet playing, Nardini, who has become so famous as a virtuoso through the perfection of his playing, and Boccherini, whose merits are well enough known, did me the honor of accepting me as a violist among them. In this manner we studied quartets by Haydn (those which now

---

[28] The clause "noch einstimmiger als ihre Instrumente" is difficult to render in English. The word "einstimmig," literally "of one voice," encompasses the musical terms "concordant" and "in unison" (acoustic properties of the quartet's instruments) as well as the figurative meaning "in unanimous agreement" (the understanding shared among the quartet's players). The essay emphasizes the idea that musical understanding, achieved through "learning" and "studying," is the essential goal of the rehearsal process. This idea resonates with the statement in the previous paragraph that fluent sight-readers are often too-facile musicians; technical facility is not a shortcut to musical understanding.

make up opp. 9, 17, and 21 [*recte*: 20]) and some by Boccherini which he had just
written and which one still hears with such pleasure; and I may say myself that,
with those [pieces] that we had rehearsed [*einstudiert*] so much, we seemed like
wizards to those for whom we played. [Even] the best actor would not dare to give
a scene from a distinguished play without having often gone through it: It causes
me grief, and I must shrug my shoulders helplessly, when I hear musicians say:
"Come, let's play quartets!" just as lightly as one says in society, "Come, let's play a
game of Reversis!"[29] Then must music indeed remain vague and without meaning,
and it is no wonder, and no ground for complaint, when the audience does not
wish to hear more of it – or yawns, like – the reader of my essay.[30]

The mysteries surrounding this historically significant essay (and its putative author) compel us to make a slight detour before engaging in a close
reading. Although this account of Cambini's youthful period of quartet
collaboration with Nardini, Manfredi, and Boccherini has widely been
cited as the earliest record of a professional string quartet with stable
personnel,[31] others have doubted its veracity, because of some curious
inconsistencies and to the lack of independent corroboration beyond
Cambini's own writings.[32] The most suspicious aspect is the reference to

---

[29] Reversis is a four-person, trick-avoiding card game similar to hearts, which dates from 1601 and
was fashionable at the turn of the nineteenth century. For a cultural and historical overview, see
David Sidney Parlett, *The Oxford Guide to Card Games* (Oxford University Press, 1990), 299–
303; also John McLeod, "Rules of Games No. 5: Reversis," *Journal of the International Playing-
Card Society* 5, no. 4 (May 1977): 23–30.

[30] Cambini (?), "Ausführung der Instrumentalquartetten" (Web Doc. #2).

[31] Elisabeth Le Guin acknowledges certain irregularities in the essay's reference to Haydn's quartets
(which I discuss below) but accepts the basic account of the quartet with Nardini, Manfredi, and
Boccherini, stating that the ensemble met precisely in 1765 in Milan and that Boccherini's op. 2
quartets were created specifically for this ensemble's concert tours. Le Guin, *Boccherini's Body*,
207–8. Although Boccherini and Manfredi traveled as a duo beginning in 1766, I am not aware of
evidence of public quartet performances. Like Le Guin, Giorgio Pestelli takes the seemingly
concomitant composition of Boccherini's op. 2 as strong evidence of the quartet's existence (*L'età
de Mozart e de Beethoven*, rev. ed. [Torino: Edizioni di Torino, 1991], 141). Mara Parker does not
mention touring but does assert that the quartet performed publicly in Milan, without providing
further details (*The String Quartet: Four Types of Conversation* [Burlington: Ashgate, 2002], 29). See
also John H. Baron, *Chamber Music: A Research and Information Guide*, 2nd ed. (New York:
Routledge, 2002), 283–84; Michelle Garnier-Panafieu, "Le quatuor à cordes au temps de Mozart:
trajectoires et spécificités," in *Cordes et claviers au temps de Mozart*, ed. Peter Lang (Bern: Editions
Scientifiques Internationals, 2010), 56–57; Levy, "The *Quatuor Concertant* in Paris," 37–38; Parker,
The String Quartet, 29; Potter, "From Chamber to Concert Hall," 53; and Maurice W. Riley, *The
History of the Viola*, 2nd ed., vol. 2 (Ann Arbor: Braun-Brumfield, 1991), 185.

[32] The notion that Cambini played quartets by Boccherini, Haydn, and others with Nardini,
Manfredi, and Boccherini originates in a passing comment by Cambini in his discussion of
expressive performance in his earlier *Nouvelle méthode théorique et pratique pour le violon*
(Paris, [c. 1795–1803]; facsimile reprint Geneva: Minkoff, 1972), 22. I quote the passage in Web
Doc. #3, and an English translation appears in Le Guin, *Boccherini's Body*, 321 n. 2. Because of

Haydn's quartets opp. 9, 17, and 20 (misstated as "21"), none of which had even been composed, let alone published, when the ensemble purportedly met in the mid-1760s.[33] Indeed, Cambini's biographical record, which is based largely on his own testimony, is riddled with irregularities that suggest some pervasive fabrication or self-mythologizing.[34] Particularly bizarre is the oft-repeated story that, following an unsuccessful opera premiere in Naples around 1766 (i.e., around the same time Cambini purportedly played in the quartet), Cambini and his fiancée were captured and enslaved by Barbary pirates, eventually to be ransomed by a wealthy Venetian merchant.[35] While the narratives about the pirate abduction and the quartet collaboration make for entertaining reading, they cannot both be true – and, in all likelihood, neither one is. Cambini may have had an incentive to bolster his reputation through biographical exaggeration and name-dropping when around 1800, in the wake of various personal set-backs, he sharply curtailed his composing and turned to various writing projects.[36] The essay in the *Allgemeine musikalische Zeitung*, then, is much

the lack of independent corroboration, Daniel Heartz concludes that "the 'Tuscan' Quartet, as it has been called, did not last long, if it ever existed." Daniel Heartz, *Music in European Capitals: The Galant Style, 1720–1780* (New York: W. W. Norton, 2003), 969. A similarly cautious discussion is Chappell White, Jean Gribenski, and Amzie D. Parcell, "Cambini, Giuseppe Maria," in *The New Grove Dictionary*, 2nd ed., ed. Stanley Sadie, vol. 3 (London: Macmillan, 1980), 639–40. Dieter Lutz Trimpert charitably suggests that Cambini may simply have confused Haydn quartets he performed after moving to Paris with others he might have played while still in Italy. Dieter Lutz Trimpert, *Die Quatuors concertants von Giuseppe Cambini* (Tutzing: Hans Schneider, 1967), 10–12.

[33] Heartz notes that Nardini and Boccherini had been in Vienna, where they might possibly have obtained some of Haydn's early *Divertimenti à 4* (*Music in European Capitals*, 968–69). See also Le Guin, *Boccherini's Body*, 207–8. Unlike the 1804 essay attributed to Cambini (Web Doc. #2), Cambini's comment in the *Nouvelle méthode* (Web Doc. #3) mentions Haydn's quartets generally, without indicating any specific opus.

[34] On the problems of Cambini's biography, see White et al., "Cambini, Giuseppe Maria," in *The New Grove Dictionary*, 2nd ed., 3:639–41. For a more detailed discussion, see also Trimpert, *Die Quatuors concertants von Giuseppe Cambini*, 9–22.

[35] The original source for this anecdote is the German-born French author Baron Friedrich Grimm, whose proximity to Cambini suggests an autobiographical origin for this myth; see the entry for "août 1776" in Friedrich Grimm, *Correspondance littéraire*, 2nd ed. (Paris, 1812), 3:209. This story was widely transmitted, including in Fétis, *Biographie universelle des musiciens*, 2:162; and in George Grove, ed., *A Dictionary of Music and Musicians*, vol. 1 (London: Macmillan, 1879), 299. Some sources, including Grove, give the date of Cambini's Neapolitan opera as 1766, around the same time that he is presumed to have been touring with Boccherini, Manfredi, and Nardini. See also Trimpert, *Die Quatuors concertants von Giuseppe Cambini*, 13.

[36] Cambini's biographical record includes other dubious claims of relationships with more famous individuals, such as the (now disputed) notions that he had studied with Padre Martini and later with Haydn. In a similar vein, Janet M. Levy observes that whereas Nardini, Boccherini, and Manfredi all made their reputations as virtuoso performers, Cambini never distinguished

less a historical account of Cambini's youthful activities than a manifesto that expresses ideals of quartet performance germane to the early nineteenth century. It may have been written by Cambini – at the twilight of his musical career and curiously critiquing the amateur salon culture that had embraced him for three decades – but it could also have been forged, embellished, or ghost-written.[37]

Readers of the essay today may be surprised at such a hortatory delivery of seemingly unobjectionable ideas. Who would dispute that string quartets can be as powerful as symphonies or that a proper performance requires hours of detailed rehearsal and repeated play-throughs? Would anyone deny the value of chamber music studies to fostering musicians' interpretive sensitivity, expanding their expressive range, and cultivating their contrapuntal awareness? To this day, the study of chamber music (especially string quartets) is seen in most countries as essential training, even for musicians who do not aspire to perform chamber music professionally.

Yet all of these ideas were novel when the essay appeared in 1804. Whereas *Sperrdruck* (spaced type, reproduced here as italics) is typically limited to unfamiliar names and difficult terms, its repeated use for the verbs "learn" and "study" is almost condescendingly didactic, perhaps betraying the author's exasperation with the status quo. The very practices that the essay attacks were at the core of Parisian amateur musical culture at the end of the eighteenth century, which revolved around lovers of music gathering in salons to sight-read the newest compositions available from the city's thriving publishing houses, amid the ambiance of the salon's sophisticated society.[38] The culture

---

himself as a violinist and is remembered mainly for his Parisian compositions ("The *Quatuor Concertant* in Paris," 38). Among the various doubtful claims in Cambini's biographical accounts, it can be difficult to establish conclusively which ones originated with Cambini himself. See White et al., "Cambini, Giuseppe Maria," and Trimpert, *Die Quatuors concertants von Giuseppe Cambini*, 12–14.

[37] Heartz (*Music in European Capitals*, 969 n. 129) speculates that the essay may actually have been written by Friedrich Rochlitz, founding editor of Leipzig's *Allgemeine musikalische Zeitung*. That the article appeared prominently as the issue's lead story seems consistent with this theory. Finscher (*Studien zur Geschichte des Streichquartetts*, 296) raises the possibility that the document might be a hoax ("Mystifikation") but basically takes its authenticity for granted. I have suggested, in a separate study examining this issue in more detail, that the essay may be Rochlitz's highly embellished translation and expansion of the passage from Cambini's *Nouvelle méthode* (Web Doc. #3) referenced above, 82 n. 32. See Klorman, "The First Professional String Quartet? Re-Examining an Account Attributed to Giuseppe Maria Cambini," *Notes* 71, no. 4 (June 2015): 629–43.

[38] The salon was the natural habitat for the *quatuor concertant*, and this environment played an obvious role in that genre's formation. The essay's rebuke of the culture of the *quatuor concertant* – in which Cambini himself was an active and prodigious participant – may cast further doubt on his alleged authorship. Likewise, Paul Griffiths – who does not question

of the salon celebrated sociability and spontaneity in quartet playing (no less than in a game of Reversis), but the essay sees in this scenario a casualness that leads to poor execution, leaving listeners bored and ultimately devaluing the quartet as a genre.

The essay thus underscores the serious responsibilities that quartet players must discharge in order to perform successfully for attentive audiences. To be a curator, as it were, in the newly opened quartet wing of Lydia Goehr's "imaginary museum of musical works," one was first required to undergo a requisite, several-month-long period of intense learning and studying about quartet playing. And even after this foundational training, each successive performance would require the *Tonkünstler* to engage in hours of intensive rehearsal over multiple sessions, cultivating a deep musical understanding and refining every nuance in order to prepare a compelling performance.[39]

Instead of delighting in their individual utterances and personal characteristics, the players undergo this rehearsal process for the sake of unity, so that they become as one.[40] The essay is, in fact, one of the earliest documents to describe a string quartet as a fixed ensemble, cultivating musical cohesion and unity of expression through an extended period of rehearsal with the same four players. The statement that "after such execution of the separate parts [*Ausführung des Einzelnen*], the sense of the whole (and consequently of the composer himself) arises" describes how the quartet's players aspire to create something greater (or other) than the sum of its parts.[41] The same ideal was expounded upon just a few years

Cambini's authorship of the essay – notes the irony that Cambini, "composer of quartets by the dozen," would exhort musicians to exalt the quartet as a serious genre by rehearsing more thoroughly. Griffiths, *The String Quartet*, 85.

[39] The effect of such rehearsals on the Schuppanzigh Quartet's performance did not escape the notice of an anonymous reviewer, who wrote the following of the quartet's inaugural concert series (winter 1804–5): "Naturally it is only the most exquisite, most outstanding compositions that were performed publicly, [having been] carefully studied by these masters and only after some rehearsals" (Natürlich sind es nur die vorzüglichsten, ausgezeichnetsten Kompositionen, welche von solchen Meistern nach einigen Proben öffentlich vorgetragen werden). "Wien, Anfang des Mays," *Allgemeine musikalische Zeitung (Leipzig)* 7, no. 33 (May 15, 1805): col. 535 (Web Doc. #40).

[40] A related idea is articulated in a contemporaneous review of Beethoven's "Kreutzer" Sonata that appeared in the *Allgemeine musikalische Zeitung*; this review observes that the pianist and violinist will need to study the sonata carefully and together, not separately. *Allgemeine musikalische Zeitung (Leipzig)* 7, no. 28 (August 28, 1805): cols. 769–71 (Web Doc. #28). See Owen Jander's discussion of this review and its relation to Sulzer's notion of sonatas as musical dialogue in "The 'Kreutzer' Sonata as Dialog," *Early Music* 16, no. 1 (February 1988): 34–49.

[41] This idea that the four individual players collectively comprise a single voice (understood to be that of the composer) anticipates aspects of Cone, *The Composer's Voice*.

later in an influential essay entitled "Ueber Quartettmusik" by Johann Conrad Wilhelm Petiscus (signed "P."), also published in the *Allgemeine musikalische Zeitung* in 1810. Writing of the "beautiful harmony of the four instruments [*schönen Einklang der vier Instrumente*]," Petiscus coins the touching neologism "Viereinigkeit" (four-in-one-ness), evoking a quasi-sacred connection among the players (cf. "die heilige Dreieinigkeit," German for "Holy Trinity").[42] Indeed, some version of a four-in-one ideology remains the basis of quartet playing and teaching to this day.[43]

Mozartean spontaneity: improvisation and sight-reading

The new responsibilities involved in professional, public chamber music performance would have struck Mozart as utterly foreign. Intensive "rehearsal" in the modern sense was essentially unknown before the rise of public chamber music series, and sight-reading (or playing with only light preparation) seems to have been the norm.[44] The constant demand by music-loving families for new material to play at private gatherings is illustrated in an advertisement from the copyist Johann Traeg that appeared in the *Wiener Zeitung* on February 25, 1784:

---

[42] P[etiscus], "Ueber Quartettmusik," col. 520 (Web Doc. #23). For Petiscus, a preacher and visionary, these religious overtones were by no means accidental. His belief in quartet playing as a universalist agent of positive social relations is evinced in the passage quoted in the epigraph to Chapter 1.

[43] Members of the Guarneri Quartet, for example, describe "feel[ing] and breath[ing] as one player" and sometimes mystically experiencing "a guiding hand" or a "fifth presence" in performance. David Blum, ed., *The Art of Quartet Playing: The Guarneri Quartet* (Ithaca: Cornell University Press, 1987), 168–71. A related, twentieth-century trend is the performance of quartets from memory (notably undertaken by the Kolisch Quartet, Quartetto Italiano, and Smetana Quartet), which represents the logical extreme of the intensive preparation and ensemble unity advocated here and the polar opposite of casual, eighteenth-century norms. A yet more recent development, also related to the kind of rigorous quartet study described in the essay, is the practice of performing from full scores (rather than individual parts), made possible by playing from laptops or tablets, with foot pedals to facilitate page turns. See Daniel J. Wakin, "Bytes and Beethoven: Borromeo String Quartet and the Digital Tide," *New York Times*, January 14, 2011, www.nytimes.com/2011/01/16/arts/music/16string.html (accessed May 1, 2015).

[44] By rehearsal "in the modern sense," I refer to a period of ensemble practicing, usually over multiple sessions, involving a meticulous process of corrections and improvement, aimed at achieving a defined standard of perfection for a future concert performance on a separate occasion. Although the (pseudo-)Cambini essayist called for string quartets to rehearse this way in his 1804 article, it is difficult to document anything resembling this practice in Mozart's period with respect to chamber music.

There are many families and individuals in this very city who amuse themselves with large or small musical gatherings [*musikalische Akademien*].[45] Many of them do not wish to be overloaded with sheet music, or at very least to have an introductory hearing of things that they have a mind to buy. Inasmuch as I now possess a fine stock, which I endeavor daily to enlarge further, of the best and newest music of all types, I offer to hire out weekly either three symphonies or six quintets, six quartets, six trios, etc. for a quarterly payment in advance of three florin. If anyone wishes to give concerts twice a week and, accordingly, requires six symphonies or twelve other pieces, he can subscribe that way and pay quarterly only five florin. However, because I must strive to serve everyone fairly, no one should have misgivings at returning the pieces received directly the following day.[46]

Traeg's rental service attests to a voracious appetite for the newest compositions, many evidently to be played only once before being returned in exchange for something else. The sheer quantity of available music is suggested by Traeg's catalog of 1799, which lists around 1,100 quartets in 218 sets, by some 118 composers, plus several dozen operatic, symphonic, and concerto arrangements.[47]

Unlike the polished, carefully rehearsed performances usually heard on today's concert stages, the eighteenth-century practice of reading from individual parts, with minimal rehearsal or none, and without recourse to scores, must have lent the playing an air of adventure as well as a spontaneous, off-the-cuff quality. The remainder of this chapter accounts the prevalence of sight-reading in Mozart's day and, more speculatively, examines affinities between sight-reading and improvisation. The major challenge in constructing a history of chamber music sight-reading is scant

---

[45] The term "Akademie" was originally used to refer to societies of musical connoisseurs and subsequently for the institutions they founded to present public concerts; familiar examples include London's Academy for Ancient Music, Berlin's *Singakademie*, and (most relevant to Mozart) Baron van Swieten's *Gesellschaft der Associierten Cavaliere*. See Koch's *Musikalisches Lexikon*, s.v. "Akademie der Musik," cols. 94–96.

[46] Johann Traeg, "Nachricht an die Musikliebhaber," *Wiener Zeitung* 16 (February 25, 1784): 395–96 (Web Doc. #36). English translation adapted from Neal Zaslaw and William Cowdery, eds., *The Compleat Mozart* (New York: W. W. Norton, 1990), 117–18. Traeg's advertisement also offers "skilled musicians for large and small concerts at a very reasonable price" so long as orders are placed "at my establishment any time before midday" (ibid.). Such contracting services would likely include not only professional ensemble formations but also the hiring of individual musicians needed to complete amateur formations. That Traeg accepted requests up to the morning of a musical gathering implies that these "concerts" were sometimes arranged with little lead-time and without rehearsals in the modern sense. I thank Tom Beghin for bringing this source to my attention.

[47] Alexander Weinmann, *Johann Traeg: Die Musikalienverzeichnisse von 1799 und 1804* (Vienna: Universal Edition, 1973); cited in November, *Beethoven's Theatrical Quartets*, 36.

documentation. For one thing, a lack of evidence of rehearsals cannot, in itself, be taken as evidence of a lack of rehearsals. Yet, sources such as the (pseudo-)Cambini essay testify, by their appeals for rigorous rehearsal, to the currency of more casual practices. Before proceeding to a more detailed account of what one might call "Mozartean spontaneity," it is worth acknowledging that a significant gray area exists between playing music on first sight and performing after careful rehearsal. Although a profound contrast of attitudes is at issue here, the chamber-ensemble rehearsal practices of the past cannot be reduced to two categories, just as perform-ance situations cannot straightforwardly be classified as private or public.

Mozart's own correspondence, which provides an unusually thorough record of his activities, illuminates the ubiquity of sight-reading in his musical world and scarcely mentions anything modern readers would recognize as sustained chamber music rehearsal, even ahead of relatively formal perform-ances. Most of his explicit references to sight-reading (*prima vista*) relate to solo keyboard playing.[48] Typically these letters describe Mozart as a guest in someone's home, testing out the host's clavier by playing through whatever music was at hand and by improvising.[49] The following three excerpts are representative; each is drawn from a different letter:

I ... [went] to Herr von Hamm's, whose three young ladies each played a concerto, and I [played] one of Aichner's *prima vista*, and then went on improvis-ing [*und dann immer Phantasieren*].[50]

On going upstairs [at the home of the local magistrate Jakob Wilhelm Benedikt Langenmantel], I had the honor of playing for nearly three-quarters of an hour on a good clavichord of Stein's, in the presence of the stuck-up [*gestarzten*] young son, and his prim, leggy [*langhachsigten*][51] wife, and the simple old lady. I first impro-vised [*spielte Phantasien*], and finally played everything he had *prima vista*,

---

[48]   A well-known anecdote is L. Mozart's account of young Wolfgang's sight-reading, improvisation and figured-bass realization when he appeared before the King and Queen in London in May 1764. See Mozart, *Briefe*, ed. Wilhelm A. Bauer and Otto Erich Deutsch, vol. 1, *1755–76* (Kassel: Bärenreiter, 1962), 151. Grétry wrote superlatively in his *Mémoires* of "a young child who could play anything at sight," whom he met in Geneva in 1766; many scholars presume that the child in question was Mozart. Grétry, *Mémoires*, 1:99–100 (Web Doc. #6). English translation from Deutsch, *Mozart: A Documentary Biography*, 477. For an overview of accounts of Mozart the *Wunderkind* (including tests of his sight-reading and improvisation skills), see Katalin Komlós, "Mozart the Performer," in *The Cambridge Companion to Mozart*, 215–16.

[49]   An amply documented survey of Mozart's activities as improviser appears in Katalin Komlós, "'Ich praeludirte und spielte Variazionen': Mozart the Fortepianist," in *Perspectives on Mozart Performance*, ed. R. Larry Todd and Peter Williams (Cambridge University Press, 1991), 27–54.

[50]   W. A. Mozart to L. Mozart, Munich, October 11, 1777, in Mozart, *Briefe*, 2:47.

[51]   Various translations of Mozart's letter have rendered "langhachsig" as "prim" or even "condescending." The term is a synonym for "langbeinig," meaning "leggy." The German

[including] among others some very pretty pieces by Edlmann [*recte*: Edelmann]. Everyone was exceptionally polite, and I was equally so, for my habit is to behave toward people just as they behave toward me.[52]

At night, at supper, I played the Strassburg concerto; it went as smooth as oil. Everyone praised the beautiful, pure tone. After this a small clavichord was brought in. I preluded and played a sonata and the variations by Fischer. Then the others whispered to the Dean [of the St. Ulrich monastery in Augsburg] that he ought to hear me play in the organ style. I asked him to give me a theme; he did not want to, but one of the monks gave me one. I took it for a walk [*ich führte es spazieren*],[53] and in the middle (the fugue being in G minor) I brought it into major and in a playful [*scherzhaftes*] style but in the same tempo [*aber in nämlichen tempo*], and then finally I brought back the [original] subject only backwards [*arschling*]. At last it occurred to me, could the playful idea not [also] be used as the subject of a fugue? – I did not wonder long, but did so at once, and it went as accurately as if [the Salzburg tailor] Daser had taken its measure . . . At last someone brought me a fugued sonata and asked me to play it. But I said, "Gentlemen, this is too much, I must confess that I could not play such a sonata at sight [*die Sonate werde ich nicht gleich spielen können*]." "Yes, I think so too," said the Dean eagerly, as he was all in my favor, "it is too much; no one could do it." "In any case," said I, "I can but try." I heard the Dean muttering behind me the whole time, "Oh, you rogue! Oh, you rascal! Oh you!" – I played till eleven o'clock, bombarded and besieged, as it were, by noisy fugue themes.[54]

The frequent descriptions of sight-reading and keyboard improvisation together at the same sitting suggest that these activities were linked together as related forms of music-making; both are experienced, so to speak, in the present tense.[55] Mozart explicitly comments on this affinity in the following anecdote, which describes Abbé Georg Joseph Vogler's (evidently abysmal) sight-reading:

"Haxe" is a cognate of the English "hock." Ludwig Merkle, *Bairische Grammatik* (Munich: Heimeran Verlag, 1975), 170.

[52] W. A. Mozart to L. Mozart, Augsburg, October 14, 1777, in Mozart, *Briefe*, 2:54–55.

[53] Mozart's statement literally means he took the theme for a walk, as one would a dog. This may be a colorful way of saying he tried the theme out, or it might be a play on the Italian "Andante" for a *walking* tempo.

[54] W. A. Mozart to L. Mozart, Augsburg, October 23–25, 1777, in Mozart, *Briefe*, 2:82. Daser is identified as a Salzburg tailor in Ludwig Pohl, ed., *Mozarts Briefe* (Salzburg, 1865), 75.

[55] This is suggested by the etymology of the word "improvise," from the Latin *im-provisus*, meaning unforeseen or unprovided. This word entered the European musical lexicon (supplanting such traditional verbs as "präludiren" and "fantasiren") only in the nineteenth century, after improvisation declined as a standard practice and came to be regarded as a "marked" activity. See Stephen Blum, "Recognizing Improvisation," in *In the Course of Performance: Studies in the World of Musical Improvisation*, ed. Bruno Nettl and Melinda Russell (University of Chicago Press, 1998), 27–45.

After dinner, he [Abbé Vogler] arranged for two keyboards to be tuned to one another and sent for his piercingly boring [*gestochene langweiligen*] sonatas. He insisted that I play them and he accompanied me on the second clavier. Then, on his desperate urging, I had to fetch my sonatas. N.b., before dinner he raced *prima vista* through my concerto, the one the mademoiselle of the house had learned and which I wrote for the Countess Litzau [*recte*: Baroness Lützow; K. 246]. He played the first movement [marked *Allegro aperto*] *preßtißimo*, the Andante *allegro*, and the Rondo [marked *Tempo di Minuetto*] truly *preßtißimo*. The bass he played mostly differently from the way it is written, and once in a while he came up with entirely different harmonies and melodies. It is inevitable at that speed, [since] the eyes cannot see [the notes quickly enough] and the hands cannot execute them. So, then, what do you call this? – to play *prima vista* like this and to take a shit are one and the same to me. The listeners, I mean those worthy of the name, can't say anything, except that they have – *seen* Musique and Clavier being performed. They hear, think – and *feel* as little as – *he* does. You can easily imagine that it was hard to take, especially since I couldn't say to him: *much too fast*! Besides, it is so much easier to play a piece fast than to play it slowly; in fast passages you can drop quite a few notes without anybody noticing. But is it beautiful? – When you play with such rapidity you can make changes in your right and in your left hand without anybody seeing or hearing it; but is it beautiful? – And what does the art of *prima vista* consist of? It is this: to play the piece in correct time, just the way it is supposed to be, and to play all the notes, appoggiaturas, etc., with all proper expression and feeling, just as it says on the page, so that one could have the impression that the one who is playing the piece had actually composed it himself.[56]

Mozart's conclusion articulates a fascinating notion: an ideal sight-reader executes the piece so fluently that it seems as though he or she was the music's author and not merely its performer. By effacing the distinction between performer and composer – a distinction that was not very pronounced in this period anyway – Mozart suggests that the act of sight-reading is similar to improvisation; musical continuity is discovered (or created) spontaneously, from moment to moment, as the music is played.[57] Mozart must have considered skillful sight-reading to be a hallmark of

---

[56] W. A. Mozart to L. Mozart, Mannheim, January 17, 1778, in Mozart, *Briefe*, 2:227–28. English translation adapted from *Mozart's Letters, Mozart's Life*, 121–22.

[57] In a similar vein, Carl Czerny describes sight-reading as an activity in which a pianist's musical and manual capacities intertwine: "A thorough knowledge of harmony, which one is already capable of executing practically through the fingers, contributes greatly to sight-reading; whereas a superficial, merely cerebral knowledge of it will lead one even more astray if one chooses to apply it" (Eine gründliche Kenntniss der Harmonielehre, die man auch schon praktisch durch die Finger auszuüben vermag, trägt sehr zum A-vista-Spielen bei; wogegen aber eine bloss oberflächliche, nur erst im Kopfe wohnende Kenntniss derselben nur noch mehr irre macht, wenn man sie dazu anwenden wollte). Carl Czerny, *Pianoforte-Schule*, op. 500 (Vienna, 1839), 71.

excellent musicianship, since he frequently comments on this ability (or its absence) when assessing a player's talent.[58]

Several of Mozart's letters refer (explicitly or implicitly) to the sight-reading of chamber music as well. Here, too, the most direct references are often part of an assessment of another musician's abilities:

Last Saturday, the 4th, on the most solemn name day of His Highness the Archduke Albert, we had a small gathering [*kleine accademie*] at our lodgings [at the Schwarzen Adler inn, where Mozart and his mother were staying], which commenced at half-past three o'clock and finished at eight. M. Dubreil [*recte:* Charles-Albert Dupreille, a violinist in the Munich court orchestra],[59] whom Papa no doubt remembers, was also present; he is a pupil of Tartini's. In the forenoon he gave a lesson on the violin to the youngest son, Carl, and I chanced to come in at the time. I never gave him credit for much talent, but I saw that he took great pains in giving his lesson; and when we entered into conversation about concerto and orchestral violin playing, he reasoned very well, and was always of my opinion, so I retracted my former sentiments with regard to him, and was persuaded that I should find him to play well in time, and a correct violinist in the orchestra. I therefore invited him to be so kind as to attend our little music academy that afternoon. We played, first of all, two quintets of [Michael] Haydn, but to my dismay I could scarcely hear Dubreil, who could not play four continuous bars without a mistake. He could never find the positions, and he was no good friend to the *sospirs* [short pauses]. The only good thing was that he spoke politely and praised the quintets; otherwise – As it was, I said nothing to him, but he kept constantly saying himself, "I beg your pardon, but really I am out again! The thing is puzzling, but fine!" I invariably replied, "It doesn't matter; we are just among ourselves." I then played the concertos in C [K. 246], in B♭ [K. 238], in E♭ [K. 271], and after that a trio of mine [K. 254]. This was finely accompanied, truly! In the adagio I was obliged to play six bars of his part. As a finale, I played my last Cassation in B♭ [K. 287]; they all pricked up their ears at this [*da schauete alles groß drein*]. I played as if I had been the greatest violin-player in all Europe.[60]

Since the word "Akademie" typically indicates a somewhat formal (public or private) concert,[61] Mozart was more than a little facetious to use it for

---

[58] For example, Mozart praised Aloysia Weber in a letter a few weeks later for her fluent sight-reading of his "difficult sonatas," favorably comparing her slow, careful sight-reading to Vogler's fast, careless sight-reading. W. A. Mozart to L. Mozart, Mannheim, February 2, 1778, in Mozart, *Briefe*, 2:251–52.

[59] On the identity of Dubreil/Dupreille, see Hermann Abert, *W. A. Mozart*, trans. Stewart Spencer, ed. Cliff Eisen (New Haven: Yale University Press, 2007), 378 n. 16.

[60] W. A. Mozart to L. Mozart, Munich, October 6, 1777, in Mozart, *Briefe*, 2:40–41. The interpolated Köchel numbers are according to Abert, *W. A. Mozart*, 378.

[61] Mozart used the same term to designate concerto performances with orchestra. In a letter to L. Mozart (Vienna, March 20, 1784) outlining his busy performance calender during the Lenten

this casual sight-reading session. In an earlier letter written the day before the event, Mozart describes it more dismissively as a "kleine schlackademie" and decries the lousy clavier at the inn ("auweh! auweh! auweh!").[62] The music was clearly organized haphazardly, since he only asked Dupreille to participate the morning of the gathering and merely because Mozart happened to observe the violin lesson. There were at least some listeners in attendance, as Mozart indicates with his comment that "they all pricked up their ears" for the finale, after the middling play-through of the Haydn quintets. But his reassurances to Dupreille that "we are just among ourselves" suggest a fairly intimate company of family members and familiars, perhaps also others who were present at the inn for festivities celebrating the Archduke's name day. These attendees probably socialized concurrently with the music; it is difficult to imagine anyone listening with rapt attention for over four hours, especially given Dupreille's reportedly blundering performance. (Notice the chatty, distracted listeners at the private concert depicted in Fig. 3.1.[63]) This event was, thus, precisely the kind of concert that the (pseudo-)Cambini essayist would lambast a few decades later: a casual performance with some audience present in which the musicians sight-read with mixed success. But whereas the essay asserts

---

season, events are categorized as either *Academie im Theater,* for concerto performances with orchestra at the *Burgtheater,* or *Privat-Academie,* for solo or chamber performances at aristocratic homes.

[62] W. A. Mozart to L. Mozart, Munich, October 2, 1777 (postscript dated October 3), in Mozart, *Briefe,* 2:33.

[63] This engraving of a private concert accompanied Joseph Richter's satirical discussion of court mourning customs (*Hoftrauer*) practiced by aristocrats, whose expensive, black mourning clothes he describes as cloaking a host of insincere and unkind behaviors. Joseph Richter, *Bildergalerie weltlicher Misbräuche Bildergalerie: ein Gegenstück zur Bildergalerie katholischer und klösterlicher* (Frankfurt and Leipzig, 1785), 38–47. Judging from the posture and countenance of the dilettantes who accompany a piano solo by the daughter of the house, the music seems to leave something to be desired. Yet, according to Richter's explanation of the image, the listeners "clap their hands mechanically, since that is [demanded by] the custom." The young widow (on the right) "applauds too and is all ears, only not for the beautiful music but the beautiful words of the gallant man behind her chair who whispers into her ear"; even as she wears the proper ribbon of mourning for her late husband, she is already flirting with a suitor. The other listeners are described as being mostly consumed with trivial or irrelevant matters: a pair of men (background, right) enjoy their frozen refreshments while criticizing their host, while the plump man (seated in front of them) hears the *solo* performance and is reminded of his *solo-dog,* who just yesterday caught three rabbits *solo.* Upon seeing among the audience a guest not wearing his requisite mourning attire, the baroness swoons onto a chair (foreground, left), prompting a family friend to revive her with smelling salts while ejecting the offensive guest from the house (ibid., 46–7) (Web Doc. #29). This gathering may ostensibly depict a private concert, but the musical activities are merely a catalyst for other, less flattering forms of (anti)social interaction.

Fig. 3.1 Johann Ernst Mansfeld, *Private Concert during Court Mourning*. Engraving published in Joseph Richter, *Bildergalerie weltlicher Misbräuche: ein Gegenstück zur Bildergalerie katholischer und klösterlicher* (Frankfurt and Leipzig, 1785), 38.

that such spontaneous music-making inevitably fails to move the audience, Mozart seems to believe that a compelling, sight-read performance *is* possible with skillful players; the weak link in this case was poor Monsieur Dupreille.

A similar story, recounted from the opposite vantage point, is transmitted in a journal entry by Susan Burney, the third daughter of Charles Burney. Her "journal letter" dated August 23–26, 1788 describes her consternation at being pressured, while hosting company that included a distinguished Swiss violinist named Scheener, to perform difficult music with him without notice:

> We had tea – & then a little general conversation but it soon flagged – there were violins, & Music, & every body longing to hear Scheener – & all looked towards *me* as being the only person who c^d give him a *Base* – but think how pleasant! Terrified as I must at any rate have been to play wth Scheener alone, there was no music wth any accomp^{ts} that I c^d play except two of Pleyell's [*sic*] new lessons [i.e., sonatas], very difficult, & wch I have not above half learn'd, both of wch Mr Burney had played the eve^g before & again that Morn^g – However *pour abreger* [to cut things short] I was obliged to go thro', frightened to death, both lessons – & then accomp^d as well as I c^d a new trio of Haydn's – after wch I was half *compelled* to begin a lesson of Kozeluch's I had not seen these two years, & of wch I c^d not get thro' the first page – & after all – suffering very unpleasant sensations, & forcing myself to attempt what I knew I c^d not execute, it ended as I had foreseen in general disappointment – chiefly on the part of my dear Mrs Lock – who tho' she w^d attempt nothing herself, seemed to think *I* ought to undertake everything – believing me capable of what I am not perhaps – but indeed fear disabled me completely – & rendered things difficult to me wch alone w^d have had nothing to alarm me … I c^d not but be very sorry – & vexed – & share the disappointment which I *seemed* to have occasioned – th' only because more had been expected from me than I *could* execute.[64]

Burney's references to pieces she had "half learn'd" and "had not seen [in] two years" demonstrate but two possibilities on the continuum from sight-reading an absolutely unknown piece to performing a carefully prepared one. Her account reminds us that some players who attempted music beyond their abilitiy to sight-read – such as Dupreille – may have done so only under duress.[65]

---

[64] *The Journals and Letters of Susan Burney: Music and Society in Late Eighteenth-Century England*, ed. Philip Olleson (Farnham: Ashgate, 2012), 210–11. Olleson suggests that the Haydn trio in question is likely the Trio in E♭, Hob. XV/10 and that the cello part would have been dispensed with. The full account of Scheener's visit begins on p. 205. I thank Rohan H. Stewart-MacDonald for bringing this passage to my attention.

[65] Richard Leppert describes such performances before company as inherently risky, especially when proud parents presented their daughters: "What portended was a double bind for the girl's father. She had to have music; her social station and marriage prospects demanded it. Yet to let the girl perform in semi-public could lead to ridicule." Leppert, *Music and Image*, 60–61. Although Leppert's remarks pertain to marriagable young ladies, Burney (already married and in her thirties) would have felt a similar pressure to excel, being the daughter of a musically sophisticated family performing with a professional-musician guest.

A more favorable report of chamber music sight-reading appears in Mozart's assessment of a certain violinist "Menzl," whom he recommended for a vacant position as leader of the Salzburg court orchestra.[66] After recommending Menzl to Gottfried Ignaz von Ployer (agent of the Salzburg court in Vienna and father of Mozart's student Barbara), he followed up with a letter to his father:

> I confidentially recommended to him [Ployer] a certain *Menzl* – a handsome, young, and skilled musician. – I asked him not to reveal my name, otherwise it might not work. – He is now awaiting a decision. – He would probably get 400 gulden – and a new *suit* – I already scolded Menzl about the suit – it's so beggarly. – Should something come of it, I'll ask Menzl to take a letter from me to you, and some Musique as well; – you'll find him a very Pleasant Violinist who is also a good sight-reader; – no one in *Vienna* has played my quartets *a prima vista* as well as he has; – besides, he is the best fellow in the whole world as well, who will be delighted to make some Musique with you whenever you like – I even asked him to be in the orchestra here when I did my concerts.[67]

Apparently Mozart and Menzl were on fairly intimate terms, close enough for Mozart to offer fashion tips besides giving an enthusiastic character reference. They might have sight-read Mozart's quartets together on more than one occasion, perhaps as trial runs of the first three "Haydn" quartets, which had just been composed,[68] and Menzl's playing must have been impressive enough to elicit this enthusiastic recommendation. Mozart's idea that Menzl should meet Leopold and bring some music so they could play together sounds less like an official audition than a suggestion that the two musicians might use sight-reading as a means to forge a relationship – to break musical bread together, as it were.

Mozart offers a glimpse into one such chamber music session that took place while staying at Count Thun's palace in Prague during the wildly successful revival of *Le nozze di Figaro*:

---

[66] Dorothea Link attempts to disentangle his identity (Karl Menzel or Zeno Franz Mentzel, or perhaps these are actually the same individual) in "Mozart's Appointment to the Viennese Court," in *Words about Mozart: Essays in Honour of Stanley Sadie*, ed. Dorothea Link with Judith Nagley (Woodbridge: Boydell Press, 2005), 153–78; see Link's Table 9.2.

[67] W. A. Mozart to L. Mozart, Vienna, April 10, 1784, in Mozart, *Briefe*, 3:309–10. English translation from *Mozart's Letters, Mozart's Life*, 367.

[68] According to Alan Tyson, the "Haydn" quartets were composed in two spurts, with the first three (and possibly also the "Hunt") completed by 1783, and the remainder composed later, between November 1784 and January 1785, very shortly before the famous gatherings with Haydn, Leopold, and the Barons Tinti on January 15 and February 12, 1785. Tyson, *Mozart: Studies of the Autograph Scores* (Cambridge, MA: Harvard University Press, 1987), 103–5.

You mustn't forget the count's high and noble music after the noon meal. Furthermore, as they put a pretty good Pianoforte in my room that day, you can easily imagine that I couldn't leave it standing there in the evening, untouched, without playing it; and from that it follows quite logically that we played a little *Quatuor in Caritatis camera* (*and* "das schöne Bandel Hammera") and from there it probably follows that we lost another entire evening *Sine Linea*; well, that's exactly what happened.[69]

The silly tone of this passage betrays traces of the wine or punch that surely fueled this evening of musical revelry.[70] With a nice keyboard at hand, Mozart and his companions chose to sight-read a piano quartet ("Quatuor in Caritatis camera") and then sing the comic terzetto "Liebes Mandel, wo ist's Bandel," K. 441.[71] The terzetto (whose text translates roughly as "Where is the ribbon, dear?") is a musical inside joke that Mozart composed to sing together with his wife and their friend Gottfried von Jacquin.[72] Constanze's second husband, Georg Nikolaus von Nissen, explains: "[Mozart] often made verses, but mostly only for playful [*scherz-haften*] occasions, for example his 'Mandel, wo ist's Bandel,' a comic terzetto with keyboard accompaniment."[73]

The sight-reading of chamber music was not limited to professional musicians and serious connoisseurs; dilettantes also engaged in casual sight-reading "concerts," even with demanding repertoire, though with

---

[69] W. A. Mozart to Gottfried von Jacquin, Prague, January 15, 1787, in Mozart, *Briefe*, 4:10. English translation from *Mozart's Letters, Mozart's Life*, 385.

[70] This same letter contains Mozart's famously effusive report of *Figaro*'s popularity in Prague, including an account of the beautiful ladies who danced to arrangements of *Figaro* at Count Thun's ball the previous evening. The letter closes with Mozart christening his travel companions with nonsense (mock Czech?) nicknames: Mozart's nickname was Pùnkitititi, his wife's Schabla Pumfa, their dog's Gauckerl, Anton Stadler's Nàtschibinìtschibi, and so on. Equally silly monikers were given to Jacquin (Hinkiti Honky), his sister Franziska (Dinimininimi), and his botanist brother Joseph Franz (Blatterizi, probably from *Blatt*, or leaf). On Mozart's relationship with the Jacquin family, see Chapter 7.

[71] Spaethling (*Mozart's Letters, Mozart's Life*, 385) mistranslates *caritatis camera* as "a room free of charge." It is actually a play on the Latin expression "in camera caritatis," meaning "just among us" or "off the record." The reference in the letter is a riff on the final stanza of Mozart's "Bandel" terzetto, K. 441, which inverts the Latin expression in deference to the rhyme scheme: "Welche Wonne, edle Sonne,/ Z'lebe'n *caritatis camera,*/ Und das schöne Bandel hammer a [i.e., Viennese dialect for "haben wir auch"],/ Ja, wir habn's, wir habn's, ja!" (What joy, noble sun to live *in camera caritatis*, and we also have the pretty ribbon; yes, we have it!).

[72] For details about the terzetto, including the episode that may have inspired its composition, see below, 272.

[73] "Er machte oft selbst Verse, meistens aber nur bey scherzhaften Gelegenheiten, z.B. sein 'Mandel, wo ist's Bandel,' ein komisches Terzett mit Clavier-Begleitung." Georg Nikolaus von Nissen, *Biographie W. A. Mozarts* (Leipzig, 1828), 668. For further context for this trio and Mozart's friendship with Jacquin, see Chapter 7.

predictably uneven results. Unlike Mozart's essentially comic telling of the episode with Dupreille, the following 1788 essay from the *Journal des Luxus und der Moden* expresses serious alarm at a spate of unrehearsed performances in noisy settings of one of Mozart's piano quartets. The writer, who does not specify which of Mozart's piano quartets he is describing,[74] adopts a harshly moralistic tone to censure amateur pianists for blundering through a new Mozart composition in settings unsuitable for serious playing or listening. Note that, in this essay, the word "concerts" (*Concerten*) refers to parties and social gatherings where music was played, not public performances.

"Concerning the Latest Favourite Music at Grand Concerts, especially in regard to Ladies' Predilections in Pianoforte Dilettantism"

[. . .] A few words now on an odd phenomenon occasioned by him [Mozart] (or by his fame). Some time ago a single *Quadro* by him (for pianoforte, 1 violin, 1 viola and violoncello) was engraved and published, which is very cunningly set and in performance needs the utmost precision in all four parts, but even when well played, or so it seems, is able and intended to delight only connoisseurs of music in a *musica di camera*. The cry soon made itself heard: "Mozart has written a very special new *Quadro*, and such and such a Princess or Countess possesses and plays it!", and this excited curiosity and led to the rash resolve to produce this original composition at grand and noisy concerts and to make a parade with it *invita Minerva*.

Many another piece keeps some countenance even when indifferently performed; but this product of Mozart's can in truth hardly bear listening to when it falls into mediocre amateurish hands and is negligently played. – Now this is what happened innumerable times last winter; at nearly every place to which my travels led me and where I was taken to a concert, some young lady or pretentious middle-class *demoiselle*, or some other pert dilettante in a noisy gathering, came up with this printed *Quadro* and fancied that it would be enjoyed. But it *could* not please;

---

[74] Mozart's Piano Quartet in G Minor (K. 478) was published by Hoffmeister in 1785, and the Piano Quartet in E♭ Major (K. 493) followed in 1786, just two years before this 1788 article. Deutsch speculates that the author may refer to K. 478 (*Mozart: A Documentary Biography*, 318), but they could easily refer to either piece, since both are so musically and technically demanding as to be unsuitable for any but the most accomplished players.

The "problem" of K. 478 and its unsuitability for dilettantes is a recurring theme in Mozart scholarship, stemming from an anecdote transmitted by Nissen (but uncorroborated elsewhere). According to Nissen, Hoffmeister had originally commissioned Mozart to compose three quartets for piano and strings but presented Mozart with a "kill" fee after K. 478. The cancellation of the commission prompted him to publish K. 493 with Artaria instead and to compose no more piano quartets. Rupert Ridgewell re-evaluates this narrative in his article "Biographical Myth and the Publication of Mozart's Piano Quartets," *Journal of the Royal Musical Association* 135, no. 1 (2010): 41–114.

everybody yawned with boredom over the incomprehensible *tintamarre* of 4 instruments which did not keep together for four bars on end, and whose senseless *concentus* never allowed any unity of feeling; but it *had to* to please [*sic*], it *had to* be praised! It is difficult for me to describe to you the persistence with which attempts were nearly everywhere made to enforce this. It were too little merely to rail at an ephemeral *manie du jour*, for it went on throughout a whole winter and (according to what I have additionally learned from hearsay) showed itself far too frequently. It deserves a public rebuke in your pages, where so many another fashionable idiocy, so many a misguided ostentation has already been justly exposed. For indeed such clumsy forwardness is not only unseemly, not only useless and purposeless, but it does harm to Art and to the spread of true taste. "Is that all it is?" (thinks the half-instructed hearer of this music)[.] "This is supposed to verge on the extreme of excellence in art, and yet I feel tempted to block my ears to it frequently as I listen. What sense does that make? How am I to know in the end what I may honestly praise or find fault with in music?" – In this way is a true love of music spoiled, sound human reason and sound natural impulses misled, and that directness and thoroughness of culture obstructed without which no art can ever rise to and maintain itself on the heights.

What a difference when this much-advertised work of art is performed with the highest degree of accuracy by four skilled musicians who have studied it carefully, in a quiet room where the suspension of every note cannot escape the listening ear, and in the presence of only two or three attentive persons![75]

To read about the craze swirling around a new Mozart quartet in the German Enlightenment equivalent of *Vogue* magazine illustrates the cultural currency it evidently commanded as an icon of refinement. While the writer surely exaggerates just how frequently this piece was played at parties during the 1787–88 winter season, his report nevertheless confirms that casual sight-reading in noisy social settings, even for complex compositions, was a widespread practice. The scene depicted in Fig. 3.2, in which musicians are evidently sight-reading at a grand concert, may resemble the setting described in the essay.[76] The commingling of fashion and art receives a harsh reprimand in the *Journal des Luxus und der*

---

[75] "Ueber die neueste Favorit-Musik in großen Concerten, sonderlich in Rücksicht auf Damen-Kunst, in Clavier-Liebhaberey (An die Herausgeber des Journals)," *Journal des Luxus und der Moden (Weimar)*, (June 1788): 230–33 (Web Doc. #39). English translation from Deutsch, *Mozart: A Documentary Biography*, 317–18. About the *Journal des Luxus und der Moden*, founded in Weimar in 1786 and the first German-language fashion magazine, see Caryl Clark, "Reading and Listening: Viennese Frauenzimmer Journals and the Sociocultural Context of Mozartean Opera Buffa," *Musical Quarterly* 87, no. 1 (Spring 2004): 157–59.

[76] The complete Duclos engraving, of which Fig. 3.2 shows just a detail, is provided among the Web Resources.

Fig. 3.2 Detail from Antoine Jean Duclos, *The Concert*, 1774. Etching and engraving after Augustin de Saint-Aubin.

Moden, and the moralistic, patriarchal tone with which the author chastises his dilettante-lady-pianist readership underscores his point: An unrehearsed performance of a fine composition at boisterous parties ultimately degrades the art of music. Like the (pseudo-)Cambini essayist, this author advises players to rehearse carefully in advance, and, moreover, he cautions against playing a musically demanding work in a large social gathering.[77] Yet, contrary to the author's appeals for a dawn of musical

---

[77] It is telling that the author critiques not only the incompetent performance but also the inappropriate setting for such a sophisticated, artfully wrought composition; this commentary reflects the emerging distinction between *Hausmusik* for dilettantes and an increasingly distinct body of "serious" chamber music that migrated to the concert hall in the early decades of the nineteenth century. Neal Zaslaw summarizes the article's critique as follows: "Mozart's late accompanied keyboard music is technically and conceptually difficult compared to the repertory most amateurs played; music of such difficulty could not be adequately performed in the salons, as long as playing at sight was the norm. Even if the music were properly prepared, any noise or lack of seriousness would make comprehension difficult; and in any case, this is music for connoisseurs, not the general public." Zaslaw and Cowdery, eds., *The Compleat Mozart,* 277.

connoisseurship, it is again apparent that casual music-making was the norm and that the *liebhaberisch* status quo would not easily be broken.

It would be a mistake, however, to conclude from such polemics that no amateur players were up to the task of sight-reading challenging chamber music. A 1796 listing of musicians active in Prague and Vienna praised the Viennese banker Joseph von Henickstein – a talented amateur bass singer who also played cello in quartets and symphonies – for possessing "the great musical advantage that he can read everything at sight."[78] A report from the Viennese *Allgemeine musikalische Zeitung* asserts that, in Venice, excellent amateur performance was alive and well as late as 1817, well after the apex of domestic musical activity in the previous century:

> The instrumentalists of Venice, including the dilettantes … are characterized favorably by the fire of their execution, their steadiness, and their quick apprehension. With just two rehearsals, they perform the most difficult operas to the admiration of composers, who give preference to the Venetian Orchestra over all others in Italy. The dilettantes and professors also distinguish themselves in the precise, nuanced execution of quartets by *Haydn, Mozart, Beethoven, Krommer, Romberg*, etc., which are often played at sight with estimable perfection.[79]

This was high praise, coming from an (anonymous) Viennese critic!

So far, the present survey of documented instances of chamber music sight-reading has focused on what was then the commonest performance setting – a drawing room or music room. But what about performances in more formal concerts for which music was the purpose of the gathering? Surely, one would think, these would have been thoroughly prepared in order to deliver polished performances that would impress aristocratic audiences.

Even ahead of relatively formal, high-stakes concerts, the evidence suggests little more than a cursory run-through, and sometimes not even that.[80] Mozart offers the following account of his 1789 performance for the

---

[78] Schönfeld, "A Yearbook of Music in Vienna and Prague, 1796," 301. Several entries in Schönfeld's yearbook comment on amateur musicians' abilities as sight-readers, mostly for (lady) keyboard players and occasionally for singers. In context, it is unclear whether his praise of Henickstein's sight-reading pertains mainly to singing or encompasses playing as well.

[79] "Über den jetzigen Musikzustand in Venedigs," *Allgemeine musikalische Zeitung* (Vienna) 1, no. 14 (April 3, 1817): col. 107 (Web Doc. #38). This passage is all the more striking because instrumental music occupied a marginalized position in *ottocento* Italy, especially by comparison with Vienna. However, the critic tempers his superlative terms with a footnote that upholds the supremacy of German instrumental music.

[80] Public symphonic or concerto performances were often "rehearsed" just once, in what may have been closer to a run-through than a *bona fide* rehearsal. Even a single preparatory session could not always be taken for granted. When Haydn sent scores of his symphonies nos. 95 and

Elector Friedrich August III of Saxony in Dresden, while traveling with his friend, patron, and Masonic brother Prince Karl Lichnowsky:

My princely travel companion invited the Naumanns [*recte*: Neumanns] and Madame [Josefa] Duschek [who was also visiting Dresden] to lunch. – While we were at table, I received a message that I was to play at court the following day, Tuesday the 14th, at 5:30 in the evening – this was quite out of the ordinary, for it is difficult to get an invitation to play; and, as you know, I wasn't counting on it at all. – We had gotten a quartet together at our hotel, l'hotel de Boulogne [*recte*: Hôtel de Pologne]; – the group included Antoine Tayber [*recte*: Anton Teyber, later the Viennese court composer], who, as you know, is organist here, and Herr [Anton] Kraft, a cellist, who is here with his son [Nikolaus, age nine, also a cellist]; he is in the service of Prince Esterhazy. I introduced the Trio I wrote for Herr Puchberg at this little musicale – and we played it quite decently; Duschek sang a number of arias from *Figaro* and *Don Juan* – The next day I played my New Concerto in D [Major, K. 537 "Coronation"] at court; the following day, Wednesday, the 15th, in the morning, I received a very pretty snuffbox.[81]

From this sketchy account, it is difficult to sort out the precise repertoire and personnel for the instrumental pieces played at the "rehearsal" session at the hotel on April 13 or the performance at court the following evening.[82] It is clear, though, that the performance at court was arranged on short notice, with Mozart enlisting whoever was available, assembling a combination of local Dresden musicians (the organist Teyber, who perhaps "moonlighted" on violin, and the flutist Johann Friedrich Prinz, a member

---

96 from London to Vienna to prepare for a performance, he included a letter with the following request: "I respectfully ask Herr von Keeß [*recte*: Franz Bernhard Ritter von Kees] to have a rehearsal, because they are very delicate, especially the last movement [of the Symphony no. 96] in D, for which I recommend the softest possible *piano* and a very quick tempo." Franz Joseph Haydn to Marianne von Genzinger, London, November 17, 1791, in *Joseph Haydn: Gesammelte Briefe und Aufzeichnungen*, ed. H. C. Robbins Landon and Dénes Bartha (Kassel: Bärenreiter, 1965), 265. James Webster discusses this letter in "Haydn's Aesthetics," in *The Cambridge Companion to Haydn*, 39.

Likewise, Leopold Mozart describes the premiere performance of the Piano Concerto in D Minor, K. 466, "which the copyist was still copying when we arrived, and your brother didn't have time to play through the *rondeau* because he had to supervise the copyist." L. Mozart to Maria Anna Mozart, Vienna, February 16, 1785, in Mozart, *Briefe*, 3:373. Most striking in Leopold's report is his matter-of-fact tone, indicating that such an extreme copyist's delay was not unheard of. Apparently even a single run-through before a public performance was sometimes a luxury to be dispensed with!

[81] W. A. Mozart to Constanze Mozart, Dresden, April 16, 1789, in Mozart, *Briefe*, 4:82–83.

[82] Again the question arises as to whether the so-called "Puchberg" Trio is the string trio (K. 563, as most scholars assume) or a piano trio (K. 542). See the discussion above, 17 n. 26. It is likewise unclear whether the "quartet" in question is one of the piano quartets or string quartets.

of the Dresden Court Orchestra),[83] as well as other musicians familiar to Mozart who happened to be in town (Duschek and the father-and-son cellists Kraft).

Since this motley assortment of players seems to have only first met the day before the concert, with scant time for rehearsal, it is remarkable how superbly well their performance was received. Several accounts write glowingly of Mozart's keyboard playing; for example, the *Musikalische Real-Zeitung* reports that "his agility on the clavier and on the fortepiano is inexpressible – and to this is added an extraordinary ability to read at sight, which truly borders on the incredible."[84] Just what might Mozart have been sight-reading during this concert? A sonata with the flutist Prinz, who seemingly was not involved with the "rehearsal" the previous day? Or perhaps something requested by the Elector or another guest at court as a test of Mozart's abilities?[85] That he was sight-reading at all might reflect the limited time available for rehearsal. It is possible that this performance might also have included improvisation, perhaps on a theme chosen by the Elector or another prominent nobleperson, since such improvisations were often a highlight of Mozart's *Akademien*.[86]

[83] Prinz is not mentioned in Mozart's letter, but he is named in an account from the *Journal des Dresdener Hofmarschallamtes* (April 14, 1789). Quoted in Deutsch, *Mozart: A Documentary Biography*, 339. Prinz is listed in a roster of the Dresden Court Orchestra from 1794, which is included in Laurie H. Ongley, "The Reconstruction of an 18th-Century Basso Group," *Early Music* 27, no. 2 (May 1999): 271.

[84] Quoted in Deutsch, *Mozart: A Documentary Biography*, 347. Another superlative report of Mozart's keyboard playing appears in the *Magazin der Sächsischen Geschichte aufs Jahr 1789*, quoted in translated version in Cliff Eisen, ed., *New Mozart Documents: A Supplement to O. E. Deutsch's Documentary Biography* (Stanford University Press, 1991), 56–57. À propos questions of repertoire for this performance, none of the contemporary sources mentions Mozart as playing viola, indicating either that he did not play that instrument in this concert or (equally plausibly) that his virtuosic keyboard playing was universally deemed to be more noteworthy.

[85] Mozart's youthful appearances at court commonly included such "tests," so it is certainly possible that this was part of the Dresden performance. In this case, Mozart's reputation preceded him, as his own *Wunderkind* pupil Johann Nepomuk Hummel, then just nine, had made an impressive appearance in Dresden the previous month. Consistent with the testing of Mozart's abilities is his engaging the next day in an organ competition with the Erfurt organist Johann Wilhelm Häßler, a "grandstudent" of J. S. Bach who was well acquainted with Lichnowsky. Mozart's account of this event is in the same letter of April 16, 1789, and the above-cited *Magazin der Sächsischen Geschichte* reports that he "surpassed all who have been heard previously, including *Himmel* [sic] and even *Häßler*, according to the latter's own admission." Quoted in translated version in Eisen, *New Mozart Documents*, 56.

[86] An extraordinary account of a 1787 performance in Prague, in which the audience reportedly went into raptures over Mozart's spontaneous improvisations on "Non più andrai" (as per an audience request), is transmitted in Nissen, *Biographie W. A. Mozarts*, 517. See also the discussion in Komlós, "'Ich praeludirte und spielte Variazionen': Mozart the Fortepianist," 34–35.

The following example is a special case – somewhere between improvising, sight-reading, and performing a fixed (notated) composition. Mozart describes a 1781 concert in Vienna that was organized in characteristic haste:

Today (for I am writing at eleven at night) we had a concert, where three of my pieces were performed – new ones, of course. The Rondo of a concerto [K. 373] for [Salzburg concertmaster Antonio] Brunetti, a sonata with violin accompaniment [K. 379] for myself, *which I composed last night between eleven and twelve o'clock, but in order to have it ready in time, I only wrote out the accompaniment for Brunetti, and retained my own part in my head* [emphasis added]. The third was a rondo for [the castrato Francesco] Ceccarelli [K. 374], which was encored.[87]

The so-called "one-hour sonata" is widely believed to be the Sonata for Piano and Violin in G Major/Minor, K. 379.[88] Mozart's claim to have "composed" the piece in such a short period warrants closer examination; one hour is an exceptionally short time in which to compose *and write out* a twenty-minute sonata from scratch, even if the writing was limited to the "accompaniment" (i.e., violin) part. What he likely meant is that he *notated* just the violin part during the one-hour window, probably having conceived at least part of the piece ahead of time, either by improvising at the keyboard or simply in his imagination. The sonata's first movement in particular betrays its origins in improvisation. The movement opens with an elaborate *adagio* in G major, whose forty-nine measures comprise an exposition (with repeat) followed by a full development section; but in lieu of a recapitulation, it abruptly begins an *allegro* in G minor, which is revealed to be the true body of the movement.[89]

---

[87] W. A. Mozart to L. Mozart, Vienna, April 8, 1781, in Mozart, *Briefe*, 3:103. The wording of Mozart's list is striking: a concert rondo for Brunetti, a sonata with violin accompaniment *for myself* (n.b., not "for Brunetti and me"), and a rondo for Ceccarelli. This view of a piano-and-violin duo sonata as essentially a piano work contrasts starkly with Baillot's description of a sonata as "a kind of concerto [for violin] divested of its accompaniments" that lets the violinist "be heard alone" and "left entirely to himself" (see above, 49 n. 63, and Web Doc. #1).

[88] Robert Riggs, "Mozart's Sonata for Piano and Violin, K. 379: Perspectives on the 'One-Hour' Sonata," *Mozart-Jahrbuch* (1991): 708–15. John Irving asserts that Mozart returned to this method – writing out the violin part only and playing the piano part from memory – for the Sonata in B♭ Major, K. 454, written for a public *Akademie* given by the Mantuan virtuosa Regina Strinasacchi, which was attended by Emperor Joseph II (see W. A. Mozart, letter to L. Mozart, Vienna, April 24, 1784). Irving's argument is based on the manuscript, in which the piano part is notated in different ink and "at times very cramped, as if 'fitted-in' to an already completed 'grid' of bar-lines encompassing the violin line." John Irving, "Sonatas," in *The Cambridge Mozart Encyclopedia*, ed. Cliff Eisen and Simon P. Keefe (Cambridge University Press, 2006), 474.

[89] On the slow introduction as a "before-the-beginning" framing function, see William E. Caplin, *Classical Form: A Theory of Formal Functions for the Instrumental Music of Haydn, Mozart, and Beethoven* (Oxford University Press, 1998), 15–16. Typically, the repeat would signal that this is not

By the performance, the violin part had necessarily been set down into a fixed, written form, but the piano part remained in a malleable, pre-notated state. Mozart writes that he "retained [his] own part in [his] head," but it is doubtful that he had literally composed it note for note, to be reproduced verbatim in a run-through with Brunetti and again (identically) in the performance – although he certainly would have been able to do this, given his legendary gifts of musical memory. More likely, the sonata's performance represented a particular mode of music-making, not quite improvisation but also not quite the performance of a completed score, since Mozart was surely creating new details afresh in the piano part in each play-through.[90] One clue that Mozart probably fleshed out the sonata with improvised embellishments is the brevity of the development section, a mere twelve bars consisting solely of a *Monte* pattern (ascending sequence) and a half cadence, at which juncture Mozart might well have added an *Eingang* (a brief, improvised passage). Although neither Brunetti nor Mozart was playing at first sight in this concert, this performance must have been unusually fresh and alive, with the ink of the violin part barely dry, and that of the piano part not yet spilled.

Some concluding reflections: playing "in the present tense"

> Notation is to improvisation as the portrait is to the living model.
> – Feruccio Busoni, *Sketch of a New Esthetic of Music*[91]

How unusual was Mozart's act of playing the premiere of K. 379 without having notated the keyboard part?[92] By modern standards, it seems

---

a slow introduction but the actual body of the movement; however, this conclusion is thwarted when a new exposition begins at the *allegro*. On the retrospective reinterpretation of a formal function, see Janet Schmalfeldt, *In the Process of Becoming: Analytic and Philosophical Perspectives on Form in Early Nineteenth-Century Music* (Oxford University Press, 2011).

[90] With respect to the piano part, what Mozart had mentally composed was likely tantamount to what Schenkerians call the *foreground* but not to the fine details of *surface realization*, which remained in a malleable state. Cf. William Benjamin's perceptive description of the Schenkerian foreground as a "performance" of the middleground levels. William Benjamin, "Schenker's Theory and the Future of Music," *Journal of Music Theory* 25, no. 1 (Spring 1981): 162. See also Heinrich Schenker's essay "Die Kunst der Improvisation," in *Das Meisterwerk in der Musik*, vol. 1 (Munich: Drei Masken Verlag, 1925), 9–40; trans. Richard Kramer as "The Art of Improvisation" in *The Masterwork in Music*, vol. 1, ed. William Drabkin (Cambridge University Press, 1994), 2–29.

[91] Feruccio Busoni, *Sketch of a New Esthetic of Music*, trans. Theodore Baker (New York: Schirmer, 1911), 15.

[92] This instance is by no means unique. Another notable account is the premiere of Beethoven's Piano Concerto No. 3 in 1803, at which point the solo part remained little more than a sketch. Beethoven's friend Ignaz von Seyfried reports: "[Beethoven] invited me to turn pages. But –

extraordinary. But for Mozart, this was simply a more exaggerated instance of his usual practice, since his performances always involved an element of improvisation and embellishment, even when playing from a fully notated score. The absence of a notated keyboard part at the premiere of K. 379 was merely a sign of an open-endedness and flexibility in music-making that was habitual.

Documented situations such as this raise a philosophical question fundamental to the relationship of the composer's and performer's roles: At what point in the creative process does music become a "work"?[93] This imponderable question is akin to asking, at what point between conception and birth does life begin?[94] To extend the comparison further: Just as the moment of birth is a milestone demarcating the end of one phase of development (gestation) and the beginning of another, the moment a piece is notated is simultaneously the end of a more fluid stage of its creation (composition) and the beginning of a new phase (execution or interpretation) in the hands of the performer, who molds and sculpts the piece anew in each performance by adding nuances and, style permitting,

heaven help me – that was easier said than done. I was looking at almost empty leaves; at the most, on one or another page, a few unintelligible Egyptian hieroglyphics were scribbled down to serve as aids to his memory." Quoted in translated version in Leon Plantinga, "When Did Beethoven Compose His Third Piano Concerto?," *Journal of Musicology* 7, no. 3 (Summer 1989): 296 n. 56. According to Beethoven's pupil Ferdinand Ries, Beethoven only notated the piano part properly a year later, when Ries was to give a performance, although Beethoven refused his request to write out a cadenza (ibid., 291).

[93] The classic, English-language discussion of "workhood" is Goehr's *The Imaginary Museum of Musical Works*. Goehr's study argues that the modern "fixed-work concept" evolved after around 1800; before then, she concludes, composers created music but not musical "works." Beethoven is often regarded as the transformational figure regarding the fixed-work concept in German instrumental music. It should be noted that the practice of extemporaneous embellishment endured well into the nineteenth century in other countries, evincing a more fluid concept of "workhood." This is most clearly evident in the world of Italian opera but also to some extent in music by instrumental composer-performers such as Paganini and Chopin.

The divide between music and notated musical works is parallel to a gap Adam Gopnik describes between a master chef's dish and the written recipe thereof: "The recipe is a blueprint but also a red herring, a way to do something and a false summing up of a living process that can be handed on only by demonstration, a knack posing as a knowledge." Gopnik, *The Table Comes First: Family, France, and the Meaning of Food* (New York: Alfred A. Knopf, 2011), 56. Much of Gopnik's commentary about chefs and the home cooks who use their recipes can be applied, *mutatis mutandis*, to composers and the performers who play from their scores.

[94] Similar questions about the fixedness of musical works arise in Richard Kramer's probing exegesis of a well-known aphorism by Walter Benjamin: "The work is the death mask of conception." Richard Kramer, *Unfinished Music* (Oxford University Press, 2008), vii–ix and 367–79. Walter Benjamin, "The Writer's Technique in Thirteen Theses," in *Selected Writings*, ed. Marcus Bullock and Michael W. Jennings, vol. 1, *1913–1926* (Cambridge, MA: Harvard University Press, 1996), 459.

improvised embellishments. Whereas the performer's role is nowadays considered to be separate and different in kind from the composer's, a pre-1800 perspective would construe the performer as essentially *completing* a process already begun by the composer. Put differently, what is now called composition comprises the Ciceronian rhetorical canons of *inventio*, *dispositio*, and *elocutio*, and performance may comprise additional *elocutio* (in the form of added embellishments), *memoria*, and *pronunciatio*; but according to the rhetorical model, these overlapping activities are phases of one, unbroken creative process. Only in the nineteenth century, with the decline of improvisation and the rise of the fixed-work concept in German instrumental music, did the roles of composer and performer become more strongly divided.[95]

The problem of defining when the compositional process is "finished" is borne out in a number of examples from Mozart's *oeuvre*, such as the "Coronation" concerto, K. 537, whose holograph contains large swaths of blank measures in the solo keyboard's left hand.[96] Mozart was able to leave the left hand in such a fragmentary state since he wrote the concerto for his own use and "fleshed out" the missing material in concert, almost certainly with some variation in successive performances. Since Mozart did not finish *notating* the left hand, can he be said to have finished *composing* it? Is this a meaningful distinction? When the composer is also the performer, it is difficult to define precisely where one process ends and another begins.

Mozart often took an otherwise complete composition, originally written for himself, and wrote out embellishments for his students to play – that is, "composing" the very kind of ornaments that he himself would have created extemporaneously in performance.[97] What is the status of such "extra-notational" embellishment added to an already "finished" composition? Does it depend on whether the embellishments are improvised in concert or written out in advance (to be performed with

---

[95] For an imaginative illumination of the integrated, eighteenth-century view of improvisation, composition, and performance, see Tom Beghin, "A Composer, His Dedicatee, Her Instrument, and I: Thoughts on Performing Haydn's Keyboard Sonatas," in *The Cambridge Companion to Haydn*, 203–25. See also Tom Beghin, "'Delivery, Delivery, Delivery!': Crowning the Rhetorical Process of Haydn's Keyboard Sonatas," in *Haydn and the Performance of Rhetoric*, 131–71.

[96] See Alan Tyson's preface to the facsimile edition, included in the Pierpont Morgan Library Music Manuscript Reprint Series (New York: Dover, 1991), vii–xi.

[97] See Robert D. Levin, "Performance Practice in the Music of Mozart," in *The Cambridge Companion to Mozart*, 227–45, esp. 232–38.

sprezzatura, as if improvised)?[98] Likewise, when a musician adds ornaments to a thematic reprise, is that musician acting as a composer, performer, or both simultaneously? These questions illustrate the futility of defining the exact moment that the composer's work ends and the performer's work begins. An essential moment of overlap occurs as the baton is passed from one to the other, allowing the music to retain an open-ended state, lending live performance an open-ended spirit even though all of the notes have been determined in advance.[99]

This chapter has examined many historical accounts in which improvisation, sight-reading, and the performance of (more or less) rehearsed compositions commingled at the same event. In contrast, a modern listener of Western art music would have to go to rather disparate places to experience these various modes of music-making. By way of conclusion, consider one final anecdote attributed to the Viennese novelist and salon hostess Caroline Pichler that illustrates the blurred outlines between these categories:

[98] The term "sprezzatura" was first applied to music by Giulio Caccini in the preface to *Le nuove musiche* (1602), which advocates "a certain noble negligence [*sprezzatura*] in song." Giulio Caccini, *Le nuove musiche*, trans. H. Wiley Hitchcock (Middleton: A-R Editions, 1970), 44 n. 10. The term denotes studied carelessness, spontaneity, or nonchalance in declamation (referring both to musical timing and *seconda prattica* dissonance treatment). It traces back to Baldassare Castiglione's *Il libro del cortegiano* (Venice, 1528), in which it is defined as "that virtue opposite to affectation ... whence springs grace" (quoted in ibid.). On the more recent invocation of this term in political rhetoric, see William Safire, "On Language: Sprezzatura," *New York Times Magazine,* October 27, 2002, www.nytimes.com/2002/10/27/magazine/ 27ONLANGUAGE.html (accessed May 1, 2015).

James Webster discusses "compositional improvisation" as a musical topic, designating a passage that is fully notated but represents a kind of improvisation frozen in time. James Webster, "The Rhetoric of Improvisation in Haydn's Keyboard Music," in *Haydn and the Performance of Rhetoric*, 172–212. Komlós uses the term "*alias* improvisations" to denote a similar concept. Komlós, "'Ich praeludirte und spielte Variazionen': Mozart the Fortepianist," 34.

[99] The tension between fixedness and spontaneity in musical performance has parallels to artful conversation. Unlike modern social discourse, traditional artful conversation was a comparatively more scripted, self-conscious affair. Like musical performance, conversation was regarded as a skill that could be cultivated through study and practice, as evinced by the proliferation of treatises devoted to the art of conversation throughout the early-modern period. Peter Burke writes: "Keeping a commonplace book of material to introduce into conversations was also recommended by some, though others mocked people who collect anecdotes arranged 'in alphabetical order' and lie in wait for opportunities to insert them into a conversation." Burke, *The Art of Conversation*, 120. Yet the delivery in conversation ought to be (or, at least, to seem) spontaneous; see De Staël's remarks quoted above, 24, and in Web Doc. #31. A conversationalist who practices a joke or witty retort – in advance of the conversation in which she hopes to use them – is not unlike a keyboard player who experiments with various ways to ornament a melody in preparation for a performance in which such embellishments will be "improvised."

One day when I was sitting at the pianoforte playing "Non più andrai" from *Figaro*, Mozart, who was paying a visit to us, came up behind me; I must have been playing it to his satisfaction, for he hummed the melody as I played and beat time on my shoulders; but then he suddenly moved a chair up, sat down, told me to carry on playing the bass, and began to improvise such wonderfully beautiful variations that everyone listened to the tones of the German Orpheus with bated breath.[100]

In a musical world where a play-through of a notated piece can so easily flow into a duo improvisation, and where that improvisation could in turn have evolved into a composition – if only Mozart had written it down! – the division between performer and composer is eroded or even dissolved. What remains is a salon filled with Frau Pichler's guests, enjoying music being created just for them by Mozart and their hostess, in the present moment.

---

[100] Anton Langer, "Ein Abend bei Karoline Pichler," *Allgemeine Theaterzeitung (Vienna)* 168, (July 15, 1843): 750 (Web Doc. #16). English translation from Deutsch, *Mozart: A Documentary Biography*, 556–57. The account proceeds to describe how, in another improvisatory turn, Mozart suddenly tired of their duet and summarily began leaping over the furniture, turning somersaults, and meowing like a cat – an open-ended, convivial atmosphere for music-making indeed! However, this story should be treated with caution as it is merely attributed to Pichler by Langer, a poet and author of this tribute to Pichler published about a week after her death. Issues of authorship aside, the document in any case reports on events purported to have occurred a half-century prior and therefore reflects a mid-nineteenth-century viewpoint.

PART II

Analytical perspectives

4 | Analyzing from within the music: toward a theory of multiple agency

Certain musical passages, such as the excerpt quoted in Ex. 4.1, seem so vividly to enact a delightful exchange among familiars that it is difficult *not* to experience them in those terms. Indeed, the coquettish interplay between piano and violin seems to give this passage its *raison d'être*. Yet as palpable as this exchange may seem, traditional analytical methods focused on harmony and voice-leading are ill-equipped to capture it. Although the piano and violin are distinct *parts*, a voice-leading reduction or Schenkerian graph would depict them as constituting the same abstract *voice*.[1] Such an analysis would by no means be "wrong," but it would privilege the voice-leading structure while overlooking the musical dialogue among the parts.

What is needed, it would seem, is to develop extensions to existing musical theories inspired by the culture of the late-eighteenth-century drawing room and by the rudimentary theory of agency adumbrated in the historical texts by Johann Georg Sulzer, Giuseppe Carpani, et al. Part II of this book aims to do just that, integrating the historical perspectives examined above with sophisticated tools of music analysis, marrying style criticism and close reading. My central project is to construct a framework for analyzing chamber music as play, expressing in prose the kind of dynamic social intercourse that musicians experience while playing this repertoire.

The historical study in Part I emphasized two main themes: first, the tradition of understanding chamber music as a stylized conversation or social engagement, often with each instrument construed as a distinct character (Ch. 2); and second, the currency in Mozart's time of domestic musical practices that not only included improvisation but that also lent a quality of spontaneity to the playing of published compositions (Ch. 3).

---

[1] My distinction between *parts* and *voices* is analogous to one William Rothstein posits between *notes* and *tones*. In his usage, the former inhere concretely in a real or imagined performance; the latter exist only as mental abstractions, as in a Schenkerian middleground. William Rothstein, "On Implied Tones," *Music Analysis* 10, no. 3 (October 1991): 289–328. One study that attempts to integrate Schenkerian approaches with metaphors of musical dialogue is David Gagné, "A Dialogue among Equals: Structural Style in Mozart's 'Haydn' String Quartets," *Studi Musicali* 37 (2008): 503–27.

Ex. 4.1 Mozart, Piano Quartet in E♭ Major, K. 493, Allegretto (iii)

"Conversation" between violin and piano

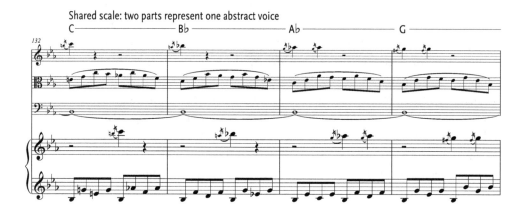

Shared scale: two parts represent one abstract voice

These two threads are, of course, deeply intertwined. Unlike modern concert performances, prepared carefully in advance and delivered by an ensemble to a formal audience of strangers, more impromptu readings by *ad hoc* groups of players at once instantiated and resembled social interaction.[2]

To develop analytical methods informed by these perspectives, I will begin by disentangling relationships among the musical characters imagined to be engaging in social interaction from the players who enact these roles and from the composed parts that constitute the "script." The present chapter addresses the following broad, conceptual questions:

(1) How could the historically inspired perspective of multiple, independent characters interact with other, more rigorous methods of musical analysis? What do metaphors of social intercourse add to existing analytical methodologies?
(2) What kind of musical roles or characters can the individual instrumental parts represent? What is the ontological status of such roles or characters?
(3) In what sense can musicians reading from fully notated parts be imagined to be quasi-improvising or exerting agency on musical events as they ensue?
(4) What are the limits to the metaphor of sociability in chamber music? In what ways is chamber music *not* like a conversation?

Examining these questions will give rise to a theory of *multiple agency*, a concept that recasts the conversation metaphor and overcomes some of its limitations. In the second half of this chapter, I will demonstrate my multiple-agency methodology with some brief analyses, each of which takes a short excerpt of music and focuses narrowly on a specific theoretical issue. The analyses in subsequent chapters will be more extensive.

Limitations of the metaphor of conversation

The notion that string quartets enact a kind of conversation has become a sort of received wisdom over the last two centuries. And like any

---

[2] Composer Noam Sivan describes improvisation as "a basic quality of human life" and notes an improvisatory element in many everyday activities, such as cooking or sightseeing. Noam Sivan, "Improvisation in Western Art Music: Its Relevance Today" (D.M.A. diss., The Juilliard School, 2010), 3–4. On conversation as improvisation, see De Staël's remarks quoted above, 24, and in Web Doc. #31.

metaphorical idea, it has proven its worth by illuminating important qualities in the object of primary interest, in spite of the obvious differences that exist between one domain and the other (such as that conversation uses words, where chamber music uses notes). Yet the quartet-as-conversation metaphor need not be taken on faith and accepted without careful scrutiny. An examination of what the metaphor overlooks can help us refine our terms for the sociable aspects of music and aid development of more sophisticated theories of musical interaction. I begin by discussing two uncommonly perceptive critiques of the "conversation" tradition in quartet criticism, from Gretchen Wheelock and W. Dean Sutcliffe.[3] The following remarks focus on quartets – the genre most commonly described as conversational – but the argument applies broadly to other chamber music genres.

Wheelock enumerates three significant reservations about the conversation metaphor as it pertains to Haydn's quartets: (1) its application has tended to be highly selective, favoring sonata-style first movements and tending to exclude other movement types such as arias, fantasias, minuets, and finales; (2) the comparison to specifically *refined, artful* conversation is too narrow and belies the diverse range of venues, players, and audiences for Haydn's quartets as well as the role of the "middle" and "low" styles in his music;[4] and (3) the paradigm of conversation *within* a quartet tends to neglect the audience.[5] Wheelock's first point rightly indicates that certain moments in string quartets may seem conversational in the same way that other moments may evoke oratory, opera, virtuoso spectacle, or courtly dance; no single concept should be regarded as the genre's exclusive stylistic referent. Regarding her second point, it should be noted that artful conversation is not a single, exclusively elevated style. On the contrary, many manuals of conversation invoke a principle called *accommodation*, which prevails upon speakers to adapt the register and topics of conversation to suit the company and reflect whether their listeners are "old or

---

[3] Wheelock, "The Rhetorical Pause"; and W. Dean Sutcliffe, "Haydn, Mozart and Their Contemporaries," in *The Cambridge Companion to the String Quartet*, 185–209.

[4] Hans-Joachim Bracht raises the same issue: "Which type of verbal interaction is the basis for the term quartet 'conversation'? Can we still understand the conversation-*topos* in terms of the art of conversation, or should we apply a completely different model of conversation in its place?" (Welcher Typus sprachlicher Interaktion liegt dem Begriff des Quartett-"Gesprächs" zugrunde? Läßt sich der Gesprächstopos nach wie vor von der Kunst der Konversation her verstehen, oder ist an deren Stelle eine ganz anderes Gesprächsmodell zu setzen?). Hans-Joachim Bracht, "Überlegungen zum Quartett-'Gespräch,'" *Archiv für Musikwissenschaft* 51, no. 3 (1994): 169–70.

[5] Wheelock, "The 'Rhetorical Pause,'" 68–72.

young, nobles or commoners, learned or ignorant, clergy or laity, men or women."[6] Nevertheless, since accommodation was not so great as to permit base or vulgar language, Wheelock's basic point that Haydn's music incorporates "low" elements to a greater degree than did artful conversation is well taken.

Wheelock's most serious objections pertain to her third point, about the exclusion of listeners:

My chief reservation about our use of the conversation metaphor is that it focuses attention almost exclusively on the discourse of the players and seldom takes other listeners into account. Perhaps as a consequence, musical analysis tends to elide the role of physical gesture in performance . . .

Performative gestures and address to the listener are . . . subjects of interest to students of rhetoric. On the face of it, rhetoric would seem to have little in common with conversation. In its public mode of address, rhetoric is in general construed as the work of a single orator, whose impassioned speech is calculated to move an audience . . . [T]he "wordless oration" [in Haydn's quartets] is impoverished without the gestural language of the body, and that attention to music in performance can bring conversation and rhetoric closer together in addressing the interplay between players and listeners. Of particular interest here are the ways in which rhetorical gestures affect the conversation among the quartet players themselves and with those supposedly contingent listeners, the audience . . .

[I]f there is a potential conflict between conversation and music, it is that the audience must abandon their own conversations and attend to that of the players . . . It is perhaps ironic that . . . demands for silence call attention to the boundaries between players and audience, reminding listeners that they are "outsiders" to the primary conversation of the players. Perhaps it is this distance that the metaphor of conversation tries to erase, at the same time that it extends to the audience the responsibility of listening carefully.[7]

Wheelock's concern with the status of the audience leads to a seeming contradiction in her argument. Dissatisfied with the paradigm of an *intra*-quartet conversation, which relegates the audience to outsider status, she turns to the performative gestures of classical rhetoric to extend the discourse beyond the quartet's enclosed circle. Yet, as Wheelock notes, rhetoric is a decidedly one-way mode of address that would seem to preclude an active role for the audience. Moreover, since rhetorical delivery

---

[6] Burke, *The Art of Conversation*, 101–2. The earliest known usage of the term "accomodazione" is in Stefano Guazzo, *La civil conversazione* (Brecia, 1574), and the concept is echoed in many subsequent treatises. See summary in Burke, *The Art of Conversation*, 101–2, 110–11, and 114.

[7] Wheelock, "The 'Rhetorical Pause,'" 71–73.

is performed by a single orator, this concept effaces the quartet's four separate personas, the root of the very conversational aspect that Wheelock seeks to refine.[8] While Wheelock laudably draws attention to the physical and embodied aspects of quartet playing,[9] her claim that these gestures – like the proverbial tree falling in the woods – require an outside observer in order to have meaning is, at best, overstated.[10] The statement that "the audience must abandon their own conversations to attend to that of the players" seems to be rooted in modern conceptions of concert audience-hood and listening, in concert halls among strangers. Depictions of historical concerts in social settings (as in Figs. 1.5 and 3.2), on the other hand, exemplify a kind of parallel play between concurrent musical and non-musical discourse. As Hunter nicely puts it, chamber music serves both to "stimulate . . . [and] simulate" convivial social relations.[11]

Sutcliffe eloquently challenges a number of assumptions about the quartet-as-conversation model, chiefly the widespread tendency to equate speech with melodic utterance only.[12] This overly melodic conception of

---

[8] On the distinction between rhetoric and conversation as forms of discourse, see above, 21–26. A performance of a string quartet may include aspects of both, but they are nevertheless conceptually distinct.

[9] Cone likewise discusses "kinetic-sonic correspondences that underlie instrumental gestures" in *The Composer's Voice*, 136ff. See also Robert S. Hatten's sophisticated theory of gesture in *Interpreting Musical Gestures, Topics, and Tropes: Mozart, Beethoven, Schubert* (Bloomington: Indiana University Press, 2004), 97–234.

[10] Wheelock makes a related (in my view, overstated) point in an earlier study of Haydn's quartets. Discussing the false ending of Haydn's "Joke" quartet, which ends *in medias res*, she imagines "the first reading of the finale . . . [in which] four string players in private chambers might have been confounded before they were amused by the extended rests in their individual parts . . . *Still, it is in the playing of the work before others that the joke finds its point* [emphasis added]." Wheelock, *Haydn's Ingenious Jesting*, 13. In describing the players' sight-reading as merely a warm-up to the "real" performance for an audience, Wheelock seems to overcorrect what she regards as a traditional bias favoring intra-quartet exchange.

[11] Hunter, "The Most Interesting Genre of Music," 56. Describing the string quartet as a "genre fundamentally about participatory performance" (ibid.), Hunter's remarks focus on the bonds forged among quartet players themselves. But her basic point can be extended to listeners and to other genres of chamber music. The impression in Figs. 1.5 and 3.2 that the music helps to stimulate social interaction among the company resembles what Arnie Cox calls a "mimetic" engagement in music listening. For Cox, the implicit questions "what's it like to do that" and "what's it like to be that?" are fundamental to the experience of listening. Arnie Cox, "Embodying Music: Principles of the Mimetic Hypothesis," *Music Theory Online* 17, no. 2 (July 2011), www.mtosmt.org/issues/mto.11.17.2/mto.11.17.2.cox.html.

[12] Like many historical authors surveyed in Chapter 2, Charles Rosen regards musical dialogue as an aspect of melody and positions it in opposition to harmony. Writing eloquently of the opening of Haydn's String Quartet in E Major, op. 54, no. 3, he observes: "This passage is like a model for a dramatic and yet conversational dialogue in a comedy, in which the content of the words has become irrelevant to the wit of the form (although I should not wish to imply that

musical dialogue has led to distorted accounts of interaction among the parts in Haydn's and Mozart's quartets.

Conversation is often associated with one of the articles of faith about the string quartet, that there should be four equal parts. This is almost always defined in terms of distribution of melodic lines. Yet any literal equality of melodic material is barely possible in later eighteenth-century instrumental style, premised as it is on accessible and "natural" homophonic textures. The most common disposition will feature the melodic line at the top ... The melodic lead will of course alternate, but this rarely approaches statistical equality; and where it does, the results risk sounding contrived and mechanical, just the opposite of the imagined democratic ideal. A more fundamental principle is to establish separate identities for the four players, to lend them a sense of autonomy or individuality or agency, and this can be more consistently and subtly served by the "intrinsic" compositional thinking outlined above.

A melody-centered view also accounts for some of the difficulties of the conversational metaphor ... Given the logical difficulty that such conversations would literally imply the near-continual talking of all the protagonists, the tendency has been to equate speech with melody, or more broadly thematic material, and listening with accompaniment. Yet this understanding breaks down for the same reason as does the notion of melodically based equality – that it does not allow for the flexible boundaries between different constituents of a quartet texture.[13]

Indeed, if conversation is defined exclusively in terms of melodic statements, and if it furthermore requires a near-equal exchange, then it is doomed to vastly exaggerate its claims and, worse, to overlook the contributions of non-melodic elements within the texture.[14] To that end, Sutcliffe charts a course between two extremes found among historical authors, namely, between the Scylla of near-exclusive attention to melody (as in writings by Carpani, Anton Reicha, and Pierre Baillot) and the Charybdis of an overstated equality among the parts (as in those by Heinrich Christoph Koch). Sutcliffe's reference to the

---

the harmonic significance of this opening does not contribute to its vitality)." Rosen, *The Classical Style*, 142.

[13] Sutcliffe, "Haydn, Mozart and Their Contemporaries," 186–87. Elsewhere, Sutcliffe has made much the same point with respect to Mozart's chamber music with keyboard: "Aided by passages where each line conveys a strong sense of agency ... an apparently subordinate part can suddenly take the lead ... Although not melodically 'active' – the normal terms for assessing a place in a textural hierarchy – such elements can form the most eloquent part of the discourse." W. Dean Sutcliffe, "The Keyboard Music," in *The Cambridge Companion to Mozart*, 64.

[14] For example, Carpani's narrow attention to melodic utterance only leads to his caricatured account of the roles of the second violin, viola, and cello in Haydn's quartets (see above, 41–42). The ideal of an egalitarian exchange, measured in terms of equitable distribution of melodic activity, was more nearly achieved within the Parisian *quatuor concertant* repertoire and in Boccherini's quartets and quintets than in those by Haydn and Mozart.

apparent "near-continual talking of all protagonists" raises some essential questions: If a quartet is regarded as a form of musical conversation, must every instrumental utterance be equated to speech? Could other aspects of social intercourse be encoded musically, such as body language and physical gestures (mentioned by both J. J. de Momigny and by Wheelock)? Could the quartet-as-conversation paradigm be formulated in a more sophisticated – and less literal – way, to overcome some of the logical problems that Sutcliffe enumerates?[15]

Beyond "conversation": toward a theory of multiple agency

What do we talk about when we talk about chamber music as being conversational? To examine this question, let us pose an analysis of a passage from the finale of Mozart's String Quartet in G Major, K. 387 (shown in Ex. 4.2) and then analyze the analysis.

The movement opens in stile antico, with each instrument entering in turn with *overlapping statements of a five-measure fugal subject. Suddenly (m. 17) the first violin changes the topic, breaking out into a flurry of virtuoso fiddling, to which the remaining parts provide a simple, chordal accompaniment. Not wanting to be outdone, the second violin immediately jumps in (m. 23), repeating his colleague's statement exactly in a moment of "anything you can do, I can do better." Soon the viola chimes in (m. 29), though somewhat less virtuosically, echoing just the passage's tail. But the cello, who is the quartet's resident expert in the harmonic/ cadential plan of sonata form, seems to be fed up with this time-consuming rivalry, which has delayed the necessary modulation to the subordinate key by keeping the movement locked in a tonic-key holding pattern. And so he barges in (m. 31), subito forte, turning the fiddling figure into the model for a sequence that leads the way toward the new key, achieving a half cadence (m. 39) and standing-on-the- dominant that prepares for his statement of the subordinate theme in m. 51.[16]*

---

[15] Sutcliffe's concern about "near-continual talking" of multiple speakers mirrors the opinion of Rousseau, who held that fugues are unintelligible because they depict many voices speaking at once. But Johann Nikolaus Forkel turned Rousseau's idea on its head, arguing that fugues are both natural and powerful precisely because they represent the emotions of many people, unlike arias, which artificially represent just one person. See discussion in Sisman, *Mozart: The "Jupiter" Symphony,* 70.

[16] Throughout this chapter, analyses given in italics and block quotations are by me. I use this formatting to separate these analyses from my critiques of them in the main text. On m. 39 as a half cadence (as opposed to m. 51), see Caplin's distinction between "stop" and "end." William E. Caplin, "The Classical Cadence: Conceptions and Misconceptions," *Journal of the American Musicological Society* 57, no. 1 (Spring 2004): 97–103 and *passim.* In the parlance of Warren Darcy and James Hepokoski's Sonata Theory, m. 39 commences "dominant lock," which

Ex. 4.2 Mozart, String Quartet in G Major, K. 387, Molto allegro (iv)

Subject entries by each instrument in turn *(stile antico)*

Violin I changes topic (virtuoso fiddling)

Violin II repeats fiddling music exactly

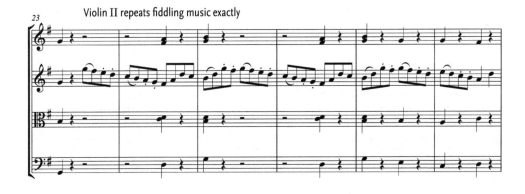

Ex. 4.2 (cont.)

This discussion engages certain familiar analytical categories, such as harmony, form, and musical topics, but it describes musical events as the actions or statements of four separate personas, represented in this case by the individual instrumental parts. The analytical text explicitly treats these parts in anthropomorphic terms, using the pronouns "who" and "he" and describing the parts as posessing both consciousness and volition.

The above analysis is unusually concerned with which instrument utters a particular musical statement and how the others respond. For instance, it is significant that the virtuoso music introduced by the first violin (m. 17) is repeated verbatim by the second violin (m. 23), rather than stated twice by the same part. Some listeners might not even notice the exchange of parts unless they are listening (or, in a concert, watching) carefully. But the antiphonal exchange is felt acutely by the *players* themselves, who might bring a quality of one-upmanship to their inter-pretation or, more directly, to the execution of their parts (recalling Koch's notion of *Wettstreit*).[17] Perhaps the two violinists may have squabbled over who should play which part, motivating the second violinist to prove that he is fully equipped to manage first-violin-caliber passagework. Unlike the later imitations of this material by the viola and cello, the second violin repeats the first-violin material exactly, without adding, subtracting, or changing anything. This is consistent with Car-pani's caricature of the second-violin character as taking his lead from the first, capable of imitation but not invention.

Although the analysis describes the cello as the agent triggering certain key events in m. 31 (i.e., the *subito forte* and the sequence that modulates to the dominant), this claim should be examined more closely. The cello is clearly the most prominent part at that moment, not only because of his rhythmic activity but also because he takes over and reformulates motivic materials that had "belonged" to the upper parts at precisely this juncture. Just as the fugal subject had been passed among all four instruments, the fiddling music is also stated successively, and the cello's "turn" comes at m. 31. However, it is actually the first violin who initiates the *subito forte* on the downbeat, before the cello enters. The first violin's entrance effects textural and topical events as well, resuming *stile antico* elements (note the

---

obtains until the "medial caesura" in m. 51. James Hepokoski and Warren Darcy, *Elements of Sonata Theory: Norms, Types, and Deformations in the Late-Eighteenth Century Sonata* (Oxford University Press, 2006).

[17] The rivalry between the two violins once again recalls that between the two sopranos Madame Herz and Mademoiselle Silberklang from Mozart's *Der Schauspieldirektor*.

rising chain of leapfrogging suspensions in the violins, reminiscent of Pergolesi's *Stabat mater*), leaving the cello and viola as a pair with their continued development of the fiddling material.[18] This passage thus illustrates an issue one encounters often: A first impulse to ascribe control solely to the melodic instrument's persona is revealed to be oversimplified, since the dynamic, topical, textural, and metrical events occur through the actions of multiple instruments.

Our discussion has shifted away from musical conversation *per se*, yet it retains certain elements that many authors have discussed under that banner. Fundamentally, when chamber music is described as conversational (or, alternatively, operatic),[19] I believe most authors refer to a way of experiencing a musical passage or composition as embodying *multiple, independent characters – often represented by the individual instruments – who engage in a seemingly spontaneous interaction involving the exchange of roles and/or musical ideas*. This simple formulation scales back some of the more specific claims that have been made about the affinity between late-eighteenth-century chamber music and contemporaneous styles of conversation. I leave it to other scholars with more specialized expertise to assess whether quartets by composer X might be fruitfully compared to artful conversation as described in author Y's etiquette manual or as illustrated in playwright Z's dialogue.[20] The present formulation, general as it may be, will suffice for the analytical method I wish to develop.

We have arrived at a definition for which we have not yet coined a term. The formulation above avoids the word "conversation" advisedly, since this traditional comparison can obscure as much as it elucidates and is furthermore burdened by over two centuries of history. Important similarities between our concept and conversation include the notion of multiple personas engaged in discourse that are understood to act autonomously

---

[18] Another example of a topically bifurcated texture occurs in the theme and variations from Mozart's String Quartet in A Major, K. 464. In the sixth variation, the cello plays a drumbeat figure against sustained, hymn-like music in the upper parts.

[19] References to Mozart's chamber music as "operatic" usually refer not to specifically operatic elements (e.g., recitatives) but more generally to elements suggestive of the vibrant, often witty interplay of his celebrated ensemble numbers. Two exemplary articles that analyze Mozart duets in terms of the interaction between two characters are Charles Burkhart, "How Rhythm Tells the Story in 'Là ci darem la mano,'" *Theory and Practice* 16 (1991): 21–38; and David Lewin, "Figaro's Mistakes," in *Studies in Music with Text* (Oxford University Press, 2006), 5–18. Comparisons between late-eighteenth-century instrumental music and *opera buffa* also feature prominently throughout Rosen's *The Classical Style*.

[20] Burke points out that treatises merely transmit the precepts of conversation as it was taught. Other sources, such as dialogue in novels and plays, may come closer to actual practices. Burke, *The Art of Conversation*, 93 and 120.

and to possess the consciousness and volition necessary to determine their own statements and actions. I therefore propose the term *multiple agency* to designate this concept. This term captures the notion that a chamber music score is, above all, something to be *played*, an encoded musical exchange in which each player assumes an individual character, similar in many respects to a theatrical script.[21] To hear a string quartet as multiple agency is not to conceive some derivative imitation of conversation in which words have been replaced by notes. Rather, the resemblance between chamber music and artful conversation arises because they are both diverting forms of social intercourse among cultured individuals. As members of this common, superordinate category, they share a sibling rather than descendant relationship.[22]

Several of Sutcliffe's objections to equating string quartets with conversation are resolved by substituting multiple agency for conversation. The quartet-as-conversation paradigm reveals its limitations as the comparisons become increasingly literal. As a case in point, Sutcliffe mentions the illogicality of all instruments "speaking" nearly continuously, which underscores an undisputable fact: unlike melodies in quartets, speakers in a conversation do not require "accompaniment." Yet, as a stylized, specifically musical form of social intercourse, why should one expect a string quartet to adhere strictly to the same norms as literal, verbal discourse?[23] In polite conversation, listeners might show their engagement with a speaker by remaining quietly attentive, maintaining eye contact or perhaps nodding, and offering clever comments or questions at appropriate junctures. But in musical discourse, the act of providing a supportive accompaniment for

---

[21] To extend the comparison: If a chamber music score is like a full script, individual instrumental parts resemble cue scripts, which contain only a single character's lines (plus a few cue words from the previous speech). A recent movement has revived the original practice of performing Shakespeare plays from cue scripts, with little or no rehearsal (thus "sight-reading"), which is often described as "first folio technique" or "unrehearsed Shakespeare." See Don Weingust, *Acting from Shakespeare's First Folio: Theory, Text and Performance* (New York: Routledge, 2006) and Patrick Tucker, *Secrets of Acting Shakespeare: The Original Approach* (New York: Routledge, 2002).

[22] I am adopting the terms "sibling" and "descendant" from Byron Almén's account of the relationship between music and narrative. Almén, *A Theory of Musical Narrative* (Bloomington: Indiana University Press, 2009), 12–13.

[23] Along similar lines, audiences willingly accept highly stylized conversations among operatic characters without questioning why their discourse is in verse or why it distinguishes between recitative and set numbers, to say nothing of why they are singing at all. Since overtly diegetic singing (as in Cherubino's arietta "Voi che sapete") is the exception rather than the norm, it must be concluded that operatic characters inhabit a world in which normal discourse is both poetic and sung – clearly a different world from our own.

another instrument's melody could be construed as a sign of engagement with the primary melodic part. That is, *not* remaining quiet may be the way to show supportive attention in a musical exchange, precisely the opposite of conversational etiquette. It would seem that musical and conversational arts operate according to their own respective conventions, as related but decidedly distinct forms of social intercourse. Framing our discussion in terms of multiple agency, rather than conversation, will help avoid distorting our analyses with unduly literal comparisons.

Another departure from the conversation model pertains to the relationships among the melodic and accompanimental instruments, which have often been compared to the roles of speakers and listeners respectively.[24] In chamber music, the so-called accompanimental parts can actually exert considerable influence over the course of events within a phrase putatively "spoken" by the melodic instrument, which relies on the others' harmonic and cadential support to achieve certain musical goals. The reason for this is that the essentially single-line nature of most instruments used in this repertoire means that the expression of a harmony, achievement of a cadence, establishment of a meter or texture, etc., usually involves the participation of multiple parts,[25] who generally act in cooperation. But this interdependence also means that accompanimental parts can surprise the melodic instrument and even thwart its expectations by contributing unanticipated accidentals, harmonizations, or cadential elisions that nudge the phrase off the expected course (as in Ex. 4.6, discussed below); the excerpts selected for analysis in this book tend to feature such moments, which I take as evidence of the parts' autonomy. Such examples illustrate the high degree of influence wielded by non-melodic instruments to affect the trajectory of a passage,

[24] This issue raises the question of precisely what is meant by the roles "melody" and "accompaniment." As discussed in Chapter 2, some historical authors (e.g., Koch) understand the texture to comprise melodic and accompanimental *roles* that can be freely exchanged among all *instruments*, but most (e.g. Carpani, Momigny, and Baillot) regard each instrument as having inherent predisposition toward melodic or accompanimental roles. A further complication arises from the historical terms used for chamber music with keyboard, in which the term accompaniment (*Begleitung*) denoted the non-keyboard instrument(s). My usage corresponds most closely to Koch's theory of textural roles: I will use "melody" to denote the primary voice *at a given moment* within a homophonic texture (equivalent to Koch's *Hauptmelodie*), and I will use "accompaniment" to refer to the role played by all other voices (comprising Koch's bass line and "accessory melodies").

[25] A rare example within Mozart's chamber *oeuvre* of a piece written for two instruments that are each, so to speak, self-sufficient and that are handled equally is the Sonata for Two Pianos in D Major, K. 448. See Sutcliffe, "The Keyboard Music," 67–68.

demonstrating that the analogy between melody/accompaniment and speaker/listener is approximate at best.

A related issue is the tendency of the first violin to monopolize the melodic role (at least to some degree, and often to a great degree), which would seem to belie descriptions of the string quartet as a conversation among equals.[26] Surely the first violin is not to be construed as a loquacious speaker who rudely dominates the discourse in violation of etiquette. Rather, as Sutcliffe observes, this is the usual state of affairs in this genre on account of the instruments' registral arrangement. It is normal, in a string quartet, for the first violin to predominate to a greater degree than any one person typically would in artful conversation. The important point that distinguishes late-eighteenth-century chamber music from earlier styles is the *potential* for exchangeability of roles, notably with respect to the cello part, which in earlier styles of chamber music had been restricted narrowly to the *basso continuo* role – a *Grundstimme* rather than *Hauptstimme* role.[27] I refer not to a literal equality of roles but to a certain ideal of egalitarianism whereby differences among the various parties do not preclude their free participation. Jürgen Habermas makes a parallel observation about the claims of equality within the emerging public sphere (*Öffentlichkeit*) during the Enlightenment:

However much the literary societies [*Tischgesellschaften*], *salons*, and coffeehouses ... may have differed from each other ... they were all based on a kind of social intercourse that, rather than presupposing equality of status, disregarded status altogether. The manners of equality tended to assert themselves over the ceremony of rank. Parity – the sole basis on which the authority of the better argument could assert itself against social hierarchy and in the end carry the day – meant, in the common understanding of the time, the parity of "simple humanity" [*bloß Menschlichen*] ... *Not that this idea of the public sphere* [Idee des Publikums] *was realized in earnest through the coffeehouses, salons, and societies; but as an idea it was institutionalized and thus established as an objective standard. To this extent a certain power, if not [full] reality, was bestowed on it* [emphasis added].[28]

---

[26] See, for example, Gagné, "A Dialogue among Equals."

[27] This notion of role exchange is discussed in detail by Koch. See above, 30–40, and Web Docs. #11 and #16.

[28] "Wie sehr sich Tischgesellschaften, Salons und Kaffeehäuser im Umfang und Zusammensetzung ihres Publikums, im Stil des Umgangs, im Klima des Räsonnements und in der thematischen Orientierung unterscheiden mögen, sie organisieren doch allemal eine der Tendenz nach permanente Diskussion unter Privatleuten; sie verfügen daher über eine Reihe gemeinsamer institutionelle Kriterien. *Zunächst* ist eine Art gesellschaftlichen Verkehrs gefordert, der nicht etwa die Gleichheit des Status voraussetzt, sondern von diesem überhaupt absieht. Gegen das Zeremoniell der Ränge setzt sich tendenziell der Takt der Ebenbürtigkeit durch. Die Parität, auf deren Basis allein die Autorität des Arguments gegen die der sozialen Hierarchie sich behaupten und am Ende auch durchsetzen kann,

Egalité, it seems, has always been more of an ideal than a reality. A similar tension between the ideal of equal participation and the reality of certain fixed, hierarchical roles exists in manuals of conversation. As Peter Burke notes, "the many references to equality and reciprocity in conversation [treatises] are matched by other references to the social hierarchy and marks of respect, and advice is often given about ways of speaking to one's superiors and inferiors. These references are a reminder that early modern European society was more hierarchical, and above all more openly hierarchical, than our own."[29]

The most fundamental incongruity between chamber music and conversation pertains to a certain goal-oriented, teleological aspect of "Classical" form and tonality that is without parallel in social discourse. Salon conversation, as a form of divertissement, emphasizes style over substance; unlike classical rhetoric, it is undertaken for its own sake and not burdened with the serious goal of presenting an argument. Whereas an oration is supposed to adhere to its primary subject, the open-ended nature of conversation allows it to freely follow a meandering path, with new

meint im Selbstverständnis der Zeit die Parität des 'bloß Menschlichen.' Les hommes, private gentlemen, die Privatleute bilden das Publikum nicht nur in dem Sinne, daß Macht und Ansehen der öffentlichen Ämter außer Kraft gesetzt sind; auch wirtschaftliche Abhängigkeiten dürfen im Prinzip nicht wirksam sein; Gesetze des Marktes sind ebenso suspendiert wie die des Staates. Nicht als ob mit den Kaffeehäusern, den Salons und den Gesellschaften im Ernst diese Idee des Publikums verwirklicht worden sei; wohl aber ist sie mit ihnen als Idee institutionalisiert, damit als objektiver Anspruch gesetzt und insofern, wenn nicht wirklich, so doch wirksam gewesen." Jürgen Habermas, *Strukturwandel der Öffentlichkeit: Untersuchungen zu einer Kategorie der bürgerlichen Gesellschaft*, 2nd ed. (Frankfurt: Suhrkamp Verlag, 1990), 96–97. See also the English translation published in *The Structural Transformation of the Public Sphere: An Inquiry into a Category of Bourgeois Society*, trans. Thomas Burger (Cambridge, MA: MIT Press, 1989), 36.

In addition to (1) *disregard of status*, Habermas describes two additional common elements in the incipient public sphere: (2) the *domain of common concern* as a subject for public critical attention (independent of the state or church), and (3) a *principle of inclusivity* in public discourse. Like the egalitarianism within the quartet, these lofty principles existed more as ideals than literal practices, and feminist critiques of Habermas have pointed out a "number of significant exclusions." Nancy Fraser, "Rethinking the Public Sphere: A Contribution to the Critique of Actually Existing Democracy," *Social Text* 25/26 (1990): 59.

[29] Burke, *The Art of Conversation*, 92. Habermas's and Burke's observations are borne out in the following advice from the German musician Jakob Greber, who had been in London in 1703–4: "If after the meal one is invited to remain when they [the noblemen] begin to drink, one sometimes accepts but sometimes leaves, which pleases them, for although one mixes freely with them, one is not on equal terms. It is better if one joins the wives and drinks tea or coffee with them"; cited in Leppert, *Music and Image*, 57. Greber's advice, offered to a fellow German musician who was about to travel to London, exemplifies a partial disregard of status while remaining decidedly on unequal terms.

twists and turns introduced with phrases such as "by the way."[30] If a conversation stumbles onto a touchy subject or disagreement, a sensitive hostess might offer a disarming joke and deflect the discourse onto a lighter topic, lest matters become unduly heated. Not so in musical discourse, where certain tonal events are essential for the completion of the form and require the participation of all parties.[31] Even when structural, form-defining cadences are temporarily evaded, the process of cadential delay merely serves to dramatize the eventual, obligatory achievement of closure.[32] This gives sonata form a strong sense of mission and trajectory toward its essential goals that is quite different from conversation, which can easily be interrupted midstream by the arrival of a new guest or the serving of a meal. That tonal form requires the achievement of various tasks – such as completing a cadence or accomplishing a modulation at the phrase level, or completing the sonata structure at the movement level – may suggest metaphors of human action rather than utterance, though I will draw from both of these categories.[33]

Chamber music personas as self-determining agents

In what sense can the players of a chamber work be said to determine their own statements and actions or to exhibit agency to influence the outcome of musical events? Are they not simply executing notes that were chosen in advance by the composer? How, then, can their fully preordained exchange seem to be spontaneous? To unravel these apparent contradictions, a first step is to sort out various classes of agents and the levels at which they operate more precisely. To begin with an analogy to the world of opera: A singer who performs the title role of *Don Giovanni* attends weeks of

[30] See De Staël's commentary from her essay "L'esprit de conversation," quoted above, 24, and in Web Doc. #31.

[31] On this teleological aspect of sonata form, cf. Hepokoski and Darcy, *Elements of Sonata Theory*, which models sonata form as a series of action-spaces directed toward essential cadential goals, a view that is based partly on Koch's punctuation-based model of form. Chapter 5 will provide a detailed account of form analysis from a multiple-agency perspective.

[32] On "avoidance of cadence" as a means of intensification and thematic extension, see Rosen, *The Classical Style*, 50.

[33] Whereas Cone famously asks, "If music is a language, then who is speaking?" (*The Composer's Voice*, 1), Anthony Newcomb poses the alternate formulation: "If music is (or represents) actions and events, who is acting?" Anthony Newomb, "Action and Agency in Mahler's Ninth Symphony, Second Movement," in *Music and Meaning*, ed. Jenefer Robinson (Ithaca: Cornell University Press, 1997), 131.

rehearsals and becomes familiar with the complete opera, from beginning to end, including other characters' parts as well as his own. When the curtain rises for each successive performance, he maintains his omniscient vantage point, remaining fully aware that the opera's plot is predetermined and its music already composed. But although this is true for the *singer*, it is not so for his *character*, who experiences the opera in the present tense as the action unscrolls. The character Don Giovanni possesses a consciousness limited to the past and present, with no foreknowledge of events yet to come, including future actions by other characters. Moreover, since he has no knowledge of a world outside his own, he is unaware of either Mozart or Da Ponte[34] and therefore perceives that he himself determines his own statements and actions. In Edward T. Cone's words, the operatic characters are "like Petrouchkas, brought to life by the composer but thenceforth driven by their own wills and desires"[35] and able to act freely within the confines of the opera's fictional frame. So far as the character Don Giovanni is aware, he is the author of his own verse and the composer of his own music.

This operatic scenario suggests some parallel observations one could make about four players sight-reading a composition for string quartet in an eighteenth-century musical salon. Like the singer portraying Don Giovanni, our quartet's second violinist is also enacting a role – that of a second violinist in a string quartet. The distinction between the second violinist and role is by no means trivial. A similar distinction holds, for example, between the *person* Jerry Seinfeld and the *character* Jerry Seinfeld in the eponymous sitcom; both are comedians living in New York who share the same name and appearance, but they are not exactly the same person.[36] As for the quartet: The real-life violinist is aware that he is

---

[34] That Don Giovanni actually does hear some music by Mozart – the wind band's performance of "Non più andrai" during the banquet scene – is a comic reminder that he is a Mozartean character with no knowledge of, and who is seemingly indifferent to, Mozart. Set in seventeenth-century Spain, the opera takes place well before Viennese *Harmoniemusik* arrangements were in vogue (and certainly before arias by Sarti, Martín y Soler, and Mozart were composed). The joke lies in a boundary play between inside and outside the opera's world, between Seville and Vienna/Prague, between "then" and "now."

[35] Cone, *The Composer's Voice*, 23. Cone's original point was in reference to the characters portrayed by singers in art song, not opera (in which the dramatic element is all the more vivid).

[36] A more historically suitable example is the book authored by Laurence Sterne but published with the title *A Sentimental Journey through France and Italy by Mr. Yorick*, 2 vols. (London, 1768); Sterne's name does not appear on the title page. That Sterne shared his narrator's profession as a parson – and that he furthermore published collections of sermons under both names – suggests a permeable boundary between the real and fictional worlds and a partial conflation of author and narrator. See Elizabeth K. Goodhue, "When Yorick Takes His Tea; Or,

reading notes off a page that has been composed in advance, but within the quartet's fictional frame the persona of the second violin engages in a present-tense exchange with the others, all of whom seem to create the piece, moment to moment, through their collective actions and interactions.

The perceived "realness" of these personas is heightened by the near-identity of the instrumentalists and the roles they play. Unlike the singer portraying Don Giovanni, who must wear a costume and make-up to get into character, the instrumentalist playing the role of the second violin is, in a sense, simply playing himself (or a stylized version of himself).[37] Furthermore, unlike opera singers, who know the plot in advance yet portray characters ignorant of future events, quartet players who sight-read their parts together are genuinely discovering the piece for the first time, in the moment, as they play. These circumstances afford the ensemble's play-through a quality of exploration, and the players may actually feel as though they are creating the music extemporaneously through a process of group improvisation.[38] The sense of the players fictionally improvising their musical exchange is parodied in the video "Endless Coda" by the musical-comedy duo Igudesman & Joo (Web Fig. 4.1 ▶).

Does the fact that the musicians are playing from fully notated parts – tangible evidence that they are not literally improvising – shatter this illusion of spontaneity and self-determination? Not according to Cone, who writes:

If a lieder singer impersonates a protagonist, if an accompanist tries to create an effect of spontaneity, how can we tolerate – as we often must – their use of scores? Isn't the illusion bound to fail under these circumstances? Oddly enough, the illusion does not fail, even under apparently more difficult conditions. "Readings"

---

the Commerce of Consumptive Passions in the Case of Laurence Sterne," *Journal for Early Modern Cultural Studies* 6, no. 1 (Spring/Summer 2006): 51–83.

[37] Musicians' propensity to identify with the parts they play may relate to Cox's theory of "mimetic engagement" (Cox, "Embodying Music: Principles of the Mimetic Hypothesis"). Although Cox focuses on listeners, as in an audience, it applies by extension to performing musicians, who are also listeners to their own performances. Their physical performing gestures are a highly tangible "mimicking" of the imagined sounds, gestures, and actions encoded into their parts.

[38] Raymond Monelle, critiquing Cone's emphasis on the composer's agency, makes a parallel point: "The composer's voice has disappeared. There is a voice, there are multiple voices, there is a controlling voice; yet all voices are roles, including the central voice of the 'complete persona' ... The listener to music hears, not the voice of the composer but that of the performer ... It is the performer who has absolute control over all the events in the piece, although these events are 'predetermined' by the composer." Raymond Monelle, *The Sense of Music: Semiotic Essays* (Princeton University Press, 2000), 168.

of plays, in which the characters [*recte*: actors?] openly read their parts from a script, are often effective, and oratorio performances, with no semblance of staging or acting, can be dramatically convincing. To a certain extent such success is due to the familiarity of the convention: we accept these modes of performance and in a sense overlook them.[39]

Cone's slight solecism – writing that *characters* read from scripts, rather than *actors* – underscores the point: The play's actors (and their scripts) reside in the real world but their characters dwell within the fictional frame, where the events are still unfolding, the ending is not yet written, and the script therefore does not exist. The unstaged (or lightly staged) reading of a play approximates the setting of a chamber music salon, in which the players "read" from their own parts, primarily for the enjoyment of airing an unfamilar work in a kind of proto-performance. When the same chamber work is performed for an audience in a modern concert hall, it takes on a more dramatic, performative quality, more like a rehearsed, theatrical dialogue than an actual, spontaneous one. However, even in this public performance setting, the quartet retains its potential for multiple agency, with characters who enjoy the same ontological status as those of opera or theater.

The various categories of agents and personas sketched out here, in Cone's ideas and my own, can be formalized more rigorously using a model recently developed by Seth Monahan.[40] In a lucid meta-study of musical action and agency, building on earlier work by Fred Everett Maus,[41] Monahan defines as agential those descriptions of music event-successions that appeal to "psychodramatic or anthropomorphic" rationales and that "regard musical objects or gestures as volitional, as purposive, in such a way that is indicative of psychological states."[42] Monahan proceeds to enumerate the types of agency invoked by music scholars and systematically to organize them hierarchically into four classes, listed here in order from highest to lowest rank:

(1) Analyst
(2) Fictional Composer
(3) Work-Persona
(4) Individuated Element.

---

[39] Cone, *The Composer's Voice*, 64.

[40] Seth Monahan, "Action and Agency Revisited," *Journal of Music Theory* 57, no. 2 (Fall 2013): 321–71.

[41] Fred Everett Maus, "Music as Drama," *Music Theory Spectrum* 10 (Spring 1988): 56–73; and "Agency in Instrumental Music and Song," *College Music Symposium* 29 (1989): 31–43.

[42] Monahan, "Action and Agency Revisited," 325.

Individuated element refers broadly to "any discrete component of the musical fabric that can be construed as having autonomy and volition ... [such as] individual themes, motives, gestures, keys, chords, topics, and even pitch classes."[43] The *work-persona* is a unitary, continuous consciousness that represents "the work itself, personified"; like the individuated element, it "dwells in an *intra*musical world," its awareness limited to the musical past and present, with no foreknowledge of future events.[44] The next agent class, the *fictional composer*, refers to "the person postulated by the analyst as the controlling, intending author of the musical text"; this agent is based on, but not coextensive with, the actual, historical composer.[45] Finally, the highest-ranking agent class is the *analyst*, who "in many respects ... stands in the same relation to the analytical text as the fictional composer stands in relation to the musical work: our task in reading is to interpret that text as an intelligible action of some analyzing agent, some plausible intending subject."[46]

Monahan defines the relational logic of the four agency classes as a nested hierarchy: "Any fictional agency called forth in an analysis may also be understood by the reader as an action of any or all of the higher-ranking (but not lower-ranking) agent classes, whether or not they have been made explicit by the analyst."[47] To demonstrate this, let us analyze the applicability of the following statement with respect to Ex. 4.2:

In m. 17, the quartet casts off the opening stile antico *counterpoint and abruptly begins a virtuoso fiddling theme.*

This wording of this assertion describes the individuated elements (the "*stile antico* counterpoint" and "virtuoso fiddling theme") as the utterances of the work-persona ("the quartet"). Implicitly, this statement also invokes a fictional composer ("Mozart"), who composed the quartet, as well as an analyst ("I" or "we"), the author of the analytical text.

But the very same statement could be read in a slightly different way if the words "the quartet" are understood in reference not to the composition itself but to the four players as a corporate entity (activating the ambiguity inherent in such terms as duo, trio, quartet, and symphony). Let us reread the statement with this new interpretation:

---

[43] Ibid., 327.   [44] Ibid., 328.

[45] Ibid., 329. Monahan's distinction between the *historical* and *fictional* composer figures is based on Michel Foucault's parallel distinction between *writers* (who are actual human beings) and *authors* (who are interpretive constructs). See Foucault, "What is an Author?," in *The Foucault Reader*, ed. Paul Rabinow (New York: Pantheon Books, 1984), 101–20.

[46] Monahan, "Action and Agency Revisited," 332.   [47] Ibid., 337.

In m. 17, the quartet [i.e., the four players as a corporate entity] casts off the opening
stile antico *counterpoint and abruptly begins a virtuoso fiddling theme.*

This new reading captures a certain, highly tangible type of action: In any performance, it is the physical movements of the players that cause the realization of a musical event, such as a change of topic, to occur.

At this point I should pause to consider whether this statement, in either interpretation, truly expresses agency or whether it is merely a non-purposive, chronological reporting of events.[48] It is possible for language to *seem* agential without actually describing the volitional, purposive action of a plausible, sentient agent. For example, the statement "the Mozart Bridge traverses the Salzach River" uses an action verb but would not ordinarily be construed as agential.[49] As for the statement above about the K. 387 finale (Ex. 4.2), it is *potentially agential* if the analyst conceives of the event – the abandonment of one musical topic and the introduction of another – as the volitional, purposive act of the four, sentient fictional characters within the quartet. To that end, the extended description of this same passage presented earlier in this chapter (above, 118) is more overtly agential, since the account of the first-violin persona introducing virtuoso music to show off and of the second-violin persona repeating it to best his colleague treats the instruments as explicitly anthropomorphic.

Normally the burden is on the analyst to provide signals in the analytical text that a potentially agential statement is intended as truly agential. For instance, in the sentence "the second violin brazenly repeats the first violin's fiddling theme," the adverb "brazenly" serves to anthropomorphize the second-violin persona in what would otherwise be a neutral, non-purposive statement. However, in this book, the underlying premise is that I will *always* view the individual, real-world players as enacting sentient, fictional personas – personas whom I imagine to invent their own parts. This renders their every utterance as a fictionally volitional and (at least marginally) purposive action or statement.[50] To put it the other way around, I will *always* view each musical utterance as the volitional and (at least marginally)

---

[48] Monahan discusses such "pseudoagential figural language" in ibid., 324–25.

[49] This example is adapted from ibid., 363–64.

[50] As an example of a *marginally* purposive agential action, imagine a conversationalist who gasps or raises her eyebrows upon hearing a surprising remark. These (at least partly) volitional actions by a sentient person do serve a modest purpose – to communicate astonishment – even if they may be less interesting or noteworthy than the remark that elicited them. Just as the gasp or raised eyebrow meets Monahan's minimum definition for agency (as the purposive, volitional action of a sentient persona), the analytical perspective advanced in this book regards every musical utterance within a chamber work as meeting at least this baseline standard.

purposive action of a fictional persona, a role that is enacted in the real world by an instrumentalist.[51] I intend these fundamental premises as blanket statements, applying to all of the analyses that follow.

What is the status of the fictionalized performer personas according to Monahan's model? To understand this, let us compare two similar statements about Ex. 4.2:

> In m. 31, the sequence boldly forges the way for a modulation to the dominant.
>
> In m. 31, the cellist boldly forges the way for a modulation to the dominant.

In the first version, the *sequence* (an individuated element) is described as the intending subject of an action (the modulation to the dominant). The second version expresses essentially the same observation but refers to the *cellist*, the instrumentalist who plays the sequential material, as the intending subject. Monahan's model would describe the cellist as an *avatar* of the individuated element, since he is a real-world person who is substituted in the analytical text for an agent at the individuated-element level. Paraphrasing Monahan, "This substitution works . . . [because this 'cellist'] is predicated not on any real or imaginary . . . musician, but on attributes . . . [we] hear in the music itself";[52] that is, it is the *forte*, sequential music that is regarded as exhibiting a bold quality, not the cellist.

Monahan's explanation holds true in conventional, score-based music analysis, since the object of analytical study has typically been the work *per se*; when an analyst writes about the cellist's actions in m. 31, it is traditionally meant as a statement about the composition rather than the instrumentalist. But if the object of study is a (real or imagined) *performance* of the quartet, then matters have shifted.[53] Statements about the cellist can now potentially refer to several things at once:

---

[51] These two conversely related statements are not redundant. Together, they are meant to avoid an ambiguity that plagues Momigny's analysis of K. 421 (see above, 52–70): whereas Momigny considers the entire first-violin part to represent Dido's speech, he only fleetingly considers utterances by the other parts to represent a human character (Aeneas, Dido's sister, members of her entourage), and he struggles to define what they are the rest of the time. For my purposes in this book, every musical utterance is regarded as the utterance of some fictional persona; there are no musical sounds that are merely "scenery."

[52] Ibid., 348. While Monahan observes that avatars of the individuated element are most ubiquitous in analytical literature, he discusses avatars of all four agency classes in ibid., 347–53.

[53] This temporal perspective – regarding a musical work as something that exists in time, in a performance – resonates with the eighteenth-century musical perspectives discussed in the previous chapter. In contrast, the modern culture of music analysis often places more emphasis

(1) the cellist as a fictional persona that represents the personification of the cello part (an individuated element);

(2) the cellist as a real-world instrumentalist, who performs this fictional role;

(3) the cellist as a co-composer of the work, to the extent that the cellist may feel like the author of his own part;[54] and

(4) the cellist as an analyst of the work, to the extent that playing the piece involves a cognitive process of observing events as they occur and understanding them in relation to the whole.[55]

Our analytical statement about the cellist's actions thus refers to a conflation of the real-world player and the fictional character. If the cellist, acting as an analyst, hears a quality of boldness in the sequential material, he may ascribe this quality to the fictional cello persona who utters the material. But he may furthermore vicariously experience this boldness as well, since he is enacting that role and since the role is a stylized version of himself.[56] This circular network of relationships partly effaces the distinction between the real and fictional worlds. The player may feel as if he *is* his own character, improvising his own part within the quartet's fictional frame, even while he is actually located in the real world, sight-reading from a fully notated part. From this point forward, I will refer in my analyses to "the cello" as shorthand for the combined persona of the real-world cellist, the fictional cello persona, and the cello part (i.e., the utterances of that persona). Moreover, I will grant him the dignity of human pronouns, which underscore his anthropomorphic status.[57]

---

on the musical score than on its realization in performance, reflecting post-1800 (especially German instrumental) notions of workhood.

[54] Aside from *feeling* (internally) like the author of his own part, the cellist necessarily *is* (externally) a co-composer inasmuch as the act of performing involves adding nuances and performance choices that cannot be notated in scores.

[55] On performers as analysts, see, for example, Joel Lester, "How Theorists Relate to Musicians," *Music Theory Online* 4, no. 2 (March 1998), www.mtosmt.org/issues/mto.98.4.2/mto.98.4.2 .lester.html.

[56] The relationship between the actual cellist and his fictional counterpart is analogous to that between the historical and fictional composers. In both cases, the fictional personage is the one described by the analyst as the composer or performer of the work, respectively. Furthermore, in both cases, a single analytical statement can refer simultaneously to an actual and a fictional figure. For instance, "Mozart introduces a new theme" can refer to either or both Mozarts, just as "the cellist plays a sequence that modulates to D major" can refer simultaneously to the real and fictional cellists.

[57] Since string players were virtually always male in this period, I will use male pronouns to refer to this combined cello/cellist persona. Nevertheless, the gender of an instrumentalist need not be identical to the gender of the musical part he or she plays (to the extent that the musical

How does Monahan's model interpret the tradition of comparing quartets to conversation and the notion of multiple agency developed in this chapter? Monahan's major contribution is to clarify the multiple classes of agency as they exist along the *vertical* axis of his hierarchy. Authors who compare quartets to conversation conceive of multiple agents along a single, isolated slice of Monahan's model, since these various fictionalized performer personas all share the same hierarchical rank. From my own vantage point as outside analyst, I recognize that these characters' discourse constitutes a musical work and that this work was itself created by a composer. But once these points are acknowledged as given, I can elect to turn my attention to a single level that is salient for the analysis.[58] One does this tacitly with the statement "Don Giovanni attempts to seduce Zerlina" as a shorthand for "Mozart and Da Ponte wrote a duet in which the fictional character Don Giovanni attempts to seduce the fictional character Zerlina." An analyst who resides outside the fictional frame, in full awareness of the existence of the composer and the score, can nevertheless analyze the work by imagining how events appear, moment to moment, from the vantage points of the fictional performer personas. Is this mode of analysis not what highly skilled musicians do implicitly when they play a piece of chamber music from individual parts – experiencing first-hand an interplay among fictionalized versions of themselves, anticipating how their colleagues might respond to their statements and actions, and interpreting the meanings of these events in the still-unscrolling musical whole?

Refining multiple agency

If music analysis has traditionally placed the locus of attention at the levels of the work-persona and fictional composer, the multiple-agency perspective developed in this book directs our attention to a lower level, where a

persona is understood to be gendered). For instance, that the slow movement of Mozart's "Dissonance" Quartet, K. 465, is often performed at weddings suggests that some listeners hear the duets between the first violin and cello (mm. 13–20, 39–44, and 58–69) as an exchange between a woman and a man. This impression is presumably not dependent on the genders of the players.

[58] Monahan's nested hierarchy of agency classes has parallels with the Schenkerian theory of structural levels. Musical events may attract a Schenkerian analyst's attention to a given level of middleground, but this does not negate the existence or explanatory power of other (higher or lower) levels. In both Schenkerian theory and Monahan's model of agency classes, observations made about any one level often contain implicit statements about other levels.

more individuated, heterogeneous landscape emerges.[59] Multiple agency thus emphasizes that the musical fabric is produced through the interaction of all parts within the texture, correcting a tendency in music analysis to view scores from an omniscient, outside vantage point.[60] It constitutes a radical focusing of analytical attention on a single level, that of the various fictional personas that (usually) correspond to the individual players.[61] But perhaps it seems radical only by the standards of analytical practice for instrumental music, since in the analysis of opera, it is perfectly commonplace to interpret musical events in terms of the statements, actions, or desires of individual characters. It can be challenging to make analogous interpretations of music lacking such explicit characters or plots. This chapter concludes with a series of brief analyses that examine various problems in the application of multiple agency to instrumental chamber music.

Since the domain of harmony, by definition, involves all musical voices sounding at a particular moment, it would seem paradoxical to interpret harmonic events through the lens of multiple agency. However, in certain passages, an unexpected harmony may seem to arise at the instigation of a single part, especially one that introduces a significant chromatic note. Such a harmony may seem less a collectively planned event than a surprise to some part(s), who recognize(s) and react(s) to it only as it happens. An example of such a passage occurs at the permeable boundary between the exposition and development in the first movement of Mozart's Duo in B♭ Major for Violin and Viola, K. 424 (shown in Ex. 4.3). As the development opens, the violin and viola still muse on the simple V^7–I cadence that had

---

[59] The concept of "work-persona" approximates the unified, monological model of musical personification advanced in Cone, *The Composer's Voice*. Monahan perceives an implicit bias toward post-1800 music in this concept: "Though Cone never says so outright, the hermeneutic of personification he develops in *The Composer's Voice* is an outgrowth of, and consequently geared toward, experiences of Romantic music and its attendant aesthetic of emotive communication." Monahan, "Action and Agency Revisited," 323 n. 3.

[60] This "inside" analytical vantage point recalls a shift in analytical attitude described by David Lewin: "We [analysts] tend to imagine ourselves in the position of *observers* when we theorize about musical space; the space is 'out there,' away from our dancing bodies or singing voices . . . In contrast, the transformational attitude is much less Cartesian . . . [and is] by and large the attitude of someone *inside* the music, as idealized dancer and/or singer. No external observer (analyst, listener) is needed." David Lewin, *Generalized Musical Intervals and Transformations* (Oxford University Press, 2007), 159.

[61] Although my analyses usually interpret each instrument as a distinct musical agent, I will discuss other possibilities below (e.g., if a group of instruments is interpreted collectively as a cohort or if the two hands of a single keyboard instrument may be construed as two independent personas).

Ex. 4.3 Mozart, Duo in B♭ Major for Violin and Viola, K. 424, Allegro (i)

ended the exposition. These bars may, indeed, be heard as an extension of the exposition by cadential repetition.[62] Lest these repetitions continue indefinitely, the violin abruptly shifts to minor in m. 84, substituting an A♭ for the expected A♮. The dumbfounded viola drops out, while the violin ponders the note A♭ ("hmm, that was a clever trick . . . but what can I do with this note?"). The *pianissimo* marking, rare in Mozart's chamber music, seems like an operatic aside ("da sè"). With the A♭ isolated and in a melodic register, the violin cleverly treats it as 5̂, inviting the viola back in

---

[62] A listener who does not follow the score may be confused upon hearing mm. 81–82 ("did they play that figure more than once the first time through? It's hard to remember"). This ambiguity is less palpable for the players, who have the visual cue of their parts, which clearly indicate the location of the repeat sign.

for a new, *dolce* theme in D♭ major. As that theme begins, the viola might not yet realize about the new key – his notes (F–A♭) are the common third between F-minor and D♭-major triads, so he could still be expecting F minor – but he surely gets the message by m. 89, where he begins playing E♭s and G♭s. As soon as the new key is confirmed by an arrival on a root-position local tonic chord (m. 93), the key is immediately destabilized by a sequence instigated by the simultaneous syncopated *sforzandi* in both parts.

The impression of independent action is heightened in passages in which individual characters seem to be working toward opposing ends. The following analysis of a passage from the first movement of Schubert's "Arpeggione" Sonata (shown in Ex. 4.4) addresses the agential autonomy of melody and accompaniment, an issue that Cone returned to throughout his career in his many studies of Lied accompaniment.[63]

By m. 60, both arpeggione and piano seem to be en route toward a grand cadence in C major, with the virtuoso arpeggione climbing higher and higher (showing off his vast range) as the piano eagerly supports it with cadential $^6_4$ chords. In m. 62, as the piano ceases her motoric rhythms, the arpeggione soars to his highest register, reaching a climactic G as part of a sweeping, operatic gesture that strives for a perfect authentic cadence (PAC) on the following downbeat. The piano's lack of rhythmic activity in this measure encourages the arpeggione to stretch his high note, relishing the climactic moment and heightening the drama of the ensuing cadence.

But on the following downbeat, as the arpeggione resolves his melody to the cadential tonic note, the piano resolves deceptively, with a secondary leading-tone chord (VII of V) in place of the expected cadential tonic.[64] After the arpeggione hears the piano's harmony, which signals the failed cadence, he sings a lyrical melody, beginning in minor (m. 63) but blossoming into major (by m. 65), perhaps striving to console the piano and to convince her to affirm C major with a successful cadence. Since this melody reprises m. 49, where it led to a deceptive cadence in m. 51 and a PAC in m. 53, the arpeggione expects a PAC in m. 67 based on precedent from the earlier passage. But when the piano once again makes a deceptive resolution, matters seem more desperate, since the continued failure to cadence in C major threatens the entire expositional trajectory. The arpeggione thus strengthens his appeal, repeating his melody in a higher register and reaching up to a higher note (compare the

---

[63] See overview in Monahan, "Action and Agency Revisited," 361 n. 67.

[64] Regarding deceptive cadences ending on VII of V (instead of the more familiar VI harmony), see Caplin, *Classical Form*, 28; and William Rothstein, *Phrase Rhythm in Tonal Music* (New York: Schirmer, 1989), 254. Their more-inclusive usage is in accordance with a variety of seventeenth- and eighteenth-century authors (Rameau notably excepted), and stems ultimately from Gioseffo Zarlino's *cadenza fuggita*.

Ex. 4.4 Schubert, Sonata in A Minor for Arpeggione and Piano, D. 821, Allegro moderato (i)

Ex. 4.4 (*cont.*)

Deceptive resolution again; prompts
arpeggione to appeal to higher register

PAC (at last!)

figuration in m. 69 to that of m. 65), and successfully persuades the piano to
complete the cadence in m. 71. Both instruments celebrate the shared arrival with
a codetta of grand chords.

Throughout the excerpt, the arpeggione is the exclusive melodic protagonist and the piano is fixed in an accompanimental role, an arrangement that
imitates the orchestral accompaniment to an aria or concerto. Beginning at
m. 60, both instruments initially seem to be united in their intention to
effect a PAC. The arpeggione player, reading off his own part, would have
every reason to expect his C on the downbeat of m. 63 to be harmonized
with a tonic chord to complete the cadence. The deceptive resolution that
appears instead is caused by the piano alone and only becomes apparent to
the arpeggione *after* he hears the diminished-seventh harmony on the
downbeat.[65]

This analysis does not speculate as to *why* the piano circumvents
authentic cadences in mm. 63 and 67 or why it ultimately cooperates in

---

[65] This interpretation is suggested by the notation of Schubert's holograph in the parallel passage
in the recapitulation (m. 182), in which the arpeggione completes his would-be PAC in *forte*,
even as the piano makes a *subito piano* on the downbeat. Schubert marked the dynamics less
clearly in m. 63.

m. 71. It does not claim, for instance, that these actions are in retaliation for some alleged wrong that the arpeggione had committed earlier in the piece. Multiple-agency analyses can focus on fleeting moments of interaction without necessarily subsuming them into a broader narrative arc spanning an entire movement or composition. Perhaps, if the analytical purview were broadened to a longer excerpt, there might be compelling reasons to make a bolder interpretation of the piano's behavior in this passage, but as the analysis stands, the piano's reticence to cadence is not presented as part of a pervasive pattern of behavior throughout the composition. It nevertheless exemplifies multiple agency because it conceives of two independent personas, interacting spontaneously, volitionally, and purposively.[66]

In other contexts, however, an analyst may be less inclined to interpret agential autonomy between melody and accompaniment. The subordinate theme from the first movement of Mozart's Clarinet Quintet, K. 581 (shown in Ex. 4.5) is introduced by the first violin and restated in a transformed version by the clarinet. Whereas the original version is a diatonic melody with gentle accompaniment in the lower strings, the mood changes as the clarinet takes over. Who is responsible for the change of atmosphere? The string accompaniment changes to *agitato* syncopations in *pianissimo* dynamic just after the downbeat of m. 49, before the clarinet enters, and the viola shifts the mode to minor on the following downbeat, after the clarinet's entrance but before his first minor-inflected note.

Do the strings *oblige* the clarinet to make a statement in minor or do they *foretell* the mood he is about to convey? Since agency is not a property of the music itself but a property of how an analyst describes the events (or how a player or listener experiences them), there is no single, "correct" explanation. The important point is that agency attribution is not clinched by the signals in the strings that precede those in the clarinet. An interpretation focused on the passing of the melodic role from first violin to clarinet could treat each soloist's agency as primary and view the accompaniment as reflecting (or preparing) the moods of their respective melodic statements; Momigny's comparison of the *accompagnemens* to the melody's entourage seems apt (see above, 60). As the violin completes the first "pass" through his carefree theme, the clarinet enters with his own, more affecting version (signaled by his *dolce* marking and chromaticism),

---

[66] An alternative, non-agential explanation would describe the successive deceptive resolutions generically as imitations of operatic "one-more-time" repetitions or the analogous *Spielepisoden* of a concerto's first movement. See Janet Schmalfeldt, "Cadential Processes: The Evaded Cadence and the 'One More Time' Technique," *Journal of Musicological Research* 12, nos. 1–2 (1992): 1–52.

Ex. 4.5 Mozart, Clarinet Quintet in A Major, K. 581, Allegro (i), subordinate theme

... introduce diatonic version of new theme

Shift to minor as clarinet enters; whose agency?

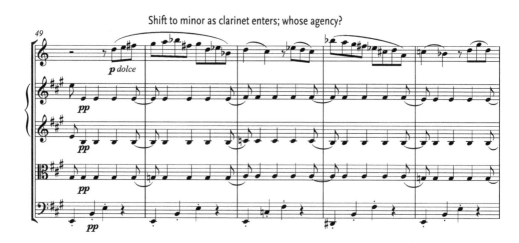

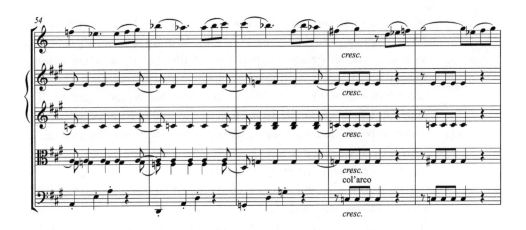

Major mode restored; exchange of 16ths shows enthusiastic ...

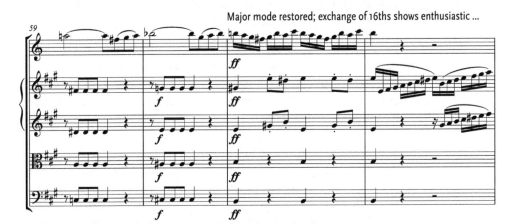

... participation
in cadential action

Group trill marks
hard-won cadence

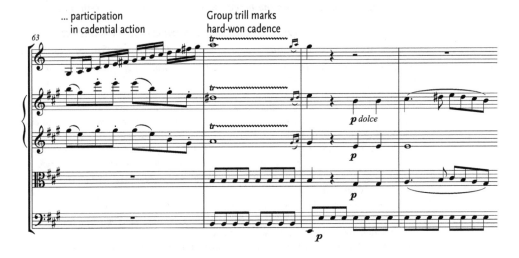

offering his wisdom and experience as a response to the violin's inno-
cence.[67] Unlike the Schubert passage analyzed in Ex. 4.4, here there are few
signals to encourage an interpretation of the strings as acting autonomously or subverting the intentions of the melody, since they are strictly
accompanimental from m. 49 on (until just before the cadence). The
ambiguity in this example seems to arise from a metrical offset between
the melody and accompaniment, since the melodic groups begin *after* the
hyperdownbeats established by the accompaniment, giving the impression
that the melody follows rather than leads.[68]

  It is also possible for a melodic instrument to begin a theme, initially
receiving straightforward accompanimental support, only to be blindsided
by unexpected or even subversive statements from the other instruments.
Such is the case in the subordinate theme from the first movement of
Mozart's Piano Quartet in E♭ Major, K. 493 (shown in Ex. 4.6a).

*The piano incipit (mm. 28–29) proposes an initial melodic idea for the violin to
develop as a subordinate theme. As the violin's melody gets underway (m. 30), the
piano's right hand assumes an accompanimental role, forming a nascent duo-sonata
texture that conspicuously lacks a bass line. As the bass belatedly enters in m. 31, the
piano's left hand resolves deceptively, making a submediant harmony (a minor
sonority) in place of the root-position tonic chord that the violin probably expects.
As the bass line continues in a cadential progression (D–E♭–F),[69] it suggests an
intention to resolve to B♭ on the downbeat of m. 35, which would provide the
required weak cadence (imperfect authentic cadence) for this would-be antecedent
phrase. But the bass line again surprises the violin with another deceptive resolution
(m. 35). By this point, the repeated avoidance of root-position tonic chords has
become palpable, arising from the piano's mischief or perhaps her reticence.*

*As the passage continues (and the viola and cello enter), the bass line attempts to
initiate an expanded cadential progression (note the motion from D to E♭ in
mm. 35–36). However the harmony over the E♭ is not the requisite predominant*

---

[67] A less colorful interpretation might point to the mixture of concerto and chamber music norms
   in this composition, with the strings serving the role of orchestral accompaniment. In this case,
   the timbral difference reinforces the clarinet's distinctive role, but concerto elements are
   possible even in homogeneous compositions such as string quartets or even solo-keyboard
   sonatas, as in the finale to the Sonata in B♭ Major, K. 333. On the concerto style in string
   quartets, see Floyd K. Grave, "Concerto Style in Haydn's String Quartets," *Journal of Musicology*
   18, no. 1 (Winter 2001): 76–97.

[68] Eric McKee discusses this aspect of the passage in "Extended Anacruces in Mozart's
   Instrumental Music," *Theory and Practice* 29 (2004): 14–15. See also Roger Kamien,
   "Conflicting Metrical Patterns in Accompaniment and Melody in Works by Mozart and
   Beethoven: A Preliminary Study," *Journal of Music Theory* 31, no. 2 (1993): 311–48.

[69] On the bass line $\hat{3}$–$\hat{4}$–$\hat{5}$–$\hat{1}$ as an "expanded cadential progression," see Caplin, *Classical Form*,
   20 and *passim*.

Ex. 4.6 Mozart, Piano Quartet in E♭ Major, K. 493, Allegro (i), subordinate theme

a. Score

but a V_2^4 chord, which exerts pressure for a downward resolution in the bass (from E♭ back to D), frustrating the potential cadential trajectory. The V_2^4 harmony is supplied by the piano's right hand and reinforced by the viola's sustained F, a note that stubbornly negates any possibility of a predominant-functioning chord. The repeated neighboring progression $I^6-V_2^4-I^6$ (mm. 35–38) makes for continued

Ex. 4.6 (*cont.*)

Violin adds C♯ · Viola cadential idea: to G minor? · No! Piano's ...

... deceptive resolution prevents G minor cadence (swerves to E♭, global tonic).
But how to return to B♭ to complete the subordinate theme?

Piano emerges as concerto soloist, leads way back to B♭

tonic prolongation, *stalling the progress of the theme toward a cadential conclusion.
The repetitions in the violin part suggest some hesitation, especially once the motive is
distilled down to a single pitch, with the repeated Cs (mm. 39–40).*

*Since the momentum toward a B♭ cadence has dissipated, the viola acts to break the
harmonic stasis. His rise to F♯ (m. 40) intensifies the harmony and nudges toward
the relative minor, suggesting a harmonic association with the earlier deceptive*

Cadence achieved

resolutions to G minor chords (mm. 32 and 35). The violin follows suit, contributing a C♯ (m. 41), which forms an augmented sixth over the bass, bolstering the swerve toward a cadence in G minor. (The viola's F♯ and the violin's C♯ are both doubled in the piano's right-hand accompaniment; the viola obliges the violin by accompanying the latter's C♯ with G, also doubled in the piano.) The augmented sixth emphatically forces the bass-note E♭ to resolve once again downward to D, but the latter note now has a new harmonic function as dominant in G minor (m. 42).

At this point, the original expectation of a simple, diatonic route to a cadence in B♭ seems like a distant memory. Perhaps the violin's failure to successfully lead the group to that goal motivates him to drop out at this juncture and to relinquish the melodic role for the remainder of the theme. The dark-hued viola comes to the fore (m. 42), resolving the violin's C♯ and initiating a cadential figure that aims toward a would-be PAC in G minor in m. 44, attempting to complete the pessimistic swerve he had begun some bars earlier. Yet, to the viola's surprise, the bass line has a trick up its sleeve: another deceptive resolution (m. 44) impedes the viola's attempted G-minor cadence, deflecting this potentially serious moment back toward major keys (in contradistinction to earlier deceptive cadences, which had swerved toward minor chords).

After a brief thematic restatement in E♭ major (m. 44), complete with the now de rigueur *deceptive resolution* (mm. 44–45), the piano reintroduces A♮ as part of an inverted F dominant-seventh chord, as if she reminds the strings of the original need

*to cadence in B♭ major, goading them to join in this process and "treading water"
with increasing frenzy until they finally get the message. With their entrance in
m. 51 – in crescendo – the strings prod the piano out of her loop. With the arrival on
a root-position dominant (m. 52), coinciding with the climactic e♭³ in the piano's
right hand, the piano emerges as a virtuoso concerto soloist, quite at odds with the
theme's modest opening as a duo sonata. As the piano makes one final deceptive
resolution (m. 54), she seems to be reenacting a juncture we have encountered
before, trying hard to get it right this time, and at long last successfully progressing
to a II⁶ harmony (m. 54, and stretched with an Eingang through m. 56). The piano
continues as a charismatic soloist, leading the way to the long-awaited cadence in
m. 59, supported by the strings' affirmative accompaniment.*

Before discussing the above analysis, let us begin by considering a normalized version of the theme (shown in Ex. 4.6b), which can be used as a
benchmark to interpret how and why significant detours occur in the
actual passage. This normalized model presents the theme as an eight-
bar, antecedent-plus-continuation hybrid.[70] In the actual composition, the
antecedent portion (mm. 30–35, played by the violin and piano only)
adheres reasonably closely to this model, although it is extended to six
bars from the paradigmatic four. This extension occurs because the
first bars of the basic idea and of the contrasting idea are each stretched
out to double their normal length (see Ex. 4.6c), seemingly by the melodic
violin, using a technique described by Johann Philipp Kirnberger
(see Ex. 4.7).[71] But the continuation/cadential segment (mm. 36–59, played
by all four instruments) is expanded beyond recognition, because of the
initial loss of cadential momentum and detour to G minor before the piano
ultimately emerges as concerto soloist to reinitiate the cadential process.

To be sure, it is typical for subordinate themes to be loosely knit and to
postpone their cadences, but the important point is that the process of
veering off and delaying in this passage can be understood through the

---

[70] Caplin designates this type as "Hybrid 1" (*Classical Form*, 59–61). A brief introduction to
sentences, periods, and hybrids is included in the "Notes on Sonata Form," provided among the
Web Resources.

[71] Kirnberger writes that "a phrase [*Einschnitt*] of four measures can be transformed into units
[*Rhythmen*] of five measures through the lengthening [*Verlängerung*] of certain principal notes
that are to be given a special emphasis" (ein Einschnitt von 4 Tackten durch Verlängerung
gewisser Haupttöne, auf denen ein besonderer Nachdruck soll gelegt werden, in Rhythmen von
5 Tackten verwandelt werden kann). Johann Philipp Kirnberger, *Die Kunst des reinen Satzes in
der Musik* (Berlin, 1776), vol. 2, pt. 1, 145. See also English translation in David Beach and
Jürgen Thym as *The Art of Strict Musical Composition* (New Haven: Yale University Press,
1982), 411. Whereas Kirnberger defines this technique in terms of lengthened *notes*, I have
extended his concept to lengthened (abstract) *tones* and *harmonies*. On notes vs. tones, see
above, 111 n. 1.

Ex. 4.6 (*cont.*)

b. Normalized model (antecedent plus continuation)

c. Expansion of basic idea and contrasting idea

Ex. 4.7 Phrase (*Einschnitt*) expansion through partial rhythmic augmentation (from Johann Philipp Kirnberger, *Die Kunst des reinen Satzes*, vol. 2, pt. 1 [Berlin, 1776], 146)

a. Four-bar model

b. Five-bar expansion

interplay among our cast of characters. This becomes clear when one considers events from the violin's perspective. Since the theme initially began in a duo-sonata texture, the violin might have expected this pair to complete a simple version on its own, which would subsequently be repeated (and likely extended) in a version by the full ensemble (similar to Ex. 4.5, from the Clarinet Quintet). What a surprise, then, when the violin is unable to see the initial statement through to completion and other instruments come to the fore, most notably the piano, who emerges as a concerto soloist! Since the first signs of "trouble" began in the bass line and were followed by those in the viola, this theme illustrates the importance of looking beyond the main melody for agential efficacy.

The analysis describes the characters' actions rather neutrally, without much speculation as to their motivations. A bolder version of this analysis might investigate the intentions of the piano, who initially proposes a theme to the violin (saying "why don't you tell us a nice story about this musical motive?") only to eclipse the violin and position herself as soloist. Such an interpretation might point to the piano's repeated deceptive resolutions (mm. 32 and 35) as initial signs of the piano's doubt or sabotage. The viola, with his F♯ in m. 40, might be taking advantage of a moment of hesitation in the violin's leadership, participating in an effort to oust the violin from a position of melodic dominance. As the viola emerges unexpectedly into a melodic position, he nearly manages to effect a G-minor cadence in m. 44, which would throw the theme quite a bit off course. More ambiguous is the motivation behind the piano's swerve to E♭ major at this juncture. On the one hand, this harmony prevents the viola from completing a gloomy, G-minor cadence. However, the piano's thematic presentation in E♭ major is also subversive act, since this theme ought not to appear in the global tonic key until the recapitulation. Furthermore, the harmony in m. 47, where the piano restores A♮ in the bass, has the potential to function as a predominant (specifically, secondary dominant) in E♭ major, before action is taken to correct the course back toward B♭ major by m. 52 (where the F dominant-seventh chord appears in root position). Nevertheless, I am reluctant to fully endorse this interpretation and am reticent to impute such devious motives and strategies to the piano. After all, the violin shows no signs of harbored ill feelings as he quite willingly supports the piano's final cadence in mm. 57–59 and proceeds to play a friendly duet with the piano immediately afterward (not shown in Ex. 4.6a). The multiple-agency perspective is well suited for explaining individual moments within a composition, but these moments may not always cohere into a comprehensible, continuous plot.

The interaction among the characters is highly stylized, lacking the explanatory story lines of opera. The identities of the fictional instrumental personas are less robust and less precisely defined than those of operatic characters.

The analysis of Ex. 4.6a prompts an additional theoretical clarification: There is not always a literal, one-to-one correspondence between the (fictional) personas and the (actual) instruments or instrumentalists. This is most obvious in cases of doublings within the part-writing. For instance, the cello's entire part in this example doubles the bass line in the piano's left hand, which indicates a lack of agential autonomy; statements about the "bass line" refer to a composite character encompassing both parts.[72] Furthermore, although the analysis describes the introduction of F♯ (m. 40) and C♯ (m. 41) as actions by the viola and violin, respectively, these notes are doubled in the piano's right-hand figuration. Does this indicate that the analysis is focused on abstract musical voices rather than literal parts? Not exactly, or at least not consistently. For instance, the analysis describes how the violin fails to resolve his C♯, prompting the viola to swoop in with his D (m. 42) in an effort to effect a G-minor cadence. This interpretation depends on the fact that C♯ and D are played by two different instruments, even though a Schenkerian voice-leading analysis would view them as a single, abstract voice.

An alternative solution for analyzing doublings would be to deem one part as primary and agential and the other as a passive doubler. This distinction could be made on the basis of salience criteria, considering such factors as register, timbre, status as *Hauptmelodie*, and continuity. For instance, the violin, as *Hauptmelodie*, occupies a privileged status and higher register relative to the piano's inner-voice C♯ (m. 41). The viola's F♯ (m. 40) is a more difficult case since it shares the piano's register and textural status; however, the onset of his F♯ precedes that of the piano and he holds the note more continuously, on account of his enhanced capacity for sustainment. Furthermore, the viola's timbral salience on this long note could be enhanced through vibrato, which would help him emerge into the melodic role two bars later. In other situations, an analyst may prefer to simply regard a pair of doubling voices as a kind of cohort (as with the cello and piano's left hand), without conferring privileged status onto either one.

---

[72] The cello and piano's left hand are, of course, longstanding colleagues from their traditional, doubled role in basso continuo practice. This doubling appears commonly in chamber music for piano and strings by Haydn and Mozart.

Another related issue arises from the treatment of the piano's two hands. While they, of course, belong to a single player, they may often be fruitfully regarded as separate characters.[73] The analysis of Ex. 4.6a adopts this perspective when it suggests that the piano's left hand is attempting to initiate a cadential progression in m. 36 (with upbeat), even as the piano's right hand provides a harmony that negates this effort. Subsequent analyses in this book will treat the two hands separately when there is a compelling reason to do so.[74]

However counterintuitive it may seem, it is even possible for the two hands to engage in a kind of friendly competition or *Wettstreit* (as described by Koch),[75] even though these two fictional characters are both realized by the same real-world musician. Let us examine this aspect in a passage from the first movement of Mozart's Sonata for Piano in A Minor, K. 310 (shown in Ex. 4.8).[76]

By the middle of m. 31, with the bass poised on $\hat{3}$, the stage is set for an expanded cadential progression to achieve expositional closure. As the predominant function lasts for two measures rather than one, the left hand shows his eagerness to proceed by adopting sixteenth-note figuration in m. 33, which he continues, Alberti style, over the dominant function in the following measure. The right hand supplies the conventional cadential trill, signaling that the expected cadence should occur on the downbeat of m. 35.

But no: When the downbeat arrives, the right hand elides her final note, a light-hearted trick that overturns the left hand's expectations and leaves the cadential process incomplete. A second cadential attempt is made in m. 39,

---

[73] This issue calls to mind C. P. E. Bach's publication in 1788 of three "quartets" for flute, viola, and clavier, H. 537–39, a designation that counts the piano's two hands separately.

[74] According to Anton Schindler (not always a trustworthy source), Beethoven conceived his op. 14 sonatas as dialogues between the pianist's two hands, which represent a man and his wife or lover and his mistress. Schindler holds that this characterization is "very forcibly expressed" in the opening of the Sonata in G Major, op. 14, no. 2, in which he claims Beethoven designated "the [right hand as] *entreating* and the [left hand as] *resisting* [emphasis in original]." Schindler adds that Beethoven's performance of his op. 14 sonatas "was a sort of musical declamation, in which the two principles were as distinctly separated as the two parts of a dialogue when recited by the flexible voice of a good speaker." Anton Schindler, *Biographie von Ludwig van Beethoven* (Münster, 1840), 224 and 229. English translation from Ignaz Moscheles, ed., *The Life of Beethoven* (London, 1841), 123 and 131. Schindler's discussion of op. 14 is partially excerpted in Carol MacClintock, ed., *Readings in the History of Music in Performance* (Bloomington: Indiana University Press, 1979), 385–88. See also Hatten, *Interpreting Musical Gestures, Topics, and Tropes*, 313 n. 44.

[75] See above, 36–40.

[76] For this analysis only, I will designate the left and right hands with male and female pronouns, respectively, to emphasize the multiple personas enacted by the single player.

Ex. 4.8 Mozart, Piano Sonata in A Minor, K. 310, Allegro maestoso (i), end of exposition

again with both hands' participation – the cadential bass line and the melodic trill – but this time it is the left hand who elides his final bass note on the downbeat of m. 40. Perhaps this elision was born of a desire to repeat the right hand's trick ("two can play at that game!"). This idea of swapping

Ex. 4.8 (*cont.*)

Cadence in both hands (but left hand in wrong register)

Left hand reaches
C (great octave)

roles continues with the material in mm. 40ff., in which the two hands exchange their parts from mm. 35ff.

Finally, by m. 44, it seems that both hands truly intend to cadence in earnest, their bolstered resolve signaled by their new, more extreme registers, leading to the completed cadence in m. 45. This arrival in the exposition's closing theme is marked by a reprise of primary-theme material (the dotted rhythm) in the right hand, while the characteristic sixteenth notes of the subordinate theme continue in the left. Although m. 45 is without a doubt a successful cadence, it has one slight defect: the bass note is c^1 rather than C (great octave), the bass note that would best complete the cadential bass line in the previous measure, given the octave leap from G to GG. Throughout the closing theme, as the left hand descends lower and lower, he finally achieves the missing C (great octave) in the final measure, an arrival marked by a triple hammerstroke.

Without the multiple-agency perspective, this passage could be interpreted rather neutrally as an example of what James Hepokoski and Warren Darcy call deferral of the essential expositional closure (EEC), that is, the postponement of the structural cadence that marks the end of the subordinate theme and the arrival of the closing theme.[77] However, the added attention to the interplay between the two hands, each of which is viewed as a sentient, volitional persona, renders the discussion far more vivid.

This analysis shows that the multiple-agency concept applies to a broader repertoire than the chamber music examined in this book. While the concept is inspired by the circumstances of playing one part per person and sight-reading, without access to full scores, multiple agency is not fully dependent on this literal premise. If it were, the spontaneous interplay among the characters would disappear the moment a piece is played for the second time – or, for that matter, with every expositional repeat.[78] The concept is instead robust enough to survive even the most trying scenario: a single player, whose score shows the complete texture, can still enact a right-hand persona that tricks and surprises that of the left hand.[79] If this is true, then there is hope that our own performances, in modern concert halls, can be infused with the same spirit of spontaneous interchange that players enjoyed sight-reading Mozart's brand-new works in Enlightenment salons. Though they are no longer new to us, though we certainly never sight-read in today's concert performances, the surprises of "the music of friends" are there to be enjoyed, again and again.

---

[77] See "Notes on Sonata Form" among the Web Resources for Chapter 5. I will discuss the concept of EEC and its potential for deferral in that chapter. Hepokoski and Darcy's discussion of this passage is in *Elements of Sonata Theory*, 170.

[78] Although I have emphasized the ubiquity of sight-reading in Mozart's musical world, David Lewin has persuasively argued that the experience of a musical present tense it not limited to the first hearing (or, *mutatis mutandis*, the first playing). See David Lewin, "Music Theory, Phenomenology, and Modes of Perception," in *Studies in Music with Text* (Oxford University Press, 2006), 53–108. On multiple hearings of the same piece, see also Edward T. Cone, "Three Ways of Reading a Detective Story – Or a Brahms Intermezzo," in *Music: A View from Delft*, ed. Robert P. Morgan (University of Chicago Press, 1989), 77–93.

[79] This very point has been argued by W. Dean Sutcliffe, who emphasizes that musical sociability does not depend on a literal exchange among individual players. In "The Shapes of Sociability," he analyzes a sociable interplay – specifically between an assertive opening gesture and the ensuing gracious riposte – drawing equally from solo-keyboard, small-ensemble, and orchestral examples. An effort to recast notions of musical sociability and to decouple them from traditional metaphors of conversation (especially in their most literal versions) has motivated Sutcliffe's significant contributions to this topic.

5 | Multiple agency and sonata form

The past two decades have seen tremendous advances in the analysis of sonata form. William Caplin's sophisticated recasting of Schoenbergian *Formenlehre* offers precise models and vocabulary for analyzing the internal structures of individual themes and their interthematic functions in complete movements.[1] Two major studies, by James Hepokoski and Warren Darcy[2] and by Janet Schmalfeldt,[3] offer notably dynamic, temporal accounts of what might be called the "experience" of musical form. Hepokoski and Darcy's Sonata Theory in particular is striking for its present-tense, in-time perspective, which resonates with the eighteenth-century sensibilities examined in Chapter 3. Their often richly hermeneutical language overtly invokes an agential or quasi-narratological perspective:

A sonata is a metaphorical representation of a perfect human action. It is a narrative "action" because it drives through a vectored sequence of energized events toward a clearly determined, graspable goal, the ESC [essential structural closure]. It is "perfect" because ... it typically accomplishes the task elegantly, proportionally, and completely. It is "human" primarily within eighteenth-century European conceptions of humanness. By "representation" we do not refer to the presence of unequivocal, concrete imagery or extramusical stories. Instead, the sense of representation in sonatas is for the most part suggestive, inlaid (as part of the sonata "game") into their chains of dramatic, linear modules, into their calculated impression of pulling insistently for attention at our sleeves, as if at some deeper level each of them must somehow also be "about" processes that are fundamental to Western European experience.[4]

Hepokoski and Darcy's "perfect human" actor is the sonata itself, what Monahan would call the work-persona (see above, 130–31). The "sonata game" refers to the hypothetical genesis of the composition through a

---

[1] Caplin, *Classical Form.*   [2] Hepokoski and Darcy, *Elements of Sonata Theory.*
[3] Schmalfeldt, *In the Process of Becoming.* This book is an expansion of Schmalfeldt's earlier article "Form as the Process of Becoming: The Beethoven-Hegelian Tradition and the Tempest Sonata," in *Beethoven Forum 4*, ed. Lewis Lockwood, Christopher Reynolds, and James Webster (Lincoln: University of Nebraska Press, 1995), 37–71.
[4] Hepokoski and Darcy, *Elements of Sonata Theory,* 252.

series of choices made by the composer (or *fictional* composer), so to speak, as the piece progresses, choosing at each juncture among a menu of possible continuation choices.[5] In short, such an analysis is essentially an imagined enactment of the sonata's improvisation.

In orthodox Sonata Theory, the sonata game is conceived as a form of solitaire, with all creative decisions made by the monolithic "Invisible Hand of the Composer." But what if we conceived of these choices as being made by the multiple agents within the composition? How could Sonata Theory be extended and enriched by shifting the focus from the unitary level of the fictional composer to that of the diverse instrumental characters who engage in dialogue not only with conventional defaults and norms *but also with one another*?

Of special analytical interest are passages in which these characters exhibit a capacity for agential independence, engaging at times in friendly interplay or mischievous intrigues that unfold through the musical discourse. These elements of rivalry among the instrumental personas recall Sulzer's description of a trio consisting of three instruments concerting *against* one another (*gegen einander concertiren*) and Koch's reference to concerting (*concertirend*) instruments as competing among themselves (*unter sich selbst ... wettstreiten*).[6] I distinguish such rivalries or one-upmanship among personas *within* a composition from what other scholars call "negactants," or elements interpreted as antagonists to the central work-persona itself.[7] As the characters play the "sonata game" together, I posit as given (for the purposes of this book) that none of them wishes the game itself to fail. All participants intend for the group to collectively achieve certain essential musical goals for each round of the game, even if temporary detours occasionally arise from some friendly competition (or even serious squabbles) that may arise along the way.

---

[5] Ibid., 606–7. Whereas the notion of composition as a "game" has many eighteenth-century antecedents (see above, 15 n. 23), Hepokoski and Darcy also use an alternate metaphor that is highly anachronistic yet in many ways apt: "For novice-composers, one might wittily fantasize – provided that the image is not taken too literally – something on the order of an aggressively complex 'wizard' help feature within a late-eighteenth-century musical computer application, prompting the still-puzzled apprentice with a welter of numerous, successive dialog boxes of general information, tips, pre-selected weighted options, and strong, generically normative suggestions as the act of composition proceeded" (ibid., 10).

[6] See above, 36–40.

[7] See discussion of "negactants" in Monahan, "Action and Agency Revisited," 328–29 and 343–44. The term was introduced into musical scholarship by Eero Tarasti (*A Theory of Musical Semiotics* [Bloomington: Indiana University Press, 1994]), who borrowed it from A. J. Greimas.

This chapter examines form in two movements by Mozart from the perspective of the interacting characters within each work. Although both analyses place some emphasis on actions required to achieve the essential expositional closure (EEC), a concept drawn from Hepokoski and Darcy's Sonata Theory, I also draw from Caplin's theory of formal functions. In this chapter, I do not wish to directly enter the debate about these two theories, which, for all their significant points of departure, can nevertheless offer a rich account when used in tandem.[8] I will therefore use certain corresponding terms synonymously, although I remain fully aware that their respective meanings are not identical. This pluralism offers an advantage for our present goal: to imagine how all theories of sonata form could be fruitfully expanded by adopting a multiple-agency vantage point. It is my hope that readers who are strongly committed to any particular formal model (including traditional "textbook" approaches) will not be deterred by this terminological and conceptual commingling.

For the benefit of readers unfamiliar with recent approaches to sonata form, a brief primer entitled "Notes on Sonata Form" is provided among the Web Resources. It introduces all of the important concepts and terms used throughout this chapter and may serve as helpful preliminary reading.

Multiple agency and the EEC: Sonata for Piano and Violin in E Minor, K. 304, Allegro (exposition only) ▶

In any sonata-form exposition, a principal tonal goal is to achieve a perfect authentic cadence (PAC) in the secondary key area. This first, successful PAC in the new key is often so laden with structural and rhetorical import that Hepokoski and Darcy have dubbed it the "essential expositional closure" (EEC), forming the point of demarcation between the spaces of the subordinate and closing themes;[9] their EEC corresponds broadly to Koch's *Schlußsatz*, which is likewise a structurally significant, new-key

---

[8] A thorough examination of the interface among recent approaches to sonata form is William E. Caplin, James Hepokoski, and James Webster, *Musical Form, Forms, and* Formenlehre: *Three Methodological Reflections*, ed. Pieter Bergé (Leuven University Press, 2009). Another lucid, comparative critique is Markus Neuwirth, "Joseph Haydn's 'Witty' Play on Hepokoski and Darcy's *Elements of Sonata Theory*," *Zeitschrift der Gesellschaft für Musiktheorie* 8, no. 1 (2011): 199–220.

[9] Hepokoski and Darcy, *Elements of Sonata Theory*, 120–31. These authors cite Rothstein as the first modern scholar to identify the importance of the *first* PAC in the subordinate key area. See Rothstein, *Phrase Rhythm in Tonal Music*, 116–17.

cadence that completes the essential part of the exposition prior to the optional appendix (*Anhang*).[10] Hepokoski and Darcy describe the EEC as both *hard-won* and *fragile*, since it is often achieved with effort or through multiple attempts and since events that follow a plausible EEC candidate can mitigate or even cancel its effect, necessitating one or more subsequent PACs to close the exposition more decisively:

> To be sure, the first-PAC rule is more of a guideline than a "rule"; it is anything but inflexible. Composers devised a number of strategies to override that implication – in other words, to demonstrate that the first PAC was being reopened – and to defer the EEC to the next PAC by means of immediate thematic repetition or variation, the continuation of an accompaniment figure, the later placement of a nonelided cadence, and the like.[11]

These techniques of deferral lead to their full definition of EEC as *the first successful new-key PAC that moves on to new material.*

When an attempted EEC is deferred, whose action effects the deferral? One could reformulate the notion of deferral from a multiple-agency perspective as follows: If one party (an instrument or group of instruments) attempts to effect the EEC prematurely, it is possible for another party to "cancel" the effect retroactively using such means as immediate thematic repetition, accompanimental continuation, or cadential elision. An attempted EEC can likewise be thwarted preemptively if some party (usually melody or bass) interferes with the cadential formula, substituting either a different note (as in the deceptive cadences of Ex. 4.6) or a rest (as illustrated in the cadential elisions of Ex. 4.8). Even a keyboard instrument, which has the harmonic capacity to make a cadence on her own, will rarely present the EEC unilaterally in any chamber work, since conventional decorum requires that all parties "consent" to a structural cadence, either by participating in it directly (as in Ex. 4.5, mm. 61–65)[12] or, as often happens in sonatas or concerto-style works, by endorsing the cadence in an immediate repetition.[13]

---

[10] Koch, *Versuch*, 3:304–6. See English translation in *Introductory Essay*, 210.

[11] Hepokoski and Darcy, *Elements of Sonata Theory*, 123. See also ibid., Ch. 8 (pp. 150–79), which takes up the topic of EEC deferral in detail.

[12] An exception that proves the rule is the Adagio from Mozart's Sonata for Piano and Violin in G Major, K. 379. The subordinate theme (mm. 20–31) is a loose-knit sentence played almost exclusively by the keyboard; the violin enters briefly to support the second statement of the basic idea with sustained harmonic filler (mm. 22–24). The violin then drops out for the entire cadential process, only to re-enter for the brief closing theme (mm. 31–33). Such a scanty use of the violin, at least in the Adagio, marks this as a duo sonata of a particular kind.

[13] This procedure – whereby the solo piano makes a cadence on her own and the *ripieno* strings repeat the cadence – resembles Hepokoski and Darcy's notion of "tutti affirmation," discussed in *Elements of Sonata Theory*, 113–14. Sutcliffe likewise points to the involvement of

That the achievement of expositional closure within a chamber work involves interplay among multiple parties raises the possibility that various characters will pursue different strategies as to where, how, and under what terms it should be achieved. Even once an exposition has ended, they may retrospectively hold different views about precisely where the EEC occurred or who deserves credit for this important accomplishment. In such cases, although an analyst may be tempted to arbitrate as to whose interpretation is "correct" (serving as what Carl Schachter might call the Commissar of Expositional Closure),[14] it may be more fruitful to interrogate the various participants' motivations and where each would consider the EEC to have occurred.

From this multiple-agency perspective, let us examine the path to the EEC in the first movement of Mozart's Sonata in E Minor for Piano and Violin, K. 304 (shown in Ex. 5.1), an early work that was composed in Paris, possibly in connection with the sudden death of the composer's mother.[15] The piece begins with a plaintive, E-minor theme in Baroque style – like a melody in the manner of a bass line,[16] as in "The People that Walked in Darkness" from Handel's *Messiah* – introduced in bare, unison octaves (mm. 1–12) and then restated by the violin with piano accompaniment (mm. 13–20). The serious mood continues as the piano plays a codetta to the primary theme (mm. 20–28). Although the piano part for the codetta is self-sufficient, the violin adds two significant elements: the pedal tones and the Neapolitan-tinged "commentary" figures. These pedal tones are the second time the violin has assumed a bass role, the first being the shared bass of the unison opening; his encroachment on the usual business of the piano's left hand foretells later events. Also in the codetta, the violin's semitone "commentary" figures (mm. 23–24 and 27–28), evoking a conventional symbol of pain, intensify the harmony by

all parties in significant cadences in string quartets by Haydn and Mozart. He describes "heavily elaborated cadence points, *often featuring a distinctive contribution from an inner part* [emphasis added]" as a way of "affirming ... that there are four individuals involved" and "enact[ing] the balance between individual consciousness and social obligation that is part of any conversational ethos." Sutcliffe, "Haydn, Mozart, and Their Contemporaries," 187–88.

[14] Cf. Carl Schachter's "Commissar of Metrics," fleetingly postulated in his "Rhythm and Linear Analysis: Aspects of Meter," in *Unfoldings: Essays in Schenkerian Theory and Analysis*, ed. Joseph N. Straus (Oxford University Press, 1999), 101.

[15] Several of this sonata's features suggest a serious character, including its minor mode (unique among Mozart's sonatas for keyboard and violin) and most notably the lament topic of the second movement.

[16] The melodic figure that ends the first phrase (mm. 7–8) is a conventional cadential bass-line formula: $\hat{3}$-$\hat{4}$-$\hat{5}$-$\hat{5}$-$\hat{1}$.

Ex. 5.1 Mozart, Sonata in E Minor for Piano and Violin, K. 304, Allegro (i), exposition ▶

Unison opening

Codetta:

Violin contributes pedal tones and Neapolitan-tinged "commentary"

transforming the piano's would-be subdominant chords into the more poignant Neapolitan harmonies.

But the piano summarily casts off the tragic tone as her *forte* chords (m. 29) herald the arrival of the brief transition and usher the sonata into

Ex. 5.1 (*cont.*)

Forte chords herald transition; piano comes to the fore

Piano leads subordinate theme; violin adds *leggiero* "commentary"

Shift to minor; violin's agency?

Piano dismisses violin's doubts, restores major, and demonstrates a simple path to EEC

Piano evades cadence... inviting violin to join for one-more-time repetition

Lovebirds' duet (mostly parallel tenths)

the world of *opera buffa*. Even the conventional break for the medial caesura (m. 36) is smoothed over by the violin's caesura-fill eighth notes, which continue as a *leggiero* accompaniment while the piano introduces the subordinate theme (m. 37).[17] With such a smooth path to G major, one might expect an easy route to cadential closure, which would solidify the exposition's triumph of G major (and its attendant *buffa* topic) over E minor (and its serious, Baroque-inspired thematic materials).

At this point, one could speculate that the violin has a more pessimistic temperament than the piano, since the violin played a leading role in much of the E-minor music, whereas the piano came to the fore in the major-mode transition and subordinate theme. That characterization is indeed strengthened when, shortly after the subordinate theme gets underway, the violin answers to the piano's G-major presentation statement (mm. 37–40) in the parallel minor (mm. 41–44).[18] The piano, unfazed, dismisses the violin's doubts out of hand by restoring the major mode and instigating an expanded cadential progression (mm. 45ff.), as if to show the violin a simple path to completing the theme as a loosely knit compound sentence and to achieving the EEC; this demonstration is replete with a celebratory cadential trill (m. 50). However, since decorum forbids the piano from making the EEC alone, she evades the cadence with a V_2^4 harmony (m. 50), ushering in a one-more-time repetition to invite the violin to join in the cadential action.

The violin accepts the invitation, joining the piano in melodic octaves (mm. 51–52) and in the homorhythmic, *leggiero* gestures that (mostly) form parallel tenths (mm. 53–56), a conventional operatic symbol of love or agreement. But lest the two lovebirds become too absorbed in their own private moment, the piano's left hand – seemingly acting as a third character, perhaps a blustering busybody *à la* Dr. Bartolo – barges in *subito forte* (m. 56), providing a comically urgent reminder that the cadential progression remains stalled on the predominant harmony and needs to continue.[19] All parties seem to be in accord as the piano makes a jubilant cadence (m. 59), vigorously accompanied by the violin.

---

[17] Although the same "tune" appears in mm. 29–30 and in mm. 33–34, these occupy the transition. Only in m. 37, with the subordinate theme, does a stable, G-major thematic presentation commence.

[18] An alternative hearing would hold that the piano, not the violin, instigates the shift to the minor mode, since the piano introduces the pitch B♭ (m. 41) before the violin introduces the pitch E♭ (m. 42). The issue is similar to Ex. 4.5 since, in both cases (1) a major-mode theme is inflected to minor precisely as a new melodic soloist repeats it, but (2) the first minor-inflected note appears in the accompaniment.

[19] On the possibility of interpreting the piano's hands as two separate characters, see above, 152–55.

The EEC has been achieved ... or has it? The violin immediately disturbs the nascent cadence, shaking the putative EEC with his insistent, syncopated open Ds (mm. 59ff.). Whereas a successful EEC usually entails a pointed change in texture, the violin's syncopations sustain an accompaniment figure over the cadential boundary, albeit with a heightened articulation and slight change of rhythmic notation.[20] Moreover, the cadence is susceptible to retroactive weakening on account of the short duration of the piano's cadential bass note, the quarter-note G on the downbeat of m. 59. In the *alla breve* meter of the movement, the violin's syncopations disturb the cadence before it has settled for a full, half-note beat.[21] Furthermore, once the piano's bass drops out, the violin's Ds emerge as the lowest-sounding voice for several measures, and this usurpation of the bass role and register leaves the ensuing tonic prolongation to unfold over a weaker, quasi-$^6_4$ sonority.[22] In spite of the piano's efforts to bring about a cadence in G major with her colleague's cooperation, the violin wastes no time in undermining the cadence and its bid to close the exposition. This juncture recalls earlier moments in which the violin had assumed a bass role, either alongside the piano (at the movement's opening) or alone (with the pedal tones of mm. 20–22 and 24–26).

But while the violin is occupied with attempting to subvert the cadence in m. 59, the piano nevertheless acts as though the EEC has been successfully achieved. Her reuse of eighth-note figures based on mm. 8–12 shows that she believes it is already time for the closing theme, where primary-theme materials commonly recur.[23] This, then, is the moment of maximum formal dissonance: the piano is convinced that a satisfactory EEC has occurred, even as the violin strives to unmake the cadence with his self-absorbed syncopations.[24] The conflict is not sustainable. As the tension

---

[20] As noted above, Hepokoski and Darcy mention the continuation of an accompanimental figure as a device that can defer a would-be EEC. See *Elements of Sonata Theory*, 123.

[21] On the exceptional nature of cadences with such brief closing chords, see Carl Schachter, "Rhythm and Linear Analysis: A Preliminary Study," in *Unfoldings*, 25.

[22] Although the violin's d¹ pedal notes (mm. 59ff.) are an octave higher than the piano's cadential bass notes (small octave d and g, mm. 57–59), it should be noted that the violin is playing his lowest-available D. After the piano's left hand drops out, although the bass *tone* G is retained abstractly for the ensuing tonic prolongation, the literal *note* G is absent in the bass register, resulting in the impression of a quasi-$^6_4$ chord.

[23] Hepokoski and Darcy discuss the "rounding effect" of what they call a "P-based C," that is, one in which primary-theme-based material is recovered in the closing theme. *Elements of Sonata Theory*, 184–85.

[24] The momentary switch of parts between the violin and piano (right hand) in mm. 63–64 is a generic duo-sonata technique, and is difficult to account for in terms of the characters I have posited in this analysis.

builds, the violin repeats his syncopation gesture, now with insistent octaves (mm. 65–66), until the passage erupts into a deceptive resolution, with the piano shockingly stating the second-theme motive in E minor (mm. 67–68), the original key and the very last place the sonata ought to be at this juncture. What began as benign stubbornness or indifference on the violin's part (mm. 59ff.) now threatens to endanger the exposition's ability to break free of its original key.[25]

Still, the piano maintains composure (as indicated by the *piano* marking and the textural simplicity), and shows how to set things right by making a tidy cadence in G major using three simple harmonies (II^6–V^7–I, mm. 69–70). Of course this cadence by the piano alone cannot suffice. Once again, the cadence is interrupted after just a quarter note as the violin and piano repeat it together (mm. 70–73), now in full cooperation, to make the expositional closure complete. Perhaps in deference to the violin, the piano's right hand plays an octave lower this time, allowing the violin to carry the melodic line into the cadence.[26] Compared to the flamboyance of the piano's previous attempts to cadence in G major (mm. 45ff. and especially mm. 51ff.), the cadence in m. 73 is notable for its simplicity and clarity.

The violin obliges in turn, providing a rich tonic pedal to consummate the cadential arrival. This open-G pedal may be heard as a foil to the earlier dominant pedal (m. 59), in which the violin's *agitato* syncopations strove to undermine the piano's attempted EEC. Whereas the violin's open-D pedal constituted a bass statement that excluded the piano's left hand, the open-G pedal in mm. 73–76 is shared with the piano,[27] reflecting their mutual affirmation of expositional closure.

---

[25] Cf. Ex. 4.6, which likewise tonicizes the global tonic during the subordinate theme. Such tonicizations can signify that an exposition is "off course" since the subordinate theme ought not to be heard in the global tonic until the recapitulation.

[26] This is an inversion of the typical arrangement for unison or homorhythmic passages in Mozart's duo sonatas for piano and violin; cf. mm. 51–56 and mm. 63–64, where the piano is in the higher register. To that end, mm. 1–8 are also exceptional, since the violin is higher than the piano's right hand; in this case, the reason is because each part (including the piano's right hand) is playing in its lowest register, reflecting the "bass-line" topic (see above, 160).

[27] Throughout this passage, Daniel Gottlob Türk would advise the pianist to hold the Gs in the left hand for the duration of each slur, which bolsters the sense of tonic pedal. Daniel Gottlob Türk, *Klavierschule* (Leipzig, 1789), 355. See also English translation in *School of Clavier Playing*, trans. Raymond H. Haggh (Lincoln: University of Nebraska Press, 1982), 344–45.

The role of thematic events in sonata form: Piano Quartet in E♭ Major, K. 493, Larghetto ▶

The seeds of the debate over how to conceptualize sonata form – in terms of cadential punctuation or thematic design – were sown even before the form had a name. Since Leonard Ratner's revival of Koch's punctuation-based model, the pendulum has swung toward emphasizing the achievement of cadential goals as the central, form-defining principle.[28] Nevertheless, melodic ideas (sometimes called "themes" in the old-fashioned sense of that word) interact with cadential requirements of punctuation form, and a complete account of the sonata-form experience must fully integrate these aspects as well.[29]

Caplin defines the term "theme" as follows: "A unit consisting of a conventional set of initiating, medial, and ending intrathematic functions. It must close with a cadence."[30] This precise definition breaks from eighteenth-century notions of *Thema* in several respects, notably by broadening the concept beyond its melodic aspects and by requiring cadential closure. A theme is far more than just the main "tune" of a movement or section; it is the sum total of the musical material that transpires from an initiating function to the subsequent cadential function, encompassing not only melodic ideas (sometimes several), but also bass lines, harmonies, textures, and so on.

Caplin's definition of theme, whereby a cadence is an essential component, helps to reconcile the longstanding dialectic of melodic vs. tonal criteria for form analysis, since themes are understood to be the very

---

[28] Ratner, *Classic Music*. Leonard Ratner first called for a revival of what he called a "harmonic" model of form, inspired by Koch, several decades earlier in an article entitled "Harmonic Aspects of Classic Form," *Journal of the American Musicological Society* 11 (1949): 159–68. More recent scholarship, recognizing the form-defining role of cadences, has introduced the modern locution "punctuation form" as a cognate of Koch's "Interpunction" and "interpunctisch." Carl Dahlhaus used the related term "Interpunktische Form" (e.g. in Dahlhaus, "Der rhetorische Formbegriff H. Chr. Kochs und die Theorie der Sonatenform," *Archiv für Musikwissenschaft* 35, no. 3 [1978]: 155–77), and the term entered English-language usage in a series of publications on Mozart's piano concertos by Karol Berger, beginning with "The Second-Movement Punctuation Form in Mozart's Piano Concertos: The Andantino of K. 449," *Mozart-Jahrbuch* (1992): 168–72.

[29] Rosen perceptively critiques both exclusively thematic and exclusively tonal models of sonata form: "The isolation of the harmonic structure, while an advance over a basically thematic definition of 'sonata form,' is . . . generally unsatisfactory . . . [since] themes are absurdly seen as subsidiary – decorations added to emphasize, or even to hide, a more basic structure." Rosen, *The Classical Style*, 33.

[30] Caplin, *Classical Form*, 257.

agents that establish the requisite cadences of punctuation form. To use a traveling metaphor, if the cadences required by punctuation form are milestones and resting points within a long journey, the themes (as defined by Caplin) are the paths by which these subsidiary destinations are reached.[31] Even Hepokoski and Darcy's Sonata Theory, which is heavily influenced by Koch's punctuation model of form, emphasizes the role that melodic signals play in defining a cadence's structural meaning; for instance, their definition of EEC as the first satisfactory PAC in the subordinate key *that moves on to new melodic material* uses melodic markers to interpret the significance of a cadence in the overall form.

In the following analysis of the Larghetto movement from Mozart's Piano Quartet in E♭ Major, K. 493, I will draw particular attention to the interactions between the piano and the string cohort, and how these characters use specific melodic ideas to help achieve major cadential goals. Specifically, the characters seem to struggle to achieve the EEC using the movement's main thematic materials, running into detours and false starts at every turn until a new musical idea is introduced specifically to achieve this purpose.

As an aside: Throughout this A♭-major movement, the note G♭ frequently appears in passages that are rhetorically marked and that impact the shape of the form. I will make note of these throughout and will provide an overview of "the adventures of a G♭" at the end of the chapter in Fig. 5.1.[32]

Thematic breakthrough in the exposition (K. 493)

One of just a handful of movements that Mozart wrote in the key of A♭ major,[33] the Larghetto begins with a richly voiced (*vollstimmig*) tonic

[31] Cf. Hepokoski and Darcy, who describe a sonata as "a linear journey of tonal realization, onto which might be mapped any number of concrete metaphors of human experience. Since a central component of the sonata genre is its built-in teleological drive – pushing forward to accomplish a generically predetermined goal – the sonata invites an interpretation as a musically narrative genre." Hepokoski and Darcy, *Elements of Sonata Theory*, 251.

[32] I borrow this phrase (and pitch class) from Carl Schachter, "The Adventures of an F-Sharp: Tonal Narration and Exhortation in Donna Anna's First-Act Recitative and Aria," in *Unfoldings*, 221–35. See also Patrick McCreless, "The Pitch-Class Motive in Tonal Analysis: Some Critical Observations," *Res Musica* 3 (2011): 52–67.

[33] A conservative composer in terms of key choice, Mozart seldom composed in keys with more than three sharps or flats. Useful comparisons could be made between this movement and the second movement of his String Divertimento in E♭ Major, K. 563, which is a stormy, flat-laden movement in A♭ major. Several late-eighteenth-century authors described dark, severe associations for the key of A♭ major, among them Abbé Vogler ("the Plutonian realm"), Christian Friedrich Schubart ("the key of the grave") and Justin Heinrich Knecht ("black like the night"). See Rita Katherine Steblin, *Key Characteristics in the Eighteenth and Early Nineteenth Centuries*, 2nd ed. (University of Rochester Press, 2002), 115–28.

Ex. 5.2 Mozart, Piano Quartet in E♭ Major, K. 493, Larghetto (ii), exposition ▶

Presentation of "piano" idea

New presentation of "strings" idea,
piano "commentary" on alternate measures

Piano "commentary" comes
to the fore; strings defer

Strings' presentation of "piano"
idea, viola introduces G♭

Continuation/cadential segment
begins, but piano makes deceptive
resolution after strings drop out

Ex. 5.2 (*cont.*)

Rich I⁶ chord suggests potential for cadence

Piano stops on tentative harmony   Breakthrough idea   Piano joins in full communion ...

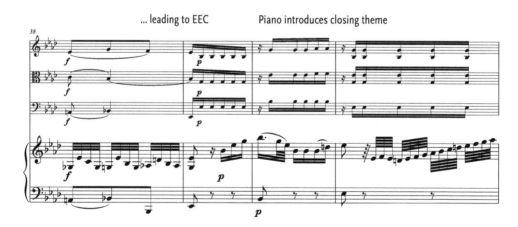

... leading to EEC   Piano introduces closing theme

chord in the piano, heralding a four-bar solo statement that comprises the presentation segment of a would-be sentence (hereafter, the "piano" idea). Although the piano politely invites the strings in (with the left hand's upbeat lead-in to m. 5), the strings opt to reject her statement, responding not with the expected continuation/cadential segment needed to complete the sentential theme but with a new presentation of a different basic idea (mm. 5–8, the "strings" idea). The new material has little to do with the piano idea beyond sharing its rhythm. Still less geared to coherence is that the strings never quite manage to complete their theme either; although they do *stop* on the downbeat of m. 9, they drop out before their theme has reached its *end*.[34] Compared to the assured confidence of the piano's original presentation is the strings' more tentative presentation, which is characterized by slower harmonic rhythm and simplified harmonic vocabulary. (The strings' harmony consists of alternating I and V_5^6 chords, with a slight intensification as the viola adds the note G♭ in m. 7 – the first of many significant G♭s throughout the movement.)

Why do the strings allow their nascent theme to stop prematurely, without bringing it to a cadence? Do they somehow lose their train of thought, unable to muster the energy to continue? Or perhaps they are edged out of the limelight by the piano's soaring commentary embellishing the V_5^6 chords in mm. 6 and 8. It is as if the descanting piano is so

---

[34] On the distinction between "stopping" and "ending," see Caplin, *Classical Form*, 51.

captivated by her own asides that she cannot stop herself, and the strings defer (even though it is supposed to be their "turn"). The piano's statement in mm. 9–10 stands as a kind of truncated continuation to the strings' presentation (in the sense that the piano achieves a half cadence). But it is telling that the piano's statement does not develop the strings' basic idea in any way and is instead based on her own thirty-second-note commentary figures, perhaps an indication of her self-absorption.

With their next entrance (m. 11), the strings redouble their efforts but this time have recourse to the piano idea, which is restated with a considerably intensified harmonization. In particular, the viola's piercing G♭ (m. 11) heightens the tonicization of the II harmony; compared to the milder tonicization in the piano's version, the strings express a greater urgency by underscoring the cadential predominant, suggesting a heightened desire to lead to a conclusive cadence. This sense of increased urgency is also established by the accelerated harmonic rhythm and heightened activity level in the accompanying voices (compared to the piano's homorhythmic version), suggesting exertion, struggle, or even agitation on the viola and cello's part.[35]

As the passage continues, it seems that the cello in particular has the foresight that is needed to help move the form along. Whereas the violin and viola parts in m. 14 could have been harmonized as part of a tonic harmony, the cello seems to know that this would be redundant with m. 4 and, instead, effects a deceptive cadence, which he emphasizes by tonicizing VI. Again, agency for this tonicization can be ascribed specifically to the cello, since the act of raising its E♭ to E♮ produces the tonicization, decisively eliminating the possibility of an authentic resolution on the next downbeat.[36] This deceptive cadence is significant in the movement's form since the submediant harmony serves as a convenient pivot chord toward the dominant key area, the exposition's ultimate tonal goal. The cello even shows that he is aware of this fact with

---

[35] It is open to interpretation whether the strings are best understood purely as a unified cohort or whether it is the viola and cello specifically who intensify the piano's original version of the theme, since they are the instruments responsible for the reharmonization. That is, it is possible that the violin might expect a harmonization similar to mm. 1–4, only to be surprised by the new harmonies that occur instead. In performance, the viola and cello could bring their sixteenth notes to the fore to heighten the *agitato* friction that their parts make against the violin.

[36] If the cello had instead held his E♭ throughout the end of the bar, it would have formed a V^7 harmony with the upper parts, a more conventional harmonization that the violin and viola most likely would have expected, and that could have led to a PAC on the next downbeat.

the lead-in he plays into m. 15, which arpeggiates a V^7 harmony in the dominant key (and invites the piano to enter, returning the same courtesy that the piano had extended leading into m. 5).

With the exposition having firmly arrived in the dominant key area, the piano enters (m. 15) with a version of the strings idea, adapted to be presented over a dominant pedal, and with the violin playing the commentary figures on alternate measures, a reversal of roles from the first appearance of this idea. In contrast with the strings' original presentation of this idea (wherein they were unable to progress to a "normal" continuation since the piano had cut them off), the piano's presentation (mm. 15–18) flows naturally into the continuation/cadential segment (mm. 19–22). Having arrived at a I^6 harmony in m. 20, the piano seems poised on the cusp of an expanded cadential progression that could achieve expositional closure, and the heightened anticipation of this moment is intensified by the melody's bold leap to a climactic register (eb^3).[37] But at the last instant (m. 22), the piano steers the phrase toward a deceptive cadence instead.

Why would the piano make a deceptive cadence at this juncture, when expositional closure had appeared to be so close at hand? First of all, in general terms, subordinate themes tend to be looser than primary ones and to delay or postpone the cadence several times before it is ultimately completed; simply put, an EEC at this juncture would have seemed "too soon," throwing the exposition out of proportion. Beyond this generic explanation, there are also some additional clues specific to this piece. For instance, even if the piano had completed a PAC in m. 22, she would have made the cadence entirely by herself, with no participation from the strings, who had dropped out two bars before. Questions would therefore linger about whether the strings had fully accepted a cadence made by the piano alone, and the cadence would require subsequent repetitions by the strings for reinforcement.

It may seem odd that the strings break off in the middle of the continuation segment of the phrase, which is usually an uninterrupted,

---

[37] This melodic high point is striking because of the ways it contradicts convention. That is, in the continuation segment of this sentence, the falling sixth of the basic idea is transformed into a falling fifth (as in m. 19). Using the conventional techniques of fragmentation and melodic sequence, the piano could have followed suit in m. 20, with a falling fifth from bb^2 to eb^2. Instead, the piano actively chooses to transfer the Eb to a higher register, an impressive "reaching" gesture that underscores the exalted potential of this moment to lead to the cadential closure in the subordinate key. (This same pitch – eb^3 – had been anticipated previously, in m. 9, though its later iteration in m. 20 has a stronger rhetorical impact.)

Ex. 5.3 Recomposition of mm. 19–22

four-measure unit. In so doing, they leave the piano exposed in an uncom-
fortably weak position, with both of her hands in the treble register.[38]
As the cello had been doubling the bass line since m. 15, the piano would
have expected the strings to continue their support for a strong cadence, as
Ex. 5.3 (a recomposition of mm. 19–22) shows. Instead, when the piano is
abandoned by the strings and left alone in a weak register, it is understandable why she would be reluctant to proceed to a PAC.[39]

   The strings' reticence to support the piano through the end of the phrase
can also be understood as symptomatic of a larger issue, namely, a certain
stiffness or formality in the piano and strings' interactions throughout the
movement so far. Up to this point, there has been a loose pattern of
alternating entries by piano and strings at intervals of about four measures
(with some deviations and extensions, such as the piano completing the
strings' first entrance). Texturally, these two groups have remained, for the
most part, very distinct.[40] There have been, for example, no instances of

[38] It might be objected that the piano's left hand is in an adequately low register to supply a bass
line and, in fact, that a listener is not aware of whether it is notated in treble or bass clef.
However, if our analytical method is inspired by the perspective of musicians playing in time off
of individual parts, then the notated clef is significant to the subjective experience of the pianist.
Simply put, if the pianist feels that she is in a weak position to make a cadence, this is relevant to
her psychological state in this passage.

[39] The cello's change of register in m. 19 – where he joins the piano's left hand at pitch
after previously doubling it an octave lower – may prefigure his premature exit in m. 20, on
the I⁶ chord that, potentially, could have initiated a progression to a successful cadence.
Since the cello's erstwhile low register facilitated the piano's playing with both hands in the
treble range, his shift to a higher register could be heard as a withdrawal of bass-line
support.

[40] This division between piano and strings can only partly be attributed to the concerto-like
features of this piece. In both of Mozart's piano quartets, the division between soloist and
ripieno is the sharpest in the finales but somewhat less pronounced in the slow movements. In
the first movement of K. 493 in particular, the distribution of material among all parts is

close counterpoint or parallel-thirds duets between the piano and any of the individual strings.[41] Even when the piano and violin have made commentary during each other's melodies (the piano in mm. 6ff. and the violin in mm. 16ff.), the commentary has been composed of material that contrasts with the main melody, rather than being a direct, mutually engaged conversation (although this will change later in the movement, notably in the recapitulation).

Most unusually, each successive entrance by the piano or strings up to this point has consistently "changed the subject" – that is, has entered with an idea that contrasts with the one just stated, suggesting some kind of obstacle or barrier to cooperation. This finally changes, however, with the strings' entrance in m. 23, which is the first time that the strings enter with the same material as the piano's previous entrance (m. 15). There is a harmonic continuity as well; whereas the piano's statement had begun with motion toward a cadence in E♭ major but swerved toward C minor for a deceptive cadence, the strings' statement begins with continued tonicization of C minor (mm. 23–24) and then "reverses course" to E♭ major (mm. 25–26). The exuberance of the arrival on E♭ in m. 26 – the first appearance of a root-position local tonic in the subordinate key area – is underscored by the depth of the cello register. The cello's E♭ (great octave), the lowest pitch in the movement so far, could be intended to compensate for its withholding of bass-line support in mm. 21–22. Since a strictly sequential bass line would have placed this pitch one octave higher (as in Ex. 5.4), the use of the lower register appears as a specific initiative of the cello.

Emboldened by the strings, the piano enters (m. 27) with a stunningly rich, eight-note I^6 chord (recalling the sonority of m. 1), once again poised to initiate an expanded cadential progression. In terms of texture, it is notable how seamlessly the piano connects to the cello's bass register and rhythm. For the first time, the hand-off from strings to piano feels like a true continuation rather than a new beginning; one can sense this continuity by comparing mm. 23–27 with the slight recomposition shown in Ex. 5.4. With this newfound cooperation, momentum, and sheer sonic

considerably more equitable than in any of Mozart's piano concerti (see analysis of Ex. 4.6 above, 144–51). As for the present movement, I will discuss details in the recapitulation that suggest an evolving, progressively more intimate relationship between piano and strings.

[41] So far, the only obvious example of direct conversation can be found in the aforementioned lead-in figures, whereby the piano invites the strings (upbeat to m. 5) and the cello later invites the piano (upbeat to m. 15). This figure is suggestive of a relatively formulaic, standard courtesy extended among polite company, rather than a more spontaneous, intimate interaction.

Ex. 5.4 Recomposition of mm. 23–27

weight, it would appear that expositional closure must surely be at hand. When the strings once again drop out so close to the cadence (m. 29, coinciding with the *subito piano*), the piano tries a new tactic, stopping the phrase in m. 31 on V_3^4 of IV as a musical dare to the strings. In expressing this harmony, the piano introduces the pitch D♭ ($♭\hat{7}$ in the local key) to match the viola's G♭ from m. 7 and m. 11 ($♭\hat{7}$ in the original key). Just as the viola had originally used that note to intensify the tonicization of a predominant chord in hopes of making a cadence, here too the piano tonicizes the subdominant as a means to induce the strings to complete the phrase.[42]

The strings accept the piano's challenge, entering in m. 32 with a new idea, which I will call the "breakthrough" idea, whispered in *pianissimo*. This idea picks up almost the same harmony that the piano had just ended with,[43] demonstrating the strings' earnest effort to foster continuity. The chorale texture of this material may suggest a hymn or prayer topic,[44]

[42] It is instructive to compare the piano's different reactions to the two instances in which the strings prematurely dropped out as a cadence in E♭ major was imminent. In mm. 21–22, the piano steered the phrase toward a deceptive cadence, allowing the phrase to end and the potential for an authentic cadence to fully dissipate. But this time (mm. 30–31), the piano does not give up so easily, and the piano's V_3^4 of IV is not a phrase ending but merely a stopping point, intended specifically to invite the strings in so they can lead the way to a cadence.

[43] That is, the strings' VII⁶ of IV contains three of the four notes of the piano's V_3^4 of IV, with the outer-voice pitches retained. Tellingly, it is the viola specifically that picks up the piano's D♭, the linchpin of the piano's musical "dare" that was offered in response to the viola's G♭ from m. 11.

[44] By "chorale texture," I do not refer literally to the syllabic settings of Lutheran practice. Rather, I borrow this usage from Sutcliffe's discussion of string quartets: "What I call a 'chorale' texture arises when all parts proceed in relatively homogeneous, even note values, generally in a fairly low tessitura and at a subdued dynamic level. The lack of rhythmic differentiation and the strong tendency towards stepwise voice-leading emphasise the way in which full harmony is created from parts with pronounced linear 'integrity.'" Sutcliffe, "Haydn, Mozart, and Their Contemporaries," 188.

and the homorhythmic texture effaces any sense of roles or hierarchy within the group, with the three strings speaking together as a unified cohort. The specialness of this idea is further marked not only by the extreme dynamic but also by unique articulation and timbre, since the use of such long slurs in a slow tempo calls for the strings to use a supremely airy, almost fragile bow stroke.

The strings' first statement of the breakthrough idea, culminating in a deceptive cadence in m. 35, represents the potential for the impending EEC. But the critical breakthrough moment comes in full force when the piano joins the strings for a second pass (mm. 36–39). In the context of a movement composed mainly of alternating, separate statements by piano and strings, this pivotal moment is striking for its homogeneity among all four instruments, since the piano has melded herself in full communion with the strings' chorale texture. The sense of "communion" is manifest tangibly through a direct doubling of the string parts within the piano's figuration.

The initial version of the breakthrough idea undergoes some notable transformations when the piano joins the strings for the second statement. The melody remains almost exactly the same (save for the chromatic adjustment of B♭ to B♮), but the bass line and resulting harmonic progressions are new (see Ex. 5.5). The harmonies group strongly into pairs, with the first chord of each pair resolving to the second; the violin part features

Ex. 5.5 Transformation of the breakthrough idea

Ex. 5.6 Identical scale degrees in opening and closing themes

Ex. 5.7 A subtle motivic repetition (Bb–C–D–Eb)
a. Breakthrough idea (violin)

b. Closing theme (piano, right hand)

compelling half-step motions (G–Ab, B♮–C, and D–Eb), which are mirrored in the contour of the viola part as well. This grouping articulates a hemiola measure (that is, a measure of quasi-$\frac{3}{4}$, expressed over two notated measures of $\frac{3}{8}$), a device that traditionally anticipates a cadence of high structural or formal rank.[45]

With growing confidence throughout this passage, embodied by the notated *crescendo,* the ensemble finally achieves the EEC in m. 39. The piano marks the occasion by introducing a closing theme that bears a resemblance to the movement's opening. Ex. 5.6 compares the piano's right-hand *grupetto* from m. 1 (5̂–1̂–3̂–5̂) to the beginning of the closing theme (upbeat to m. 40), which contains the same scale degrees in the local key. But perhaps the most interesting detail is found toward the end of the closing theme. Once the theme has undergone liquidation, the strings have dropped out, and the piano is left alone for a moment of private euphoria over repeated V^7–I cadences. After two statements of the closing theme's "tail," she makes a variation on the third and final statement, expanding the leap of a seventh (in mm. 42 and 43) to a leap of a ninth up to c^3 (m. 44). This c^3 is beautiful unto itself, but it more significantly hearkens

---

[45] I will discuss hemiola – and its distinction from *imbroglio* – in more detail in Chapter 6.
It is noteworthy that the hemiola grouping is not present in the first, string-only statement of the breakthrough idea; note the viola's suspension in m. 33, which renders the downbeat stronger than the second eighth note. The hemiola grouping nevertheless becomes evident in m. 36, seemingly through the piano's influence.

back to the violin's part from the breakthrough idea, where the notes bb^2–c^3–d^2–eb^2 were heard; the piano's statement now duplicates three of these four notes in their original register (see Ex. 5.7). If the repeated cadences of a closing theme can represent a celebration of hard-won cadential closure, the piano can be understood in this passage to be reflecting on the role that the breakthrough idea had played in forging the way toward the EEC, perhaps even expressing gratitude to the strings for discovering it. It is telling that the piano quotes specifically the initial version of the breakthrough idea, which the strings had played alone.[46]

Rotational form and the development section (K. 493)

The sense of balance and completeness brought about by the EEC arises not only because it represents the principal tonal goal of the exposition but also, according to Sonata Theory, because the EEC serves to forecast the essential structural closure (ESC) that will eventually be achieved in the recapitulation with a home-key cadence at the end of the subordinate theme.[47] This notion of foreshadowing pertains not only to the parallelism of structural cadences between exposition (EEC) and recapitulation (ESC), but in many pieces also to a close parallelism of the melodic sequence of events. Hepokoski and Darcy coin the term "rotational form" to describe this concept, writing that "the exposition's *rhetorical* task, no less important [than its harmonic task], is to provide a referential arrangement or layout of specialized themes and textures against which the events of the two subsequent spaces – development and recapitulation – are to be understood."[48] Simply put, the musical experience of the exposition provides a kind of roadmap to help guide the players through the journey of the recapitulation. In the recapitulation, their major challenge will be to rework the

---

[46] This is clear since the piano's statement appears in the register that the violin had used in the first statement of the breakthrough idea (mm. 32–35). In the second statement of the idea, the violin drops an octave lower and also adjusts its Bb to B♮.

[47] Hepokoski and Darcy refer to the exposition as a "structure of promise," with a "central mission [of] laying out the strategy for the eventual attainment of the ESC." In parallel fashion, they refer to the recapitulation as "a structure of accomplishment." Hepokoski and Darcy, *Elements of Sonata Theory*, 17.

[48] Ibid., 16. This notion of the exposition as the referential rotation was anticipated in eighteenth-century theories of musical rhetoric, notably in Sulzer and Koch. A substantial section of Koch's *Versuch* (vol. 3, Ch. 4) is devoted to describing the typical plan (*Anlage*) for full-scale movements in various musical genres. See especially Koch's description of the first movement of the symphony, which can be understood as representative for all two-reprise instrumental forms. See Koch, *Introductory Essay*, 199–202.

transition materials so that the subordinate theme occurs in the home key. After that point, they can achieve the ESC essentially by following the exposition's precedent – though, to be sure, many recapitulations deviate from this, the simplest possible path.

The developmental section, however, is another matter. As Hepokoski and Darcy have shown, many development sections begin with some material based on the primary theme followed by material based on the subordinate and/or closing themes, thus retracing an arc or "rotation" that approximates the exposition's order of events.[49] But compared to the predetermined tendencies and format of the standard recapitulation, in which familiar themes generally retain their roles and ordering from the exposition, with the requisite tonal adjustments, a fully rotational develop-ment section can be a more disorienting mix of the familiar and unfamil-iar. Even though the sequence of thematic events roughly parallels the exposition, these thematic references are usually stripped of their associ-ation with specific tonal milestones. The primary theme may return, but it might no longer be part of a stable presentation. Or a theme that helped in the exposition to achieve the EEC may recur but, this time, in a context that obfuscates rather than clarifies.

The German term for the development section, *Durchführung* (literally "leading through"), connotes a musical journey that forges a path between the relatively more stable exposition and recapitulation. With respect to rotational form in a development section, the effect of experi-encing familiar materials in a recognizable sequence but in a strange tonal context can be like becoming disoriented while traveling down a familiar road, perhaps passing landmarks that one has seen many times before but now with a vague sense that things are somehow not in the right place, perhaps even throwing into question whether one is traveling in the right direction. For that matter, the "right direction" is itself often unclear and undefined in development sections, which lack the established tonal plans of expositions and recapitulations. Some sonata developments begin by searching for a key for the development's main section or "core"; Caplin coins the term "pre-core" for these unstable interludes, which often hint at several possible keys before ultimately committing to one.[50] One of the tasks of such an interlude is to search for

---

[49] Hepokoski and Darcy, *Elements of Sonata Theory*, 195–218.

[50] Caplin, *Classical Form*, 141–55. The notion of "core" was first discussed by Erwin Ratz, whose term was "Kern der Durchführung." Ratz uses the term "Einleitung" for what Caplin calls "pre-core." See Erwin Ratz, *Einführung in die musikalische Formenlehre: Über*

an appropriate key for the core, sometimes choosing among many viable candidates. It is possible for different personas within the ensemble to each nudge the phrase toward different keys, like a vehicle full of backseat drivers, none of whom has a reliable map, but who nevertheless all wish to navigate.[51] Returning to the slow movement of K. 493, the path through this development section is a perilous road indeed, as progressively more flats are added throughout.

From the very instant the development begins (see the score in Ex. 5.8), it is clear that all is not well; compare the rich stability of the tonic chord on the downbeat of m. 1 to the stinging shock of the A° $\frac{4}{3}$ chord in m. 47. Since these two chords occupy a parallel position, each opening one of the movement's two reprises, they are marked for comparison, sharing an extremely rich voicing and even harmonizing the same melody. After the piano's retransition in mm. 45–46, the music that opens the development sounds like a "wrong" version of the movement's opening, as if the expositional repeat were erroneously taken one time too many and this somehow results in the strange notes mixed into the harmony (A♮ and G♭). Yet, in another sense, m. 47 sounds like an *intensified* version of m. 1, which had also tonicized B♭ minor. It is notable that the two "wrong" notes of m. 47 were the first two accidentals introduced in this movement (A♮ in m. 1 and G♭ in mm. 7 and 11, respectively).

Jolted by the sound of her own unstable harmony, the piano seeks more stable ground by initiating a cadential progression in B♭ minor, stopping in m. 48 on the local subdominant. This choice of harmony necessitates a conspicuous adjustment to her melodic statement, ending on G♭ (compared to F in the parallel place, m. 2). The piano seems to invite an answer from the strings that would complete the harmonic motion toward B♭ minor. A recomposed string response is shown in Ex. 5.9, whereby the violin picks up the piano's G♭ and the strings solidify the key of B♭ minor by completing the second statement of the basic idea, thus preparing for a continuation/cadential segment in that key. Compared to Ex. 5.9, the strings' actual response seems downright devious. The violin does indeed take the piano's G♭ but, through sleight of hand, reinterprets it in D♭ major as $\hat{4}$ (just as the piano's D♭ in m. 3 was $\hat{4}$ in A♭ major).

Formprinzipien in den Inventionen und Fugen J. S. Bachs und ihre Bedeutung für die Kompositionstechnik Beethovens, 3rd ed., enl. (Vienna: Universal, 1973), 33.

[51] See, for example, David Gagné's analysis of the development from the first movement of Mozart's String Quartet in G Major, K. 387, "A Dialogue among Equals," 511–19.

Ex. 5.8 Mozart, Piano Quartet in E♭ Major, K. 493, Larghetto (ii), development ▶

But who actually controls this sudden veering toward D♭ major? The violin part in m. 49 could very possibly have been harmonized in B♭ minor (as Ex. 5.9 shows). Perhaps the violin might have anticipated, prospectively, that her statement in that measure would continue in B♭ minor, only to be surprised by the cello's choice of A♭ for a bass note, a note that changes the function of the violin's G♭, outlining a dominant seventh that shifts the phrase toward D♭ major. "All right," the violin thinks as he hears the cello, "I'll adjust my plan for m. 50 to support an arrival in D♭!" Since m. 50 is parallel to m. 4, the violin might have expected a single harmony to prevail for the entire measure. He would therefore be

Strings' canon figure recalls "break-through"
idea's characteristic leap ($\hat{6}$ to $\hat{7}$),
piano's 32nds recall its figuration

New energy-build toward dominant pedal

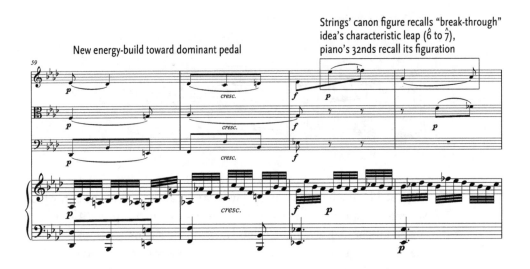

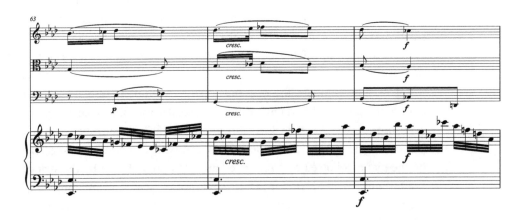

Major mode restored,
new canon begins

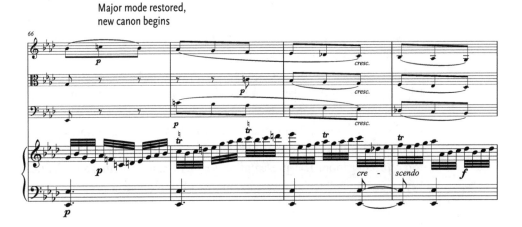

Ex. 5.9 Recomposition of mm. 47–50

surprised by the harmony in the lower voices at the end of the bar, which yet again transforms a would-be consonance in his part (A♭) into a dissonant chordal seventh. Curiously, the piano's entrance in m. 51 elides the resolution to E♭ minor, pointing instead toward a dominant seventh in F minor. In short, five measures of music have hinted at motions toward four possible keys – B♭ minor, D♭ major, E♭ minor, and now F minor – of which the first three have already been revealed to be illusory *Scheintonarten*, evaporating as soon as they are implied. Compared to the stable presentation in mm. 1–4, the passage on which this material is based, the opening of the development seems to be almost desperately unsettled.

Let us now compare the openings of the exposition (mm. 1–10) and development (mm. 47–51) in a different, broader way. Our analysis of the exposition noted a certain formality or standoffish distance between the piano and the strings. The exposition began with a presentation segment by the piano, followed by a separate, unrelated presentation by the strings (with a new basic idea), but the strings were prevented from completing their phrase by the piano's self-involved commentary and cadenza. Although the exposition's opening enjoyed ideal conditions for completing sentence theme-types – namely, a clearly defined tonality and a largely diatonic environment – it took almost the duration of the exposition and the invention of a special breakthrough idea for the piano and strings to truly find each other by converging onto a PAC.

The opening of the development, in contrast, represents a more frightening, obstacle-laden situation and is more a series of fragments than a coherent presentation segment; above all it lacks a stable, clearly defined key. Without a definite (if merely local) tonal center, the attempted presentation retains its basic format but is robbed of its essential tonal function: tonic prolongation. If a presentation segment cannot manage to define a key, it is impossible for a continuation to bring about a proper cadence;

a malformed presentation thus threatens the integrity of the entire sentence. Perhaps it is this alarming prospect that motivates the strings to enter more urgently in this passage (in m. 49), after just two bars (compared to four bars in the exposition), to help right the tonal ship after the piano's jarring diminished-seventh chord.[52] But when the violin's hopeful attempt to secure relief in Db is undermined, raising the frightening prospect of a move toward the distant, flat-laden key of Eb minor, the piano desperately enters with a rare third statement of the second half of the basic idea (m. 51), an urgent, fragmented version that directs the phrase toward F minor, as if to exclaim: "Any port in a storm!"[53]

The piano's dominant-seventh chord represents the *potential* for a cadence in F minor, and the strings seek to realize this potential by invoking the breakthrough idea (mm. 52–55), the very idea that had unified the ensemble and attained cadential closure in the exposition. "Surely," the strings might think, "if we try this idea for four bars, ending on a deceptive cadence, then the piano will join us for the next four bars

---

[52] In m. 49, a statement of the basic idea in Bb minor could have set the sentence back on a normal course. Although the violin and viola could be heard at first as continuing in that key, the cello's Ab forces a swerve toward Db major.

[53] Of the keys locally tonicized in mm. 47–51, Bb minor (II) and Db major (IV) are normal keys for a piece in Ab major, whereas Eb minor (Vb) is an extremely distant relation from the perspective of Abbé Vogler's or Gottfried Weber's conceptions of key relationships. Perhaps the prospect of a modulation to such a remote key prompts the piano's statement in m. 51, which deflects the passage back toward F minor (VI), a far more typical destination. An implied or actual modulation to the submediant is common in development sections and harkens back to Baroque two-reprise forms. Nevertheless, the rising pitch of the three successive "questioning" gestures (in m. 48, m. 50, and "too soon" in m. 51) imbues this modulation with a sense of rising despair. Note the effect of the repeated "questioning" figures, compared to the movement's opening, in which an ascending "question" (m. 2) is balanced by a descending "answer" (m. 4).

Although it is generically appropriate for development sections to modulate to (or hint at) remote keys, these keys may still represent a frightening or dangerous prospect for the characters within the piece, in the same sense that it is dangerous for children in fairy tales to venture into the deep, dark woods, even though they often do so. To connect this simile to rotational form: the expositional rotation, with its preordained tonal scheme, is like Hänsel and Gretel's first venture into the woods, in which their trail of pebbles guides them to a safe destination. But the developmental rotation – wherein familiar thematic events recur but often in disorienting ways – is like their second excursion, in which their trail of breadcrumbs is eaten by birds, leaving them unable to find their way home. Although the woods are by now slightly familiar, the children are nevertheless lost and wander deeper into the woods, unknowingly toward the dangerous witch. This sense of danger may be manifest in Mozart's piano quartet by the retransition (mm. 61–69), which begins in Ab minor, the minor tonic, or *Schwarze Gredel* in the language of contemporaneous music theory. See Gretchen A. Wheelock, "*Schwarze Gredel* and the Engendered Minor Mode in Mozart's Operas," in *Musicology and Difference: Gender and Sexuality in Music Scholarship*, ed. Ruth A. Solie (Berkeley: University of California Press, 1992), 201–21.

Ex. 5.10 A comparison of breakthrough idea statements
a. Original statement

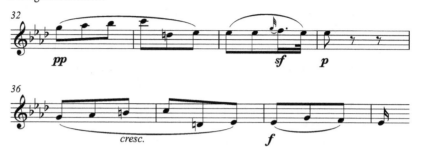

b. Development

leading to a PAC (just like in the exposition), and we can put this whole unstable episode behind us!" In other words, the strings seem to be relying on the central premise of rotational form, namely, that the arrangement of the exposition may provide a guide to events yet to come in the development.[54] However, it is the nature of rotational form that tried-and-true strategies from the exposition might not necessarily work the same way in subsequent rotations. Let us begin by comparing the parallel statements of the breakthrough idea from the exposition and development (see Ex. 5.10).

To examine the antecedent unit first, mm. 52–55 clearly recall the original breakthrough idea (mm. 32–35), but with a significant transformation of the melody. The contour of the first measure has been

---

[54] In Hepokoski and Darcy's terms, this development section is a full rotation, since it opens with material based on the primary theme (P-zone) in mm. 47–51 followed by material based on the breakthrough idea, which is part of the subordinate theme (S-zone) in mm. 52–61. I will argue presently that the retransition (mm. 61–69) is also derived from elements of the subordinate-theme and closing zones, which bolsters the sense of rotation.

(approximately) inverted, the prominent minor seventh (m. 33) has become an anguished diminished fourth (m. 53), and a troublesome accidental (G♭) has been added on the *sforzando* that thwarts the anticipated deceptive cadence. The inversion of the first measure significantly alters the overall melodic shape. Whereas, in the original version, the violin seems to climb and soar while seeking expositional closure in E♭, this time the phrase seems to sink, perhaps reflecting the growing uncertainty about whether a PAC in F minor will materialize and, for that matter, whether such a cadence is even an important goal for the movement.

The viola and cello parts share the generally "sinking" contour, and bear little resemblance to their parts in the parallel passage from the exposition.[55] Among the strings, it is perhaps the cello who is the most committed to making a deceptive cadence, since his part could have been harmonized with a motion from V to VI in mm. 54–55. However, the violin and viola deviate from the rotational-form "script" precisely on the *sforzando*, creating a VII$_5^6$ of IV harmony that resolves to IV^6 on the downbeat. (The dissonant *sforzando* chord is an inversion of the piano's chord from the beginning of the development section.) The violin and viola therefore divert the passage away from F minor by preemptively avoiding the cadential dominant at the last possible moment.[56] Caplin coins the term "abandoned cadence" to describe "the failure to realize an implied authentic cadence by eliminating the cadential dominant in root position."[57] In this instance, one might reasonably speak of an abandoned *deceptive* cadence, based on the precedent from the exposition. Instead of a deceptive cadence, the strings make no cadence at all, and the phrase simply stops in m. 55 on a tonicized B♭-minor chord.

If the rotational-form script had promised that a deceptive cadence by the strings would help bring about a PAC when the piano joins the ensemble, what will happen now that the strings have deviated from the script? What will it take to overcome the troubling G♭ that had

---

[55] It is indeed remarkable how intuitively a listener can identify this passage as the return of the breakthrough idea, considering that the melody is significantly altered and the accompanying parts are completely rewritten. The resemblance is found in other elements instead, such as the *pianissimo* dynamic, homorhythmic texture, eighth-note harmonic rhythm, and legato articulation. Less obvious, but also important, is the articulation of a hemiolic, quasi-$\frac{2}{8}$ metric level, which is suggested strongly in the contour of the cello part. In the exposition, this hemiola was absent in m. 32 but became evident starting in m. 36.

[56] This "swerve" away from the expected cadence in F minor is remarkable because, by the cadential $^6_4$ on the second beat of m. 58, a resolution to the root-position dominant had seemed nearly inevitable.

[57] Caplin, *Classical Form*, 253.

Ex. 5.11 Recomposition of mm. 56–59

bedeviled the strings in m. 54, throwing the phrase off course? When the piano joins the strings, all traces of the original breakthrough idea's melody are effaced – notably the distinctive downward leap that had always appeared in the second bar – leaving a (mostly) chromatic, descending scale in the violin, shadowed by the piano. Compared to the original presentation of the breakthrough idea in the exposition (where the melody suggested reaching and striving toward a goal), the violin seems deflated this time, too burdened by challenging circumstances to sculpt a proper melodic contour.

The ensemble, following the rotational-form script, once again attempts to use a *crescendo* to gain control and to bring the phrase to completion. By the *forte* arrival, the niggling G♭ is accommodated within a Neapolitan-sixth harmony, cementing the strong presumption of a conclusive PAC in F minor on the following downbeat[58] – a cadence that would close the door on a troublesome, tonally ambiguous *Hauptperiode*, as imagined in Ex. 5.11. It is astonishing, then, when the violin and the viola once again abandon the cadence on the third beat of m. 58, spoiling the dominant at the moment of its anticipated arrival. And again, the pitch G♭ plays a decisive role.[59]

[58] Regarding the Neapolitan-sixth chord in this phrase: the propensity of various predominant chords to progress to a dominant harmony can be measured roughly according to the number of tendency tones they contain. By this measure, a Neapolitan is a relatively intense predominant – more so than a diatonic II or IV harmony, but less so than VII⁷/V or an augmented-sixth chord. A ♭II chord contains two tendency tones, one of which (♭$\hat{2}$) must normally move downward to the leading tone. Since the previous phrase was derailed by a G♭, it is significant that this phrase strives to accommodate that pitch within a Neapolitan chord, a harmony that would seem to guarantee a progression to a dominant harmony and therefore to a cadence.

[59] The violin's E♭ is also curious. Strictly speaking, the violin's G♭ from the beginning of the bar (♭$\hat{2}$) was required to move down to E♮ for the cadential dominant; the F passing tone in between should not have impacted this syntactical requirement for the grammar of the Neapolitan harmony. It is puzzling to tease out precisely who is the agent in this turn of events. At the beginning of the bar, is the violin ignorant of the viola's plan to undermine the cadential

The forestalled cadence leaves the phrase at an odd juncture. According to the rotational-form script, the breakthrough music ought to have lasted exactly eight measures (four measures of the strings alone, then four measures of strings and piano together), culminating in a PAC on the downbeat of m. 59. Instead, the unusual harmonic turn renders m. 59 as an appoggiatura chord to a IV^6 harmony (Rameau's chord of the augmented fifth), which would be an awkward place for the phrase to stop. Instead, the phrase is forcibly extended by two bars. The opportunity to make a PAC in F minor in m. 59 having passed, the ensemble abandons F minor as a goal altogether and sets its sights instead on a dominant pedal in the movement's original key. Dynamics point out the changes of course. If the *crescendo* in m. 57 represents a growing confidence about reaching the anticipated PAC in F minor, the *subito piano* in m. 59 marks the waning of F minor with a sudden loss of sonic energy; but as the ensemble finds new momentum toward the dominant in mm. 60–61 (by way of the circle-of-fifths bass line), a new *crescendo* appears. One important dimension of a successful dominant is the cancellation of G♭ in favor of G♮, the chordal third and leading tone. This task falls to the viola (mm. 59–61), who first introduced G♭ in the exposition and continued to be associated with it at key moments.

The dominant arrival in m. 61 is marked by a canon in the severe style, with each of the string instruments entering in succession with a motive that outlines A♭ minor, the darkest, most flat-laden key on the circle of fifths.[60] After suffering through such a turbulent development section, the strings seem to use this motive to express pent-up angst. The canon motive can be understood as a variant on the breakthrough idea's motive (5̂–6̂–7̂–1̂), with prominent downward leap from 6̂ to 7̂, as shown in Ex. 5.12. Both passages also share a legato texture with mostly eighth-note motion in the strings and the piano doubling in thirty-second-note figuration. The *crescendo* marking is yet another element in common with the breakthrough idea. Whereas the original breakthrough statement had been a *tutti* utterance, intoned in *pianissimo* and in chorale texture, the canonic entries of this version emphasize the individual roles, and the severity of the motive is made vivid by the prominent diminished-seventh leaps, a

---

dominant? Or does their shared use of G♭ (combined with their cadence-destroying actions in m. 54) provide enough circumstantial evidence to suggest collusion?

[60] That is, A♭ minor is the minor key that has the greatest number of flats within the conventional circle of fifths, which includes keys signatures containing only up to seven accidentals. It is, of course, also possible for pieces to modulate to keys with more than seven sharps or flats.

Ex. 5.12 Breakthrough motive ($\hat{5}$–$\hat{6}$–$\hat{7}$–$\hat{1}$) in the retransition

a. Original breakthrough idea (violin)

b. Canonic treatment in the retransition

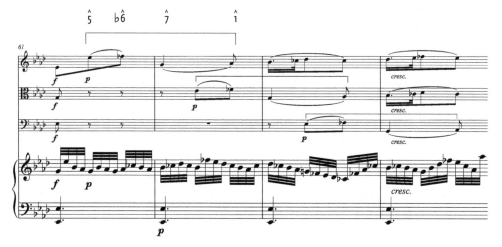

token of painful *Affekt*. The strings seem to bemoan the failure of the breakthrough idea to secure a cadence earlier in the development.

In terms of rotational form, it is instructive to regard the canonic passage as parallel to – even as a foil to – the piano's solo statements at the end of the exposition. I noted earlier that the exposition's closing theme ends with the piano invoking the breakthrough idea in a transformed version at mm. 44–45, translating a *tutti* idea into an individual's private reflection (recall Ex. 5.7). The effect is quite different when the same breakthrough motive (5̂–6̂–7̂–1̂) returns here over a dominant pedal, which is a prolongation of the final harmony of the development, and thus a position analogous to the exposition's closing theme. The canonic entries of the motive transform its effect, at once emphasizing each string instrument's individual statement while also subsuming them all within the broader canonic event. (For comparison, imagine how much more human and personal this passage would sound if the melody were played by the violin alone, without canonic imitation in the viola and cello.) The "dehumanizing" aspect of canon, whereby individual identities are partly effaced, contributes to the severe, monolithic effect.

Ultimately, the tension dissipates in m. 66, as the strings reject the intensity of A♭ minor and introduce a new, gentler canon of descending diatonic scales in A♭ major, counterpointed beautifully by ascending gestures in the piano. The gesture and texture of all three string instruments simultaneously playing descending scales in flowing, legato eighth notes, counterpointed with thirty-second notes in the piano, recalls mm. 56–60 (the breakthrough idea), but this time the diatonic content of the scales and the harmonic support of the dominant pedal create a warmer, more comforting mood. Any concerns pertaining to tonal ambiguity or chromaticism earlier in the development are by now laid to rest. The string entrances, set at intervals of two eighth notes, subtly articulate a quasi-$\frac{2}{8}$ meter, which is matched in the piano's right hand by the patterns of figuration and the trill markings. Eventually this metric articulation is manifest as a *bona fide* hemiola (see the piano's left hand in mm. 68–69). Together, the hemiola, the breakthrough-idea texture, and a *crescendo* mark the beginning of the recapitulation, just as the same features marked the earlier structural boundary of the EEC.

Recapitulation and the adventures of a G♭

Undergoing a tumultuous development section seems to have bonded the members of the piano quartet closer together, since the recapitulation reveals an intimacy between the strings and piano that was absent in the exposition. As the piano begins the recapitulation (see Ex. 5.13), the violin immediately chimes in with engaged, supportive commentary, interacting

Ex. 5.13 Mozart, Piano Quartet in E♭ Major, K. 493, Larghetto (ii), recapitulation ▶

Recapitulation: piano adds skipping ornamentation, violin adds engaged "commentary"

Piano adds new commentary

Piano statement recalls breakthrough idea

Piano's and viola's G♭s fulfill
prophesy of mm. 31–32

Ex. 5.13 (*cont.*)

without threatening or upstaging the piano in any way. It is the first time in the movement that any instrument has provided commentary figures that directly engage the main melody.

Soon after, the piano returns the same courtesy to the strings (mm. 80–83). The piano's second comment is extended to comprise two measures of additional material that have no parallel in the exposition (mm. 84–85).[61] Significantly, these extra measures also recall the break-through idea, quoting three notes in exact register (c^3–$d\natural^2$–eb^2). These two measures represent the recapitulation's only significant departure from the *Anlage* of the exposition, and the remainder of the recapitulation is an almost literal replica of the exposition (aside from the requisite transposition of the subordinate theme to the tonic key).

The movement's coda is rife with symbols of mutual affection between the piano and the violin, the latter serving as representative of the entire string cohort. The coda begins like the opening of the development, but the piano wisely circumvents her earlier mistake by avoiding Gb in m. 118 (cf. m. 48), restoring the proper version of this melody (cf. m. 2) and cadencing in the tonic. It is as if the piano's four-bar statement says: "I no longer have a care in the world! If I ever encounter another A$\natural$ diminished-seventh chord again, I'll just use it to tonicize II and lead comfortably to a reassuring PAC. When life gives you lemons … " The strings enter to repeat the same material straightaway, bolstering the shared feeling of fondness and mutual support. Compared to the solo-piano statement, the strings' version is more intense because of added appoggiaturas in the violin part and the viola's and cello's inner voices.[62] The strings reinforce the piano's statement as if saying, "Even when life gives us *very* sour lemons, we can still make a PAC!" And PACs they do make, again and again, supported by gently flowing arpeggios in the piano as the movement draws to a

---

[61] In the parlance of Sonata Theory, these bars could be heard as providing a medial caesura that is arguably absent in the exposition, if the exposition is interpreted as continuous. What I have called the subordinate theme (mm. 15–39, following Caplin) might in terms of Sonata Theory be interpreted as merely a "thematically profiled … 'S-like' module." Hepokoski and Darcy, *Elements of Sonata Theory*, 58 n. 7 and *passim*. In many instances, this subtle distinction seems to be one of degree rather than of kind. In the present movement, another plausible Sonata Theory analysis (suggested to me by L. Poundie Burstein) would treat the exposition as two-part, interpreting m. 10 as the medial caesura (I:HC) and mm. 11–14 as S^0, with $S^{1.0}$ beginning in m. 15. On introductory S^0 and $S^{1.0}$ modules, see ibid., 142–45.

[62] In m. 117, note that the piano's right hand is missing its customary chordal arpeggiation (compared to the parallel material in the opening measures of the exposition and development). But when the passage is repeated with the strings added, the viola and cello supply some of the notes that would have been in the piano's right hand. Yet again, the viola is associated with the troublesome note Gb in what turns out to be its final appearance.

sublime, *pianissimo* close (a reference to the dynamic of the breakthrough idea). What a distance the ensemble has traveled psychologically, from their stiff formality at the movement's opening to their warm relations in the coda!

As an overview of the rhetorically significant G♭s encountered at critical junctures throughout the movement, Fig. 5.1 provides a summary.

Exposition

m. 7	The viola introduces G♭ as part of a tonicization of IV, providing an intensified variation of m. 5.
m. 11	The viola again introduces G♭, this time tonicizing II. The new tonicization adds intensity to the phrase and invigorates the attempt to reach a cadence.
m. 31	In the piano, D♭ as ♭$\hat{7}$ in the local key of E♭ major corresponds to G♭ in the home key. It is central to the piano's "dare" that elicits the strings' breakthrough idea, leading to the EEC. In the recapitulation, D♭ will return as G♭ (m. 102).

Development

m. 47	The piano's "shock" chord pairs G♭ with A♮, the first two accidentals presented in the exposition. This harmony gestures toward a true modulation to B♭ minor, in which key a cadential progression is begun but subsequently abandoned. The reharmonization changes the sound of the melody from mm. 1–2: notes that were formerly stable are now dissonant.
m. 48	The piano's melody substitutes G♭ for the expected F.
m. 49	The violin takes up the piano's G♭, while the lower strings elect to reharmonize it as $\hat{4}$ in D♭ major.
m. 54	A G♭ in the violin undermines the anticipated cadence in F minor by undoing dominant harmony.
m. 58	As the breakthrough idea is repeated, the violin's G♭ is harmonized with ♭II^6 (a cadential intensifier), but another G♭ in viola and piano at the end of bar thwarts the cadence. The ensemble gives up on F minor as a tonal goal.
m. 59	The viola rectifies G♭ with G♮ to facilitate the dominant of A♭. The ensemble is back on track toward the development's true tonal destination, the dominant pedal in mm. 61–69.

Fig. 5.1 The Adventures of a G♭ in Piano Quartet in E♭ Major, K. 493, Larghetto (ii)

Recapitulation

mm. 76 and 80	As in the exposition, the viola monopolizes G♭.
m. 102	Fulfilling the promise of m. 31, G♭ appears as part of the piano's "dare." The viola accepts the dare in the following measure.

Coda

m. 117	As in the development, the piano's "shock" chord pairs G♭ with A♮, but, tellingly, G♭ is avoided in the following measure. G♭ is no longer a "problem": the ensemble has discovered how to resolve it properly.
m. 121	The viola (doubled in the piano) contributes the movement's last G♭ and supplies its final resolution. (The chord containing G♭, tonicizing II, is the first and only statement of the "shock" chord by the strings.) The remainder of the coda is completely diatonic.

Fig. 5.1 (*cont.*)

6 | Multiple agency and meter

Mozart's music has often been mischaracterized as "symmetrical" and "balanced," even "simple" – including by otherwise quite sophisticated musicians and writers – despite the subtle and important irregularities that exist in its rhythm. Edward Lowinsky pointed out some of these irregularities around the bicentennial of Mozart's birth, at a time when modern meter studies were in their infancy.[1] Since then, a burgeoning interest in rhythm and meter has seen the development of new analytical methods and terminologies that have helped to clarify what is asymmetrical and complex in the metrical dimension of Mozart's compositions.[2] Fred Lerdahl and Ray Jackendoff's influential *A Generative Theory of Tonal Music*, in particular, showed the way to distinguish grouping and meter and opened metrical perception to the theoretical model of preference rules.[3] Adapting Lerdahl and Jackendoff's definitions, this chapter will use a series of "metrical preference rules" (MPRs), listed in Fig. 6.1, to shed light on how metrical events play out in Mozart's chamber music through the intercourse among the parts.[4] A brief introduction to Lerdahl and Jackendoff's

---

[1] Edward Lowinsky, "On Mozart's Rhythm," *Musical Quarterly* 42 (1956): 162–86.

[2] This resurgence of attention to meter was stimulated in large part by Carl Schachter's and William Rothstein's inquiries into the implications of Heinrich Schenker's theories. Schachter's trilogy of articles entitled "Rhythm and Linear Analysis" originally appeared in *Music Forum*, vols. 4–6, and is reprinted in *Unfoldings*, 17–117. Rothstein's *Phrase Rhythm in Tonal Music* is partly based on his "Rhythm and the Theory of Structural Levels" (Ph.D. diss., Yale University, 1981).

[3] Fred Lerdahl and Ray Jackendoff, *A Generative Theory of Tonal Music* (Cambridge, MA: MIT Press, 1983). Their discussion of grouping preference rules (GPRs) appears on pp. 43–55, and that of metrical preference rules (MPRs) on pp. 74–96.

[4] The first ten MPRs listed in Fig. 6.1 correspond to those of Lerdahl and Jackendoff, except that I have adopted some simplified names and borrowed formulations from David Temperley and Rothstein. See David Temperley, *The Cognition of Basic Musical Structures* (Cambridge, MA: MIT Press, 2001), 30–39; and William Rothstein, "Metrical Theory and Verdi's Midcentury Operas," *Dutch Journal of Music Theory* 16, no. 2 (2010): 95–98. Regarding MPRs 5a and 5e: the distinction between literal *notes* and abstract *tones* is discussed above, 111 n. 1.

The eleventh MPR listed in Fig. 6.1 ("First Statement Stronger") is Rothstein's refined formulation of what he calls "Tetzel's rule," named for the little-known German theorist

1) **Parallelism**	Prefer to assign parallel metrical structures to parallel segments.
2) **Strong Beat Early**	Weakly prefer to assign the strongest beat relatively early in a group.
3) **Event**	Prefer to align strong beats with onsets of notes.
4) **Stress**	Prefer to align strong beats with relatively stressed notes.
5) **Length**	Prefer to align strong beats with the inception of long events, such as: **a.** a relatively long note; **b.** a relatively long duration of a dynamic; **c.** a relatively long slur; **d.** a relatively long pattern; **e.** a relatively long tone (i.e., an abstractly prolonged note); **f.** a relatively long harmony.
6) **Bass**	Prefer a metrically stable bass. (This rule intensifies other MPRs as they apply to the bass.)
7) **Cadence**	Strongly prefer a metrically stable cadence. NB: This rule does not prefer cadences to fall on weak or strong beats; it merely prefers for them to fall on beats.
8) **Suspension**	Strongly prefer a metrical structure in which a suspension is on a stronger beat than its resolution. This rule applies to the suspended sixth and fourth in a cadential $\frac{6}{4}$ chord.
9) **Stability**	Prefer to align stronger beats with the onsets of relatively stable harmonies and weaker beats with less stable harmonies. This rule also applies to stable and unstable notes (i.e., non-chord tones such as passing and neighbor tones are preferably aligned with relatively weak metrical positions).
10) **Duple Bias**	Prefer duple over triple relationships between metrical levels.
11) **First Statement Stronger**	When a motive is immediately repeated at the same or another pitch level, prefer to align the strongest beat in the first statement with a stronger metrical position than the strongest beat in the second statement.

Fig. 6.1 Metrical preference rules (MPRs), adapted from Lerdahl and Jackendoff

Eugen Tetzel who first articulated it about a century ago. Tetzel's original statement runs as follows: "The initial statement of a motive or phrase, in relation to its later imitations [or repetitions], falls on the strong point, even if the motive itself begins with an upbeat (for example the main theme of Beethoven's Fifth Symphony)" (*Das erstmalige Auftreten eines Motivs oder einer Phrase* geschieht gegenüber deren Nachahmungen beim Schwerpunkt, auch preference-rule-based model of meter and other concepts fundamental to this chapter appears in the "Notes on Metrical Theory," provided among the Web Resources.

Mozart's chamber music, alongside Haydn's, has proven to be especially fertile ground for the analysis of meter and hypermeter.[5] The central concern of many such analytical studies is to determine *the* correct metrical or hypermetrical interpretation of a musical passage. To ask the question, "How should one count the measures as strong and weak?" (for example) is to posit an ideal, qualified listener – often a thinly veiled straw man for the analyst – whose intuitions, habits, and biases are explained in the analysis.[6] When a passage contains conflicting metrical cues that allow for two or more plausible interpretations, the traditional argument goes, *the* listener's cognitive processing determines *the* preferred interpretation, against which the contravening elements are heard as syncopations, shadow meters, or other secondary phenomena – eddies swirling against the main current's overwhelming flow.[7]

wenn sie auftaktig gebildet sind [z.B. das Hauptthema von Beethovens c moll-Symphony]), emphasis in original. Tetzel, "Der Große Takt," *Zeitschrift für Musikwissenschaft* 3 (1920–21): 609. English translation from Rothstein, "Metrical Theory and Verdi's Midcentury Operas," 96. Temperley incorporates a similar principle into his version of the parallelism rule, but since Lerdahl and Jackendoff's version (their MPR 1) contains no such idea, I have chosen to treat it as a separate rule.

[5] See Danuta Mirka's elegant *Metric Manipulations in Haydn and Mozart*, which focuses on their chamber music for strings. Chamber music by Haydn and Mozart also figures prominently in Rothstein's *Phrase Rhythm in Tonal Music* and in articles by Ryan McClelland and by Eric McKee. Ryan McClelland, "Extended Upbeats in the Classical Minuet: Interactions with Hypermeter and Phrase Structure," *Music Theory Spectrum* 28, no. 1 (2006): 23–56; and "Teaching Phrase Rhythm through Minuets from Haydn's String Quartets," *Journal of Music Theory Pedagogy* 20 (2006): 5–35. McKee,"Extended Anacruses in Mozart's Instrumental Music."

[6] A notable exception is Andrew Imbrie, who outlines the interpretations of "radical" and "conservative" listeners, without identifying himself as a member of either camp. See Andrew Imbrie, "'Extra' Measures and Metrical Ambiguity in Beethoven," in *Beethoven Studies*, ed. Alan Tyson (New York: W. W. Norton, 1973), 45–66. On the tendency of other theorists to "take sides" in a metrical conflict, see William Rothstein, "Beethoven with and without 'Kunstgepräng': Metrical Ambiguity Reconsidered," in *Beethoven Forum* 4, 173 n. 18 and esp. 178–79.

[7] The concept of "shadow meter" was introduced by Frank Samarotto in a paper delivered at the Second International Schenker Symposium in 1992 that was subsequently published as "Strange Dimensions: Regularity and Irregularity in Deep Levels of Rhythmic Reduction," in *Schenker Studies 2*, ed. Carl Schachter and Hedi Siegel, 222–38 (Cambridge University Press, 1999). See also Rothstein, "Beethoven with and without 'Kunstgepräng.'" The image of meter as a wave is inspired by the writings of Victor Zuckerkandl: *Sound and Symbol: Music and the External World* (New York: Pantheon Books, 1956), 169–80; and *The Sense of Music* (Princeton University Press, 1959), 99–138.

In this chapter, I take a different approach, shifting the focus toward meter as experienced by the various players *within* a chamber ensemble. Oftentimes in Mozart's chamber music, metrical play is tantamount to metrical interplay: moments of metrical ambiguity or manipulation commonly arise through conflicting signals expressed by individual parts. Meter is therefore not so much an abstract structure to be inferred by the outside listener or analyst as something the players *do* or *make* through their moment-to-moment utterances and interchanges. Unlike an outside listener, the fictional instrumentalist personas are *agents* capable of producing musical events that bolster, resist, or even supplant the prevailing meter. More to the point, they can support or resist *one another*, enabling their metrical manipulations to be interpreted through metaphors of social interaction.

The chapter begins with an overview of the dynamic model of in-time metrical projection advanced by Danuta Mirka in *Metric Manipulations in Haydn and Mozart*, which informs my approach. A number of brief analyses follow, laying out the theoretical bases of what I call a *decentered* view of meter, one that emphasizes the independent vantage points and actions of individual instruments as they pertain to the metrical structure and its manipulation. The metrical ramifications of multiple agency are then explored fully in the final three analyses, which tell the sometimes contentious metrical "stories" of extended passages from three compositions by Mozart: (1) the "Dissonance" Quartet, K. 465; (2) the Sonata in G Major for Piano and Violin, K. 379; and (3) the "Kegelstatt" trio, K. 498.

First, a word to any readers who choose to skim the theoretical portion of this chapter and focus on the discussion of the musical examples. To have a visceral experience of the analyses, I recommend listening to a given excerpt several times, and successively directing one's attention to different instrumental parts (imagining what it would feel like to play each one) or to different metrical signals (e.g. melodic groupings or harmonic rhythm). A good way to do this is to conduct alternative interpretations of the hypermeter on repeated listenings, even trying interpretations that initially seem "wrong." In essence, this chapter's analytical prose aims to explain the hypermetrical counting (or countings) of the musical examples based on the activation of specific metrical preference rules by the various instrumental parts. For music rife with metrical manipulations and conflicts, the question "how do I hear the hypermeter?" is often less illuminating than the alternative query "which metrical signals rub against the prevailing hearing?" It is in this spirit of metrical play that the chapter is written.

Meter as a process of becoming: toward an in-time model of metrical analysis

Whereas Lerdahl and Jackendoff are concerned only with the listener's final analysis,[8] Mirka offers a more dynamic account of a listener's in-time metrical processing. She describes Lerdahl and Jackendoff's end-state perspective, which brackets off in-time processing, as a "disadvantage" for the analysis of metrical manipulations in eighteenth-century music:

> As a result of this methodological option, the model of meter developed by Lerdahl and Jackendoff is inherently static. The only aspect of metrical manipulations it can capture is the difference between *clear* and *vague* sensation of meter. Clear meter arises if the cues provided from the musical surface are regular and mutually supportive ... But this does not suffice to account for all metric manipulations ... [examined in Mirka's book] since many of them induce the listener to develop several representations of one musical passage successively. To provide just one analytical description of a passage when in fact the listener hears the passage in different ways as it continues results not only in obscuring a very important aspect of the listener's experience but also in ignoring a crucial part of the composer's strategy. *What is needed for the description of such metrical manipulations is a dynamic theory of musical processing as an extension of Lerdahl and Jackendoff's model* [emphasis added].[9]

Mirka's interest in the in-time experience of metric manipulations leads her to adopt two significant extensions to Lerdahl and Jackendoff's methodology. The first is *parallel multiple-analysis*, whereby a listener entertains multiple, conflicting metrical interpretations simultaneously until some point when one preferred analysis is decisively selected and the other(s) "pruned."[10] This model permits the analyst to speak in nuanced terms

---

[8] Lerdahl and Jackendoff state this explicitly: "Instead of describing the listener's real-time mental processes, we will be concerned only with the final state of his understanding. In our view it would be fruitless to theorize about the mental processing before understanding the organization to which the processing leads." Lerdahl and Jackendoff, *A Generative Theory of Tonal Music*, 4.

[9] Mirka, *Metric Manipulations in Haydn and Mozart*, 16–17. Mirka's critique may be placed in the broader context of a growing trend toward methods that go beyond goal-state analysis to model the temporal experience of music. Notable examples include theories of form by Hepokoski and Darcy and by Schmalfeldt, and psychologically oriented studies by Leonard Meyer, Eugene Narmour, Robert O. Gjerdingen, and David Huron.

[10] Parallel multiple-analysis was first formulated by Jackendoff in a study subsequent to his collaboration with Lerdahl: "The idea behind this theory is that when the processor [i.e., listener] encounters a choice point among competing analyses, processing splits into simultaneous branches, each computing an analysis for one of the possibilities. When a

Fig. 6.2 Metrical Projection (from Danuta Mirka, *Metric Manipulations in Haydn and Mozart*, Ex. 1.13)

about prospective and retrospective metrical processing and to model the experience of metrical surprises. An unexpected metrical signal may prompt a listener to analyze retrospectively, to reanalyze retrospectively, or even to lose her bearings.[11] Mirka's interest in prospective hearing leads to her second significant extension to Lerdahl and Jackendoff's theory: the concept of *projection*.[12] The underlying premise of projection is that a listener does not merely process available information passively but "actively *awaits* further information on the basis of the information collected earlier ... [such as] by projecting the time interval between two earlier attacks into the future, so as to anticipate the moment of the third attack [as in Fig. 6.2]."[13]

particular branch drops below some threshold of plausibility, it is abandoned." Ray Jackendoff, "Musical Processing and Musical Affect," in *Cognitive Bases of Musical Communication*, ed. Mari Riess Jones and Susan Holleran (Washington, DC: American Psychological Association, 1992), 62. Jackendoff originally published a version of this article as "Musical Parsing and Musical Affect," *Music Perception* 9, no. 2 (Winter 1991): 199–230.

This model of parallel multiple-analysis resembles the concept of *Mehrdeutigkeit* as described by Abbé Vogler and Gottfried Weber, which is the basis of instruction on modulation in modern theory textbooks. While hearing a modulatory passage in time, the so-called "pivot chord" or "pivot area" is the last point in which multiple tonal analyses remain tenable. Subsequent events, such as a cadence in a key, will confirm the analysis, encouraging the listener to select the final analysis accordingly.

[11] Mirka discusses these possibilities in *Metric Manipulations in Haydn and Mozart*, 20–23.

[12] Projection was first conceived by Moritz Hauptmann in *Die Natur der Harmonik und der Metrik* (Leipzig, 1853) and was revived by Christopher F. Hasty in *Meter as Rhythm* (Oxford University Press, 1997).

[13] Mirka, *Metric Manipulations in Haydn and Mozart*, 24. Mirka's conception of projection departs from Hasty's in two significant ways. Hasty defines projection as "the process in which a mensurally determinate duration provides a definite durational potential for the beginning of an immediately successive event" (Hasty, *Meter as Rhythm*, 84). In his theory, a projection is the psychological motion from a first impulse to a later one, and his interest lies in the gradually growing duration as the listener awaits the next, projected event. Mirka, on the other hand, conceives of projection as a span between timeless points, a perspective that grows out of late-eighteenth-century German metrical theory and the theory of Lerdahl and Jackendoff – that is, the very tradition that Hasty critiques.

The second important difference between Hasty's and Mirka's notions of projection lies in their respective models for processing. Hasty's analyses conform to the "serial single-choice" model whereas Mirka adopts "parallel multiple-analysis." These terms were coined by Jackendoff, who rejects the former for logical inconsistencies and advocates the latter. See discussion in Mirka, *Metric Manipulations in Haydn and Mozart*, 27–30.

The notion of meter as a process – whereby listeners actively create imagined, projected events that are subsequently realized (or not) by actual events as they occur – assumes a radically different orientation from Lerdahl and Jackendoff's methodology in *A Generative Theory of Tonal Music*. Whereas these authors are concerned only with the final analysis, Mirka's interest in the intermediate stages offers a more elaborate, psychological account of the moment-to-moment metrical experience – meter as a process of becoming, to paraphrase Janet Schmalfeldt.[14] Mirka's book virtuosically unites these fundamental concepts with other principles drawn from historical theories of meter. With this methodology, she develops detailed analyses that model how a listener finds the meter at the beginning of a composition and processes later events that challenge, change, or stop the meter. She focuses exclusively on meter up to the level of the measure. Hypermeter, the focus of the present chapter, is beyond the scope of her book.[15]

Decentering meter

Whereas Mirka's book focuses on meter as experienced by outside listeners, my interest in chamber music as a social practice and in performance settings in which players formed their own primary audience leads me to focus on metrical interplay *within* ensembles. The various player-personas within a chamber ensemble are not only metrical *listeners* (or "processors") but also metrical *agents* too: the very notes they play constitute the signals used by themselves and their colleagues to induce the meter. Their metrical processing may be informed not only by what they have heard in the past and are hearing in the present, but also by what they *wish to hear* or *wish to make happen* in the future.[16] Some

---

[14] Cf. Schmalfeldt, *In the Process of Becoming*.

[15] Mirka, *Metric Manipulations in Haydn and Mozart*, xi. Mirka has announced plans to address hypermeter in a future volume.

[16] A precedent for analyzing meter by looking independently at individual characters or instrumental parts is Thrasybulos G. Georgiades's notion of *Polymetrik*, discussed in "Aus der Musiksprache des Mozart-Theaters," in *Kleine Schriften* (Tutzing: Hans Schneider, 1977), 9–32. Although Georgiades addresses what he regards as the metrical autonomy of various characters, his concept does not include the agential aspect examined in this chapter. Georgiades's perspective recalls a famous moment from Mozart's operas: the three metrically independent, on-stage ensembles during the ball scene from *Don Giovanni*.

metrical processes, conflicts, and resolutions can therefore be analyzed with an agential perspective that describes the vantage points of distinct ensemble members and speculates as to the psychodramatic intent behind their metrical actions.[17]

To acknowledge that each instrumentalist might have a unique metrical experience is to move toward a *decentered* conception of meter. The phenomenon is most palpable when individual parts express conflicting metrical cues, as often happens during hypermetrical transitions[18] or in passages containing displacement dissonances in some parts that rub against the notated meter supported by other parts.[19] For Mirka, only one ideal listener is required because processing is based on a single input: the sound of the complete ensemble.[20] My perspective aims to capture the unique vantage point of each instrumentalist, as suggested by metrical cues residing in their respective parts.

[17] Among various listeners present while a chamber piece is played, there will almost certainly be variation in their processing of meter. That one listener may be more attentive to melodies and another to bass lines may prompt certain elements within the texture to seem more salient and prioritize certain metrical signals. William Rothstein examined this point in his unpublished study "Clash of the Titans: What to do when Tovey and Schnabel Disagree about Hypermeter in Beethoven's Piano Sonatas," (paper presented at the Music Theory Society of New York State and the New England Conference of Music Theorists, New Haven, CT, April 26, 2003). Even factors external to the music proper could potentially play a role. For instance, if, among the listeners within our eighteenth-century salon, one is married to the second violinist or another used to play the cello, these considerations might direct their attention to particular parts and to privilege metrical signals contained therein.

[18] David Temperley, "Hypermetrical Transitions," *Music Theory Spectrum* 30, no. 2 (2008): 305–25.

[19] On displacement dissonance, see Harald Krebs, *Fantasy Pieces: Metrical Dissonance in the Music of Robert Schumann* (Oxford University Press, 1999), 33–34. See also Schachter's related discussion of Schumann's *Davidsbündlertänze*, which critiques the concept of "the" meter and "the" hypermeter and suggests the possibility of simultaneous meters expressed by different elements within the texture. Schachter, "Aspects of Meter," in *Unfoldings*, 97–102.

[20] It is assumed, in Mirka's analyses – as well as in Lerdahl and Jackendoff's and Hasty's – that the listener does not have access to any visual inputs, either from the score or from watching the performers. It is further assumed that the listener hears only a faithful, "pure" realization of the musical score, with little impact from the nuances of any particular performance or interpretation. The paradigm thus models the experience of listening to a MIDI file, in a laboratory, using headphones. Lerdahl and Jackendoff occasionally mention the influence of a performer's realization, usually in connection with MPR 4, which governs performed stress; see, for example, *A Generative Theory of Tonal Music*, 25. Regarding the performer's influence on perceived grouping structure, see ibid., 63–64. On the impact of performers' choices on hypermeter, see Alan Dodson, "Performance and Hypermetric Transformation: An Extension of the Lerdahl–Jackendoff Theory," *Music Theory Online* 8, no. 1 (February 2002), www.mtosmt.org/issues/mto.02.8.1/mto.02.8.1.dodson_frames.html.

Ex. 6.1 Mozart, String Quartet in F Major, K. 590, Menuetto: Allegretto (iii)

a. Score

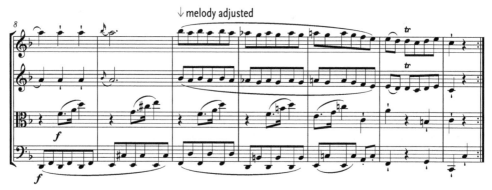

Consider the minuet from Mozart's String Quartet in F Major, K. 590 (shown in Ex. 6.1a): As the first violin completes the first bar of his melody, it is not clear whether the measure is strong or weak at the two-bar hypermetrical level. Should the opening measures be counted "one–two, one–two," or "two–one, two–one"? A weak, default preference for early strong beats (MPR 2, favoring m. 1 as strong) is neutralized by another weak preference for hearing an initial, unaccompanied measure as an anacrusis (favoring m. 1 as weak).[21] Helpfully, the second violin clarifies the meter at his entrance

---

[21] The tendency to hear unaccompanied melodic figures as gestural upbeats involves MPRs 3 and 6 – that is, the lack of events in the bass suggests a position of relative metrical weakness. Janet M. Levy has discussed this tendency to hear extended upbeats in passages in which an established texture is reduced to an unaccompanied melodic line. Janet M. Levy, "Texture as a Sign in Classic and Early Romantic Music," 498–99. But McClelland points out that unaccompanied openings are not necessarily hypermetrical or even gestural upbeats. McClelland, "Extended Upbeats in the Classical Minuet," 26. See also Rothstein, *Phrase Rhythm in Tonal Music,* 39–40, and the discussion of Ex. 6.14 below, 241–50.

b. Recomposition of consequent phrase

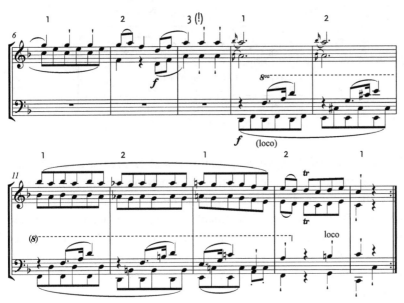

with several signals that establish m. 2 as strong and retroactively render m. 1 as an upbeat measure: the second violin's entrance initiates both an accompaniment pattern (MPR 5d) and a relatively long slur (MPR 5c), and, within the accompanimental figure (F–A, G–B♭, A–C), the tonic chord tones in the even measures are heard as harmonically stable and metrically strong relative to the passing tones in m. 3 (MPR 9). These cues are all amplified since the second violin is the active bass part (MPR 6). The first violin seems immediately to accept the even-strong interpretation,[22] since his repetition of m. 2 in m. 3 supports the former measure as strong (MPR 11). Once the even-strong hypermeter is established, it is maintained up through the hypermetrically unaccented cadence in m. 7.

However, a disagreement between the violins and the lower pair brings about a significant conflict in the following phrase. With the unison, *forte* upbeat to m. 8, the violins seem to invite a *tutti* thematic repetition in which the lower parts would take over the role formerly played by the second violin. If this thematic repetition followed the model of the first phrase, it would appear as in Ex. 6.1b. Measures 8–9 of this recomposition create a parallelism

---

[22] The terms "even-strong" and "odd-strong" were coined by Temperley ("Hypermetrical Transitions") as shorthand for a metrical structure in which metrical accents fall on downbeats of even-numbered or odd-numbered measures, respectively.

Ex. 6.1 (*cont.*)

c. Durational reduction (Carl Schachter's analysis from "Rhythm and Linear Analysis: Aspects of Meter," in *Unfoldings*, Ex. 3.8b.)

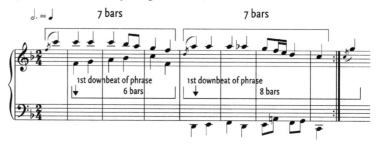

with mm. 1–2 (MPR 1), whereby m. 9 would be favored as strong for the same reasons as m. 2: the inception of a new accompaniment pattern (MPR 5d) and long slur (MPR 5c), the harmonic stability of the D-minor chords relative to their applied dominant (MPR 9), the preference for a stable bass (MPR 6), and the first-statement-stronger rule (MPR 11). The problem with this version, however, is that the two consecutive weak bars in mm. 7 and 8 violate duple bias by departing from the established, even-strong hypermeter (MPR 10).

Perhaps to prevent this from happening, the viola and cello in Mozart's version (Ex. 6.1a) elect to join the consequent phrase one measure earlier than the second violin did in the antecedent phrase. This action aligns their signals of metrical strength with the prevailing even-strong hypermeter; parallelism with mm. 1–2 (MPR 1) is violated in favor of observing duple bias (MPR 10). Since metrical signals in the bass tend to supersede those in the melody (MPR 6), the violins' would-be upbeat measure is forcibly transformed into a hyperdownbeat. This compels the violins to shorten their melody, omitting the repetition of the dotted half note from m. 3, in order to reach the cadence in time with the accompaniment (m. 14). That this cadence is metrically accented, unlike its predecessor, serves to set up the repeat of m. 1 as a weak bar, and so erases (or mitigates) the very ambiguity that incited the passage's metrical interplay in the first place.

This end-state hypermetrical analysis, as it stands in retrospect after the first playthrough of mm. 1–14, is demonstrated in a durational reduction by Carl Schachter (reproduced in Ex. 6.1c), whose analysis inspired the present discussion.[23] Although Schachter and I arrive at the same final analysis of this passage, my discussion puts a greater emphasis on the

---

[23] Schachter, "Aspects of Meter," in *Unfoldings*, 94–96. Schachter's analysis refines Lowinsky's earlier discussion of the same passage, which describes the pair of seven-bar phrases as

autonomous actions of the individual personas and on the ambiguities they experience from moment to moment. The essential difference between Mozart's version (Ex. 6.1a) and my recomposition (Ex. 6.1b) is that in Mozart's version, the viola and cello "choose" to commence their accompaniment at a different point relative to the antecedent-phrase model, prompting the violins to curtail their melody. It is not clear how to characterize the motivation behind this action. Is the lower pair *correcting* the second violin, implying that his error in the antecedent has resulted in an odd, seven-bar phrase? Or are they simply *being helpful* by trying to avoid consecutive weak bars in mm. 7–8? Perhaps they *make a mistake* themselves – a wrong entrance (relative to the antecedent phrase) whose fortuitous effect of resolving a metrical problem reveals itself afterwards? As discussed in Chapter 4, since agency is a property an analyst ascribes to musical events, rather than a property of the music *per se*, it is not possible to isolate one "correct" form of agency attribution. Since the quartet players are the principal analysts of their own parts – in time, while they play – such agency attribution may be an ongoing, tacit process of interpreting the meaning(s) of each musical gesture and riposte.[24]

One musical context that invites a decentered metrical interpretation is the overlapping entrances of imitative polyphony. Heinrich Schenker makes the following observation in a discussion of the fugue in C♯ minor from Bach's *Well-Tempered Clavier*, Book I:

As long as musical content moved principally in imitations of canonic and fugal forms, it was somehow illogical to presuppose a metric scheme. Each of the numerous imitations, after all, involved [a 4 = 1] reinterpretation ... Where would we find ourselves if we were to pursue the idea of reinterpretation in the manner indicated [in Ex. 6.2]? We can ... clearly see that subject or answer can appear in such contradiction to the original [hyper]metric scheme that the new ordering amounts to a complete change of that scheme. This is of special significance for fugue writing![25]

For Schenker, the starting note of a statement of the subject so strongly indicates a hypermetrical "1" (due to parallelism, MPR 1) as to effect

exemplifying the "studied irregularity," or balance between symmetry and asymmetry, characteristic of Mozart's rhythm. Lowinsky, "On Mozart's Rhythm," 163–64.

[24] This book thus takes up a subject that Seth Monahan explicitly brackets off, namely, "the relationship of agency to performance or real-time audiation." His study focuses exclusively on "how agency is modeled *in analytical prose only* [emphasis in original]." Monahan, "Action and Agency Revisited," 326.

[25] Heinrich Schenker, *Der freie Satz* (Vienna: Universal Edition, 1935). English translation from *Free Composition*, trans. Ernst Oster (New York: Longman, 1979), 126.

Ex. 6.2 Bach, Fugue in C♯ Minor from *The Well-Tempered Clavier*, Book 1 (hypermetrical analysis from Heinrich Schenker, *Free Composition*, Fig. 149, 8a)

repeated 4 = 1 metrical reinterpretations, even in close succession. Such pervasive violation of duple bias (MPR 10) effectively forestalls the establishment of a meaningful hypermetrical level, in Schenker's view. Nevertheless, the metrical conflicts are relatively short-lived – and can be resolved through metrical reinterpretation – since the subject and answer overlap for just one note.

A more pervasive conflict occurs in a canon *per arsin et thesin*, wherein notes that fall on strong metrical positions in the *dux* are imitated on weak metrical positions in the *comes* (and vice versa).[26] Such imitation results, by definition, in conflicting metrical signals expressed by the ongoing violation of parallelism (MPR 1) between the two parts. Each voice expresses its own individual meter, while also contributing to the composite meter. An outside listener may be temporarily disoriented, unsure whether she will be rewarded for relying on the *dux* or *comes*.

Consider the opening of the minuet from Mozart's Serenade in C Minor for Wind Octet, K. 388 (shown, in short score, in Ex. 6.3).[27] Since the *pas de menuet* is counted in six beats, many minuets are composed with two-measure groupings that may also suggest a two-bar hypermetrical level. Examining the oboes' part of this minuet, such a two-bar grouping is suggested by the hemiola unit of mm. 1–2 and by the melodic sequence in mm. 3–4. These groups can furthermore be construed as metrical units: the downbeat of m. 1 is preferred over that of m. 2, which lacks an attack (MPR 3), and the downbeat of the sequential model in m. 3 is preferred as

---

[26] Mirka discusses displacement dissonances relating to imitation, including canons *per thesin et arsin*, in *Metric Manipulations in Haydn and Mozart*, 189–98. She gives the term as "imitatio per thesin et arsin" following Koch's *Musikalisches Lexikon*, cols. 1039–40. The term is more commonly stated as "imitatio per arsin et thesin," following Friedrich Wilhelm Marpurg, who coined this usage in *Abhandlung von der Fuge*, vol. 1 (Berlin, 1753), 8. Earlier theorists, such as Zarlino and Morley, used the same term in an unrelated way to refer to melodic inversion (i.e., down and up are reversed in terms of melodic contour rather than metrical downbeat and upbeat).

[27] This composition may be more familiar to some readers in Mozart's later transcription for string quintet (K. 406).

Ex. 6.3 Mozart, Serenade in C Minor for Wind Octet, K. 388, Menuetto in canone (iii), oboes and bassoons only

stronger than that of m. 4 (MPR 11). A looser parallelism also exists between the first two beats of m. 5 (a slurred ascending fourth) and those of m. 6 (a slurred descending fifth); if m. 5 is heard as the model of m. 6, the first-statement-stronger rule (MPR 11) will tend to favor the former as strong. Cutting across this odd-strong, two-bar hypermeter is the unexpected tie from m. 6 to m. 7, which suggests a kind of hemiola syncopated against the established odd-strong hypermeter in the oboes' part.

Since the bassoons imitate the oboes at a one-bar interval, the very signals that suggest an odd-strong hearing in the oboes point to an even-strong hearing of the bassoons' part, resulting in a clear, ongoing hypermetrical conflict between *dux* and *comes*. Listening to both parts together, the default advantage that the oboes receive simply by being first (MPRs 2 and 11) is counteracted by the preference for a metrically stable bass (MPR 6, which augments all of the metrical signals contained in the bassoons' part). As a result of this conflict, one might conclude that there is no universal, two-bar hypermeter in this passage, even though the oboes and bassoons each express their respective hypermeters quite clearly for the first several measures. This conflict emphasizes the one-bar level by default, since every measure is strong in either the oboes or bassoons, and therefore contributes a certain heaviness to this minuet. Moreover, this conflict may be a catalyst for the breakdown of the oboes' and bassoons' respective two-bar hypermeters around m. 7.

Another canon *per arsin et thesin* appears in the coda to the finale of Mozart's String Quartet in G Major, K. 387, beginning in m. 282 (see Ex. 6.4; the opening of this movement is shown above in Ex. 4.2). The coda opens with a passage of supreme stillness. Whereas much of the movement will tend to be counted in one-bar beats organized into four-bar hyper-measures, the relative sparsity of rhythmic activity and the pattern of imitation at two-bar intervals beginning in m. 268 encourage counting in two-bar units or "double measures," such that four hyperbeats are counted

Ex. 6.4 Mozart, String Quartet in G Major, K. 387, Molto allegro (iv), coda

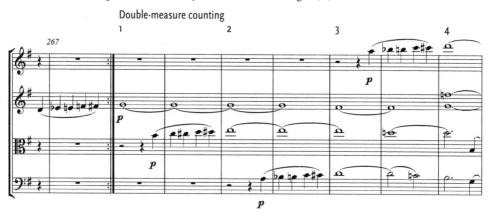

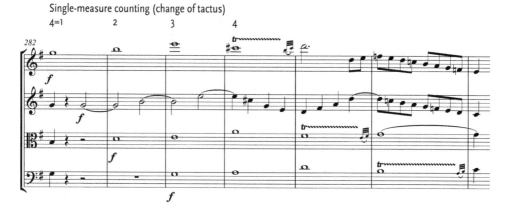

over eight notated measures.[28] Note the viola's suspension at this slow level in mm. 272–73.[29] But the salience of this slow hypermeter begins to diminish in m. 276 as the rhythmic activity picks up (coinciding with the *crescendo*) and as the first violin resumes suspensions at the normal, one-bar level. Any lingering suspicion of eight-bar hypermeter is eliminated in m. 282, due to the resumption of the movement's principal motive, which throughout the movement begins on hyperdownbeats at the four-bar level (MPR 1). The status of m. 282 as a hyperdownbeat is further bolstered by the first violin's *forte* marking (MPR 5b).[30] A listener who had continued counting in double measures would thus hear m. 282 as a 4 = 1 reinterpretation with a change of tactus.

However, whereas this principal motive has heretofore appeared in successive, non-overlapping four-bar statements aligned to commence on hyperdownbeats, the imitations by the lower parts beginning in m. 282 comprise a canon *per arsin et thesin* that renders the metrical situation more complex. The second violin – who has challenged the first violin throughout this movement (see discussion of Ex. 4.2) – now commences a final act of *Wettstreit* by imitating the first violin at a half-bar interval. From the vantage point of the second violin, his mid-bar attacks (MPR 3), commencing with a re-marked *forte* dynamic (MPR 5b), attempt to make his mid-bars seem equal to the first violin's attacks on the notated downbeats.[31] Given that the motive previously commenced on notated

---

[28] The passage is modeled after the opening of the development, as if the coda were an *ersatz* "extra" repeat of the second reprise. These are the only two passages in the movement that invite such slow counting. Danuta Mirka discusses "double measures" (a single *composed* measure comprising two *notated* measures) in "Topics and Meter," in *The Oxford Handbook of Topic Theory*, ed. Danuta Mirka, 357–80 (Oxford University Press, 2014). On the changing tactus within the K. 387 finale, see Wye Jamison Allanbrook, *Rhythmic Gesture in Mozart: Le Nozze di Figaro and Don Giovanni* (University of Chicago Press, 1983), 19–20; and Mirka, *Metric Manipulations in Haydn and Mozart*, 225–30.

[29] The interpretation of mm. 268–75 as two slow hypermeasures (at the four-double-measure or eight-notated-measure level) is bolstered by the harmonic rhythm (MPR 5f) and by the placement of relatively stable and unstable harmonies throughout the passage (MPR 9).

[30] Strictly speaking, this *forte* is not the inception of a *new* dynamic but a reinforcement of the *continued* dynamic that began four bars earlier. Many composers (especially Beethoven) tend to align such re-marked dynamics with positions of metrical strength. Arguably, these markings stand more as visual cues in the score and parts than as audible events for the listener; the same is true of inception points of *crescendos* and *diminuendos*. However, in this passage, the *forte* markings in all four parts are coordinated with motivic imitations (parallelism, MPR 1) and encourage each player to use a bolder articulation (stress, MPR 4). To this extent, they become audible because they are coordinated with other metrical cues.

[31] Further supporting the association of this motive with hyperdownbeats at the four-bar level: Whenever the motive appears in *piano* throughout the movement, it is marked with a four-bar slur (MPR 5c). Mozart omits the slur when the motive appears in *forte* to permit the players to

downbeats, this syncopated usage violates parallelism (MPR 1), as if the second violin aims to place "his downbeats" in notated mid-bars, directly contradicting the metrical structure expressed by the first violin. Meanwhile, the viola challenges the first violin's hypermeter at the two-bar level (entering in a weak bar for the first-violin part), and the cello does the same at the four-bar level.

But how "real" is the second violin's challenge to the established, notated meter? As far as a listener from outside the ensemble is concerned, it surely poses little threat. An impartial listener can appraise all of the metrical cues within the texture and resolve metrical conflicts by weighing all the evidence and letting the strongest case prevail.[32] Here, the four-bar hypermeter has remained unchallenged through most of the movement, and the two-bar hypermeter and the notated meter have been sacrosanct. Exposed to that endorsement of duple bias (MPR 10), the listener will tend to remain entrained with at least the two-bar and one-bar levels of pulse as established and so hear the viola and second violin as syncopated on those levels, respectively.[33] But unlike an outside listener, the individual players attend, by degrees, to the musical whole *and* to their own particular parts; the latter occupy each player's attention in a unique way.[34] The second violin knows he cannot singlehandedly change the meter, and the notated bar lines within his part provide visual confirmation that "his meter" is but a syncopation against the true meter.

---

use a fuller sound and more incisive articulation. But it is arguable that the "conceptual" slurring, which defines the motive as a group, applies even when it is not literally marked.

This same principle may be useful in the analysis of vocal music, in which the slur markings of an instrumental introduction might be applied to later repetitions of the same material in a vocal part, even when the slurs are not literally present. The justification in that case is that the slurring of a vocal part is determined by the syllabification of the text, a technical notation similar to the bowing in this passage.

[32] The notion of "weighing the evidence" is implicit in Lerdahl and Jackendoff as an analytical strategy for passages with conflicting metrical signals, although the authors concede that this is an underdeveloped aspect of their theory: "We have not completely characterized what happens when two preference rules come into conflict. Sometimes the outcome is a vague or ambiguous situation; sometimes one rule overrides the other, resulting in an unambiguous judgment anyway." Lerdahl and Jackendoff, *A Generative Theory of Tonal Music*, 54.

[33] On entrainment, see Candace Brower, "Memory and the Perception of Rhythm," *Music Theory Spectrum* 15, no. 1 (1993): 19–35; and Justin London, "Loud Rests and Other Strange Metric Phenomena (or, Meter as Heard)," *Music Theory Online* 0, no. 2 (April 1993), www.mtosmt .org/issues/mto.93.0.2/mto.93.0.2.london.art.

[34] Any seasoned socialite has encountered some garrulous conversationalists who are concerned only with their own contributions and others who are more sensitive to the full company's discourse. So too, *mutatis mutandis*, do chamber musicians vary in the degree of attention they focus on their own part versus the whole ensemble, especially while sight-reading.

Yet an earnest bid for change allows these three measures of metrical *Wettstreit* to function like the exalted opposition (*concertare*) of choir sections that add to the grand spectacle of the passage.[35]

A more complex example of canon *per arsin et thesin* is found in the first movement of Brahms's Sonata in E♭ Major for Piano and Clarinet, op. 120, no. 2 (shown in Ex. 6.5a). In this movement, the canon – which appears as the subordinate theme (mm. 22ff.) and expresses a conflict between the clarinet and piano – poses a serious threat to perceived meter, at least as the passage is heard in time.[36] The sonata opens with a fairly regular, four-bar hypermeter (mm. 1–8, resumed in mm. 11–14), although the legitimacy of the notated bar line is briefly called into question in mm. 15–17, which sound like two quasi-$\frac{3}{2}$ measures.[37] Within these quasi-$\frac{3}{2}$ measures, the bass is syncopated, placing the long notes on the second part of each half-note beat (MPR 5a, amplified by MPR 6). The piano's bias toward the second halves of half notes foreshadows events yet to come during the subordinate theme.

Measures 18–21 restore the normal $\frac{4}{4}$ meter,[38] and these bars may be heard as restoring the normal, four-bar hypermetrical level on account of parallelism (MPR 1, comparing m. 18 to the hyperdownbeats in m. 1 and m. 11), the *forte* marking in m. 18 (MPR 5b), and the relatively long slurs in the clarinet in m. 18 and in the piano's left hand in m. 20 (MPR 5c).[39]

---

[35] The reality of the opposition within a canon *per arsin et thesin* would be more vivid in an actual Renaissance choral work (compared to this later instrumental imitation), since bar lines are not notated and motivic parallelisms are reinforced by the text. In a score such as Mozart's, with notated bar lines, any attempt to change the meter at the level of the notated measures is an uphill battle. But at the hypermetrical level, it is anybody's game since levels above the notated measure are unnotated and far more manipulable.

[36] Whereas my analytical prose engages metrical and hypermetrical ambiguities that arise as the passage is heard in time, the notated bar lines indicate the end-state meter (i.e., the "real" meter), which is clarified to the listener around m. 28. The counting numbers in Ex. 6.5a likewise represent an end-state hypermetrical analysis.

[37] The impression of quasi-$\frac{3}{2}$ bars arises on account of melodic parallelism (MPR 1) and harmonic considerations, since the harmonies on B♭ (m. 15) and C (m. 16, third beat) are relatively long (MPR 5f) and the harmonic stability favors the C-minor harmony over the diminished-seventh chord that precedes it (MPR 9).

[38] Several factors establish the downbeat of m. 19 as a metrical downbeat and not the third beat of a quasi-$\frac{3}{2}$ bar, including (1) the first-statement-stronger rule favoring the downbeat of m. 19 over the middle of the bar (MPR 11), and (2) the inception of a new pattern of accompaniment in both the piano and clarinet beginning in m. 19 (MPR 5d, amplified by MPR 6 in the piano's left hand).

[39] The status of mm. 18–21 as a four-bar hypermeasure is somewhat undercut by other signals that prefer m. 19 over m. 20, including (1) the commencement of an accompanimental pattern in m. 19 (MPR 5d), (2) the introduction of the clarinet's triplet figure in m. 19, which is preferred as stronger than its (loose) imitation in m. 20 (MPR 11), and (3) the *diminuendo*

Ex. 6.5 Brahms, Sonata in E♭ Major for Piano and Clarinet, op. 120, no. 2, Allegro amabile (i)
a. Score

Ex. 6.5 (*cont.*)

b. Alternative barring of mm. 22–29, following the piano part ▶

The meter becomes less clear after m. 21, where the grand pause invites the players to take extra time for the sound to fade before the next entrance. As the clarinet begins the *sotto voce* theme, it may not be obvious whether his first quarter note is an upbeat or downbeat, especially because of the softness of his attack and the lack of accompaniment. This ambiguity is exacerbated when the piano enters in canon one quarter note later. The formerly reliable half-note level – which had remained steady even in the quasi-$\frac{3}{2}$ measures – is thus called into serious question.[40]

marking (MPR 5b). In light of these conflicting metrical cues, a listener might experience parallel multiple-analysis at this juncture, awaiting further metrical clarification in the music that follows.

[40] Regarding the reliability of the half-note level within much of this exposition: Lerdahl and Jackendoff use mm. 9–10 from this movement to theorize their concept of tactus, which they define as a "perceptually prominent level of metrical structure . . . [that is] the minimal metrical level that is required to be continuous." Lerdahl and Jackendoff, *A Generative Theory of Tonal Music*, 71–72. Whereas their definition points to the salience of the quarter-note level as the *minimum* metrical level *required to be* continuous, my discussion notes the prominence of the half-note level as the *maximum* metrical level that *actually is* continuous up to this point.

William Rothstein has recently challenged the notion that any one level can be established as *the* tactus, on the grounds that individual listeners will perceive different levels as perceptually

An outside listener would struggle to choose between the clarinet's and the piano's respective metrical cues and might sustain two plausible, parallel analyses for several measures. Ex. 6.5b shows a plausible alternative meter that a listener might perceive based on cues in the piano part. Although Brahms's notated meter is supported by the clarinet's status as *dux* (MPRs 2 and 11), the piano's "false" meter draws credence from the piano's bass role (MPR 6) and the harmonic advantage (MPR 9) of the piano's B♭ (the tonic) over the clarinet's concert F (the dominant).

Harmonic rhythm (MPR 5f), often a decisive consideration in such conflicts, is challenging to interpret in this passage, at least at first, on account of the lack of explicit harmony for the clarinet's first note. Since the clarinet's concert F (m. 22) immediately follows an augmented-sixth chord, it may seem to represent a fleeting dominant harmony and so be heard as an upbeat to the piano's entrance one beat later, with its unequivocal tonic harmony (MPR 9). The ambiguous harmonic rhythm continues in the following measure. Brahms's notated meter suggests that a C-minor harmony commences on the downbeat of m. 23, against which the piano's downbeat notes are heard as suspended from the previous harmony. But another possible hearing (based on Ex. 6.5b) shifts the harmonic rhythm one quarter note later, interpreting the harmonies as commencing with the piano's quarter notes (Brahms's notated second beats, shown as downbeats in Ex. 6.5b); accordingly, the clarinet's notated downbeats are interpreted in Ex. 6.5b as upbeats and anticipations. In the absence of a fixed point of reference (and without looking at Brahms's notation), it is not immediately obvious which instrument is expressing "the" meter. What scant clues exist to articulate the half-note level tend, at first, to lead the listener *away* from the notated meter (Ex. 6.5a) and toward the renotated version in Ex. 6.5b. Tellingly, the piano's putative anticipations (shown on the final eighth notes of Ex. 6.5b, mm. 22 and 24) behave more idiomatically than do the upward-resolving suspensions (retardations) in Brahms's original version (on downbeats in Ex. 6.5a).

By mm. 26–27, the interpretation in Ex. 6.5b begins to seem less plausible, although the piano's slurring continues to advocate for the shifted bar lines (MPR 5c). At m. 28, as the theme repeats, Brahms's

---

prominent, so much so that one listener's tactus may be another's hypermeasure ("Hypermeter Reconsidered," paper presented at the Society for Music Theory, New Orleans, LA, November 1, 2012). On the historical meaning of tactus (which differs from Lerdahl and Jackendoff's definition), see George Houle, *Meter in Music, 1600–1800: Performance, Perception, and Notation* (Bloomington: Indiana University Press, 1987), 4.

notation is finally confirmed as the "true" meter. Whereas one could question the location of the bar line at m. 22, no such ambiguity remains at m. 28.[41] The thematic repetition thus allays any lingering doubts about the notated meter, which is in turn confirmed retroactively. The piano accompaniment continues to favor the second beats – note the short-long accompaniment rhythm beginning in m. 28 (MPR 5a) – but these long notes are clearly heard as syncopations against the notated meter. The clarinet, it turns out, had been right all along.

An important aspect of parallel multiple-analysis is that, even though the correct meter is ultimately inferred and the "wrong" interpretation discarded, the weighing of alternative metrical structures is an important part of the experience of hearing (or playing) the passage in time. Indeed, the interpretation in Ex. 6.5b may for a moment seem more plausible than the "real" meter or, perhaps better, the metrical interpretation that ultimately proved to be lasting. The end-state metrical structure, like history, is determined by the victor, and only after the conflict has ended.

Schenker would encourage the pianist to play up this metric mischief by emphasizing the counter-metrical cues within her part:

> It is the responsibility of the performer primarily to express the special rhythmic characteristics of a composition, *as they sometimes coincide with the meter, sometimes oppose it* [emphasis added]. Today, not only the failure to recognize rhythmic relationships but also sheer indolence creates a preference for the metric scheme alone – a dismaying evidence of decline.[42]

The role of a performer who projects a meter he or she knows to be "wrong" is comparable to that of the hypothetical singer performing the role of Don Giovanni (discussed in Chapter 4). The fictional character Don Giovanni believes it is his prerogative to seduce women with impunity, even as the singer knows that the moral of the opera (according to its alternate title, *Il dissoluto punito*) is that such behavior will ultimately be punished. Likewise, while the character Donna Elvira takes her own

---

[41] Unlike the downbeat of m. 22, the downbeat of m. 28 has its own eighth-note upbeat, which clarifies that the clarinet's quarter note on the downbeat is preferred as stronger (MPR 5a). Moreover, whereas it had been unclear in m. 22 whether a long tonic harmony commenced on the downbeat or on second quarter, there is a clear change of harmony on the downbeat of m. 28 from dominant to tonic (MPR 5f).

[42] Schenker, *Free Composition*, 126. See also the discussion later in the chapter of D. G. Türk's and L. Mozart's recommended performance practice for slurs and ties that oppose the meter. The instruction to emphasize what modern scholars call rhythmic dissonances in performance is analogous to the practice of emphasizing certain intervallic dissonances (e.g., strong-beat dissonances such as suspensions and appoggiaturas), which is described by these same authors.

moralizing most seriously, the soprano who portrays her is aware that her function in the opera is largely comic. In the case of Brahms's sonata, the piano *persona* plays the role of the counter-metrical agent, even if the piano *player* is surely aware of the true meter, which is apparent from the notated bar lines.

The foregoing analyses of the canons in Exx. 6.3, 6.4, and 6.5 begin to demonstrate the possibilities of a decentered approach to metrical analysis, which I posit as a general phenomenon that is not limited to canonic imitation. In the remainder of this chapter, I will explore the intersection between a decentered view of meter and the concept of multiple agency.

Establishing, sustaining, and changing (or challenging) meter

In order to speak of meter as multiple agency, it is necessary to consider the circumstances in which an analyst can assign responsibility for activating a metrical preference rule to a particular part or cohort. Mirka describes an outside listener's processing of meter as involving three phases: (1) finding meter, (2) monitoring meter, and (3) changing meter. These same phases could be reframed in terms of the players' actions as (1) establishing, (2) sustaining, and (3) changing or challenging meter.[43] Passages in which an established meter is sustained and relatively unchallenged are likely to be analyzed non-agentially, using non-purposive reporting.[44] This corresponds to Mirka's notion that the listener's process of parallel multiple-analysis "hibernates" during the phase of monitoring meter.[45] The most palpably agential analytical language will therefore correspond either to the phrases of the initial phase of establishing meter or to subsequent events that change or challenge an established meter. The multiple-agency perspective is particularly fruitful in passages in which one radical character (or cohort) acts decisively to attempt to change the existing meter, while another, conservative character (or cohort) stubbornly holds onto it. Such passages will be heard by an outside listener as metrically ambiguous or as a hypermetrical transition, depending on whether the radical character successfully persuades his colleagues to entrain with him.

---

[43] Exx. 6.4 and 6.5 demonstrate that an instrument can *challenge* an established meter without successfully *changing* it.

[44] Monahan, "Action and Agency Revisited," 325.

[45] Mirka, *Metric Manipulations in Haydn and Mozart*, 23.

Ex. 6.6 Mozart, String Quartet in G Major, K. 387, Allegro vivace assai (i)
a. Score

In the opening of Mozart's String Quartet in G Major, K. 387 (shown in Ex. 6.6a), a highly regular initial hypermeter is disrupted through the actions of the first violin, prompting a period of metrical uncertainty until all parties act to restore the meter. The opening of this movement is

characterized by a strongly in-phase relationship between grouping and meter. In this example, and throughout the remainder of this chapter, brackets indicate grouping[46] and numbers indicate hypermeter in an end-state hearing. Numbers are suspended during some passages of ambiguity or hypermetrical transitions, which often arise from conflicting signals among individual parts.

Throughout the primary theme (mm. 1–10), an extended sentence, the placement of resting points or cadences in the middle of most even-numbered bars strongly groups the passage into two-bar units. The sentential structure of the theme suggests that these groups establish

---

[46] Whereas Lerdahl and Jackendoff assume one grouping structure for the complete texture, I sometimes show brackets in individual parts to reflect their distinct grouping structures. In this respect, my analyses resemble what Georgiades ("Aus der Musiksprache des Mozart-Theaters") calls *Polymetrik*, although his concept could more properly be called "poly-grouping." That is, although Georgiades assumes congruence between groups and metrical units, a group may or may not be a metrical unit.

Ex. 6.6 (*cont.*)

b. Alternative barring of mm. 13–19

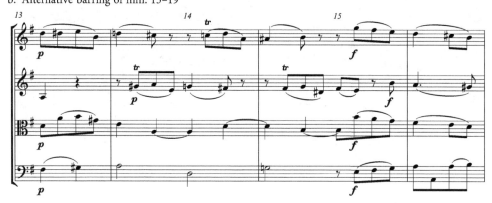

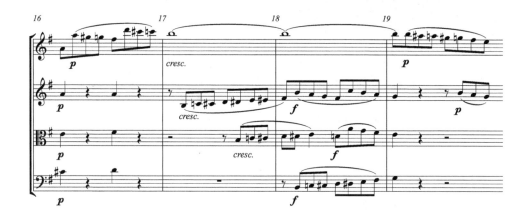

a two-bar hypermeter; note the parallelism of the basic idea (mm. 1–2) and its repetition (mm. 3–4; MPR 1). The greater harmonic stability of the downbeat of m. 1 compared to that of m. 2, as well as that of m. 3 compared to that of m. 4, provides further support for this two-bar hypermeter (MPR 9). That said, this theme might sound hopelessly four-square were it not for another opposing stream of mid-bar stresses caused by appoggiaturas (mm. 1–7) and by *crescendos* that partly counteract Mozart's slurs (m. 8 and m. 10).[47] The appoggiaturas (which trigger MPR 4) reside primarily in the first-violin part. Although it hardly seems

---

[47] See William Rothstein, "National Metrical Types in Music of the Eighteenth and Early Nineteenth Centuries," in *Communication in Eighteenth-Century Music*, ed. Danuta Mirka and Kofi Agawu (Cambridge University Press, 2008), 141.

that the first violin is attempting to supplant the notated meter – he observes a supportive alternation of *forte* and *piano*, for instance (MPR 5b) – his mid-bar stresses create a significant shadow meter. (Here, metrical conflict is found within a single instrumental part.) Without posing an existential threat to the notated meter, the mid-bar placement of these stresses becomes established as a norm under the principles of parallelism (MPR 1) and duple bias (MPR 10).

As m. 11 gets underway, it seems that the established, odd-strong hypermeter will continue. The new phrase begins as a restatement of the primary theme – by the second violin, one octave lower than the original – but soon proves to be the transition. Thus, the parallelism between m. 11 and m. 1 (MPR 1) and the momentum of the established hypermeter encourages the continued expectation (projection) of a continued, odd-strong hypermeter (fulfilling MPR 10). But just as the second violin begins his statement of the theme, the first violin introduces a pronounced hypermetrical conflict by imitating the same figure in the original register in m. 12. Having politely ceded the floor to his colleague, the first violin seems to renege after just one bar ("hey, that's my theme!"). Elbowing his way back into the melodic role, the first violin attempts to "overwrite" the second violin's statement, forcing a metrical reinterpretation, so to speak, by fiat. Since the theme has previously commenced on hyperdownbeats (cf. m. 1 and m. 11), the first violin attempts to make m. 12 into a hyperdownbeat through parallelism (MPR 1). This action is not merely an attempt to thwart the prevailing hypermeter; it is a flagrant contradiction of the second violin's incipient statement.

While the first violin's strategy – attempting to trump duple bias (MPR 10) with parallelism (MPR 1) – may seem dubious, he cavalierly believes he can pull it off by virtue of his rank as the quartet's "leader."[48] He manages to sway the cello, who treats m. 13 like m. 2 (compare the cello's part in those two measures), a parallelism that is reinforced by the *subito piano* in m. 13 (cf. m. 2). Once an analogy is established between m. 2 and m. 13, it may seem that the counterpart to m. 1 must have been the first violin's statement in m. 12 and not the second violin's statement in m. 11, as it had originally seemed. Is the crafty first violin

[48] Despite the first violin's exalted role within a string quartet, there is no official metrical preference rule that favors him over the second violin, though for some listeners, a first-violin statement may seem uniquely salient. The only metrical preference rule that favors one persona over the others is MPR 6, which prefers "a metrically stable bass," granting a slight advantage to the lowest-sounding instrument (usually the cello).

trying to make it seem like it was the second violin, and not he himself, who spoke out of turn?

By m. 13, it is clear that either m. 11 or m. 12 was an "extra" bar. The individual personas, with their unique vantage points, may have different perceptions of which bar is extra and how the anomaly came about. Thus, even as the first violin enters in m. 12, the second violin may still hope to complete his melody and so prefer a conservative hearing – interpreting the first violin's statement in m. 12 as a metrically weak imitation of his own (MPR 11). The second violin indeed treats most of m. 12 as parallel to m. 2, despite the first violin's rude interruption. The first violin, on the other hand, pursues a radical course, whereby m. 12 is a *restarting* and therefore metrically strong (as parallel to m. 1, MPR 1). This conflict serves to break down the formerly reliable hyper-meter, inviting the outside listeners (as well as the viola and cello) to engage in parallel multiple-analysis until future signals re-establish the metrical structure.

The rivalry between the two violins plays out further in their imita-tions during mm. 13–14. The passing of the eighth-note figure (from the first violin to the second violin within each measure) could support the notated measure under the first-statement-stronger rule (MPR 11). (On a higher order, the same rule also favors m. 13 as stronger than m. 14, which is a motivic repetition.) However, other signals point to a temporary breakdown of the notated meter, such that the middle of m. 13 sounds like a downbeat, as shown in Ex. 6.6b. The first violin's quarter-note D may be preferred as a downbeat on several grounds: (1) it is longer than the eighth notes that precede it, which therefore tend to sound anacrustic (MPR 5a); (2) it will likely be stressed in performance, as an appoggiatura and as the inception of a two-note slur (MPR 4);[49] and (3) harmonic stability favors the A-major triad over the D dominant-seventh chord that follows (MPR 9). More subtly, a new (albeit short-lived) pattern of accompaniment begins in the middle of m. 13 in the cello and viola, with their circle-of-fifths intervals and syncopated rhythms (MPR 5d). This patterning is matched by the imitation between the violins at the same half-note periodicity. The first violin, conspiring with the viola and cello, has managed to make the shadow meter of the opening phrase seem, ever so briefly, like the real meter, with the notated mid-bar appoggiaturas heard as real

---

[49] Note, however, that this slur does not trigger MPR 5c, since it is shorter than the immediately preceding slur.

downbeats.[50] The first-statement-stronger rule (MPR 11) still obtains in this interpretation, since the first violin's initial appoggiatura (middle of m. 13) is heard as stronger than its imitation in the second violin (downbeat of m. 14).[51]

After all four parts quit their patterns in m. 14, the *subito forte* of m. 15 signals resolve, perhaps toward restoring the original meter.[52] On the downbeat of m. 16, the lower parts change to *piano* (MPR 5b) and briefly take up a new accompaniment pattern (MPR 5d). Meanwhile, the first violin spins an extended anacrusis, which finds its definitive downbeat at m. 17 with a two-bar-long note (MPR 5a) that reaffirms the notated meter and begins to re-establish the two-bar hypermeter. The hypermeter garners further support from the pattern of imitation among the lower parts: motivic entries mark every half note in mm. 17–18 and stop on the downbeat of m. 19 (MPR 5d). Finally, the half-cadential arrival during m. 20 confirms the restoration of odd-strong, two-bar hypermeter, matching previous cadence placements on the second half of even-numbered bars (MPR 1; cf. mm. 8 and 10, as well as lesser arrivals in mm. 2, 4, and 6).

Setting the rules: MPRs in the chamber

Which MPRs are most germane to the analysis of interplay in chamber music? Lerdahl and Jackendoff conceived of MPRs as universal models of

---

[50] Alternatively, a conservative hearing could cite the parallelism between mid-bar stresses in mm. 1–10 and in mm. 13–15 as favoring the notated meter (MPR 1).

[51] In the struggle for dominance between the two violins, one factor favoring the first violin – besides his general prominence by virtue of being leader and playing in a higher register – is that his part is more interesting. That is, whereas the second violin's statement in m. 11 begins as an exact repetition of the first violin's theme (save for the registral change), the first violin *develops* the melody by substituting C♯ for C♮ in the middle of m. 13, precisely the moment where the bar line may be heard as shifted. This difference between the two violins' behavior is consistent with Carpani's characterization of the first violin as a character who can invent and the second as one who can merely imitate. Moreover, whereas the second violin's verbatim repetition seems to be stuck in the primary-theme area, the first violin signals that the transition has already commenced. In other words, his charisma as the quartet's leader grows from his attention to where the movement is going (D major), rather than where it has been (G major), and may thus tend to attract his colleagues' attention.

[52] In another sense, the *subito forte* underscores a different kind of grouping by dynamics. Whereas the movement's primary theme began with alternating *forte* and *piano* bars, the transition (mm. 11ff.) begins with two *forte* measures followed by two *piano* measures, which would encourage a listener to project a change to *forte* on the downbeat of m. 15. However, whereas the primary theme's dynamic alternation was amplified by its coordination with other regular elements of metrical patterning, the lack of such regularity or coordination in the transition tends to mask the two-bar alternations of *forte* and *piano*.

metrical perception for tonal music; only their suspension rule (MPR 8) is described as idiom-specific.[53] This assumption of universality is challenged in William Rothstein's recent research on meter in Italian opera, which concludes that the relative weighting of various metrical preferences varies with genre and style.[54] Since my subject is German instrumental music, Lerdahl and Jackendoff's MPRs (as adapted in Fig. 6.1) serve as an appropriate point of departure, but I wish to underscore two MPRs that are especially relevant to chamber music idioms.

Modules of patterned activity (MPR 5d) and cycles of imitation

Frequent changes of texture and patterning – which figured prominently in the foregoing metrical analysis of Ex. 6.6, especially of the transition – are an essential stylistic feature of string quartets.[55] The onset of what I call a *module of patterned activity* is strongly preferred as a position of metrical strength (MPR 5d).[56] A module of patterned activity typically involves all accompanimental parts, if not the entire ensemble. All participating parties are "on duty," as it were, meaning that their every utterance is part of the patterned activity within the module. Since these patterns often involve interlocking or complementary rhythms among the parts, I prefer the term "patterned activity," which captures this interplay more vividly than Lerdahl and Jackendoff's term "pattern of articulation" for MPR 5d.

The opening eight-bar phrase of Haydn's String Quartet in F Major, op. 77, no. 2 (shown in Ex. 6.7) is structured as a four-bar group

---

[53] Lerdahl and Jackendoff discuss universality and idiom-specificity in *A Generative Theory of Tonal Music*, 278–81. On suspensions, see ibid., 89–90.

[54] Rothstein discusses "MPRs *all'italiana*" to correct for what he regards as a bias among music theorists toward the norms of German instrumental music: "It may be an exaggeration to claim that different nineteenth-century repertoires require different lists of MPRs, but the same MPRs must surely be weighted differently for Verdi than they would be for Schumann or Chopin, Brahms or Bruckner, Dvořák or Tchaikovsky." Rothstein, "Metrical Theory and Verdi's Midcentury Operas," 108.

[55] Texture figures prominently among the "generic fingerprints" of the late-eighteenth-century string quartet described in Sutcliffe, "Haydn, Mozart and Their Contemporaries," 187–88. See also the historical authors surveyed in Chapter 2.

[56] This notion accords with a traditional teaching of fifth-species counterpoint. Students are advised to avoid "square" rhythms (such as two half notes followed by four quarters) since the tendency of changes in rhythmic values to parse music into sections is undesirable in that context. But in free composition, composers use essentially this very technique when the commencement of a module of patterned activity confers a metrical accent on the inception point (MPR 5d). See Felix Salzer and Carl Schachter, *Counterpoint in Composition*, 2nd ed. (New York: Columbia University Press, 1989), 101–4; and Schenker, *Free Composition*, 122.

Ex. 6.7 Haydn, String Quartet in F Major, op. 77, no. 2, Allegro moderato (i)

overlapping with a five-bar group.[57] The grouping overlap, whereby m. 4 is both an ending and a beginning, arises partly from the new pattern that commences on the downbeat of that measure, which effects a metrical reinterpretation (4 = 1 due to MPRs 5d and 11). The importance of m. 4 as a turning point is particularly clear in the first-violin part, given the introduction of the dotted-rhythm motive that continues for the remainder of the phrase. As for the accompanying cohort, several modules are apparent, defined by rhythms, dynamics, and bowing style. In one sense, the accompaniment in mm. 3–4 is a rhythmic repetition of mm. 1–2 (especially in the second violin and viola), but the switch to sustained bowing and a *piano* dynamic marks the downbeat of m. 3 as the start of a distinct module (MPRs 5b and 5c). Another module spans m. 4 through the downbeat of m. 6, and, by way of overlap, yet another emerges in mm. 6–7 (where the chords might be played using all downbows). Inceptions of modules are often coordinated with changes of playing style,

---

[57] See Rothstein's analysis in *Phrase Rhythm in Tonal Music*, 34–36.

Ex. 6.8 Cycles of imitation in chamber music for strings
a. Mozart, String Quartet in C Major ("Dissonance"), K. 465, Allegro (i), retransition

conferring upon them an embodied or felt salience, and thus metrical accent, for the players.[58]

An especially strong metrical preference is activated by a particular kind of module of patterned activity that I call a *cycle of imitation*. A cycle of imitation occurs when a motive is imitated by each instrument at a regular time-interval. Imitative entrances typically take place in order from lowest to highest (or vice versa) and often involve overlapping entries with long notes. In cycles of imitation, the strongest beat of the first statement is normally stronger than the parallel beats of all subsequent entries. This principle has an obvious relation to the first-statement-stronger rule (MPR 11), but it involves MPR 5d as well since a cycle of imitation constitutes a module with a unified pattern (canonic imitation) that terminates after the final imitative statement.

---

[58] This principle is true for modules that commence on beats. Offbeat beginnings are a special case.

b. Beethoven, Quartet in C Minor, op. 18, no. 4, Allegro (iv), *maggiore* theme

module of patterned activity

Several passages from K. 387 examined above contain cycles of imitation. A textbook example is the opening of the finale's coda (shown in Ex. 6.4), since the canonic entrances at two-bar intervals define the eight-bar hypermetrical level. The opening sixteen bars of the same movement (shown in Ex. 4.2) also comprise a cycle of imitation. In the first movement (shown in Ex. 6.6a), mm. 17–18 employ a variant of this device, since only the lower three instruments make imitative statements while the first violin holds a long note. The first violin seems like a *de facto* participant, since the points of imitation in the lower parts derive from his part in m. 16. Although there is no canonic entry at the end of m. 18, the lower three instruments play three stepwise eighths in contrary motion, in imitation of the same figure. A new cycle begins in m. 19 with the potential to last for two full measures, but it breaks off to allow for a cadence in the middle of m. 20; note the simultaneous entrance of viola and cello.

Ex. 6.8 (*cont.*)

c. Tchaikovsky, Sextet in D Minor ("Souvenir de Florence"), op. 70, Allegro con spirito (i)

Cycles of imitation are ubiquitous in chamber music, especially in music for strings, since they exploit the ensemble's timbral homogeneity. Ex. 6.8 shows additional examples from compositions by Mozart, Beethoven, and Tchaikovsky.

Slurs (MPR 5c)

Mozart's slurs, marked with meticulous care in his autograph manuscripts, are often revealing metrical signals. One factor that heightens the salience of slur markings in this style is their tendency to be performed with stress. Türk describes the customary execution of slurs with the following commentary about Ex. 6.9:

> In [Ex. 6.9], example (a) all eight notes are slurred [*geschleift*], and in example (b) four and four are slurred. The note on which the slur marking [*Bogen*] begins is very mildly (barely noticeably) accented. In example (g) there is also this mild emphasis (against the customary rule [*sonst zu befolgende Regel*]) on the weak notes [*schlechten Noten*] marked with the (+) sign. In example (h) the F♯, D, and B [receive a similar mild emphasis].[59]

The emphasis that is normally placed on the first note of a slur – in the absence of any marking to the contrary – means that MPR 5c and MPR 4 (stress) tend to be triggered concurrently. This synergetic effect is especially true of short, two-note slurs that resemble appoggiaturas.[60] Sometimes, a two-note slur will fail to activate MPR 5c – if it is surrounded by longer slurs – though it might well receive more stress in performance (MPR 4). But in passages with fairly regular slur lengths, the durations of slurs can have a quasi-metrical status and influence the listener's (or especially the performers') counting. For instance, at the start of K. 387's first movement

---

[59] Türk, *Klavierschule*, 355 (Web Doc. #37). See also the English translation published in *School of Clavier Playing*, 344. The idea of slightly accenting the first note of a slur appears in nearly every eighteenth-century treatise on performance, by such authors as J. J. Quantz, L. Mozart, C. P. E. Bach, and D. G. Türk. A detailed discussion appears in Sandra P. Rosenblum, *Performance Practices in Classic Piano Music* (Bloomington: Indiana University Press, 1988), 158–82. The execution of slurs was essentially the same for the string family and for keyboard instruments. As Rosenblum notes, some treatises explicitly instruct keyboard players to execute slurs by imitating the bowing of string instruments. The earliest statement of this idea appears in Samuel Scheidt's *Tabulatura Nova* (1624), which includes the marking "Imitatio Violistica" for some slurred passages (see ibid., 172–73). The association between slur markings and bowings may be implicit in the German word *Bogen* (literally "arc"), which refers to both bows and slurs.

[60] In a discussion of the gestural meaning of slurs in late-eighteenth-century keyboard music, Robert S. Hatten describes the two-note, descending slur as the "prototypical slurred gesture of the *galant* style." Hatten, *Interpreting Musical Gestures, Topics, and Tropes*, 140.

Ex. 6.9 Examples of slurs (from Türk, *Klavierschule*, p. 355)

Ex. 6.10 Slurs as equivalents of rhythmic values (from Lerdahl and Jackendoff, *A Generative Theory of Tonal Music*, Exx. 4.27 and 4.28)

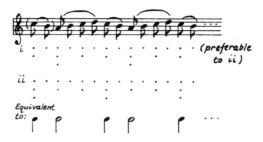

(Ex. 6.6a), the preponderance of slurs of half-note length promotes counting by half notes, establishing what might be called the "basic pace" of bowing that holds for much of the movement.[61]

Türk's advice to emphasize the first note of a slur even when it is on an offbeat, "against the customary rule" about "good" and "bad" notes, hints at a principle that Lerdahl and Jackendoff have made more explicit, namely, that the duration of a slur is equivalent to a rhythmic value (as shown in Ex. 6.10). By extension, a slur that commences on a weak beat is equivalent to syncopation at the relevant metrical level. The opening phrase of Haydn's Piano Sonata in C Major, Hob. XVI:50 (shown in

---

[61] I am adopting the term "basic pace" from Channan Willner, "Sequential Expansion and Handelian Phrase Rhythm," in *Schenker Studies 2*, 192–221.

Ex. 6.11 Haydn, Piano Sonata in C Major, Hob. XVI:50, Allegro (i)

a. Score

b. Voice-leading derivation of m. 3

Ex. 6.12 Ties across bar lines (from Leopold Mozart, *Versuch einer gründlichen Violinschule* [Augsburg, 1756], 259)

Ex. 6.11a), illustrates the point. Ex. 6.11b shows the derivation of m. 3 from fourth-species syncopations. The same syncopation is inherent in the leaps A–D and G–C in mm. 1–2, but the slurs beginning with the upbeat to m. 3 amplify the effect.

The related phenomenon of ties across bar lines is discussed by Leopold Mozart in the following terms:

Nowadays there are certain passages in which a clever composer brings about the expression in a completely unusual and unexpected way [shown in Ex. 6.12] ... Here the expression and the intensity [*Stärke*] of sound is placed on the last quarter of the bar, and the first quarter of the following bar will be completely calm and without emphasis. One thus does not distinguish these two notes at all with the bow; rather, one plays them as if they were just a half note.[62]

---

[62] L. Mozart, *Versuch*, 259 (Web Doc. #20). See also the English translation published in *A Treatise on the Fundamental Principles of Violin Playing*, 221. Although this example contains only ties, it immediately follows a discussion of slurring.

In terms of eighteenth-century performance practice, Leopold Mozart's commentary generally applies equally to *slurs* across bar lines.[63]

The capacity of slurs to challenge the notated meter is illustrated in the first trio from Mozart's Clarinet Quintet (shown in Ex. 6.13). A characteristic feature of this trio's design is the placement of two-note slurs on each beat during the opening – from 3 to 1 (first violin), from 1 to 2 (viola and cello), and from 2 to 3 (second violin) – creating a kaleidoscopic effect. If each slur is executed with emphasis on the first note (as generally advocated by Türk, Leopold Mozart, and other eighteenth-century authors), the result is an un-dancelike impression of relative equality among the three beats that contrasts with the minuet and especially with the *schwungvoll, Ländler*-like second trio. The slur markings seem as if each party wishes the onset of its slur to sound like a downbeat, especially in the lower three parts, following the principle of decentered meter developed above. The cello and viola, who support the notated bar lines, have the advantage of the established meter from the preceding minuet (MPR 10), which is further supported by the stability of the root-position chords for the beginning of each slur on the downbeat (MPR 9). The cello receives an additional advantage as bass (MPR 6). Many of the second violin's slurs, if his part is analyzed in isolation, are bolstered by the stability rule (MPR 9) as well, especially those that commence on chordal roots (e.g., mm. 1, 3, 4, and 5).[64]

It is the first violin, however, who seems to believe the least strongly in the metrical stream suggested by his slur patterns. While the onset of his initial slur coincides with a change of dynamic (MPR 5b) and is favored by a preference for early downbeats (MPR 2), these factors are outweighed both by entrainment with the previous meter from the minuet (MPR 10) and by the tendency to hear $\hat{5}$ to $\hat{1}$ idiomatically as an upbeat-to-downbeat gesture, especially in light of the lack of accompaniment (MPRs 3 and 6).

---

[63] Modern string players generally observe ties as indicated, but it is common to take extra bows within slurs (especially long slurs). However, this practice might be challenged since, according to Ex. 6.10, the (audible) changing of the composer's slurring is tantamount to changing the rhythm. (It is also equivalent to adding syllables into the declamation of vocal music.) The notated slurs are especially important in music before around 1800, when a trend toward smoother bowing and longer lines began to emerge. The evolution from eighteenth- to nineteenth-century approaches to articulation and phrasing is encapsulated in Beethoven's description of Mozart's keyboard playing (according to Carl Czerny) as "choppy and staccato [*gehackte und kurz abgestoßene*]." Carl Czerny, *Erinnerungen aus meinem Leben* (1842), ed. Walter Kolneder (Strasbourg: Éditions P. H. Heitz, 1968), 15. See also Houle, *Meter in Music*, 96.

[64] The stability rule (MPR 9) properly applies to verticalities, but I have extended it here to consider the second-violin part in isolation.

Ex. 6.13 Mozart, Clarinet Quintet in A Major, K. 581, Trio I (iii)

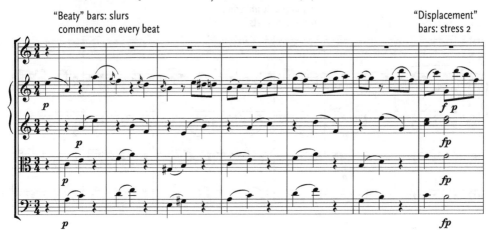

"Beaty" bars: slurs
commence on every beat

"Displacement"
bars: stress 2

"Beatless" bars:
6-beat quasi-slur

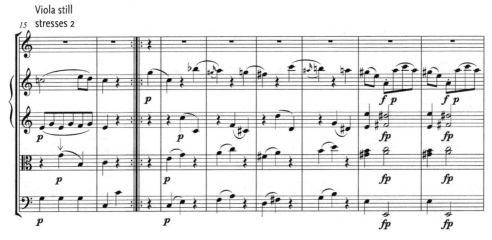

Viola still
stresses 2

Ex. 6.13 (*cont.*)

Viola's canonic imitation
stresses 2nd beats

Literal 6-beat slur (cf. mm. 9–10)

Only uncontested
one-bar slur

By the upbeat to m. 4, the first violin's upbeat-to-downbeat slurs have disappeared, leaving only the competition between the cello/viola, who favor the notated downbeats, and the disputing second violin, who prefers the notated second beats.

The pattern of emphasis on the notated second beat becomes a fixation in mm. 7–8; the half notes with *fortepiano* markings trigger metrical preferences for stress (MPR 4) and length (MPR 5a), while harmonic stability (MPR 9) still favors the downbeats. The first violin responds in mm. 9–10 with an undifferentiated, two-bar module of figuration (MPR 5d) that has an effect similar to that of a two-bar slur; one can compare the reprise of the same material (mm. 34–35), where a literal two-bar slur is performed by the inner voices as they shadow the first violin (MPR 5c). After these figures repeat (mm. 11–12 and 13–14), the ensemble joins together in relative metrical conformity for the cadence (mm. 15–16). The violins' bar-long slurs (matched by the cello's tones, if not his articulation) are the first in the trio. Only the viola provides a subtle reminder of the trio's tendency toward emphasized second beats, perhaps foreshadowing his canon during the reprise (mm. 25–31). Tellingly, the only uncontested one-bar slur appears in m. 40, leading to the trio's final cadence.

In summary, the preponderance of short slurs strongly marks the longer, two-bar slurs in mm. 34–35 (and the related, two-bar module in mm. 9–10) for consciousness. Whereas two-bar slurs in $\frac{3}{4}$ meter sometimes suggests an *imbroglio* between groupings of $3 \times \frac{2}{4}$ and $2 \times \frac{3}{4}$,[65] this trio establishes a more idiosyncratic contrast between three types of measures: (1) "normal" bars with each quarter emphasized by a different part, as in the opening;[66] (2) bars with one main emphasis displaced to the second beat, as in mm. 7 and 8; and (3) comparatively beatless two-bar units comprising a six-beat, descending scale, as in mm. 9–10. In establishing these contrasts in performance, the execution of slurs is a decisive factor.

---

[65] See, for instance, the opening of Mozart's String Quartet in A Major, K. 464. Mirka carefully distinguishes the Galant technique of *imbroglio* (or *Verwirrung*) from the older concept of hemiola (*Metric Manipulations in Haydn and Mozart*, 135–51 and 159–64). See also Floyd K. Grave, "Metrical Dissonance in Haydn," *Journal of Musicology* 13 (Spring 1995): 168–202. On grouping dissonance, see Krebs, *Fantasy Pieces*, 31–33.

[66] Cf. Koch's concept of *Metrum* (regularity of beats), discussed by Mirka, *Metric Manipulations*, 93–99. See also Joseph Riepel's related concept of alive (*lebendige*) and dead (*todte*) notes, discussed in *Anfangsgründe zur musicalischen Setzkunst*, vol. 1, *De Rhythmopoeïa, oder von der Tactordnung* (Regensburg, 1752), 5. See English translation in Treitler, ed., *Strunk's Source Readings in Music History*, 757.

Multiple agency: three analyses

The test for any analytical method is whether it bears fruit in practice.[67] In the following three analyses, I intend to show more fully how a multiple-agency methodology illuminates aspects of meter that may be overlooked by other, unitary approaches to metrical analysis. Recordings and videos of all three of the excerpts analyzed are provided among the Web Resources.

Before proceeding to the analyses, one theoretical concern deserves mention because of its relevance to all three excerpts. This has to do with the separation of grouping and meter. Many analysts of phrase rhythm assume that listeners prefer groups (such as phrases) that begin with a metrical "1"; such groups or phrases are said to observe a "rule of congruence" between grouping and meter.[68] However, end-accented phrases are not unusual, and are moreover common in certain repertoires and contexts.[69] The first bar of a four-measure phrase group – or *Vierer*, in eighteenth-century parlance[70] – may well begin on a hypermetrical "1,"

---

[67] The notion of "fruitfulness" is adopted from Matthew Brown, *Explaining Tonality: Schenkerian Theory and Beyond* (University of Rochester Press, 2005). Brown's other (equally important) criteria for assessing a theory are accuracy, scope, consistency, simplicity, and coherence.

[68] This rule of congruence is central to the Schenkerian tradition of hypermetrical analysis. See Schenker, *Free Composition*, 121; Schachter's "Rhythm and Linear Analysis" trilogy in *Unfoldings*, 17–120; Rothstein, *Phrase Rhythm in Tonal Music*, and "Beethoven with and without 'Kunstgepräng.'" The term "rule of congruence" originates in Rothstein's "Kunstgepräng" article.

But Rothstein's recent studies of French and Italian music have led him to question the application of this rule, which he now regards as a style-specific preference that is most relevant to German music after around 1800. Rothstein, "National Metrical Types"; and his "Metrical Theory and Verdi's Midcentury Operas."

[69] On end-accented organization in sonata-form closing themes, see David Temperley, "End-Accented Phrases: An Analytical Exploration," *Journal of Music Theory* 47 (Spring 2003): 125–54. This tendency of closing themes to employ end-accented phrases is almost certainly related to conventions of Italian text setting. Within a set piece in Italian opera, a typical line of verse has its main accent on the penultimate syllable, which is known as the *accento comune*; such a line is called a *verso piano* ("plain"). But a stanza-ending line usually contains one fewer syllable and ends on an accented syllable (*verso tronco*, "truncated"). For example, the opening couplet of the so-called champagne aria from *Don Giovanni* is as follows: "Finch'han dal **vi**-no / cal-da la **te**-sta / u-na gran **fes**-ta / Fa' pre-pa-**rar**!" There is no *a priori* relationship between textual and metrical accentuation, and the *accento comune* is placed in both weak and strong hypermetrical positions over the course of the aria. However, the aria's final *verso tronco* ("de-vi au-men-**tar**") is set as an end-accented phrase, concluding on a hyperdownbeat that coincides with the launch of the final orchestral *tutti*. The effect resembles the end-accented phrases that Temperley observes in closing themes of sonatas, a position analogous to an aria's final *tutti*.

[70] Riepel, *Anfangsgründe zur musicalischen Setzkunst*, 1:2. See English translation in Treitler, ed., *Strunk's Source Readings*, 751. See also Koch, *Musikalisches Lexikon*, s.v. "Vierer."

"2," "3," or "4."[71] Thus the ensuing analyses assume nothing about the relation of grouping and hypermeter (as indicated by brackets and numbers, respectively).

Nonetheless, the rule of congruence may influence some readers' hearing of the excerpts for analysis. Such readers will be quicker to hear "departure" meter (whereby phrases begin in metrically strong positions and end in weak ones) than "arrival" meter (whereby phrases begin in metrically weak positions and end in strong ones).[72] For them, the following analyses may seem counterintuitive in places, or certain metrical ambiguities may be difficult to detect as described. Partly with this in mind, I recommend to all readers multiple hearings of each passage, during which alternative hypermetrical interpretations can be tried. (Several suggested listening strategies for repeated hearings were enumerated at the outset of this chapter.) Certain metrical features are too easily masked by existing inclinations and preconceptions yet may be uncovered by cultivating flexible listening habits.

String Quartet in C Major, K. 465 ("Dissonance"), iii ▶

I wish to discuss two possible ways of hearing the hypermeter in the minuet from Mozart's "Dissonance" Quartet, K. 465. According to one version, the minuet comes off as clear cut and highly regular; according to the other, it teems with hypermetrical ambiguities. To begin with the more regular interpretation, I turn to a published analysis by Ryan McClelland, reproduced as Ex. 6.14a.[73] Although McClelland describes the unharmonized first measure as a *gestural* upbeat, he argues that it is a *hypermetrical* downbeat based on two factors: (1) the submediant harmony in m. 2, which is less stable than the (assumed) tonic in m. 1, and (2) the grouping boundary between m. 4 and m. 5. Once m. 1 is interpreted as a hyperdownbeat, McClelland

---

[71] Eric McKee has demonstrated this possibility in "Extended Anacruses in Mozart's Instrumental Music." His excellent analysis of the finale to the Piano Concerto No. 21 in C Major, K. 467 (pp. 15–34), demonstrates what he calls the "metrical rotations of a melody," whereby the same four-measure basic phrase (*Vierer*) appears metrically as "1–2–3–4," "2–3–4–1," or "4–1–2–3," all within the same movement. That is, Mozart's *Vierer* always commences with its first measure – how could it do otherwise? – but hypermetrically this measure appears variously as a "1," "2," or "4."

[72] The elegant terms "departure" meter and "arrival" meter were introduced by Andrew Wilson, "Meter in the Sarabande: Equal or Unequal, Consonant or Dissonant?," paper presented at the Society for Music Theory, Milwaukee, WI, November 7, 2014. The term "departure" meter denotes *beginning*-accented structures that observe the rule of congruence between grouping and meter, whereas the term "arrival" meter refers to *end*-accented structures that violate such congruence.

[73] McClelland, "Extended Upbeats in the Classical Minuet," 27–29.

Ex. 6.14 Mozart, String Quartet in C Major ("Dissonance"), K. 465, Menuetto: Allegro (iii) ◣
a. Hypermetrical analysis by McClelland ("Extended Upbeats in the Classical Minuet," Ex. 2)

b. Opening renotated in $\frac{2}{4}$

proceeds to analyze the entire minuet as a regular, four-bar hypermeter that is disrupted only in m. 24, where a grouping overlap results in a 4 = 1 reinterpretation. Two tacit analytical preferences seem to inform McClelland's interpretation: (1) a strong preference for an in-phase relationship between grouping and meter, per the "rule of congruence" (i.e., group beginnings in mm. 1, 5, and 9 are interpreted as hyperdownbeats at the four-bar level), and (2) a moderate preference for "conservative" readings that minimize hypermetrical reinterpretations.

Together with the adoption of an end-state (rather than in-time) analytical perspective, McClelland's analytical preferences cause certain factors to be downplayed.[74] For example, although mm. 1–4 certainly comprise a four-bar group, it does not automatically follow that this group is a hypermeasure or that m. 1 is metrically stronger than m. 2.[75] Abandoning the assumption that a four-bar group is preferred as a four-bar hypermeasure – and thus the assumption that phrase endings normally fall on weak hypermetrical positions – reveals a more nuanced metrical story that belies the phrase-rhythmic regularity in this piece.

From the very outset, little is clear about this movement's metrical structure even at the level of the notated measure. The first violin's opening gesture, if played "straight," could be heard as in Ex. 6.14b. This hearing is suggested by preferences for early strong beats (MPR 2) and for duple over

---

[74] Although both end-state and in-time methodologies are valid, the tendency of the former to disregard factors conflicting with the ultimate interpretation is unfortunate. See the discussion of Mirka's *Metric Manipulations* above, 186–88.

[75] While Riepel, Kirnberger, and Koch all describe a counting of bars for the comparison of phrase lengths, their counting does not entail a concept of metrical accent and therefore refers to grouping (phrase lengths) rather than hypermeter. Koch's "rhythmic relations of phrases" (*rhythmischen Vergleichung der Sätze*) refers neutrally to a counting of phrase lengths as a means to track expansions, contractions, and reinterpretations that manipulate basic phrases. Heinrich Christoph Koch, *Versuch*, vol. 2 (Leipzig, 1787), 427 and *passim*. See English translation in Koch, *Introductory Essay*, 42. (My Ex. 4.7, excerpted from Kirnberger's *Die Kunst des reinen Satzes*, illustrates such an expansion, whereby a four-bar model is transformed into a five-bar idea.) In modern parlance, this counting of phrase units refers to grouping structure only; the numbers 1–2–3–4 or 1–2–3–4–5 merely indicate where a group (phrase) begins and ends, not necessarily which measures are metrically strong or weak. Mirka draws a sharp line between this non-metrical, compositional counting of phrase lengths and the truly metrical counting experienced by listeners. Danuta Mirka, "Metre, Phrase Structure and Manipulations of Musical Beginnings," in *Communication in Eighteenth-Century Music*, 108 n. 10.

triple metrical relationships (MPR 10) as well as by the melodic contour of four ascending notes followed by four descending ones.[76] The first violin may choose to clarify the $\frac{3}{4}$ meter with a slight accent on the downbeat (MPR 4); such emphasis is encouraged by the accidental F♯, although it is discouraged by the slur.

As the lower parts enter in m. 2, their harmonic rhythm (MPR 5f) belatedly establishes the $\frac{3}{4}$ meter, retroactively clarifying the meter of the first violin's opening figure. But what of hypermeter at the two-bar level? Since the extended *gestural* upbeat in m. 1 may or may not be a *hypermetrical* upbeat, subsequent events are needed to clarify its status. Compared to the implied tonic harmony in m. 1, the submediant harmony in m. 2 is less stable (MPR 9), supporting odd bars as hypermetrically strong. However, by m. 3, it becomes apparent that m. 2 was the beginning of a module of patterned activity (MPR 5d), which in turn retroactively favors an even-strong hearing (MPR 11). As the phrase continues, the metrical cues remain in conflict: the inception of a three-bar-long V^7 harmony in m. 4 (MPR 5f) favors the even-strong hearing, but the upbeat to m. 5 commences a new dynamic and texture (MPRs 5b and 5d), favoring odd-strong interpretation. While the parallelism rule (MPR 1) favors an identical status for mm. 5 and 7, it is difficult to say whether these measures are identically strong or identically weak at the two-bar level. By this point, the continued lack of metrical clarity at the two-bar level must be a little frustrating for the characters within the piece, who cannot tell, so to speak, which way is up and which way is down. After all, locating the initial hyperdownbeat – where dancers would imagine commencing the first *pas de menuet* – is no academic question for eighteenth-century listeners, even in a stylized, art minuet such as this.

McClelland argues that "the hypermetric structure is sealed by the forceful beginning of a sequential passage in m. 9."[77] However, in my view, the passage remains ambiguous since what McClellend calls the beginning of a sequence is arguably its middle. That is, a cycle of imitation commences *in m. 8* whereby the same figure is imitated by all four instruments in succession, which strongly predicts mm. 8–11 as a four-bar hypermetrical unit (MPRs 5d and 11) – but the cycle is undercut in m. 9 by the *subito forte* (MPR 5b) and the introduction of new

---

[76] Lerdahl and Jackendoff's *Grouping* Preference Rule 3 (n.b. not *Metrical* Preference Rule 3) is triggered by a change of register, dynamic, articulation, or length and could be expanded to observe this change in melodic direction.

[77] McClelland, "Extended Upbeats in the Classical Minuet," 27.

countersubject motive in the first violin (MPR 11), both of which point to that measure as strong.

A listener who cues into the cycle of imitation in mm. 8–11 is rewarded by the conspicuously long, *sforzando* note in m. 12 (MPRs 4 and 5a), seemingly the strongest signal of hypermetrical strength in the movement so far. McClelland's analysis interprets this measure as a hypermetrical "4," partly out of conservative hearing and partly because of what comes before and after: m. 13 features a change of dynamic, motive, and pattern of accompaniment (MPRs 5b, 5d, and 11) and is more harmonically stable than m. 14 (MPR 9). In short, as soon as m. 12 seems to finally confirm an even-strong hearing, the following measure again suggests the odd-strong alternative. A listener influenced by the rule of congruence will tend to hear the cadences in mm. 16 and 20 as metrically weak – the "4" of a four-bar hypermeter, as in McClelland's analysis. But another listener, attuned to the tendency for some closing themes to feature end-accented phrases, might hear them as hyperdownbeats, consistent with hearing the *sforzando* in m. 12 as a hyperdownbeat (MPR 4).[78]

The minuet's first reprise seems to me altogether ambiguous at the two-bar level, to say nothing of the four-bar level shown in Ex. 6.14a. Almost every bar can claim some metrical preference rule in favor of its hypermetrical strength, but on cross-examination other arguments must be conceded that indicate hypermetrical weakness. Whereas minuets intended for dancing are counted in groups of six beats, suggesting the presence of a two-bar hypermetrical level, conflicting metrical signals in this art minuet forestall any sustainable two-bar level.[79]

Perhaps this lack of order motivates the characters to attempt to resolve the hypermeter in the second reprise. My analysis (shown in Ex. 6.14c) focuses on two moments in which the cello and first violin (respectively) act decisively to establish hyperdownbeats. Although the opening four bars of the second reprise are modeled after mm. 1–4, the metrical structure of the movement's opening was never established; therefore, the parallelism

---

[78] Temperley, "End-Accented Phrases: An Analytical Exploration." Temperley's discussion of end-accent in closing themes is merely an observed tendency, not a rule, and it pertains more to sonata-form or concerto movements than to minuets. Nevertheless, Temperley's observations are a helpful corrective against overrelying on the rule of congruence. Lerdahl and Jackendoff's cadence rule (MPR 7) likewise offers no preference for phrases as ending in positions of metrical strength or weakness; it merely prefers that cadences be metrically stable – on a beat, rather than syncopated.

[79] A similarly balanced example – equally countable as even- or odd-strong – is Beethoven's famous Minuet in G Major, WoO 10, no. 2. I thank William Rothstein for showing me this aspect of Beethoven's minuet.

Ex. 6.14 (*cont.*)

c. Alternative hypermetrical analysis (second reprise only)

rule (MPR 1) cannot clarify the status of mm. 21–24. Moreover, the use of unison texture beginning in m. 21 nuances the hypermeter, since the switch to unison texture constitutes the beginning of a pattern (MPR 5d, amplified by MPR 6).[80] Nevertheless, if m. 21 seems initially to be a hyperdownbeat, the nascent odd-strong hearing is immediately challenged since the first-statement-stronger rule favors m. 22 over m. 23 (MPR 11). Harmonic stability (MPR 9) also favors as strong the implied local-tonic harmony in m. 22.[81]

The cello, wielding the authority of MPR 6 (as bass) and fed up with this pervasive hypermetrical ambiguity, takes action in m. 24 by holding B♭ over the bar line to produce the longest note so far, thereby activating the length rule (MPR 5a) and influencing the harmonic rhythm (MPR 5f). This pivotal moment is the first juncture in which any individual instrument has acted so defiantly and independently to activate a metrical preference rule, making it the most palpably purposive moment in the movement so far.[82] The cello's action, which establishes m. 24 as strong, achieves the first moment of real hypermetrical clarity.[83] By forcing an overlap against the existing grouping, the cello reveals himself as the quartet's most radical member. The first violin, in contrast, seems metrically conservative since he continues his four-bar melodic statements, undeterred by the cello's action. This results in a conflict of parallelism: whereas the first violin begins parallel melodic groups in both m. 21 and m. 25, m. 21 tends to sound metrically strong whereas m. 25 is decidedly metrically weak.

Although the even-strong hypermeter is established in mm. 24–27, the metrical structure of mm. 28–34 is once again difficult.[84] In order to clarify

---

[80] Whereas the entrance of a bass in m. 2, after its absence in m. 1, tends to support hearing m. 1 as an upbeat (MPRs 3 and 6), these considerations do not apply in the opening of the second reprise since all four parts enter in unison in m. 21.

[81] Thus, despite the melodic parallelism (MPR 1) between mm. 1–2 and mm. 21–22, other metrical preferences cut across that correspondence. Namely, as noted above, harmonic stability (MPR 9) favors m. 1 as strong but disfavors m. 21, even though these represent corresponding bars. The parallelism between the second bars of each reprise is likewise undercut by MPR 5d, since m. 2 represents the inception of a new texture (the chordal accompaniment) whereas m. 22 continues the unison texture that had been established in the previous measure.

[82] Up to this point, nearly all of the contradictory metrical signals have been among various metrical preferences rather than among personas within the ensemble. It is telling that m. 24 is the one juncture in which McClelland departs from conservative counting to read a 4 = 1 reinterpretation.

[83] The hypermetrical strength of m. 24 is supported by the stability rule (MPR 9), which favors the triad in m. 24 over the augmented-sixth chord in the following measure. This newfound, even-strong hypermeter seems to be clinched by the cadential $^6_4$ in m. 26 (preferred by MPR 8 as strong).

[84] If a listener remains entrained with the even-strong hypermeter established in mm. 24–27 (MPR 10), the first-statement-stronger rule (MPR 11) would favor m. 28 as stronger than m. 30,

the hypermeter in time to prepare the recapitulation, and perhaps as an answer to the cello's long note in mm. 24–25, the first violin adopts the same strategy (with an even longer note) to effect a 4 = 1 reinterpretation in m. 35. In addition to the length of the first violin's note (MPR 5a), the hypermetrical strength of m. 35 is supported by the inception of the dominant pedal (MPR 5f) and the re-entrance of the cello (switching from string-trio texture back to quartet texture; MPR 5d). During the ensuing standing-on-the-dominant (mm. 35–39), the inner voices anticipate frag- ments of the main theme (upbeats to mm. 36 and 38). These bars are clearly weak due to the harmonic rhythm (MPR 5f) and stability (MPR 9, which favors the dominant chords in mm. 35 and 37 over the embellishing harmonies). The second violin and viola's statements thus sound anacrus- tic, from weak to strong, like the first violin's statement of the same figure in m. 25 – and unlike the unison statement in m. 21 or the cello's statements in mm. 28 and 30. In short, even as the characters are preparing for the thematic recapitulation, they have yet to reach an agreement regarding the preferred metrical status of the main motive.

That the recapitulation is preceded by a five-bar dominant pedal (mm. 35–39) complicates its metrical status. After the 4 = 1 reinterpret- ation in m. 35, duple bias (MPR 10) favors the onset of the recapitulation (m. 40) as weak. Yet the recapitulation is expressed as a cycle of imitation, which favors the violins' initial statement in m. 40 as stronger than the viola's imitation in m. 41 (MPR 11). Hypermeter remains unclear in mm. 44–50 due to the same same conflicting metrical signals found in the parallel passage (mm. 5–11). Measure 51 (like its analog, m. 12) is favored as strong due to the long, stressed note (MPRs 4 and 5a), but unlike m. 12, it is also favored as strong because of the harmonic progression, since the bass line F–F♯–G–G (mm. 51–54) favors the odd bars as strong (MPR 5e).[85] Moreover, harmonic stability (MPR 9) favors m. 51 over m. 52, and the

establishing a four-bar hypermeasure for the first time in my analysis. But this hypermeasure is cast into doubt by the stability rule (MPR 9), which favors the triads in mm. 29 and 31 over their respective, preceding dominant sevenths; according to this radical, odd-strong hearing, the first-statement-stronger rule (MPR 11) would favor m. 29 over m. 31, since it favors the *strongest beat* within the model over that within the copy – not the entire model over the entire copy. Having achieved hypermetrical clarity in mm. 24–27, and possibly having lost it in mm. 28–31, the upper parts initiate a module of patterned activity in m. 32 (MPRs 5d and 11) that bolsters the ongoing, even-strong interpretation and, thus, provides retroactive support for hearing mm. 28–31 as a hypermeasure after all.

[85] MPR 5e pertains to abstractly prolonged *tones* as opposed to literal *notes* (as in MPR 5a). In the cello part during this passage, the tone F governs mm. 51–52 and the tone G governs mm. 53–54. On the distinction between notes and tones, see above, 111 n. 1.

suspension rule favors the cadential $^6_4$ in m. 53 over the dominant-seventh in m. 52 (MPR 8). The lack of a cello note in m. 54 further suggests a weak measure (MPR 3, amplified by MPR 6). This hearing renders the coda (mm. 55–63) in end-accented phrases. Although the coda could alternatively be heard in beginning-accented phrases, an interpretation that is supported by the dynamic markings in m. 52 and on the upbeat to m. 60 (MPR 5b), the preponderance of metrical preferences points to the end-accented interpretation. Whether this evidence is retroactively admissible to help interpret the parallel music in the hypermetrically ambiguous first reprise – depends on the rules of the court as set by the judge.

Sonata in G Major for Piano and Violin, K. 379, ii ▶

A lively hypermetrical exchange ensues between the piano and violin in the subordinate theme from the exposition of the second movement of Mozart's Sonata in G Major, K. 379 (see Ex. 6.15). After the *Sturm und Drang* primary theme, the piano singlehandedly makes a concise transition to the mediant, reaching the medial caesura (III:HC) in m. 77. Precisely on this arrival, she begins her fluttering *tremolo*, an orchestral effect that initially sounds like caesura-fill but continues for seven measures as an accompaniment to the new theme. The inception of this figure suggests a 4 = 1 reinterpretation (MPR 5d), setting the stage for an odd-strong subordinate theme.[86] Her left hand introduces the new subordinate-theme motive, which she trades back and forth with the violin for several measures.[87] But whose statements are metrically strong? The passage sounds like a hypermetrical debate between the piano's left hand (even-strong) and the violin (odd-strong); the piano's right hand, having raised the subject in m. 77, politely stays out of the crossfire – twiddling her thumbs, so to speak.

The sentential structure of the subordinate theme adds another layer to the hypermetrical disagreement between the violin and the piano's left

---

[86] Cf. Beethoven, Piano Sonata in F Minor, op. 2, no. 1, m. 20. In that passage, the commencement of the (written-out) tremolo effects a 2 = 1 reinterpretation and provides the dominant pedal over which the subordinate theme begins.

   Although Ex. 6.15 shows a 4 = 1 reinterpretation in m. 77, an alternative analysis might adopt odd-strong counting beginning in m. 74 – that is, to regard the transition as end-accented. This is suggested by the harmonic rhythm and the rhythm of the bass line (short-short-short-long), as well as by the stress of the suspensions in m. 75.

[87] This rhythm of this motive bears a strong resemblance to that of the primary theme (cf. m. 50), despite the slight difference in notation.

Ex. 6.15 Mozart, Sonata in G Major for Piano and Violin, K. 379, Allegro (ii), transition and subordinate theme ▶

Ex. 6.15 (*cont.*)

hand. Although it is not a hard-and-fast rule, the intrathematic grouping structure of a normal, eight-bar sentence tends to correspond to its hyper-metrical structure – or, simply put, the presentation and continuation/cadential segments tend to commence on hypermetrically strong measures. Thus the rule of congruence generally holds good for sentences.[88] Here, the piano's sentence (commencing in m. 78) and the violin's sentence

---

[88] Rothstein (personal communication) has noted that German instrumental music of the last quarter of the eighteenth century saw the rise of both the sentence structure and of "departure" meter, whereby grouping and meter are normally in phase. Wilson's "departure" meter is synonymous with Rothstein's "German" meter; see Rothstein, "National Metrical Types."

(commencing in m. 79) are dueling sentences supporting conflicting hypermetrical agendas, similar to the canons *per arsin et thesin* discussed above.

The first-statement-stronger rule (MPR 11) favors the piano's original statement in m. 78 over the violin's imitation in m. 79. Yet, other factors point to an odd-strong hearing: the inception of a dominant pedal and accompaniment figure in m. 77 (MPRs 5d and 5f) and the weak V_2^4 harmonies in mm. 78, 80, and 82 (MPR 9).[89] The preference for a metrically stable bass (MPR 6) is rendered moot in this passage, since it strengthens both the first-statement-stronger rule (MPR 11, favoring the even-strong hearing) and the stability rule (MPR 9, favoring the odd-strong hearing).

The impasse is resolved by m. 83, where the continuation/cadential segment commences in both the piano and violin parts. Despite their presentation segments having been offset by one measure, congruence is achieved for the continuation/cadential segment when the piano defers to the violin's odd-strong meter. (The piano plays an extra measure of material in m. 82 – an incipient third statement of the basic idea – to allow the violin to catch up.) That m. 83 is a mutual hyperdownbeat is particularly clear because the continuation/cadential segment (mm. 83–86) constitutes a module of patterned activity (MPR 5d) with quarter notes in the two outer parts, initially moving in parallel sixths.[90] Measure 83 also represents a return to "normal" texture, with the piano's left hand providing a supportive bass line instead of challenging the violin. The conflict being resolved, the piano's right hand finally feels free to re-enter the conversation, moving in counterpoint with the violin in mm. 85–86. The newfound accord between the violin and piano is further exemplified in their sharing the cadential voice-leading: the violin's F–E♭–D (m. 84) connects to the piano's C–B♭ (m. 85) and back to his own A–B♭ (mm. 85–86).

---

[89] The progression V–V_2^4–I⁶ most naturally treats the V_2^4 harmony as a metrically weak passing chord, on account of stability (MPR 9). But other factors could make the alternations of V_2^4 and I⁶ sound like an appoggiatura (accented neighbor) chord and its resolution, respectively. Cf. the first movement of Mozart's Symphony No. 40 in G Minor, K. 550, mm. 9–13. Lerdahl and Jackendoff offer two alternative analyses of these measures in *A Generative Theory of Tonal Music*, 24.

[90] This pattern would be highlighted further if the violin part contained a two-bar slur in mm. 88–89, as it does when the figure is repeated in mm. 91–92. Mozart's autograph manuscript curiously omits the slur in m. 88, showing a one-bar slur in m. 89; the parallel passage in the recapitulation, mm. 159–60, is marked with two one-bar slurs. These inconsistent slur markings may relate to the considerable haste with which Mozart prepared the manuscript of this sonata (see above, 103–4).

As the sentence arrives at its cadence (and, prospectively, the EEC) in m. 86, the piano's left hand initiates a new, tonic-pedal tremolo, again effecting a 4 = 1 reinterpretation that befits this (apparent) closing theme (MPR 5d).[91] The roles of the three parts now seem to be more fittingly assigned: the piano's left hand plays the pedal point while the two melodic upper parts trade the motivic imitations. One indication of mutual support between the upper parts is their tag-team expression of the *Quiescenza* ($\hat{8}$–$b\hat{7}$–$\hat{6}$–$\natural\hat{7}$–$\hat{8}$) figure, a typical closing-theme gesture.[92] However, it soon becomes apparent that these imitations are not the repeated cadential formulas of a closing theme but a repeat of the dueling-sentence idea heard earlier.[93] But an important difference is that, unlike m. 77, m. 86 marks the beginning of both the tremolo and the first sentential statement, this time in the violin, with the piano answering one measure later. Unlike the previous phrase, these imitations pose no conflict between the first-statement-stronger rule and harmonic stability, because the first statement enters over tonic harmony.

Similar to the piano's five-bar presentation in the previous phrase (mm. 78–82), the violin's five-bar presentation (mm. 86–90) allows the piano to "catch up" for the joint continuation/cadential segment beginning in m. 91. Since m. 86 (the beginning of the violin's presentation) and m. 91 (the beginning of the continuation/cadential segment) both initiate beginning-accented groups, the two-bar hypermeter is disrupted during this five-bar presentation passage, a violation of duple bias (MPR 10). This contrasts with the piano's earlier, five-bar presentation (mm. 78–82), which was revealed in the final analysis not to be a metrical unit and therefore did not interfere with the odd-strong hypermeter in that passage.

Since the four-bar continuation/cadential segment of a sentence normally begins on a strong measure, there are two ways to effect a hypermetrical transition to allow for a metrically accented cadence and to prepare an end-accented closing theme: (1) a 4 = 1 reinterpretation, as in m. 86, or (2) an extension of the continuation/cadential segment that "spills over" into the

---

[91] A conservative hearing that remained entrained with the bass's even-strong hearing since m. 78 would be rewarded by the hyperdownbeat in m. 86, which would be achieved without the reinterpretation shown in my analysis.

[92] B♭–A♭–G is in the violin, answered by G–A♮–B♭ in the piano's right hand. On the *Quiescenza* schema, see Gjerdingen, *Music in the Galant Style*, 181–96. See also Hepokoski and Darcy, *Elements of Sonata Theory*, 103–5.

[93] This parallelism supports hearing the dotted quarters in mm. 86–90 as group beginnings, as shown in Ex. 6.15. Otherwise, as relatively long notes, they might tend to be heard as group endings.

following hyperdownbeat, as in m. 91 through the downbeat of m. 95. This latter strategy affords a two-measure module of patterned activity (mm. 91–92) involving contrary motion between the outer voices, followed by a quasi-hemiola cycle (mm. 93–94) articulated by the bass contour and harmonic rhythm. The effect is one of great metrical unity and a collective effort to prepare a grand cadence, potentially to serve as EEC. This sense of unanimity is heightened by the partial doubling of the violin part in the piano's right hand (Eb–D–C–Bb–A in mm. 93–94).[94] The excitement only grows as the cadence is evaded, prompting a series of one-more-time modules.

Although the evasion begins in the piano's left hand with the V_2^4 harmony at the end of m. 94, it becomes mutual when the upper parts elect not to resolve a^1 to bb^1 on the downbeat of m. 95. The piano's right-hand rest, which constitutes an elision,[95] allows her to make a new entrance for her swirling *Spielepisode* modules. The parallel statement in m. 98 effects a 4 = 1 reinterpretation, which may prompt some (radical) listeners to count in three-bar units and project a new hyperdownbeat at m. 101, whereas other (more conservative) listeners will continue counting in fours. Two hypermetric countings are provided for mm. 101–5 in Ex. 6.15. The upper option will appeal to listeners habituated to the rule of congruence ("departure" meter) and who favor conservative hearing (MPR 10). Consistent with this hearing, m. 102 is favored as strong because of the new dynamic and pattern of articulation (MPRs 5b and 5d) and as the first statement of a motive repeated in the following measure (MPR 11). The alternative option may appeal to listeners habituated to hearing end-accented phrases in closing themes ("arrival" meter) and who favor radical hearings; it is supported by the parallelism between mm. 97–98 and mm. 100–101 (MPR 1), which may encourage a listener to project three-bar units and to hear m. 101 as a "1" bar. This end-accented hearing is further supported by harmonic stability, which favors the tonic harmony in m. 101 over the submediant in m. 102 (MPR 9).

Trio in Eb Major for Piano, Clarinet, and Viola ("Kegelstatt"), K. 498, ii (Trio) ▶

On the heels of a minuet composed largely in regular two- and four-bar hypermeter,[96] the trio of Mozart's "Kegelstatt" trio is rife with

---

[94] Cf. the "breakthrough" idea in the slow movement of K. 493 (Ex. 5.5).
[95] Cf. m. 35 and m. 40 of the first-movement exposition in K. 310 (Ex. 4.8).
[96] For a hypermetrical analysis of the minuet, see Chapter 7.

Ex. 6.16 Mozart, Trio in E♭ Major for Piano, Clarinet, and Viola ("Kegelstatt"), K. 498, Trio (ii) ▶
a. Trio

hypermetrical intrigue (see score in Ex. 6.16a). As in Ex. 6.14, the interplay grows out of the ambiguous metrical status of the first measure (m. 42) and its imitations throughout the trio. As an unaccompanied, *gestural* upbeat, it could be heard as an anacrusis to m. 43 (MPRs 3 and 6). Yet entrainment with the four-bar hypermeter of the previous minuet (MPR 10), along with

Ex. 6.16 (*cont.*)

a preference for early strong beats (MPR 2), favors m. 42 as a hyperdownbeat, rendering the initial four-bar group (mm. 42–45) as a hypermeasure,
in keeping with the rule of congruence.

The viola, with his entrance in m. 43, attempts to clarify the hypermeter
by establishing a hyperdownbeat that would retroactively render m. 42

b. Voice-leading derivation of mm. 43–45

an upbeat measure. He does this by adding a bass that establishes a new pattern of accompaniment (MPRs 3 and 5d, amplified by MPR 6). Together with the piano, he outlines a prolongation of the dominant; since the apparent G-minor chord in m. 44 derives from a $\frac{5-6-5}{3-4-3}$ pedal progression (see Ex. 6.16b), harmonic stability (MPR 9) and harmonic rhythm (MPR 5f) favor dominant chords in mm. 43 and 45 as metrically strong. The piano's short-short-short-long rhythm also favors m. 44 as an upbeat to m. 45 (MPR 5a), supporting the hearing of the clarinet figures as hypermetrically weak.

Harmonic rhythm remains ambiguous as a result of the lack of explicit harmony in m. 42. Since the clarinet's unharmonized concert D immediately follows the final cadence of the minuet, it is initially heard in connection with the preceding B♭ harmony but subsequently reinterpreted as expressing the dominant in the emerging key of G minor (especially once it is recognized as the central tone of a key-defining $\hat{5}-♭\hat{6}-♯\hat{4}-\hat{5}$ figure).[97] Depending on whether one hears the dominant pedal as commencing in m. 42 (implicitly) or in m. 43 (where it becomes explicit), harmonic rhythm would favor one or the other measure as a hyperdownbeat (MPR 5f). Ex. 6.16c shows how the interpretation of the implied harmony in m. 42 would influence the hypermetrical counting of the passage. The counting numbers in the score (Ex. 6.16a) show the same two alternative hypermetrical interpretations.

The clarinet's second entrance in m. 46, echoing m. 42, seems to inaugurate a phrase rhythm of four-bar groups (*Vierer*), even as the hypermeter remains unclear. The viola and piano's right hand certainly latch onto the four-bar phrase rhythm, responding as they did to the

---

[97] Just as the clarinet's concert D may initially be heard in connection with the B♭ harmony that ends the minuet, upon the repeat of the first reprise it likewise may (fleetingly) be heard in relation to the D-minor harmony in m. 62. Regarding the key-defining aspect of the $\hat{5}-♭\hat{6}-♯\hat{4}-\hat{5}$ figure: the figure is a variant form of what Vasili Byros calls the *le-sol-fi-sol* schema. See Vasili Byros, "Meyer's Anvil: Revisiting the Schema Concept," *Music Analysis* 31, no. 3 (2012): 273–346.

Ex. 6.16 (*cont.*)

c. Two harmonic interpretations of m. 42

clarinet's initial statement. What a surprise, then, when the clarinet tricks them by entering a bar too early, in m. 49 instead of m. 50! This immediately prompts the viola and the piano's left hand to cut off their statements early ("oops, did we play too long?").[98] Following the principle of parallelism, the viola and piano (both hands) enter in the following bar, m. 50. This could be characterized in two ways: either naïvely ("that's our cue – so it must be time to play") or more knowingly ("what a gaffe! If we enter here, that should set things right and we can just move on").

However, when the clarinet again enters "too soon" in m. 52 (the piano's right hand alongside), it is clear that something is seriously amiss. The repeated entrances at three-bar intervals raise the possibility of a triple hypermeter, especially in light of the emerging pattern of two dominant

---

[98] The idea of the clarinet surprising or interrupting the others in m. 49 should be qualified on two counts: (1) the interrupting statement involves not only the clarinet but also the piano's right hand, and (2) although the premature stopping of the viola's triplets seems to be prompted by the early entrance of the clarinet figure, the viola evidently had some foreknowledge, since he adjusted the downbeat of m. 49 to reflect the F major harmony (rather than the D major harmony he might have anticipated based on m. 45). Yet the idea is nevertheless persuasive to some musicians. In rehearsal footage by Ensemble DeNOTE, the musicians discuss the "unexpected" entries of the "interrupting" clarinet, who enters "at a higher and higher register" in this passage; unlike friendlier exchanges elsewhere in the "Kegelstatt," here the three players seem to "put each other off a bit." See the documentary *Mozart's "Kegelstatt" Trio K. 498: An Eighteenth-Century Conversation* (2013), produced by John Irving for the Institute of Musical Research, School of Advanced Study, University of London, music.sas.ac.uk/music-video/denote-videos (accessed May 1, 2015).

bars followed by one tonic bar (mm. 46–48 and 49–51). But it is not obvious which measure would be strong. Harmonic rhythm (MPR 5f) favors the dominant harmonies, which are longer, whereas harmonic stability (MPR 9) prefers the tonic chords.[99] Although each clarinet statement preferably receives a parallel metrical status (MPR 1), the status of m. 42 was never definitively established. In short, even as the emerging phrase rhythm of *Dreyer* becomes evident, the hypermeter nevertheless remains vague.

By this point, the preponderance of conflicting signals has become untenable, prompting the piano to "reckon it out" (at m. 55) by means of a four-part canon *per arsin et thesin* that develops the clarinet motive. The clarinet's original, three-note figure spirals out into an extended *imbroglio* chain that undermines the notated $\frac{3}{4}$ meter (A–B♭–G♯–A … F♯–G♮–E♭–F♮, etc., from the clarinet's concert D–E♭–C♯–D). The duply grouped quarters in the piano's soprano part might tend to articulate a 3×2 grouping over mm. 55–56, were it not for: (1) the extended slur, which articulates a quasi-$\frac{4}{4}$ rather than $\frac{3}{2}$ measure; (2) the entrance of the tenor after four quarter notes, which suggests a $\frac{4}{4}$ (or $\frac{2}{2}$) meter within the larger quasi-$\frac{4}{4}$; and (3) the opposing signals (*arsin et thesin*) in the alto and bass voices, which conflict with the soprano and tenor voices, respectively. The overall impression is of four voices within the piano part that are highly uncoordinated, oppositional, and unhinged from the $\frac{3}{4}$ meter.[100]

"Hmm," thinks the viola, "the clarinet is usually my cue, but he hasn't played for a while. I do hear his motive in the piano part, but it's hard to tell what beat *she's* on, since it's all jumbled. I guess I should just play now and see what happens." Thus the viola enters with his triplets – which normally commence on downbeats – on the second beat of m. 57. "Oh dear," thinks the piano, "he really is lost! That canon must have confused him. Maybe I can simplify my part and just beat time to help him out."

---

[99] To compare the G minor harmonies in mm. 44 and 48: Ex. 6.16b shows that m. 44 is but an *apparent* tonic derived from a pedal $^6_4$ progression and is therefore preferred as weak as per the harmonic stability rule (MPR 9). In contrast, the G minor chord in m. 48 is a *real* tonic harmony and is more stable than the dominant chords that surround it.

[100] The slurring of mm. 55–57 and the parallel passage, mm. 85–87, is misleading as shown in Ex. 6.16a, which reproduces the slur markings as shown in the *Neue Mozart-Ausgabe*. In the autograph manuscript, the beginning point of these slurs is vague since Mozart noted them by *hand* rather than by *voice*. This was Mozart's customary practice for multiple voices that appear on the same staff, as noted in Levin, "Performance Practice in the Music of Mozart," 230–31. If the passage were written on separate staves (e.g., in a string quartet arrangement), Mozart very likely would have marked each voice as commencing with a slur, in imitation of the clarinet's marking throughout the trio.

And so the piano switches to homorhythmic chords in the middle of m. 57, immediately after the viola's "wrong" entrance.

The piano's chords, like the viola's triplets, are grouped into two-beat units, but it is not clear in either part which quarters are strong. The piano's first chord might be favored as strong since it commences a module of patterned activity (MPR 5d) and because it is the beginning of the motive D–Eb–C–D (imitating the clarinet's first measure), a motive that has until now always commenced on a downbeat (MPR 1).[101] However, since the sequence features dominant chords resolving to their respective tonics (G to C, F to Bb, etc.), the stability rule slightly favors the tonic chords (MPR 9). The grouping of the viola's triplets – while clearly in two-beat units – can likewise be heard one of two ways: either (1) as a series of embellished tones, each prolonged for two beats (F, Eb–Eb, D–D, C–C), or (2) as a series of appoggiaturas (F–Eb, Eb–D, D–C). Further complicating matters is the viola's entrance on a second beat (commencing his triplets, MPR 5d) with a figure that has always commenced on downbeats (cf. mm. 43, 47, 50, and 53, MPR 1), while the sequence (a module of patterned activity, MPR 5d) commences on the following beat.[102] Whereas it is clear that a two-beat pattern is at play, it is ambiguous which beats are strong or weak and, more to the point, how this pattern relates to the ostensible $\frac{3}{4}$ meter, which has been long held in abeyance.

"All right, I've had enough fun," thinks the clarinet. "Since I caused this mess, I suppose it's up to me to fix it." With the clarinet's entrance in m. 60, the piano abandons her chords, and both parts set to work restoring $\frac{3}{4}$ meter; note the slur markings in m. 60 (MPR 5c) and the grace note that stresses the downbeat of m. 61 (MPR 4). The viola does not fully "get the memo," since he continues along with his triplets, although he does abandon the sequence in m. 60 and has the good sense to stop on the third beat of m. 62 (making a parallelism with m. 45). Several metrical signals conspire in m. 60 to predict a metrically accented cadence in m. 62:

[101] The top line of the piano solo (beginning in m. 55) contains the motivic statements A–Bb–G#–A, F#–G–Eb–F♮, D–Eb–C–D, and Bb–C–A–Bb. Since this motive properly belongs in $\frac{3}{4}$ meter, commencing on a downbeat (as in m. 42 and *passim*), it scarcely registers in this strongly duple *imbroglio* passage, especially once the piano begins her chords on the third beat of m. 57. This metrical confusion undermines the impact of parallelism (MPR 1) as a metrical signal.

[102] In m. 57, I am observing a slight distinction between Lerdahl and Jackendoff's MPR 5d (what they call a "pattern of articulation") and my "module of patterned activity." According to their rule, the commencement of the viola's triplets on the second beat begins a pattern of articulation, since the triplet rhythmic value obtains for an extended period. However, I note that a pattern of activity (i.e., sequence) coordinated between the viola and piano parts commences on the third beat.

Ex. 6.16 (*cont.*)

d. Bass-line reduction of mm. 63–68

the entrance of the clarinet with a relatively long note (MPRs 3 and 5a), the commencement of a quarter-note bass line (MPR 5d), and the quasi-hemiola in mm. 60–61. The repetition of the first reprise thus has a new context: whereas m. 42 initially followed a weak measure from the end of the minuet (suggesting that its phrase-rhythmic "1" is also a hypermetrical "1"), it now follows a strong measure (suggesting an anacrustic hearing).

With matters of hypermeter still not fully resolved, the piano sets to work in the second reprise, imitating with her two hands the interaction between the clarinet and viola from the opening. In her version, the gestural upbeat figure sounds like the hyperdownbeat of what turns out to be a triple hypermeter. A slightly simplified version of her sequential bass line is shown in Ex. 6.16d.[103] Through this fleeting triple hypermeter, she refers back to the clarinet's entrances at three-bar intervals in mm. 46–51. However, she soon rejects this metrical scheme, acting decisively to re-establish her preferred hypermeter: in m. 69, she launches into a new sequence that re-establishes a four-bar hypermeter and places the clarinet's motive decisively in the fourth bar (m. 72, left hand).[104]

"See," the piano says, playing mm. 63–68, "*this* is the mistake that you made before, which messed up the four-bar phrase rhythm." Playing mm. 69–72, she thinks to herself, "But now I've fixed it once and for all: the four-bar hypermeter is finally restored, and I've placed the extended upbeat motive on a clear '4' bar, where I wanted to hear it all along. Now, that pesky clarinet had better not mess it up again!"

But the disobliging clarinet thinks, "I don't care for being told when to play!" And so he enters with an extraneous restatement of his motive

---

[103] My interpretation of m. 63 as a hyperdownbeat is based on the abstract bass *tones* shown in Ex. 6.16d (MPR 5e), since m. 63 is the inception of the bass tone G, which is prolonged for two measures. An alternative interpretation would privilege the more literal MPR 5a, which governs *notes* and which favors the half note in m. 64 over the quarter notes in m. 63. On notes vs. tones, see above, 111 n. 1.

[104] Within this passage, there is a displacement dissonance in the piano's left hand with the three-beat motivic groups commencing on the notated second beats of m. 69 and m. 70. These coincide with attacks in the piano's right hand but not with the harmonic rhythm. This passage seems to be in dialogue with the displacements in mm. 55–59.

in m. 73, turning the piano's (would-be) perfect four-bar hypermeasure into a five-bar unit and undoing the clarity that the piano had nearly achieved. Is the clarinet's statement – which is parallel to m. 42 – heard as a hyperdownbeat since it follows the piano's four-bar hypermeasure? Or is it heard as metrically weak per the first-statement-stronger rule, since it is now positioned as a follower (MPR 11)? Whereas the piano had attempted to settle the matter once and for all, the subversive clarinet's extraneous statement reinstates the very ambiguity that had plagued the original statement in m. 42.

Upon hearing the clarinet entrance, meanwhile, the viola thinks, "That's my cue . . . finally!" and enters in m. 74, followed by the piano, in imitation of the trio's opening. Thus the ensemble's discussion as to the metrical status of the clarinet's figure reaches a climax when it becomes the subject of a cycle of imitation (mm. 77–80). This passage seems to ask the question: "Does this figure belong on the first hyperbeat? The second? The third? The fourth?" (Note that the piano's left hand still advocates its placement in the "4" measure.) The cessation of activity in the harmonic rhythm gives the impression that normal time has "paused" on a V^7 chord while the ensemble tries to work this issue out. The ensuing canonic material (mm. 85–87) and sequence (mm. 88–89) fail once again to clarify the proper placement of the clarinet's motive. The prospect of the trio concluding without having resolved its central hypermetrical issue seems to motivate the intensity of the final measures, where the Neapolitan harmony introduces the dramatic deceptive resolution of the would-be cadential dominant to a German augmented-sixth chord (mm. 91–92).

The story does not end at the double bar, since the ensuing retransition – which lightens the mood considerably with a modulation back to B♭ major – continues the focus on the clarinet figure's hypermetrical status. The viola and piano make their preference abundantly clear: they emphatically attempt to make m. 96 into a hyperdownbeat, since the piano's *vollstimmig* chord decisively activates MPR 3 (amplified by MPR 6), and the viola's triplets indicate a hyperdownbeat by parallelism (MPR 1, in comparison with m. 45, notwithstanding the "wrong" entrances in mm. 57 and 87). The clarinet, perhaps winking, finally concedes when he treats his next statement (m. 97) as an unequivocal upbeat to his long note (mm. 98–101, MPR 5a). The viola and piano celebrate this occasion with an enthusiastic little canon.[105] The canon constitutes a module of

---

[105] The overlapping canonic entries commencing on each beat recall the slurring in Ex. 6.13.

Ex. 6.16 (*cont.*)

e. Coda

patterned activity (MPR 5d) that reinforces the status of mm. 98–101 as a hypermeasure. The clarinet's *Eingang* adds one additional measure and leads the way to the *da capo*.

So has the story been resolved, the clarinet's figure established as a hypermetrical upbeat? The question is posed for the last time when the motive returns in the movement's coda (shown in Ex. 6.16e). The coda opens with a *forte*, varied repetition of the minuet's final hypermeasure (mm. 144–47, repeating mm. 140–43). The four-bar hypermeter tends to render the clarinet's reprise figure in m. 148 as a hyperdownbeat, a status that is reinforced by the change of dynamic (MPR 5b) and by the piano's repetitions of the figure in mm. 149 and 150 (MPR 11, favoring the first statement in m. 148). Perhaps at this very moment the ensemble realizes what should have been clear all along: The clarinet can play his motive in a strong bar and the piano's left hand can repeat it in a weak bar, with both statements coexisting comfortably within a four-bar hypermeasure ("aha – so we *can* have it both ways!"). The viola seems pleased with this newfound understanding, entering in m. 150 in support of the even-strong hypermeter (MPR 1). The clarinet, also enthusiastic about the new arrangement, plays skipping triplets (picked up from the viola) as a lead-in to his final motivic statement (m. 152).[106] If the piano's G♭s (mm. 149 and 153) suggest some lingering misgivings, the viola enters reassuringly to inaugurate a final, closing module. Unlike in m. 151, where the viola stopped after the cadential downbeat, in m. 155, he continues beyond the cadence repeating his figures over the prolonged tonic harmony (MPR 5d). Activating the first-statement-stronger rule (MPR 11), which favors m. 155 as stronger than m. 156, the viola invites his friends to repeat the cadence together in a joyful celebration.

---

[106] The clarinet's triplets are not quite a motivic restatement of the viola's, so MPR 11 is not triggered; but the two bars of triplets in mm. 150–51 do constitute a pattern that triggers MPR 5d, thereby bolstering the even-strong hypermeter.

An afternoon at skittles: analysis of the "Kegelstatt" trio, K. 498

In the meantime, have the skittle-alley in the garden ready because my wife is a great enthusiast of the game.

–W. A. Mozart, letter to Leopold Mozart (Vienna, July 12, 1783) before a visit to Salzburg[1]

A trio for Signora Dinimininimi, Nàtschibinìtschibi, and Pùnkitititi

The title of this chapter is rather a misnomer, since only a tenuous connection links Mozart's so-called "Kegelstatt" trio to the game skittles (known in German as "Kegelspiel" or simply "Kegel").[2] The trio's nickname seems to originate through a mix-up with another composition completed around the same time: the twelve horn duos, K. 487, whose manuscript bears the inscription "July 27, 1786, while playing skittles [*untern Kegelscheiben*]."[3] It is entirely plausible that these modest duos could have been composed while playing the game; indeed, composing for

---

[1] In Mozart, *Briefe*, 2:280.

[2] The game is a form of nine-pin bowling in which a player throws, rather than rolls, a wooden ball in order to knock over the pins. "Kegelstatt" is the Viennese term for the outdoor alley where the game is played, typically in a garden setting. (Although an indoor form of the game has survived to the present day, the fact that Mozart's skittles-related letters and compositions date from summer months point to the outdoor version, which is more commonly depicted in historical documents and images.) Among the illustrations of skittles in the Web Resources, Johann Franz Hörmannsperger's untitled gouache (1736) and Friedrich Eduard Meyerheim's painting *The Skittles Society* (1834) probably depict most closely the sort of festive, summertime scenes in which Mozart would have enjoyed the game – perhaps along with the invigorating beverages that accompanied its play.

[3] The "Kegelstatt" trio was completed about a week later. Mozart's personal works list includes an entry dated August 6, 1786 for "Ein Terzett für Klavier, Clarinett und Viola," with a four-bar incipit. The above-referenced manuscript of the horn duos contains only three of the twelve duos now catalogued as K. 487. Since Mozart did not include them in his personal works list, it is unclear whether the remaining nine are indeed by him; all twelve were published posthumously as *Douze Pièces pour deux Cors composées par W. A. Mozart*, Oeuvre posthume (Vienna: Bureau d'Arts et d'Industrie, [1802]). These duos are often erroneously described as being for *basset* horns or violins. For a complete explanation, see Dietrich Berke's preface to the *Neue Mozart-Ausgabe* VII/21, ix–xii.

instruments associated with the outdoors while indulging in sport even makes a certain amount of sense. But exactly how and when the moniker "Kegelstatt" came to be associated with the K. 498 trio – a far more ambitious, intricate, and innovative composition – remains unclear.[4] It may be that Mozart was particularly keen on skittles during the summer of 1786 and composed more than one piece while playing the game, but most likely anecdotes postdating the composer's lifetime confused or conflated the two pieces, and the trio's spurious nickname has endured.[5]

Even if the association of this trio with sport stems from an uncorroborated myth, however, the nickname captures a certain spirit of "play" that pervades the piece and reflects the milieu in which it was conceived. The trio was written for the Wednesday-evening musical salons hosted by the family of the eminent botanist Nikolaus von Jacquin.[6] An account of the vivacious atmosphere among the younger attendees at these gatherings comes from the Viennese novelist Caroline Pichler, who in her youth had been a member of the Jacquins' circle:

Some sixty or seventy years ago, the family of the celebrated Baron von Jacquin was already a shining beacon for the scholarly world [both] inside and outside of

---

[4] The nickname is first reported in Köchel's 1862 thematic catalog. Reports of Mozart composing while playing games had already become something of a fascination in nineteenth-century Mozart reception, since they accord with images of Mozart's total absorption in music at all hours and ingenious capacities for mental composition. Georg Nikolaus von Nissen has Mozart composing numbers from *Die Zauberflöte* while playing billiards in a coffeehouse and numbers from *Don Giovanni* while playing skittles in his friend Duschek's garden (*Biographie W. A. Mozarts*, 559–61). Mary Novello's notes from her 1829 interview with Constanze Mozart likewise make mention of composing at the billiard table (*A Mozart Pilgrimage*, 95). This trope continues to influence popular depictions of Mozart (as in the 1984 film *Amadeus*) and scholarly treatments alike. For instance, Konrad Küster writes: "What is open to discussion is not so much whether Mozart played skittles while he composed (implying that his attention to the music would have been only superficial), but the complementary question: could he have stopped composing while he played skittles? – and that seems likely to deserve the answer 'No.'" Konrad Küster, *Mozart: A Musical Biography*, trans. Mary Whittall (Oxford: Clarendon Press, 1996), 237. The idea of Mozart being totally engrossed in music at all hours stems from an exaggerated reading of his remarks in a letter to L. Mozart dated Paris, July 31, 1778 (quoted in translated version in ibid.).

[5] Cliff Eisen warns that the story of the trio's composition during a game of skittles should be treated with "great caution" (Abert, *W. A. Mozart*, 708 n. 93). A somewhat more open-minded treatment of the issue appears in Küster, *Mozart: A Musical Biography*, 234–39. Küster notes that, sometime before 1786, Mozart had taken up skittles, billiards, and riding as forms of physical exercise on the advice of the Viennese doctor Sigmund Barisani, who had treated him for various ailments. For additional context, see also Colin Lawson, "A Winning Strike: The Miracle of Mozart's 'Kegelstatt,'" in *Mozart's Chamber Music with Keyboard*, ed. Martin Harlow, 123–37 (Cambridge University Press, 2012).

[6] For an overview, see Hedwig Kraus, "W. A. Mozart und die Familie Jacquin," *Zeitschrift für Musikwissenschaft* 15, no. 4 (January 1933): 155–68.

Vienna and was also sought out by many on account of their agreeable social relations. Whereas the scholars and would-be scholars [*gelehrt seyn Wollenden*] sought out the distinguished father and his [elder son, Joseph Franz] ... the younger attendees likewise gathered around the younger son, Gottfried, who possessed a lively, educated mind and an excellent talent for music linked to his pleasant voice, ... and around his sister, Franziska ... Franziska played the clavier admirably and was one of the best female students [*Schülerinnen*][7] of Mozart's, who composed the trio with clarinet for her, and she moreover sang nicely ... *Wednesday evenings* were dedicated in this house to conviviality [*Geselligkeit*] ... Learned conversation took place in the father's rooms, and we young people chatted away, joked, made music, played little games, and had a great time.[8]

Pichler thus documents that the "Kegelstatt" trio was written for none other than Franziska von Jacquin, no doubt to play with the clarinetist Anton Stadler and the composer on viola. Mozart was on intimate terms with Gottfried von Jacquin and counted Franziska von Jacquin among his finest pupils. In a letter to Gottfried, composed about half a year after the "Kegelstatt" trio, Mozart writes:

I kiss the hands of your sister – Signora Dinimininimi – 100,000 times, with the request that she practice diligently on her new piano – but this reminder is unnecessary as I must confess that I've never yet had a female student who was

---

[7] Pichler's use of the word "Schüler*innen*" – comparing Franziska von Jacquin to other *female* students specifically – should be understood in context, since Mozart's keyboard students by and large were aristocratic women, with some notable exceptions. Schönfeld's *Jahrbuch der Tonkunst von Wien und Prague* includes entries for both Pichler and Jacquin. The terse entry for Jacquin (s.v. "Laccusius," a misspelling of her married name "Langusius") describes her merely as "a good forte-piano player" (Schönfeld, "A Yearbook of Music in Vienna and Prague, 1796," 306). In contrast, Pichler (s.v. "Greiner," her maiden name) is effusively praised as "an excellent woman [who] combines remarkable qualities which grace head and heart with a high degree of musicality. She is one of Vienna's foremost lady pianists with a masterly touch, strong in execution, and is undaunted by the greatest difficulties" (quoted in ibid., 298). This disparity between these descriptions may reflect Schönfeld's appraisal of each lady's musical talents, but it could also stem from their relative visibility in musical circles c. 1796 or possibly the styles of multiple writers who may have contributed anonymously to Schönfeld's *Jahrbuch*.

[8] Caroline Pichler, *Denkwürdigkeiten aus meinem Leben* (Vienna, 1844), 1:179–81 (Web Doc. #24). *À propos* the lively atmosphere among the younger attendees, Pichler's remarks recall the separate account (attributed to her) of an episode at her own salon in which Mozart impulsively interrupted her playing in order to improvise a duet together and, once he tired of the music, began leaping and somersaulting about the room while meowing like a cat (see above, 108 n. 100, and Web Doc. #16). However, it should be emphasized that both Pichler's memoirs and the other account attributed to her were published posthumously and represent a mid-nineteenth-century recounting or mythologizing of long-past events.

so diligent and who shows so much zeal – in fact, I'm already looking forward to teaching her again in my own inadequate fashion.[9]

Mozart's effusive enthusiasm for teaching Franziska is striking; whereas he seems to have viewed teaching certain students as a chore necessitated by financial circumstances, some combination of Franziska's personal and musical qualities made theirs a particularly rewarding teacher–student relationship,[10] and she remained Mozart's student until his death.[11] The greatest evidence of Mozart's esteem for Franziska's musical gifts is to be found in the technically demanding passages in the scores he composed for her, notably in the rondo-finale of the "Kegelstatt" trio and throughout the four-hand Sonata in C Major, K. 521.[12] That Mozart composed a four-hand piano piece to play with Franziska may, in itself, bespeak some desire to become closer to her – musically, socially, and

---

[9] W. A. Mozart to Gottfried von Jacquin, Prague, January 15, 1787, in Mozart, *Briefe*, 4:11. Another excerpt from this well-known letter was discussed above, 95–96, where it was noted that "Dinimininimi" was one of the nonsense nicknames that Mozart assigned to various members of their circle, including all three Jacquin siblings, Anton Stadler, and himself. The salutation "Signora," as opposed to "Signorina," seems a curious choice for a young lady of seventeen years.

[10] Mozart was not above lavishing attention on his favorite students while treating others with relative indifference. The Viennese banker Henickstein, an accomplished amateur musician who knew Mozart well, claimed "Mozart would not take pains in giving Lessons to any Ladies but those he was in love with" (Novello and Novello, *A Mozart Pilgrimage*, 144). Henickstein's remark is consistent with Otto Jahn's portrayal of Mozart's good humor with his female students as opposed to his more reserved or casual approach with certain male students. Jahn's discussion includes reports by the following three students: (1) Joseph Frank, an accomplished amateur musician whose first lesson with Mozart was mostly spent passively observing Mozart at the keyboard rather than playing himself; (2) Thomas Attwood, whom Mozart sometimes invited to play billiards instead of having a lesson; and (3) Franz Jakob Freystädtler, who wrote in his memoirs that his theory lessons regularly took place at a table adjacent to – what else? – a game of skittles. Jahn, *W. A. Mozart*, 3:192–200. English translations of these anecdotes appear in Abert, *W. A. Mozart*, 708–10. For a more even-handed appraisal of Mozart's attention to his male students, see also Daniel Heartz, *Mozart, Haydn, and Early Beethoven: 1781–1802* (New York: W. W. Norton, 2009), 159–60.

[11] Konstanze Mozart, *Briefe, Aufzeichnungen, Dokumente, 1782–1842*, ed. Arthur Schurig (Dresden: Opal-Verlag, 1922), xxxviii.

[12] Mozart completed the K. 521 four-hand sonata on May 29, 1787 and was evidently quite eager to play it with Franziska. He sent a message to Gottfried requesting that he "be so good as to give this sonata to your sister with my compliments. She should tackle it right away, as it is rather difficult" (undated letter quoted in Mozart, *Briefe*, 4:48). When the sonata was published the following year, Mozart re-dedicated it to Nanette and Babette Natorp, daughters of a wealthy Viennese merchant and members of the Jacquin circle. Babette was also a student of Mozart and later married the elder Jacquin son, Joseph Franz.

    Mozart's nickname for Franziska – Dinimininimi – could possibly refer to fast notes and virtuosity (i.e., from "diminutio" or "minim," the equivalent of naming a student "Miss Hemidemisemiquaver" or "Mr. Fastfingers").

physically.[13] The intimate contact involved in the performance of such keyboard duets is depicted in the engraving in Fig. 7.1 and in the famous Mozart family portrait by Johann Nepomuk della Croce (see Web Resources).[14]

Considered against the backdrop of the Jacquins' salons, the "Kegelstatt" trio takes on a particular kind of social meaning as a "friendship piece" (*Freundschaftsstück*).[15] In the same sense that Mozart commonly referred to his clarinet quintet as *Stadler's* quintet, the "Kegelstatt" trio is very much *Jacquin, Stadler, and Mozart's* trio – or, perhaps better, *Signora Dinimininimi, Nàtschibinìtschibi, and Pùnkitititi's*. Its setting for the unlikely combination of keyboard, viola, and clarinet – the last an instrument that few if any dilettantes could play – reflects its conception as an occasional piece for these three friends to enjoy together rather than as a

[13] Four-hand piano duets must have carried a special meaning for Mozart, who popularized the genre with his sister during their youthful European tours. Stanley Sadie, *Mozart: The Early Years, 1756–1781* (Oxford University Press, 2006), 72. On Mozart's compositions for piano duet, see Sutcliffe, "The Keyboard Music," 66–69.

[14] Playing four-hand duets was surely among the most physically intimate activities that a grown man and woman could partake in together in polite company. Hand-crossing between the two players – showcased prominently between Wolfgang and Nannerl in the della Croce portrait – effectively composes such contact into the score, leaving it to the players to negotiate the awkward choreography. An early example of this technique is the fifth variation of Haydn's four-hand divertimento "Il maestro e lo scolare," Hob. XVIIa:1. The potential for such physical contact to offend decorum may explain the seated man shown listening to (and therefore also chaperoning) the younger couple at the keyboard in Fig. 7.1. Charles Burney likewise prefixed an elaborate preface to his *Four Sonatas or Duets for Two Performers on One Piano Forte or Harpsichord* (London, 1777) that reassured the players that "though, at first, the near approach of the hands of the different performers may seem aukward [*sic*] and embarrassing, a little use and contrivance with respect to the manner of placing them, and the choice of fingers, will soon remove that difficulty." Burney later commissioned a six-octave harpsichord from Merlin designed expressly so that two ladies wearing hoop skirts could play duets together. For a fascinating social history of four-hand piano playing in the nineteenth century, see Adrian Daub, *Four-Handed Monsters: Four-Hand Piano Playing and Nineteenth-Century Culture* (Oxford University Press, 2014).

[15] Harlow likewise describes the trio as "a creative consequence of biographical stimuli," noting that it was "rescued for biography through an anecdote and a nickname." Harlow, "The Chamber Music with Keyboard in Mozart Biography," in *Mozart's Chamber Music with Keyboard*, 23. I borrow the neologism "Freundschaftstück" from Harald Strebel, "Mozarts 'Kegelstatt'-Trio in Es-Dur KV 498 und seine Besetzung," *Mozart-Studien* 15 (2006): 165. Mozart once used a similar expression – but as a pejorative – referring to the ballet music he composed for Jean-George Noverre as a (mere) "Freundstück," since the composition led neither to payment nor professional advancement. W. A. Mozart to L. Mozart, Paris, July 9, 1778, in Mozart, *Briefe*, 2:397. Mozart's usage probably means "a token of friendship" (similar to the more common word "Freundesdienst") but could also be read as a pun meaning "a piece [*Stück*] composed as a favor for a friend."

Fig. 7.1 Johann August Rosmaesler. Detail from title page of Franz Seydelmann, *Sechs Sonaten für zwo Personen auf Einem Clavier*. Leipzig: Breitkopf, 1781.

commercially viable publication.[16] In this respect, the "Kegelstatt" trio resembles, for example, the comic terzetto "Liebes Mandel, wo ist's Bandel," which Mozart composed to sing with his wife and Gottfried von Jacquin.[17] The terzetto, which sets an original text in Viennese dialect by Wolfgang, may be based on a true incident involving a search by the two Mozarts and Jacquin for Constanze's lost ribbon.[18] Such scores stand as scripts for

[16] Artaria published the piece in 1788 under the title "Trio per il Clavicembalo o Forte Piano con l'accompagnamento d'un Violino e Viola, Opera [*sic*] 14," with an annotation on the title page in small print stating that the violin part may also be played on clarinet. As Küstler notes, "presumably this was done with Mozart's permission, even if only commercial considerations drove him to give it." Küstler, *Mozart: A Musical Biography*, 235. Over a century later, Simrock published viola versions of all of Brahms's clarinet chamber music – not only the two op. 120 sonatas but also the Clarinet Trio and Clarinet Quintet – for essentially the same reason: to enhance their viability for a domestic market.

[17] The three vocal staves are labeled "Constanze," "Mozart," and "Jacquin" in the surviving autograph score fragment, reproduced in the *Neue Mozart-Ausgabe* X/30, pt. 4, 131. This verifies that the piece was indeed written for Gottfried *von Jacquin*, rather than Gottfried *van Swieten*, as reported in some sources such as Jahn, *W. A. Mozart*, 3:332.

[18] Abert recounts the incident as follows: "Mozart had given his wife a new ribbon that she wanted to wear while out driving with Jacquin but which she was unable to find. 'Dear little husband,

a musical/social exchange among a particular group of friends, born of their real-world, non-musical relationships and of their particular social milieu.[19]

The following analytical story of the "Kegelstatt" trio indulges in the fantasy that the interplay among the three instruments in some way reflects that of their real-world counterparts – Masonic brothers Stadler and Mozart, both professional musicians, together with Franziska von Jacquin, who besides being Mozart's talented, young, aristocratic student was also sister to one of his closest friends. A more accurate representation would be to describe the story as an analytical fiction, probably informed as much by tropes found in Da Ponte's librettos as by my imagined versions of Jacquin, Stadler, and Mozart.[20] I make no specific claims to historical authenticity in my analytical methods, nor does my interpretation of the trio attempt to decode a social script intended by Mozart. Yet, in presenting a reading that resembles my own experience of the trio as a violist, I hope to describe what it feels like to play the "Kegelstatt" and to conjure

where's the ribbon?' she exclaimed, whereupon husband and wife joined forces with Jacquin in their search for the missing item. Jacquin eventually found it but, instead of handing it over, waved it in the air, while the diminutive Mozarts struggled to wrest it from him. Pleas, vituperation and laughter all proved fruitless, until the Mozarts' dog ran barking between Jacquin's legs, prompting him to hand it over and to suggest that the scene might be the subject for a comic trio." Abert, *W. A. Mozart*, 770. The story probably originates with Constanze Mozart and was first transmitted (in a slightly different version) in Breitkopf & Härtel's *Oeuvres complettes de Wolfgang Amadeus Mozart*, vol. 5, *XXX Gesänge mit Begleitung des Pianoforte von W. A. Mozart* (Leipzig, [1799]), 5. In the Breitkopf edition, the anecdote is followed by a recommendation that the piece be sung "in the most vulgar Viennese dialects [*im gemeinsten Wiener Dialekte*]" in order to achieve the composer's intended comic effect. See also my discussion above, 96.

[19] Mozart's Musical Game in C, K. Anh. 294d/516f is now known to have been created for the Jacquin family, since Hideo Noguchi has convincingly demonstrated that Mozart's sample solution is based on the spelling of Franziska's name. See Noguchi, "Mozart: Musical Game in C, K. 516f." Among other Mozart-related compositions belonging to the Jacquin circle are a number of vocal pieces written either for or with Gottfried, who was an amateur composer and singer. A collection of six songs published as Jacquin's (*Des Herrn von Jacquin 6 deutsche Lieder beym Klavier zu singen* [Vienna, 1791]) included two that were actually by Mozart: "Als Luise die Briefe ihres ungetreuen Liebhabers verbrannte," K. 520, and "Das Traumbild," K. 530. The autograph of the former, a setting of a poem by their mutual friend Gabriele von Baumberg, is inscribed "May 26, 1787, W. A. Mozart in Herr Gottfried von Jacquin's room, Landstraße." The bass aria *Io ti lascio, oh cara, addio*, K. Anh. 245, may be mainly by Gottfried with violin parts added by Mozart. For a complete overview, see Kraus, "W. A. Mozart und die Familie Jacquin"; and Peter Clive, *Mozart and His Circle: A Biographical Dictionary* (New Haven: Yale University Press, 1993), s.v. "Jacquin, (Emilian) Gottfried von," 79.

[20] Just as Eric Blom's poetic hearing of "an Emily Brontë-like quality of smouldering passion" in the "Kegelstatt" trio is a product of his own fantasy, the narrative and metaphorical elements in my interpretation are without question creations of my own imagination. Eric Blom, *Mozart*, rev. ed. (London: J. M. Dent and Sons, 1966), 249.

an account in which the musical and the social are deeply interwoven, perhaps reflecting something of the ambiance in which the "Kegelstatt" was first played. And it goes like this:

Andante ▶

An annotated score and recording of the complete "Kegelstatt" trio are provided among the Web Resources. Readers will want to follow the score while reading the remainder of the chapter.

As the first movement gets underway, it is not yet established just what kind of composition for three instruments this will be – a piano sonata with clarinet and viola accompaniment? a quasi-clarinet concerto, with piano and viola standing in as *ripieno* ensemble?[21] In ensemble music, a keyboard can usually rely on some bass instrument to bolster her left hand, but who in this ensemble might be inclined (and able) to provide such support?[22] Whereas string quartet players might reasonably approach a new piece with certain generic expectations of how the parts will interact, here the clarinet, viola, and piano must establish the terms of their intercourse only as they go along; in so doing, they invent a new genre.[23] How will these three dissimilar instruments find common ground to "play" together (in both senses of the word)?

The movement begins as a halting exchange between two parties.[24] The unison bass-line persona (viola plus piano) makes an elaborate opening

[21] Whereas the clarinet tends to dominate performances on modern instruments (if the players do not adjust the balance accordingly), performances on period instruments benefit from a more homogeneous blend, especially between viola and clarinet. Listen, for example, to the recordings by Charles Neidich, Jürgen Kussmaul, and Robert Levin (Sony Classical SK 53 366), and Elmar Schmid, Erich Höbarth, and András Schiff (Teldec 4509-99205-2); the latter recording was made using Mozart's fortepiano and viola with a copy of Stadler's clarinet. See also John Irving's documentary *Mozart's "Kegelstatt" Trio K. 498: An Eighteenth-Century Conversation*, which includes a performance on period instruments.

[22] This issue seems to motivate the octave doublings in the piano's left hand in many passages in which the viola and clarinet both play sustained material (e.g., mm. 13–16 of the first movement and throughout much of the minuet). It may also figure into the viola joining the piano to form a composite, unison-bass-line texture in the opening of the first movement.

[23] Mozart's then-unprecedented instrumentation of clarinet–viola–piano has inspired a variety of composers to write for the same formation, notably Robert Schumann, Max Bruch, Carl Reinecke, and György Kurtág.

[24] Throughout this chapter, I take certain liberties pertaining to the number of characters. Specifically, some passages suggest hearing the piano's two hands as distinct, independent characters, whereas others suggest a unified interpretation. Moreover, in certain passages, one or both of the piano's hands may seem temporarily to have joined another part as a composite

proposition (mm. 1–2): his chordal entrance and sweeping arpeggio, suggestive of an exaggerated, almost theatrical bow, makes for an elaborate display, but his elegant *grupetto* figure and switch from *forte* to *piano* signify his efforts to adopt a refined manner as he addresses a lady. The solo-piano persona responds coquettishly (mm. 3–4): her reaction ostensibly skirts his advance by responding with a contrasting idea with *parlando* declamation ("who, me?"), but in another sense, her reply invites him back in, since her V_5^6 harmony requires a resolution.[25] And so the unison bass-line persona makes a second, harmonically intensified statement (mm. 5–6), eliciting from the piano another coy riposte (mm. 7–8).

Enter the suave clarinet, who deftly spins the *grupetto* figure into a longer idea that very nearly leads to a cadence in m. 12 . . . only to elide his cadential note at the last moment, as the piano effects a deceptive resolution from V to VI.[26] The clarinet's clever choice to rest on the downbeat of m. 12 allows him to re-enter with a lead-in that invites the piano's right hand, who all too willingly takes up the clarinet's idea and leads to a cadence in m. 16. The slight chromatic intensifications in the piano's version – B♮ in m. 13 and G♭ in m. 14 – reflect her eagerness not only to adopt but also to develop the clarinet's idea. The clarinet, for his part, participates intimately in the cadential action through a parallel-thirds duet with the piano's right hand (mm. 15–16), while the viola remains relegated to a lesser accompanimental role. It is clear who has won the lady's favor and who has been pushed aside, at least for now.

persona. What this approach loses in rigorous consistency, it gains in interpretive flexibility. A reader who is troubled by my interpretation of the piano's statement (with the viola) in mm. 1–2 as a different character from the piano's statement (alone) in mm. 3–4 could opt to reformulate my analysis as an exchange between two musical gestures instead of two instrumental personas. See also Chapter 4 for further discussion of the relevant narratological issues.

[25] In Caplin's parlance, the basic idea (mm. 1–2) plus the contrasting idea (mm. 3–4) together compose a compound basic idea, which invites a four-bar restatement (mm. 5–8) to complete the presentation of what will become a sixteen-measure sentence. The clarinet's first statement, mm. 9–12, constitutes the continuation/cadential segment, which is repeated by the piano in mm. 13–16 to complete the sixteen-bar sentence with PAC. Caplin, *Classical Form*, 69–70.

[26] Regarding the clarinet's lack of a melodic cadential note on the downbeat of m. 12, different interpretations of agency attribution are possible. Did the piano's deceptive resolution from V to VI prompt the clarinet's rest? Or did the clarinet's intention to rest somehow prompt the piano's deceptive resolution? These literalist questions recall Momigny's similar ruminations over the ontological status of the melodic and accompanimental parts. See discussion above, 60–62.

The cadential arrival in m. 16 overlaps with the first of three statements in the piano's left hand (mm. 16, 18, and 20), seemingly a new incarnation of the unison bass-line character from mm. 1–2, only now played by the piano's left hand alone. That the left-hand entrances seem to emphatically interrupt each right-hand cadence encourages the two hands to be interpreted as separate characters at this juncture.[27] "Now I will rejoin your party," the left hand seems to assert, although without much social grace. His interruptive entrances introduce a mild metrical conflict that rubs against the established, odd-strong hypermeter at the two-bar level.[28] The B♮s furthermore usher in repeated motions toward the relative minor.

Unfazed, the clarinet leads the full company in a codetta to the primary theme (mm. 17–20) that resolves each of the left-hand piano motions to C minor with a return to the E♭ tonic. "As nice as this is," thinks the piano, "we can't stay in E♭ forever. This is supposed to be sonata form, so perhaps I can use the C-minor harmony to help us move on to B♭ major for some new adventures." And so, seizing the characteristic interval of the clarinet's codetta idea (concert g^1–c^2, as in mm. 17 and 19), she uses the same interval in m. 21 to initiate a concise transition that leads to an emphatic half cadence in the dominant key (m. 24) – one that involves some conspicuous modal mixture (G♭–F).[29]

The resourceful clarinet introduces a subordinate theme based on the melodic cadence of the primary theme (first ventured by him in mm. 11–12 though only properly completed by the piano in mm. 15–16); this, in turn, is based on the movement's opening gesture (see Ex. 7.1). The viola, long since edged out of the limelight, finds his way nearer to the soloistic clarinet, at first through an inconspicuous pedal tone (mm. 28–30) and then by joining the clarinet in a close duet (mm. 31–35). The piano plays her

[27] I have temporarily adopted male pronouns for the piano's left hand for this passage. The sense of the left hand interrupting the other parts in mm. 16, 18, and 20 depends in part on the performed dynamics. The *Neue Mozart-Ausgabe* accepts the *forte* markings on these downbeats, in all parts, based on the first edition. Mozart's manuscript contains no dynamic markings in these measures. To enhance the sense of interruption, one possible performance choice would be for the left hand only to enter with *fortepiano* (imitating m. 1), while the other parts complete their cadences in *piano*.

[28] The left hand's phrase overlaps emphasize even measures using material that previously had tended to commence on odd measures, activating MPRs 1 and 5a, both amplified by MPR 6. For an explanation of MPRs (metrical preference rules), see Chapter 6. On phrase overlap, see Rothstein, *Phrase Rhythm in Tonal Music*, 44–51 and *passim*.

[29] By around m. 21, when the piano's right hand comes to the fore, one may retroactively recognize the transition as having begun already in m. 16. In other words, mm. 16ff. stand as a codetta to the primary theme that "becomes" a transition. See Schmalfeldt, *In the Process of Becoming*.

Ex. 7.1 Derivation of subordinate theme (i)
a. Subordinate theme (clarinet, concert pitch)

b. Cadential idea from primary theme (piano, right hand)

c. Opening *grupetto* gesture (viola and piano, right hand)

ornamented repetition of the subordinate theme (mm. 35ff.), accompanied by the viola and then also clarinet, and suspense begins to mount when an expansion of the predominant harmony (mm. 43–44) delays the cadence.[30] But by the arrival of the cadential $^6_4$ (m. 45), all three parties seem to be having a grand time: the piano's descending (mostly diatonic) scale is answered in good humor by a chromatic, ascending one in the clarinet. Through the *crescendo* and the simultaneous trills in the viola and piano, all parties show their zeal for the cadence in m. 47, which stands as the EEC.[31]

The music following the EEC seems parallel to the music that followed the cadence of the primary theme, with one significant hypermetrical difference: Whereas the earlier cadence (m. 16) was unaccented at the two-bar level, the EEC (m. 47) becomes accented by virtue of the phrase expansion.[32] As a result, the bass entrances in mm. 47ff., unlike those in mm. 16ff., are congruent with the odd-strong hypermeter instead of being syncopated. By the end of the exposition, the ensemble has thus managed to achieve a certain equipoise.

Or has it? The shadowy piano left-hand character begins mixing in murky tones (D♭ and E♮, mm. 51ff.) that push the harmony in an unexpected direction. Closing themes, typically, reinforce the arrival of the

---

[30] More precisely, this phrase is expanded relative to the model in mm. 25–34, an expanded sentence whose presentation phrase comprises two statements of a three-bar basic idea, followed by a typical, four-bar continuation/cadential segment. The restatement in the piano tracks the model measure for measure until m. 43, when the expansion of the continuation/cadential segment begins.

[31] About the EEC (essential expositional closure), see Chapter 5.

[32] On the tendency of closing themes to employ end-accented phrases, see Temperley, "End-Accented Phrases: An Analytical Exploration."

subordinate key in advance of the expositional repeat. Instead of emphasizing B♭ major, however, this passage lingers on a C dominant-seventh
harmony tinged with mysterious, minor-mode inflections (D♭s, heard as ♭6̂
in F minor). Whereas the bass line's *grupetto* figure had been associated
with tonal stability and establishment at the movement's opening, here he
uses it instead to ask questions: "Will the key of F minor come next after the
fermata? What happens if we skip the expositional repeat and I nudge things
over there instead?"

The clarinet, preferring to waive the expositional repeat and avoid the
minor mode at the start of the development, opts instead for a road less
traveled. Arriving via chromatic-mediant relation in A♭ major, he introduces a new statement of the subordinate theme. His choice to begin
the development with the subordinate theme reflects a parallelism he
recognizes between mm. 53–54 (D♭–C in the bass) and the cadence of
m. 24 (G♭–F); the fermata in m. 54 is thus a kind of re-enactment of the
exposition's medial caesura. As the clarinet gets underway, the viola enters
on the upbeat to m. 58 with his innocuous pedal-tone accompaniment.
But soon after he engages the clarinet in a heated exchange (mm. 60ff.) that
chromatically intensifies the discourse and nudges it toward C minor,
arriving at a half cadence in m. 64.[33] As the cadential harmony is prolonged with a pedal tone (mm. 64–69), the viola and piano right hand
finally have the exchange of the *grupetto* figure that the viola might have
hoped for at the movement's outset, although the intensity of the piano's
dissonant statements (F♯ diminished seventh over a G pedal, concurrent
with the clarinet's painful diminished fourth) suggests circumstances that
make the exchange difficult to enjoy. "How will we find our way home to
E♭ major from here?" they wonder. But together they find a solution:
The piano (mm. 70–71) transforms the G major triad into a B diminished
$\frac{4}{3}$ chord, which the viola further transforms into a B♭ dominant-seventh
chord (mm. 72–73) through the reinterpretation of B♮ as C♭.

---

[33] The cadence in m. 64 is likewise parallel to the aforementioned dominant arrivals in mm. 24
and 54; but of the three, m. 64 is the most intense and is the only one approached through an
augmented-sixth chord. The prolonged G-major harmony (mm. 64–69), locally a dominant
in C minor, serves as the harmonic goal of the development section and functions globally as
III♯ (major mediant). Development sections that arrive at V of VI as a goal (rather than the
more typical global dominant) have received extensive scholarly attention. See, for example,
Charles Rosen, *Sonata Forms* (New York: W. W. Norton, 1980), 255 and *passim*; Caplin,
Classical Form, 275 n. 8; and Hepokoski and Darcy, *Elements of Sonata Theory*, 198–205. For
a Schenkerian view, which emphasizes the harmony's status as III♯ in the main key, see David
Beach, "A Recurring Pattern in Mozart's Music," *Journal of Music Theory* 27, no. 1 (Spring
1983): 1–29.

Ex. 7.2 Comparison of opening vs. recapitulation (i)

a. Opening: a tentative exchange

b. Recapitulation: a group of friends

Compared to the exposition's tentative opening, the recapitulation is conspicuously congenial (see Ex. 7.2). The *grupetto* figure is passed around with imitations in successively higher registers on each beat, and a chuckling duet between viola and piano right hand (mm. 77–78 and 81–82) fills in what had been an awkward silence in the exposition (cf. mm. 4–5 and 8–9).

The remainder of the recapitulation proceeds more or less by the book, in line with expositional precedent. A few noteworthy moments include mm. 85–86 (where the piano's left-hand D♭–C nudges the theme flatward and recalls the earlier left-hand D♭–C in mm. 52–54) and m. 97 (the medial caesura, where the piano's left-hand C♭–B♭ recalls the viola in mm. 69–73). The viola finally gets a chance to play the subordinate theme (mm. 98–107), which ushers in a one-more-time repetition that begins in the piano's right hand (mm. 107–8) and comes to involve the complete ensemble. During the predominant expansion (mm. 109–10), the rhythmic dissonance of the viola–clarinet duet teases playfully against the piano's steady "oom-pa-pa," and chromatic scales passed from clarinet to piano, along with duetting trills, lead the way to the essential structural closure

(ESC) cadence in m. 113.[34] The coda emphasizes a friendly exchange of the *grupetto* figure among the three instruments in mm. 118–22 and 124–26. The movement ends in pure delight: the *leggiero* sextuplet figure (mm. 127ff.) is passed around four registers as the clarinet and viola, imitating a pair of horns, play "farewell" gestures. "That turned out to be pretty fun," they seem to agree, smiling. "What's next?"

Menuetto ▶

The sole minuet among Mozart's trios with keyboard, this movement gives the impression at the outset of a trio imitating a grand ballroom ensemble – a "toy" orchestra, as it were – on account of the *tutti* scoring in *forte* dynamic; the full, chordal voicing in the piano's right hand; and the doubling of both the melody (clarinet and piano's right hand) and the bass (octaves in piano's left hand). As in many stylized dance pieces, this movement's wit is found in its metrical interplay. The opening four-bar statement (*Vierer*) establishes a minor detail of rhythmic design that becomes a point of fascination throughout the piece: The three-quarter-note figure in the bass line (m. 1) is passed to the viola (m. 2), then to the melody shared by the clarinet and piano's right hand (m. 3), and back to the bass line to mark a weak cadence (m. 4). By "three-quarter-note figure," I mean a discrete measure of all quarter notes both preceded and followed by some other rhythmic value and most commonly (especially in the bass) played with detached articulation.[35]

In m. 5, the piano's left hand instigates a second cycle by parallelism with m. 1, except that the viola bungles the exchange by playing together *with* the bass (in m. 5) instead of in the *following* measure. Bereft of the regulation of the three-quarter-note imitations to reinforce the downbeats, mm. 6–7 become rhythmically freer. That is, among the eighth notes spinning forth in the melody, the greatest emphasis falls on the second beat of m. 6, and in m. 7 the bass plus viola respond with a similar emphasis by entering after a hiatus on the second beat.

---

[34] On Hepokoski and Darcy's term "essential structural closure," see above, 179–80.

[35] The minuet's three-quarter-note figures may originate in various three-eighth-note statements from the Andante first movement (e.g., second half of m. 1, m. 3, and especially mm. 25–26, which recall the detached articulation of m. 3 and anticipate that of the minuet's statements). Given the difference in tempo, the Andante eighth notes are performed at roughly the same speed as the minuet's quarters.

The metrical dissonance in this passage seems to elicit a final statement from the solo piano – a "toy" piano within our "toy" orchestra, playing in *piano* dynamic and with both hands in treble register. If mm. 1–8 imitate an orchestral *tutti*, mm. 9–12 simulate the unaccompanied upper strings of an orchestral texture, and the piano accomplishes a modulation and new-key cadence without the aid of the viola or clarinet. The piano's syncopated entrances, emphasizing the third beats, comment on earlier metrical dissonances that similarly emphasized "wrong" beats.[36] "Pay close attention, gentlemen," she says mischievously. "With this sleight of hand, I can manipulate the meter (mm. 9–10). But now (m. 11), with these three quarter notes, I can set it right again. See, that three-quarter-note figure is what you were supposed to be doing all along! And while I'm at it, I'll take care of modulating to the dominant and reaching a cadence too. No need for your help!" The clarinet offers a dismissive retort (upbeat to m. 12), "Oh, it's all in good fun. Let's play it again – follow me this way for the repeat!"

The piano's four-bar solo statement occupies a curious status: It achieves the important tasks of the modulation, new-key cadence, and restoration of the three-quarter-note motive, yet the solo-piano instrumentation, register, and dynamic confer a parenthetical quality. The statement's extraneous character is illustrated through a comparison of the following recomposition with Mozart's first reprise. Ex. 7.3 (which retains Mozart's mm. 1–4 and recomposes the rest, especially mm. 7–8) strictly maintains the pattern of passing the three-quarter-note figure every measure. This results in a highly regular, if rather foursquare, parallel period that is self-sufficient as the minuet's first reprise. By comparison, the rhythmic freedom in mm. 6–8 of Mozart's version is palpable. Since a minuet's first reprise (especially a short one) may end on either a half cadence in the tonic key or a PAC in the new key, the piano's solo statement in mm. 9–12 is in a certain sense superfluous. But therein lies the paradox: Measures 9–12 are not a post-cadential appendix, since they achieve a cadence essential to the form, conferring a formal function of "end" (rather than "after-the-end"); but experiencing the music prospectively, that cadence only comes to be essential once the piano begins the

---

[36] Moreover, the piano's "entrance" on the third beat of m. 8 is predicted by a subtle, two-quarter-note *imbroglio* rubbing against the $\frac{3}{4}$ meter. That is, a quasi-$\frac{2}{4}$ level is lightly articulated in m. 7 (by the piano's left hand with the viola) followed by m. 8 (by the clarinet with the piano's right hand), which predicts another quasi-downbeat on the notated third beat of m. 8.

Ex. 7.3 Recomposition of first reprise (ii)

modulation to the dominant. And in electing to make the modulation and new-key cadence, the piano suggests a more ambitious type of minuet, implying that more games will be afoot in the second reprise.

The second reprise is indeed richer in metrical manipulations. The opening four bars (mm. 13–16, imitating mm. 1–4) almost reinstate the passing of the three-quarter-note figure, except that the viola once again misses his turn in m. 14; this time, the other players simply proceed without him to complete the four-bar statement. These four bars hold out the prospect of a *Fonte*, in which the tonicization of II would give way to a sequential restatement on the tonic and thereafter the recapitulation. But the "toy" piano tries a different tack, echoing only the previous two measures in a harmonic swerve toward IV. This echo thus bypasses the proper place for the viola's statement of the three-quarter-note figure,[37] but the viola, suddenly alert, jumps in to provide the requisite bass line in

[37] Three possible motivations for the piano's two-bar echo in mm. 17–18 (suggested to me by Rowland Moseley) are that (1) the piano is whimsical, unexpectedly inserting a two-bar parenthesis within the established, four-bar phrase rhythm; (2) the piano is a stickler, drawing attention to the viola's previous mistakes; or (3) the piano is resourceful, finding ways to allow for the undependable viola.

m. 18 (cf. mm. 4 and 16 in the piano). The clarinet introduces a new idea in mm. 19–20: a 3 × $\frac{2}{4}$ *imbroglio* figure, which is articulated not only by his own contour but by the imitative entrances in all parts at intervals of two quarter notes. Having united as a cohort, they beat their way to the dominant with the equivalent of three incisive quarter notes in m. 21, this being the first homorhythmic, *tutti* statement of the three-note figure.

Whereas the dominant arrival at the end of a contrasting middle is typically a point of clarity in rounded binary form, here it ushers in the minuet's most ambiguous passage in terms of both phrase rhythm and formal function. Up to this point, the minuet has been composed in four-bar units (*Vierer*), save for the two-bar echo in mm. 17–18; and the metrical strength of odd bars has been unperturbed. Thus long notes in the piano's left hand commencing in mm. 22 and 24 go against the grain, seeming to force a 4 = 1 reinterpretation of the hypermeter at m. 22. The left hand's initiative has a mixed reception. The piano's right hand ignores the overlap, treating m. 23 as a hypermetrical "1,"[38] while the clarinet remains adroitly neutral, with two-bar ideas (mm. 23–24 and 25–26) that can be heard as either strong–weak or weak–strong.

This, the first serious disagreement over meter, is a setback to the movement's recapitulatory process. Energized by an argument, the bass abandons the dominant pedal for a deceptive resolution to VI, which ushers in a corrupted and misplaced return of the main theme at mm. 27–28 but in the wrong part (piano's left hand, joined by the viola in m. 28) and the wrong key (G minor). But the clarinet (mm. 28–29) insists, "Come, now: this is my tune, and the recapitulation belongs in B♭ major!"[39] The canon

---

[38] The first-statement-stronger rule (MPR 11), applied to the piano's right hand, prefers m. 23 as stronger than its (quasi-)sequential repetition in m. 24. Yet in the left hand, m. 22 triggers MPRs for the long note length (MPR 5a) and long duration of the V harmony (MPR 5f), both amplified by virtue of being in the bass (MPR 6). That the dominant pedal lasts five measures (mm. 22–26) is further evidence of a challenge to the established, odd-strong hypermeter at the two-bar level.

[39] The conflict between the bass's G-minor "recapitulation" (m. 27) and the clarinet's B♭-major one (m. 28) relates directly to the metrical conflict introduced by the bass in m. 22. By parallelism with mm. 1, 5, and 13, the recapitulation motive ought to commence on a hyperdownbeat at the four-bar level. Regarding the bass's long notes in m. 27: a conservative hearing that ignores their length would hear hyperdownbeats in mm. 19 and 23 and would be rewarded in m. 27 by the piano's left-hand statement of the recapitulation motive (amplified by the switch to *forte* dynamic and doubled octaves, and by being in the bass voice). But a radical hearing, swayed by the long notes in m. 22, would begin to hear even bars as stronger and would be rewarded by the clarinet's statement of the recapitulation motive in m. 28. The passage therefore remains hypermetrically and form-functionally ambiguous.

between the piano's left hand and the clarinet contributes to the remarkable hypermetrical unclarity in the ensuing passage; even the notated measures are contested somewhat by the clarinet's syncopations, which emphasize the third beats (mm. 32–34, recalling the piano's solo statement in mm. 9–12). The clarinet's climbing scale reaches a climax as the passage culminates in a grand hemiola cadence (mm. 35–36, leading to a PAC in m. 37).[40] Then the "toy" piano chimes in, "I bet you're wondering precisely where the recapitulation occurred back there. But never mind all that, since it's over by now. Just let me play my little solo in the tonic, and we'll be all done."[41]

But all is not done: the minuet's trio lies ahead. Since I discussed the trio in detail in Chapter 6 (above, 255–66), it mostly remains to underscore a few links between the trio and minuet. I noted previously that the trio's first measure becomes a point of fixation throughout; that measure, of course, hearkens back to the minuet's three-quarter-note figure.[42] The trio's unaccompanied first measure – standing in neutral tonal territory, at the border between the B♭-major minuet and the G-minor trio (see Ex. 6.16c) – furthermore recalls the minuet's problematic recapitulation. The trio's own recapitulation (shown in Ex. 7.4) features a similar conflict between the piano's left hand and the clarinet (return of the head motive in m. 73, anticipated in m. 72). The minuet's lighthearted conflicts thus seem to linger in the serious trio. But not too serious, since the trio's intense demeanor is soon let go in the playful transition back to the minuet (mm. 95–102).

The movement's coda (mm. 144ff.) restores the passing of the three-quarter-note figure, bar by bar – now from clarinet to the piano's left hand

---

[40] The hemiola is strongly articulated in the piano's left hand and in the viola and to some extent also in the clarinet's melodic contour. The hemiola grouping is less evident in the piano's right hand, despite the fact that it largely shadows the clarinet in parallel motion.

[41] Although the four-bar piano solos ending each reprise are parallel material, they fulfill contrasting formal functions. That is, whereas mm. 9–12 achieve a new modulation to F major and a PAC in that key, mm. 38–41 stand as a codetta, since they repeat a cadence already achieved in m. 37. As noted above, the style of both statements – the high piano register and the absence of clarinet and viola – confers a parenthetic or extraneous "feeling," but syntactically only the second statement is truly after the end.

[42] The relationship between this gesture and the minuet becomes explicit in mm. 77–80, where the three-quarter-note idea is exchanged measure by measure. A variant form of the three-quarter-note figure, involving three eighth notes with eighth rests in between, appears in the piano part in m. 44, hearkening back to the minuet (m. 21). Finally, the trio's extended *imbroglio* passages (mm. 55–59 and *passim*) are also in dialogue with these two versions of this figure – that is, the version with repeated quarter notes and the version with eighth notes and rests.

Ex. 7.4 Two problematic rounded-binary recapitulations (ii)

a. Minuet

b. Trio

to the piano's right hand.[43] The viola, who was never the best at passing the quarter-note figure anyway, has found other material with which to occupy him. "But enough of the three-quarter-note gesture," the viola thinks, "what will be our next game?"

Rondeaux: Allegretto ▶

As the "Kegelstatt" trio lacks an Allegro first movement, its Allegretto finale stands as the most spirited of its three movements. The episodic nature of rondo form allows many opportunities for the instruments to

---

[43] This juncture makes explicit the connection between the trio's materials and the minuet's bar-by-bar exchanges of three-quarter-note figures.

Ex. 7.5 $\hat{5}$-$\hat{6}$-$\hat{7}$-$\hat{8}$ motive

a. Subordinate theme, recapitulation (i; viola)

b. Rondo theme (iii; clarinet, concert pitch)

assume diverse roles and combinations throughout. The rondo theme, based on the subordinate theme from the first movement (see Ex. 7.5),[44] is introduced by the clarinet with piano accompaniment (mm. 1–8) and subsequently repeated, with embellishments, by the piano with viola accompaniment (mm. 9–16). As the first episode gets underway – a clarinet melody with piano accompaniment (mm. 17–24) that gives way to an imitation piano concerto (mm. 24–35) – it becomes clear that the poor viola is the only one who has not yet carried the melody (even as the flamboyant piano revels in the limelight). So when the clarinet begins the next section of the episode as a transposed restatement of the rondo theme (mm. 36ff.), the viola chimes in with "me too" imitations, edging his way into a close duet with the clarinet by the cadence in m. 43. The piano follows up with another extended imitation-concerto passage (mm. 43–58), showing off her virtuoso skills; in the latter half of her display (mm. 51ff.), the clarinet and viola provide amused approval in the form of laughing gestures ("ha ha ha!"). Having emerged as concerto soloist, the piano takes the liberty of presenting the second (tonic-key) statement of the rondo theme entirely on her own (mm. 59–66).

The viola, expressing his frustration at repeated slights, launches into the second episode in a stormy C minor. As the episode begins, the viola's Lombard rhythms (m. 67) and *coup d'archet* gesture on a dissonant chord

---

[44] This particular $\hat{5}$-$\hat{6}$-$\hat{7}$-$\hat{8}$ motive is originally introduced by the clarinet (movement 1, m. 28) as a varied repetition of the subordinate theme's basic idea. Although that original statement appears in B♭ major, Ex. 7.4 reproduces the theme as it appears in the recapitulation in E♭ major, which makes its resemblance to the rondo's main theme more apparent. Yet another motivic connection (suggested to me by Patrick McCreless) is at the climax of the minuet, mm. 30–35; the clarinet's scale traverses the full octave bb^1–bb^2, but the upper tetrachord ($\hat{5}$-♯$\hat{5}$-$\hat{6}$-$\hat{7}$-$\hat{8}$) receives dynamic emphasis that intensifies the drive to the highpoint.

(m. 68) express an *agitato* mood. But as the consequent phrase (mm. 71–76) modulates to E♭ major, the mood brightens and the viola lapses into an effusive singing style, accompanied by the clarinet.[45] "That's right," he says, "*this* is the key I eventually want to sing in the next time the rondo theme comes around. And, Herr Clarinet, I'm perfectly content for you to accompany me, thank you very much. So, if you please, do stay down in that chalumeau register for a while." The piano contributes the contrasting middle (mm. 77–80) in the form of a *Romanesca* sequence that prepares a return to C minor. However, as the viola recapitulates the episode's main theme (mm. 81ff.), he hardly imagines that the clarinet will swoop in out of nowhere to interrupt him in m. 85, taking over "his" theme and playing up in the clarion register, thus forcing the viola once again into an accompanimental role. "I think that's more like it," says the clarinet. "Isn't it more natural this way, with me playing the melody?"

Although the episode proper ends in m. 90, the piano initiates a retransition (mm. 91ff.) that muses on the previous two bars – that is, on the very melodic figure and triplet accompaniment over which the clarinet and viola had quarreled. In opening the subject back up, the piano seems to set the two of them off again (middle of m. 92), inciting what has turned into a three-way dispute. But somehow, as the sequence arrives in m. 97 at the goal harmony of B♭ major (the dominant that prepares for the return of the rondo theme), the ensemble's tensions seem to have been worked out and the viola is permitted to emerge as soloist in an extended, uncharacteristically ostentatious display. He even performs the important harmonic task of introducing the chordal seventh (m. 102) to signal the impending thematic return. And, lo, after his triumphal chord (m. 106), the culmination of his virtuoso labors, he finds himself alone and playing an *Eingang* to the next statement of the rondo theme (mm. 108–15). "Can it be? Is it really, finally my turn?" he gleams, almost incredulous at his good fortune. The piano joins him with a supportive accompaniment that foregrounds ornate, quasi-*extempore* triplets. But she in no way challenges the viola for the melody, and he certainly welcomes this, their first extended duet together.[46]

---

[45] The consequent phrase's effusiveness is expressed by its two extra measures (mm. 73–74) relative to its antecedent (mm. 67–70).

[46] After the viola's failed bid for a duet with the piano at the outset of the first movement, his next opportunity in the same movement (mm. 98ff.) was again thwarted by the entrance of the clarinet only three bars later. Their extended duet in the finale, spanning mm. 108–15 (with the clarinet resting), thus fulfills a long-sought wish.

All instruments having played the rondo theme and having been show-cased in various ways, the trio comes together as an ensemble in the third episode (mm. 116–67). Here, the clarinet and viola enjoy a parallel-thirds duet shadowed an octave lower by the piano's right hand. "What exactly was our earlier disagreement about?" the clarinet asks. "Oh, it hardly matters anymore," replies the cheery viola, "and besides, it's more fun to play together this way anyhow."

The final statement of the rondo refrain begins as a clarinet/piano duet (mm. 168ff.) and ends as a boisterous party (mm. 176ff.).[47] A climactic moment arrives in mm. 189–90, when all three players present the rondo theme together, in three different octaves, the piano's statement bedecked with a virtuoso run and turn ornament. The coda introduces one new game involving a *leggiero* parallel-thirds duet between clarinet and viola, interspersed with run figures in the piano's right hand (mm. 192–201), only for the roles to be reversed in the second round (mm. 201–12). Part of the fun, or perhaps the challenge, is that the runs that the piano tosses off so easily are more difficult for the others to execute, particularly for the clarinet if he observes Mozart's unslurred articulation.[48] At this point, one can scarcely recall the reserved, almost cautious way these three players interacted at the outset of the first movement. By now, clarinet, viola, and piano have become three friends having a marvelously amusing time together. Musical carousing with this much spirit, among such good friends, is better than *Kegelspiel* any day!

---

[47] Mozart, in fact, revised his original version of the passage to increase the "boisterous" element. The autograph shows that the effervescent passage in mm. 176–84 was a later insertion; mm. 175 and 185 were originally contiguous.

[48] A comparable example occurs in the first movement of Mozart's Clarinet Quintet: The arpeggio figuration of the clarinet's first entrance (mm. 7–9) is highly idiomatic for that instrument but is far more challenging for the others – who must contend with string crossings – as they exchange the same figure throughout the development section (mm. 89–114).

∼ | Epilogue

> He did not want to compose another *Quixote* – which is easy – but *the Quixote itself*. Needless to say, he never contemplated a mechanical transcription of the original; he did not propose to copy it. His admirable intention was to produce a few pages which would coincide – word for word and line for line – with those of Miguel de Cervantes.
>
> –Jorge Luis Borges, "Pierre Menard, Author of the Quixote"[1]

To play chamber music with friends is to animate an artful, social exchange for which a musical score is but a script. And by the perspective developed in this book, performers within chamber ensembles are permitted – expected, even – to pose as the very agents of their musical intercourse. Playing off the individual parts on their music stands, they are – like Pierre Menard (re)writing *Don Quixote* – readers of a text and, paradoxically, its creators too.[2] By interpreting musical discourse within chamber ensembles as the actions of diverse characters, multiple-agency analysis shifts the focus of analytical attention from the musical score (a static text) to the play-through (a dynamic, temporal group activity).[3]

---

[1] Jorge Luis Borges, "Pierre Menard, Author of the Quixote," in *Labyrinths: Selected Stories & Other Writings*, augmented ed. (New York: New Directions Publishing, 1964), 39.

[2] I am grateful to the pianist Joseph Kalichstein for suggesting to me an analogy between Menard's creative re-creation of Cervantes's text and the act of musicians re-creating a composer's work in performance. Paul Hindemith makes a parallel observation about audiences engaging in an act of co-composition as they mentally construct the piece, in real time, as they listen. See Hindemith, *A Composer's World: Horizons and Limitations* (Cambridge, MA: Harvard University Press, 1952), 16–17. I thank William Rothstein for bringing this passage to my attention.

[3] Many authors have called for greater attention to the *performer's* subjectivity, including Raymond Monelle in his critique of Cone's *The Composer's Voice*. See Monelle, *The Sense of Music*, 165–69. Although roles within chamber ensembles and the interaction among individual parts has not, to date, been a major focus of scholarly inquiry, the subject figures prominently in at least three publications by professional string quartet players: David Waterman (cellist of the Endellion Quartet), Daniel Panner (violist of the Mendelssohn Quartet), and members of the Guarneri Quartet. See Waterman, "Playing Quartets: A View from the Inside," in *The Cambridge Companion to the String Quartet*, 97–126; Panner, "The Function of the Second Viola in the String Quintets of Wolfgang Amadeus Mozart" (D.M.A. diss., City University of New York, 2003); and Blum, *The Art of Quartet Playing: The Guarneri Quartet*.

My focus on individual players (and their individual parts) offers an alternative to the conventional view of musical works and scores as representing the actions or expression of a unitary composer figure,[4] since the multiple personas within an ensemble are capable of competing with, deceiving, challenging, opposing, seducing, interrupting, or agreeing with one another. These very modes of interaction resonate with the ways many chamber musicians conceptualize the meaning of their own musical utterances while playing together. To admit such interpretations into the arena of musical analysis is to invite scholars to speculate as to the *motivation* behind each turn of phrase (much as a method actor might). Whereas one style of analysis might describe a certain accidental as effecting a modulation that circumvents an expected cadence, another could observe of the same moment a social aspect too, perhaps describing the event as "evading a question," "pursuing a tangent," or even "changing the subject" within the musical discourse.[5]

Performing analytically or analyzing performatively?

In recent decades, a chorus of scholars has critiqued the so-called "page-to-stage" analytical approach,[6] whereby an analysis of a score is undertaken in service of certain performance aims, such as evaluating, suggesting, or even demanding a particular "interpretation." Critics of this approach have decried its inherent asymmetry – a privileging of analysis over performance, intellectual knowledge over embodied know-how, musical scholarship over artistry – since page-to-stage establishes the analyst as an authority tasked with instructing performers how to make prudent,

---

[4] Two such unitary, (fictional) composer-based perspectives include Cone's notion of music as the utterance of a "complete musical persona" and Hepokoski and Darcy's notion of a "sonata game" played by the composer in dialogue with a constellation of generic norms.

[5] Such interpretations are already commonplace in the analysis of opera. For instance, a famous example of "evading the question" occurs in the celebrated Act 2 finale of *Le nozze di Figaro* when, after the gardener Antonio presents a found letter to the Count, Figaro initially flounders under interrogation. The drama is depicted musically by Figaro's halting, *parlante* statements that "follow" the harmonies of the orchestra's sequence – the ticking clock, as it were – in *piano* and with a narrow range. But as he gains control of the situation, concocting the story about taking the letter to receive the official seal ("È l'usanza di porvi il suggello"), he exerts his agency by breaking the sequence with a bold, *forte* statement that effects a tonicized half cadence.

[6] The term "page to stage" was introduced to musical scholarship by Nicholas Cook in "Between Process and Product: Music and/as Performance," *Music Theory Online* 7, no. 2 (April 2001), www.mtosmt.org/issues/mto.01.7.2/mto.01.7.2.cook.html. See also Nicholas Cook, *Beyond the Score: Music as Performance* (Oxford University Press, 2013), 33–55 and *passim*.

analytically justifiable performance choices, lest they rely on "mere" intuition. Joel Lester, writing in 1995 during the twilight of the page-to-stage hegemony, memorably observed that "something is strikingly absent from this [analysis-and-performance] literature – namely, the performers and their performances."[7] Such exhortations have happily persuaded more recent writers to adopt a wider range of critical approaches to musical performance[8] and to vastly curtail prescriptive language about performance imperatives dictated by analytical findings; indeed, this book contains no such imperatives directed at performers (though it may contain a few directed at scholars).

But as the pendulum has swung away from page-to-stage methods, it risks continuing on the upswing toward the opposite extreme. Indeed, studies of musical performance that include any score-analysis component have increasingly been viewed in certain circles with suspicion. Some have called for newly developed *performance*-centered analytical approaches to not only augment but furthermore to supplant more traditional *score*-centered methods. (This opposition of score-vs. performance-centered musicologies is useful but only up to a point, since scores surely play an integral role in any performance of composed music.) Since this book contains no analyses of recorded performances or interviews with performers – only analyses of musical scores informed by my imagined performances by hypothetical or idealized performers – I might be criticized for engaging in what Nicholas Cook has called a kind of "ventriloquism . . . [whereby] the voices of performers have not really been heard . . . [since] theorists have taken it upon themselves to speak for performers."[9] Am I a score-based analyst masquerading in a performance-studies costume?

That is not how I understand my project in this book (although it might require an entirely different sort of analyst to determine my competency to evaluate my own motivations). As a violist with a conservatory background

---

[7] Joel Lester, "Performance and Analysis: Interaction and Interpretation," in *The Practice of Performance: Studies in Musical Interpretation*, ed. John Rink (Cambridge University Press, 1995), 197.

[8] A variety of novel methodologies proliferated under the stimulus of two large-scale, multi-year research projects based in the UK that strove to develop and promote a musicology of performance: (1) the AHRC Research Centre for the History and Analysis of Recorded Music (CHARM), founded in 2004; and (2) its successor, the AHRC Research Centre for Musical Performance as Creative Practice (CMPCP), founded in 2009. Information about these projects is available, respectively, at www.charm.rhul.ac.uk and www.cmpcp.ac.uk.

[9] Nicholas Cook, "Prompting Performance: Text, Script, and Analysis in Bryn Harrison's *être-temps*," *Music Theory Online* 11, no. 1 (March 2005), www.mtosmt.org/issues/mto.05.11.1/mto.05.11.1.cook_frames.html.

who came to music scholarship later, I have had Mozart's chamber music "in my fingers" for twenty-some years, far longer than I have been analyzing it rigorously. My performance background informs my analytical perspective in a variety of ways. For instance, whereas performance-and-analysis studies have for some time been dominated by pianists, multiple agency betrays my affiliation with a single-line instrument: while playing chamber music, I *become* one of the characters within the texture. And my background specifically as a violist surely informs my advocacy for the agency of inner-voice and accompanimental parts, correcting against certain overly melodic conceptions of quartet-as-conversation advanced by many historical and modern authors.

The project of this book is thus more "stage-to-page" (or, less mellifluously, "chamber-to-page") than anything else. I mean this literally, since many analyses within these pages originated in rehearsals, coachings, performances, and especially sight-reading parties. Writing this book has entailed a process of developing these ideas and translating them from "Performerspeak" into "Theoryspeak."[10] This code-switching process was undertaken not because my musical instincts require a theorist's seal of approval but because, as a theorist, I am interested in understanding their implicit conceptual underpinnings more deeply. This, in turn, piqued my curiosity to interrogate the relationship between my intuitions and theoretical ideas and those of historical musicians and writers. If I have succeeded in articulating my performance perspectives in language that theorists and musicologists will be inclined to read and cite, then I will have succeeded in my broadest aims: to infuse analytical and music-historical scholarship with a performer's sensibility and to bring these diverse forms of musical engagement closer together.

Historicism and presentism in musical analysis and performance

Readers have surely recognized a pronounced historicist bent in this study, which is borne out in my close readings of historical texts and in my

---

[10] A perceptive examination of the language of music analysis and the (often tacit) intuitions of performers is Patrick McCreless, "Analysis and Performance: A Counterexample?," *Dutch Journal of Music Theory* 14, no. 1 (2009): 1–16. Two impressively integrated studies by performer-scholars are Le Guin's *Boccherini's Body* and Beghin's *The Virtual Haydn*, each of which is linked to recordings by their respective authors. Another "bilingual" publication is *Inside Beethoven's Quartets*, co-authored by Lockwood and members of the Juilliard String Quartet, which includes an accompanying CD and scores annotated with performance markings.

recovery of past performance settings and practices such as sight-reading. I wish to briefly address the relationship between Part I – which could be read on its own terms as a purely historical study – and the analytical method developed in Part II. A newly developed analytical method, to be sure, does not require historical support to justify its validity, but in presenting these two studies within the same volume I have implicitly positioned the one as the inspiration for the other.

Research on the history of music theory and on performance practice often raises questions about the extent to which historical concepts could or should influence modern-day analysis or performance, respectively.[11] When hermeneutics are added into the mix, matters become yet more complex since historical evidence cannot "prove" an interpretation of musical meaning to be "correct." Michael Klein has (in another context) challenged historicist enterprises that "willingly divest our interpretive energies into reviving the unknown dead," arguing that "although uncovering the contexts and interpretive strategies of the past is a viable pursuit, an impulse to defer to the dead as a means of discovering univocal meaning brings in assumptions about texts with which I do not find myself in accord."[12] In reconstructing Mozart's relationships with Stadler, the Jacquins, Haydn, and others as an interpretive entry point into his music's social interplay, am I not guilty of the very same dubious appeals to the dear departed, looking to the authority of their experiences (as I have

---

[11] On historicism and presentism in music theory, see Thomas Christensen, "Music Theory and Its Histories." On historicism in performance, see also Richard Taruskin's spirited critique of the ideology of "authenticity" that flourished during the first wave of the early-music revival. Taruskin, *Text and Act: Essays on Music and Performance* (Oxford University Press, 1995).

[12] Michael Klein, "Chopin's Fourth Ballade as Musical Narrative," *Music Theory Spectrum* 26, no. 1 (Spring 2004): 28–29. Klein's remarks arise in a critique of Hatten's announced goal of using Peircean semiotic theory in service of "the historical reconstruction of an interpretive competency adequate to understanding Beethoven's works in his time." Robert S. Hatten, *Musical Meaning in Beethoven: Markedness, Correlation, and Interpretation*, 1st paperback ed. (Bloomington: Indiana University Press, 1994), 3. Hatten's wording refers to a certain expressive and topical vocabulary that was prevalent in Beethoven's day but that mixed uneasily with structuralist modes of discourse current at the time Hatten conceived the book in the 1980s and early '90s. As a point of comparison, Ratner's *Classic Music* (published in 1980) begins with a lengthy exposition of the (now undisputed) idea that music is a form of communication (see his Part I, pp. 1–41), and his student Kofi Agawu was compelled to defend this position and bolster it with additional historical documentation in *Playing with Signs: A Semiotic Interpretation of Classic Music* (Princeton University Press, 1991), 26–34. By the time Klein's article appeared in 2004, it was no longer necessary to ask the reader's permission to discuss music as a form of expression.

imagined them)[13] rather than to my own? But perhaps the historicist and post-modern critical stances are not an entirely either/or proposition. To engage in a conversation across the ages, invoking ideas from (those whom Klein calls) the unknown dead, is not necessarily to *defer* to their authority. I cite Koch's *Wettstreit* in service of my own theory of multiple agency not out of deference but because historical precedent can be a productive point of departure to explicate one's own ideas.[14]

At the outset of this book, I stated that I was drawn to examine metaphors of conversation and sociability in chamber music because, through my performance experience, I have found these concepts corresponded to intuitions widely held among musicians with whom I have collaborated. This shared experience may result in part from a certain received wisdom, since nearly every string player has (at least once) heard a chamber coach invoke Goethe's famous comparison of quartets to conversation. But, on the other hand, Goethe's remark would not be repeated so often if it did not resonate in some way with the experiences of musicians and listeners today.[15] To understand "where we are in relation to where we have been" (as Klein nicely puts it), we must first know where we have been.[16]

So where are we, indeed, in relation to where we have been? I would hardly suggest that to recover a sociable aspect in Mozart performance we

[13] That the "Jacquin," "Stadler," and "Mozart" figures invoked in Chapter 7 are creatures of my own imagination is no small point. Recall that the musical agent that Seth Monahan calls the "fictional composer" – who is understood to have been invented by the analyst – may be based on but is not identical to the historical composer (see discussion above, 130–31. The same applies, *mutatis mutandis*, to my imagined, fictional versions of the friends for whom Mozart composed these pieces. When I invoke Stadler in my historical writing, I am careful to limit my writing to ideas supportable by historical evidence. But the fictional "Stadler" who may influence my analytical interpretations is formed less by biographical materials than by my own interpretive responses to and fantasies about the music Mozart wrote for him. This is less "deferring to the dead" than invoking his fictional persona to serve as my muse and, at times, to do my analytical bidding.

[14] Analogies could be made to Schenker's invocation of figured-bass theory as an antidote to what he saw as overly root-based theories of harmony or to recent scholars of nineteenth-century harmony developing ideas loosely based on the theories of Hugo Riemann. In either case, past ideas are invoked as a reference and a point of departure for original theories posited by the later scholars, like a willful "misreading."

[15] Even Goethe's influential metaphor does not entail a univocal meaning. In an age in which "conversations" can take place via text messages and Facebook posts, the nuances of historical comparisons of chamber music to *artful* conversation may be lost in translation.

[16] Klein, "Chopin's Fourth Ballade as Musical Narrative," 28. For instance, Chapter 3 traced the origins of public, professional chamber music concert series, by way of setting earlier, domestic settings in relief. Without knowing this history, one might tend to universalize our experience, tacitly assuming that modern concert rituals reflect the way music always has been, will be, and should be performed. A recent trend toward reviving a more social, convivial environment for chamber music – at such venues as New York City's (*Le*) *Poisson Rouge* – may, on further inspection, be revealed to be more of a return to the past.

must restore the setting of eighteenth-century salons – where music was commonly played at sight, without much rehearsal or access to scores, generally for no audience or perhaps for listeners who were (by modern standards) inattentive, and so forth. These practices are, in large part, ill suited for public concert halls, the main venue where this repertoire is performed today. But having "visited" these Enlightenment-era salons in Part I, much of what one finds there is worth pondering. At their best, such settings reveal a thriving, participatory culture of music-making among familiars amid a sociable ambiance. The music can inspire witty repartee and more serious discourse in equal measure, and the amiable discourse conversely fuels the music-making in turn. And while it is unlikely that even the most accomplished dilettantes, sight-reading new repertoire at their weekly salons, achieved the same precision and accuracy as today's polished, professional ensembles, why should they have? Perhaps some musicians today, burdened by certain tensions associated with "serious" concert culture and by a premium on accurate reproduction in musical performance, may find inspiration in the spirit of adventure, discovery, and play that pervades these salons of the past.

Multiple agency contrasted with musical narrative

Over the course of this book, I have been careful to distinguish multiple agency from various other constructs with which it may share features but should not be conflated. While it was not my intention to develop interpretations of Mozart's chamber music as narrative *per se*, some readers will rightly sense a proto-narratological or proto-dramatic quality to them. I even referred to the analysis of the "Kegelstatt" in Chapter 7 as a "story," albeit one possessing no overarching plot. Perhaps for this reason, some readers may feel these "narratives" are barely that since they stay too close to traditional modes of musical analysis, even as I suspect other readers may feel I have at times pushed the anthropomorphism too far. Such is the nature of the enterprise.

What my analyses share with more conventionally narrative approaches to music accounts are notions of *characters* possessing *agency*, or, more precisely, the interpretation of event-successions as volitional actions undertaken by sentient, anthropomorphic personas.[17] But moments of multiple agency need not cohere into a robust plot that exhaustively

---

[17] See Monahan, "Action and Agency Revisited," 324–27.

subsumes a movement or piece.[18] Such fleeting moments of agential interaction invoke many of the trappings of narrative – such as characters, conflicts, actions, and reactions – but without a plot to explain the succession from one moment to the next. Klein addresses this point eloquently: "It would seem to be miraculous . . . if we were to find that every detail of a music analysis made a one-to-one mapping onto the events in an expressive narrative."[19] I have indeed resisted the temptation to cobble together narratives from passing moments of multiple agency in which they did not occur to me naturally. Simply put, to treat an instrumental composition (as Momigny does) as if it were an opera – one whose text and plot could be recovered if only we could find the Rosetta stone – will produce a distorted picture.

Multiple-agency analysis has the most to offer in passages with polyphonic textures, the very passages that challenged Momigny.[20] Clearly, it may have less to offer when all parts seem to act in concert. The metrical analyses in Chapter 6, for instance, used vividly agential language only at special moments of metrical change or ambiguity, whereas extended passages of steady meter were reported in more neutral, non-agential vocabularies. The relative balance between these two kinds of moments varies from piece to piece and depends on which musical dimensions are under consideration. Like topic theory, multiple agency is best used as an adjunct to other analytical methods, such as the analyses of form and meter with which I have combined it in Chapters 5–7.[21]

[18] Scholarship on musical narrative usually draws on some notion of a plotline. Northrop Frye's four archetypal *mythoi* – romance, tragedy, irony, and comedy – form a central touchstone in Almén's *A Theory of Musical Narrative*. See Northrop Frye, *Anatomy of Criticism* (Princeton University Press, 1957). Most of the excerpts examined in this book are far too short to sustain a plot. Only a few of my analyses – those in Chapters 5 and 7 that trace the form over complete movements or compositions – traverse anything resembling a plot.

[19] Klein, "Chopin's Fourth Ballade as Musical Narrative," 51. Agawu expresses a similar skepticism of "quick marriages of convenience between structural patterns (emerging from theory-based analysis) and elements of expression (emerging from hermeneutics)." Kofi Agawu, "Music Analysis Versus Musical Hermeneutics," *American Journal of Semiotics* 13, nos. 1–4 (Fall 1996): 13.

[20] I mean "polyphonic texture" in the broad sense advocated in Olga (Ellen) Bakulina, "The Loosening Role of Polyphony: Texture and Formal Functions in Mozart's 'Haydn' Quartets," *Intersections: Canadian Journal for Music* 32, nos. 1–2 (2012): 7–41.

[21] The idea of topic theory as an "adjunct" concept to be used in tandem with other analytical methods was suggested to me by Kofi Agawu (personal communication). Agawu attributes this same opinion to Ratner: "For him [Ratner], the dynamism in classic music derived from trajectories of tonal and cadential action, from the establishment and disruption of periodicities, all accomplished by means of a variety of voice-leading and cadential techniques, including various partimenti. Topics were *incorporated* into this network of actions; they had no independent existence." Agawu, "Obituary: Leonard G. Ratner (1916–2011)," *Ad Parnassum* 10, no. 19 (April 2012): 192.

Although my analyses invoke psychodramatic rationales to explain certain musical events – as in the friendly rivalry between the two violins in the finale of Mozart's G Major Quartet, K. 387 (Ex. 4.2) – I avoid the kind of intensely emotive language associated with nineteenth-century musical hermeneutics and that has been revived in some recent narrative analyses of music from Beethoven to Mahler and beyond. One clear reason for this difference is the repertoire under examination. I refer here to the contrast between musical aesthetics of the eighteenth and nineteenth centuries, or, to borrow an influential metaphor, between the mirror and the lamp.[22] Part of this aesthetic divide is the gulf between a notion of musical intercourse as a kind of game and such nineteenth-century trends as explicitly programmatic plots or thematic transformation on a teleological trajectory toward apotheosis.

In the end, multiple-agency analysis and narrative analysis tend to serve divergent goals. I have not striven, in this book, to unlock hidden story lines in so-called absolute music. Rather, I have endeavored to construct a historically grounded, theoretical position on how chamber musicians understand and experience their *musical* interactions in *social* terms, in time, as they play. While critical responses to Mozart's chamber music have always emphasized its element of interplay, mainstream style criticism has often struggled to go beyond bland generalities to provide readings of any particular composition. A basic question has remained unanswered: "If this piece is like a conversation, what is the conversation about?"

Multiple agency refines the question: "If playing this piece together is a form of social interplay, what is that interplay like?" The analyses in this book examine a conversation *in* music that is also *about* music, interpreting the characters' utterances and interactions as they play out through the harmony, counterpoint, form, and phrase rhythm. But unlike conventional analyses of those musical elements, multiple agency takes seriously the idea of social interplay as an integral aspect of formal or metrical processes and frames musical events in terms of the characters' interactions and exchanges. By conducting the analysis as if from within the ensemble, we experience first-hand the witty games that Mozart composed into his scores, games that would come to life when he played these pieces with friends such as Haydn and Stadler, and games that we can know and enjoy too – as scholars, performers, and Mozart enthusiasts of all stripes – if only we are willing to play.

---

[22] M. H. Abrams, *The Mirror and the Lamp: Romantic Theory and the Critical Tradition* (Oxford University Press, 1953).

Bibliography

Abert, Hermann. *W. A. Mozart*. Leipzig: Breitkopf & Härtel, 1923–24.
Translated by Stewart Spencer, and edited by Cliff Eisen. New Haven: Yale
University Press, 2007.

Abrams, M. H. *The Mirror and the Lamp: Romantic Theory and the Critical
Tradition*. Oxford University Press, 1953.

Adams, Sarah J. "'Mixed' Chamber Music of the Classical Period and the
Reception of Genre." In *Music, Libraries, and the Academy: Essays in Honor
of Lenore Coral*, edited by James P. Cassaro, 3–20. Middleton: A-R Editions,
2007.

Adelson, Robert. "Beethoven's String Quartet in E Flat Op. 127: A Study of the
First Performances." *Music and Letters* 79, no. 2 (1998): 219–43.

Agawu, Kofi. "Music Analysis Versus Musical Hermeneutics." *American Journal of
Semiotics* 13, nos. 1–4 (Fall 1996): 9–24.

"Obituary: Leonard G. Ratner (1916–2011)." *Ad Parnassum* 10, no. 19 (April
2012): 191–94.

Playing with Signs: A Semiotic Interpretation of Classic Music. Princeton
University Press, 1991.

Allanbrook, Wye Jamison. *Rhythmic Gesture in Mozart: Le Nozze di Figaro and
Don Giovanni*. University of Chicago Press, 1983.

Almén, Byron. *A Theory of Musical Narrative*. Bloomington: Indiana University
Press, 2009.

Bacon, Francis. *Essays or Counsels, Civil and Moral*. London, 1625. Reprinted in
Francis Bacon: The Major Works. Edited by Brian Vickers. Oxford University
Press, 1996.

Badura-Skoda, Eva. "Dittersdorf über Haydns und Mozarts Quartette." In
*Collectanea Mozartiana: herausgegeben zum 75järigen Bestehen der
Mozartgemeinde Wien*, 41–50. Tutzing: Hans Schneider, 1988.

Baillot, Pierre-Marie-François de Sales. *L'art du violon: nouvelle méthode*. Paris,
1834.

"Programmes des séances de musique de chambre." www.bruzanemediabase
.com/Fonds-d-archives/Fonds-Baillot/Programmes-des-seances-de-musique-
de-chambre-Pierre-Baillot (accessed May 1, 2015).

Bakulina, Olga (Ellen). "The Loosening Role of Polyphony: Texture and Formal
Functions in Mozart's 'Haydn' Quartets." *Intersections: Canadian Journal for
Music* 32, nos. 1–2 (2012): 7–41.

"Polyphony as a Loosening Technique in Mozart's *Haydn* Quartets." M.A. thesis, McGill University, 2010.

Baron, John H. *Chamber Music: A Research and Information Guide.* 2nd ed. New York: Routledge, 2002.

Bashford, Christina. "Historiography and Invisible Musics: Domestic Chamber Music in Nineteenth-Century Britain." *Journal of the American Musicological Society* 63, no. 2 (Summer 2010): 291–360.

"The String Quartet and Society." In *The Cambridge Companion to the String Quartet*, edited by Robin Stowell, 3–18. Cambridge University Press, 2003.

Bauer, Günther G. "'... mit der Tarockkarten Tarockkarten gespielt': die Kartenspiele des Wolfgang Amadeus Mozart." *Das Blatt: Schriftenreihe der Deutschen Spielkartengesellschaft* 19 (October 1999): 17–63.

"Mozart: Spiele ohne Musik. Mozarts dokumentierte Gesellschaftsspiele, 1768–1791." *Musik und Spiel: Homo Ludens – Der spielende Mensch* 10 (2000): 135–86.

Beach, David. "A Recurring Pattern in Mozart's Music." *Journal of Music Theory* 27, no. 1 (Spring 1983): 1–29.

Beghin, Tom. "A Composer, His Dedicatee, Her Instrument, and I: Thoughts on Performing Haydn's Keyboard Sonatas." In *The Cambridge Companion to Haydn*, edited by Caryl Clark, 203–25. Cambridge University Press, 2005.

"'Delivery, Delivery, Delivery!': Crowning the Rhetorical Process of Haydn's Keyboard Sonatas." In *Haydn and the Performance of Rhetoric*, edited by Tom Beghin and Sander M. Goldberg, 131–71. University of Chicago Press, 2007.

The Virtual Haydn: Paradox of a Twenty-First Century Keyboardist. University of Chicago Press, 2015.

Benjamin, Walter. *Selected Writings.* Vol. 1, *1913–1926*. Edited by Marcus Bullock and Michael W. Jennings. Cambridge, MA: Harvard University Press, 1996.

Benjamin, William. "Mozart: Piano Concerto No. 17 in G Major, K. 453, Movement I." In *Analytical Studies in World Music*, edited by Michael Tenzer, 332–76. Oxford University Press, 2006.

"Schenker's Theory and the Future of Music." *Journal of Music Theory* 25, no. 1 (Spring 1981): 155–73.

Bent, Ian, ed. *Music Analysis in the Nineteenth Century.* 2 vols. Cambridge University Press, 1994.

Benton, Rita. "Pleyel's Bibliothèque musicale." *Music Review* 35 (1975): 1–4.

Berger, Karol. "The Second-Movement Punctuation Form in Mozart's Piano Concertos: The Andantino of K. 449." *Mozart-Jahrbuch* (1992): 168–72.

Berke, Dietrich. "Nochmals zum Fragment eines Streichtrio-Satzes in G-Dur KV Anh. 66 (562e)." *Acta Mozartiana* 29, no. 2 (1982): 42–47.

Berke, Dietrich, and Marius Flothius. Preface to *Neue Mozart-Ausgabe* VIII/21: *Duos und Trios für Streicher und Bläser,* vii–xx. Kassel: Bärenreiter, 1975.

Berlioz, Hector. *Mémoires.* Paris, 1870. Translated by Ernst Newman as *Memoirs of Hector Berlioz.* New York: Alfred A. Knopf, 1932.

Biba, Otto. "Grundzüge des Konzertwesens in Wien zu Mozarts Zeit." In *Mozart-Jahrbuch* (1978/79): 132–43.

Blom, Eric. *Mozart*. Revised ed. London: J. M. Dent and Sons, 1966.

Blum, David, ed. *The Art of Quartet Playing: The Guarneri Quartet*. Ithaca: Cornell University Press, 1987.

Blum, Stephen. "Recognizing Improvisation." In *In the Course of Performance: Studies in the World of Musical Improvisation*, edited by Bruno Nettl and Melinda Russell, 27–45. University of Chicago Press, 1998.

Bonds, Mark Evan. "Replacing Haydn: Mozart's 'Pleyel' Quartets." *Music and Letters* 88, no. 2 (May 2007): 201–25.

"The Sincerest Form of Flattery? Mozart's 'Haydn' Quartets and the Question of Influence." *Studi Musicali* 22 (Spring 1991): 365–409.

Borges, Jorge Luis. "Pierre Menard, Author of the Quixote." In *Labyrinths: Selected Stories & Other Writings*, 36–44. Augmented ed. New York: New Directions Publishing, 1964.

Bracht, Hans-Joachim. "Überlegungen zum Quartett-'Gespräch.'" *Archiv für Musikwissenschaft* 51, no. 3 (1994): 169–89.

Brook, Barry S. "The *Symphonie Concertante*: An Interim Report." *Musical Quarterly* 47, no. 4 (October 1961): 493–516.

"The *Symphonie Concertante*: Its Musicological and Sociological Bases." *International Review of the Aesthetics and Sociology of Music* 25, nos. 1–2 (June–December 1994): 131–48.

Brower, Candace. "Memory and the Perception of Rhythm." *Music Theory Spectrum* 15, no. 1 (1993): 19–35.

Brown, Clive. *A Portrait of Mendelssohn*. New Haven: Yale University Press, 2003.

Brown, Matthew. *Explaining Tonality: Schenkerian Theory and Beyond*. University of Rochester Press, 2005.

Brown, Maurice J. E. *The New Grove Schubert*. New York: Macmillan, 1983.

Burke, Peter. *The Art of Conversation*. Ithaca: Cornell University Press, 1993.

Burkhart, Charles. "How Rhythm Tells the Story in 'Là ci darem la mano.'" *Theory and Practice* 16 (1991): 21–38.

Burney, Charles. *A General History of Music*. 4 vols. London, 1776–89.

Burney, Susan. *The Journals and Letters of Susan Burney: Music and Society in Late Eighteenth-Century England*. Edited by Philip Olleson. Farnham: Ashgate, 2012.

Busoni, Feruccio. *Sketch of a New Esthetic of Music*. Translated by Theodore Baker. New York: Schirmer, 1911.

Byros, Vasili. "Meyer's Anvil: Revisiting the Schema Concept." *Music Analysis* 31, no. 3 (2012): 273–346.

Caccini, Giulio. *Le nuove musiche*. Translated by H. Wiley Hitchcock. Middleton: A-R Editions, 1970.

Cambini, Giuseppe Maria(?). "Ausführung der Instrumentalquartetten." *Allgemeine musikalische Zeitung (Leipzig)* 6, no. 47 (August 22, 1804): cols. 781–83.

Cambini, Giuseppe Maria. *Nouvelle méthode théorique et pratique pour le violon.* Paris, c. 1795–1803.

Caplin, William E. "The Classical Cadence: Conceptions and Misconceptions." *Journal of the American Musicological Society* 57, no. 1 (Spring 2004): 51–117.

Classical Form: A Theory of Formal Functions for the Instrumental Music of Haydn, Mozart, and Beethoven. Oxford University Press, 1998.

Caplin, William E., James Hepokoski, and James Webster. *Musical Form, Forms, and* Formenlehre: *Three Methodological Reflections.* Edited by Pieter Bergé. Leuven University Press, 2009.

Carpani, Giuseppe. *Le Haydine, ovvero Lettere sulla vita e opere del célèbre maestro Giuseppe Haydn.* Milan, 1812.

Casa, Giovanni della. *Il Galateo.* Venice, 1558.

Christensen, Thomas. "Music Theory and Its Histories." In *Music Theory and the Exploration of the Past*, edited by Christopher Hatch and David W. Bernstein, 9–39. University of Chicago Press, 1993.

Cicero, Marcus Tullius. *De officiis.* Translated by W. Miller. London: William Heinemann, 1913.

Clark, Caryl. "Reading and Listening: Viennese Frauenzimmer Journals and the Sociocultural Context of Mozartean Opera Buffa." *Musical Quarterly* 87, no. 1 (Spring 2004): 140–75.

Clive, Peter. *Mozart and His Circle: A Biographical Dictionary.* New Haven: Yale University Press, 1993.

Cone, Edward T. *The Composer's Voice.* Berkeley: University of California Press, 1974.

"Three Ways of Reading a Detective Story – Or a Brahms Intermezzo." In *Music: A View from Delft.* Edited by Robert P. Morgan, 77–93. University of Chicago Press, 1989.

Cook, Nicholas. "Between Process and Product: Music and/as Performance." *Music Theory Online* 7, no. 2 (April 2001), www.mtosmt.org/issues/ mto.01.7.2/mto.01.7.2.cook.html.

Beyond the Score: Music as Performance. Oxford University Press, 2013.

"Prompting Performance: Text, Script, and Analysis in Bryn Harrison's *être-temps*." *Music Theory Online* 11, no. 1 (March 2005), www.mtosmt.org/ issues/mto.05.11.1/mto.05.11.1.cook_frames.html.

Cox, Arnie. "Embodying Music: Principles of the Mimetic Hypothesis." *Music Theory Online* 17, no. 2 (July 2011), www.mtosmt.org/issues/mto.11.17.2/ mto.11.17.2.cox.html.

Czerny, Carl. *Erinnerungen aus meinem Leben (1842).* Edited by Walter Kolneder. Strasbourg: Éditions P. H. Heitz, 1968.

Pianoforte-Schule, op. 500. Vienna, 1839.

Dahlhaus, Carl. "Der rhetorische Formbegriff H. Chr. Kochs und die Theorie der Sonatenform." *Archiv für Musikwissenschaft* 35, no. 3 (1978): 155–77.

Daub, Adrian. *Four-Handed Monsters: Four-Hand Piano Playing and Nineteenth-Century Culture.* Oxford University Press, 2014.

Daverio, John. *Robert Schumann: Herald of a "New Poetic Age."* Oxford University Press, 1997.

DeNora, Tia. *Beethoven and the Construction of Genius: Musical Politics in Vienna, 1792–1803.* Berkeley: University of California Press, 1995.

Deutsch, Otto Erich, ed. *Mozart. Die Dokumente seines Lebens.* Kassel: Bärenreiter, 1961. Translated by Eric Blom, Peter Branscombe, and Jeremy Noble as *Mozart: A Documentary Biography.* Stanford University Press, 1965.

Dodson, Alan. "Performance and Hypermetric Transformation: An Extension of the Lerdahl–Jackendoff Theory." *Music Theory Online* 8, no. 1 (February 2002), www.mtosmt.org/issues/mto.02.8.1/mto.02.8.1.dodson_frames.html.

Drabkin, William. "The Cello Part in Beethoven's Late Quartets." In *Beethoven Forum 7*, edited by Mark Evan Bonds, Lewis Lockwood, Christopher Reynolds, and Elaine R. Sisman, 45–66. Lincoln: University of Nebraska Press, 1999.

   A Reader's Guide to Haydn's Early String Quartets. Westport, CT: Greenwood Press, 2000.

Edge, Dexter. Review of *Concert Life in Haydn's Vienna: Aspects of a Developing Musical and Social Institution*, by Mary Sue Morrow. *Haydn Yearbook* 17 (1992): 108–66.

Einstein, Alfred. *Mozart: His Character, His Work.* Oxford University Press, 1945.

Eisen, Cliff. "Mozart's Chamber Music." In *The Cambridge Companion to Mozart*, edited by Simon P. Keefe, 105–17. Cambridge University Press, 2003.

Eisen, Cliff, ed. *New Mozart Documents: A Supplement to O. E. Deutsch's Documentary Biography.* Stanford University Press, 1991.

Ella, John. *Musical Sketches: Abroad and at Home.* 3rd ed. Revised and edited by John Belcher. London, 1878.

Fauquet, Joël-Marie. *Les sociétés de musique de chambre à Paris de la Restauration à 1870.* Paris: Aux amateurs de livres, 1986.

Fétis, François-Joseph. *Biographie universelle des musiciens.* 2nd ed. 8 vols. Paris, 1866–67.

   Review of Soirées musicales de Quatuors et de Quintetti, données par M. Baillot. *Revue Musicale (Paris)*, February 1827, 37–39.

Finscher, Ludwig. "Hausmusik und Kammermusik." In *Geschichte und Geschichten: Ausgewählte Aufsätze zur Musikhistorie*, edited by Hermann Danuser, 79–88. Mainz: Schott Musik, 2003.

   Preface to *Neue Mozart-Ausgabe* VIII/20, Abt. 1/2: *Streichquartette*, vi–xii. Kassel: Bärenreiter, 1962.

   "Streichquartett." In *Die Musik in Geschichte und Gegenwart*, edited by Ludwig Finscher, Vol. 8, cols. 1924–90. Kassel: Bärenreiter, 1998.

Studien zur Geschichte des Streichquartetts. Vol. 1, *Die Entstehung des klassischen Streichquartetts. Von den Vorformen zur Grundlegung durch Joseph Haydn.* Kassel: Bärenreiter, 1974.

Foucault, Michel. "What is an Author?" In *The Foucault Reader,* translated by Paul Rabinow, 101–20. New York: Pantheon Books, 1984.

Framery, Nicolas Etienne, Jérôme-Joseph de Momigny, Pierre Louis Ginguene, and Charles-Joseph Panckoucke, eds. *Encyclopédie méthodique: Musique.* 2 vols. Paris, 1791–1818.

Fraser, Nancy. "Rethinking the Public Sphere: A Contribution to the Critique of Actually Existing Democracy." *Social Text* 25/26 (1990): 56–80.

Frye, Northrop. *Anatomy of Criticism.* Princeton University Press, 1957.

Gagné, David. "A Dialogue among Equals: Structural Style in Mozart's 'Haydn' String Quartets." *Studi Musicali* 37, no. 2 (2008): 503–27.

Garnier-Panafieu, Michelle. "Le quatuor à cordes au temps de Mozart: trajectories et spécificités." In *Cordes et claviers au temps de Mozart,* edited by Peter Lang, 51–71. Bern: Editions Scientifiques Internationals, 2010.

Georgiades, Thrasybulos G. *Kleine Schriften.* Tutzing: Hans Schneider, 1977.

Gingerich, John M. "Ignaz Schuppanzigh and Beethoven's Late Quartets." *Musical Quarterly* 93, nos. 3–4 (2010): 450–513.

Schubert's Beethoven Project. Cambridge University Press, 2014.

Gjerdingen, Robert O. *Music in the Galant Style.* Oxford University Press, 2007.

Goehr, Lydia. *The Imaginary Museum of Musical Works: An Essay in the Philosophy of Music.* Oxford University Press, 1994.

Goethe, Johann Wolfgang von. *Briefwechsel zwischen Goethe und Zelter in den Jahren 1796 bis 1832.* 6 vols. Edited by Wilhelm Riemer. Berlin, 1833–34.

Goodhue, Elizabeth K. "When Yorick Takes His Tea; Or, the Commerce of Consumptive Passions in the Case of Laurence Sterne." *Journal for Early Modern Cultural Studies* 6, no. 1 (Spring/Summer 2006): 51–83.

Gopnik, Adam. *The Table Comes First: Family, France, and the Meaning of Food.* New York: Alfred A. Knopf, 2011.

Grave, Floyd K. "Concerto Style in Haydn's String Quartets." *Journal of Musicology* 18, no. 1 (Winter 2001): 76–97.

"Metrical Dissonance in Haydn," *Journal of Musicology* 13 (Spring 1995): 168–202.

Grave, Floyd K., and Margaret Grave. *The String Quartets of Joseph Haydn.* Oxford University Press, 2006.

Grétry, André. *Mémoires, ou Essai Sur La Musique.* 3 vols. Paris, 1789–94.

Griesinger, Georg August. *Biographische Notizen über Joseph Haydn.* Leipzig, 1810. Translated by Vernon Gotwals in *Haydn: Two Contemporary Portraits.* Madison: University of Wisconsin Press, 1968.

Griffiths, Paul. *The String Quartet.* New York: Thames and Hudson, 1983.

Grimm, Friedrich. *Correspondance littéraire.* 2nd ed. 6 vols. Paris, 1812.

Grove, George, ed. *A Dictionary of Music and Musicians*. 4 vols. London: Macmillan, 1878–89.

Guazzo, Stefano. *La civil conversazione*. Brecia, 1574.

Guck, Marion A. "Analytical Fictions." *Music Theory Spectrum* 16, no. 2 (Autumn 1994): 217–30.

Habermas, Jürgen. *Strukturwandel der Öffentlichkeit: Untersuchungen zu einer Kategorie der bürgerlichen Gesellschaft*. 2nd ed. Frankfurt: Suhrkamp Verlag, 1990. Translated by Thomas Burger as *The Structural Transformation of the Public Sphere: An Inquiry into a Category of Bourgeois Society*. Cambridge, MA: MIT Press, 1989.

Halsey, Katie, and Jane Slinn, eds. *The Concept and Practice of Conversation in the Long Eighteenth Century, 1688–1848*. Newcastle: Cambridge Scholars, 2008.

Hanning, Barbara R. "Conversation and Musical Style in the Late Eighteenth-Century Parisian Salon." *Eighteenth-Century Studies* 22, no. 4 (Summer 1989): 512–28.

Hanslick, Eduard. *Geschichte des Concertwesens in Wien*. 2 vols. Vienna, 1869.

Harlow, Martin. "The Chamber Music with Keyboard in Mozart Biography." In *Mozart's Chamber Music with Keyboard*, edited by Martin Harlow, 1–24. Cambridge University Press, 2012.

Hartley, L. P. *The Go-Between*. London: H. Hamilton, 1953.

Hasty, Christopher F. *Meter as Rhythm*. Oxford University Press, 1997.

Hatten, Robert S. *Musical Meaning in Beethoven: Markedness, Correlation, and Interpretation*. 1st paperback ed. Bloomington: Indiana University Press, 2004.

Interpreting Musical Gestures, Topics, and Tropes: Mozart, Beethoven, Schubert. Bloomington: Indiana University Press, 2004.

Hattis, Phyllis. *Four Centuries of French Drawings in the Fine Arts Museums of San Francisco*. Fine Arts Museums of San Francisco, 1977.

Hauptmann, Moritz. *Die Natur der Harmonik und der Metrik*. Leipzig, 1853.

Haydn, Franz Joseph. *Joseph Haydn: Gesammelte Briefe und Aufzeichnungen*. Edited by H. C. Robbins Landon and Dénes Bartha. Kassel: Bärenreiter, 1965.

Heartz, Daniel. *Haydn, Mozart, and Early Beethoven: 1781–1802*. New York: W. W. Norton, 2009.

Haydn, Mozart, and the Viennese School: 1740–1780. New York: W. W. Norton, 1995.

Music in European Capitals: The Galant Style, 1720–1780. New York: W. W. Norton, 2003.

Hedges, Stephen A. "Dice Music in the Eighteenth Century." *Music and Letters* 59, no. 2 (April 1978): 180–87.

Helm, Theodor. *Beethoven's Streichquartette: Versuch einer technischen Analyse dieser Werke im Zusammenhange mit ihrem geistigen Gehalt*. Leipzig, 1885.

Hepokoski, James, and Warren Darcy. *Elements of Sonata Theory: Norms, Types, and Deformations in the Late-Eighteenth Century Sonata*. Oxford University Press, 2006.

Hindemith, Paul. *A Composer's World: Horizons and Limitations*. Cambridge, MA: Harvard University Press, 1952.

Hopkinson, Cecil. "The Earliest Miniature Scores." *Music Review* 33 (1972): 138–44.

Hosler, Bellamy. *Changing Aesthetic Views of Instrumental Music in 18th-Century Germany*. Ann Arbor: UMI Research Press, 1981.

Houle, George. *Meter in Music, 1600–1800: Performance, Perception, and Notation*. Bloomington: Indiana University Press, 1987.

Hunter, Mary. "Haydn's London Piano Trios and His Salomon String Quartets: Private vs. Public?" In *Haydn and His World*, edited by Elaine Sisman, 103–30. Princeton University Press, 1997.

——— "'The Most Interesting Genre of Music': Performance, Sociability and Meaning in the Classical String Quartet, 1800–1830." *Nineteenth-Century Music Review* 9 (2012): 53–74.

——— "The Quartets." In *The Cambridge Companion to Haydn*, edited by Caryl Clark, 112–25. Cambridge University Press, 2005.

Imbrie, Andrew. "'Extra' Measures and Metrical Ambiguity in Beethoven." In *Beethoven Studies*, edited by Alan Tyson, 45–66. New York: W. W. Norton, 1973.

Irving, John. *Mozart's "Kegelstatt" Trio K. 498: An Eighteenth-Century Conversation*. London: Institute of Musical Research, School of Advanced Study, University of London, 2013. music.sas.ac.uk/music-video/denote-videos (accessed May 1, 2015).

——— "Sonatas." In *The Cambridge Mozart Encyclopedia*, edited by Cliff Eisen and Simon P. Keefe, 467–75. Cambridge University Press, 2006.

Jackendoff, Ray. "Musical Parsing and Musical Affect." *Music Perception* 9, no. 2 (Winter 1991): 199–230.

——— "Musical Processing and Musical Affect." In *Cognitive Bases of Musical Communication*, edited by Mari Riess Jones and Susan Holleran, 51–68. Washington, DC: American Psychological Association, 1992.

Jahn, Otto. *W. A. Mozart*. 4 vols. Leipzig, 1856–59.

Jander, Owen. "The 'Kreutzer' Sonata as Dialog." *Early Music* 16, no. 1 (February 1988): 34–49.

Johnson, Samuel. *Dr. Johnson's Table Talk, or Conversations of the late Samuel Johnson*. Compiled by Steven Jones. London, 1785.

Jones, David Wyn. "Beethoven and the Viennese Legacy." In *The Cambridge Companion to the String Quartet*, edited by Robin Stowell, 210–27. Cambridge University Press, 2003.

——— "Haydn and His Fellow Composers." In *The Cambridge Companion to Haydn*, edited by Caryl Clark, 45–60. Cambridge University Press, 2005.

——— "The Origins of the Quartet." In *The Cambridge Companion to the String Quartet*, edited by Robin Stowell, 177–84. Cambridge University Press, 2003.

Jones, William. *A Treatise on the Art of Music, in which the Elements of Harmony and Air Are Practically Considered.* Colchester, 1784.

Kamien, Roger. "Conflicting Metrical Patterns in Accompaniment and Melody in Works by Mozart and Beethoven: A Preliminary Study." *Journal of Music Theory* 31, no. 2 (1993): 311–48.

Keefe, Simon P. *Mozart's Piano Concertos: Dramatic Dialogue in the Age of Enlightenment.* Woodbridge: Boydell Press, 2001.

Kelly, Michael. *Reminiscences of Michael Kelly, of the King's Theatre, and Theatre Royal Drury Lane.* 2 vols. London, 1826.

Kerman, Joseph. "Beethoven Quartet Audiences: Actual, Potential, Ideal." In *The Beethoven Quartet Companion,* edited by Robert Winter and Robert Martin, 7–28. Berkeley: University of California Press, 1994.

   The Beethoven Quartets. New York: W. W. Norton, 1966.

Kirkendale, Warren. *Fugue and Fugato in Rococo and Classical Chamber Music.* Durham, NC: Duke University Press, 1979.

Kirnberger, Johann Philipp. *Die Kunst des reinen Satzes in der Musik.* 2 vols. Berlin, 1774–79. Translated by David Beach and Jürgen Thym as *The Art of Strict Musical Composition.* New Haven: Yale University Press, 1982.

Klein, Michael. "Chopin's Fourth Ballade as Musical Narrative." *Music Theory Spectrum* 26, no. 1 (Spring 2004): 23–56.

Klorman, Edward. "The First Professional String Quartet? Re-Examining an Account Attributed to Giuseppe Maria Cambini." *Notes* 71, no. 4 (June 2015): 629–43.

Knigge, Adolph. *Über den Umgang mit Menschen.* Hannover, 1788.

Koch, Heinrich Christoph. *Musikalisches Lexikon.* Frankfurt am Main, 1802.

   Versuch einer Anleitung zur Composition. 3 vols. Leipzig, 1782–93. Partially translated by Nancy Kovaleff Baker as *Introductory Essay on Composition.* New Haven: Yale University Press, 1983.

Köhler, Karl-Heinz, Grita Herre, and Günter Brosche, eds. *Ludwig van Beethovens Konversationshefte.* 11 vols. to date. Leipzig: VEB Deutscher Verlag für Musik, 1968–.

Kollmann, Augustus Frederic Christopher. *Essay on Practical Musical Composition.* London, 1799.

Komlós, Katalin. "'Ich praeludirte und spielte Variazionen': Mozart the Fortepianist." In *Perspectives on Mozart Performance,* edited by R. Larry Todd and Peter Williams, 27–54. Cambridge University Press, 1991.

   "Mozart the Performer." In *The Cambridge Companion to Mozart,* edited by Simon P. Keefe, 215–26. Cambridge University Press, 2003.

Kramer, Richard. *Unfinished Music.* Oxford University Press, 2008.

Kraus, Hedwig. "W. A. Mozart und die Familie Jacquin." *Zeitschrift für Musikwissenschaft* 15, no. 4 (January 1933): 155–68.

Krautwurst, Franz. "Felix Mendelssohn Bartholdy als Bratschist." In *Gedenkschrift Hermann Beck*, edited by Hermann Dechant and Wolfgang Sieber, 151–60. Laaber: Laaber-Verlag, 1982.

Krebs, Harald. *Fantasy Pieces: Metrical Dissonance in the Music of Robert Schumann*. Oxford University Press, 1999.

Küster, Konrad. *Mozart: A Musical Biography*. Translated by Mary Whittall. Oxford: Clarendon Press, 1996.

Landon, H. C. Robbins. *Haydn: Chronicle and Works*. 4 vols. Bloomington: Indiana University Press, 1976–80.

Langer, Anton. "Ein Abend bei Karoline Pichler." In *Allgemeine Theaterzeitung (Vienna)* 168 (July 15, 1843): 749–50.

Lawson, Colin. "A Winning Strike: The Miracle of Mozart's 'Kegelstatt.'" In *Mozart's Chamber Music with Keyboard*, edited by Martin Harlow, 123–37. Cambridge University Press, 2012.

Le Guin, Elisabeth. *Boccherini's Body: An Essay in Carnal Musicology*. Berkeley: University of California Press, 2005.

  "A Visit to the Salon Parnasse." In *Haydn and the Performance of Rhetoric*, edited by Tom Beghin and Sander M. Goldberg, 14–35. University of Chicago Press, 2007.

Lenneberg, Hans. "Revising the History of the Miniature Score." *Notes* 45, no. 2 (December 1988): 258–61.

Lenz, Wilhelm von. *Beethoven: Eine Kunst-Studie*. 5 vols. Hamburg, 1855–60.

Leppert, Richard. *Music and Image: Domesticity, Ideology, and Socio-Cultural Formation in Eighteenth-Century England*. Cambridge University Press, 1988.

Lerdahl, Fred, and Ray Jackendoff. *A Generative Theory of Tonal Music*. Cambridge, MA: MIT Press, 1983.

Lessing, Gotthold Ephraim. *G. E. Lessings gesammelte Werke*. 2 vols. Edited by Wolfgang Stammler. Munich: Carl Hanser Verlag, 1959.

Lester, Joel. "How Theorists Relate to Musicians." *Music Theory Online* 4, no. 2 (March 1998), www.mtosmt.org/issues/mto.98.4.2/mto.98.4.2.lester.html.

  "Performance and Analysis: Interaction and Interpretation." In *The Practice of Performance: Studies in Musical Interpretation*, edited by John Rink, 197–216. Cambridge University Press, 1995.

Levin, Robert D. "Performance Practice in the Music of Mozart." In *The Cambridge Companion to Mozart*, edited by Simon P. Keefe, 227–45. Cambridge University Press, 2003.

  Who Wrote the Mozart Four-Wind Concertante? Hillsdale, NY: Pendragon Press, 1988.

Levy, Janet M. "The *Quatuor Concertant* in Paris in the Latter Half of the Eighteenth Century." Ph.D. diss., Stanford University, 1971.

  "Texture as a Sign in Classic and Early Romantic Music." *Journal of the American Musicological Society* 35, no. 3 (Autumn 1982): 482–531.

Lewin, David. "Figaro's Mistakes." In *Studies in Music with Text*, 5–18. Oxford University Press, 2006.

Generalized Musical Intervals and Transformations. Oxford University Press, 2007.

"Music Theory, Phenomenology, and Modes of Perception." In *Studies in Music with Text*, 53–108. Oxford University Press, 2006.

Link, Dorothea. "Mozart's Appointment to the Viennese Court." In *Words about Mozart: Essays in Honour of Stanley Sadie*, edited by Dorothea Link with Judith Nagley, 153–78. Woodbridge: Boydell Press, 2005.

"Vienna's Private Theatrical and Musical Life, 1783–92, as Reported by Count Karl Zinzendorf." *Journal of the Royal Musical Association* 122, no. 2 (1997): 205–57.

Lockwood, Lewis, and The Juilliard String Quartet. *Inside Beethoven's Quartets: History, Interpretation, Performance*. Cambridge, MA: Harvard University Press, 2008.

London, Justin. "Loud Rests and Other Strange Metric Phenomena (or, Meter as Heard)." *Music Theory Online* 0, no. 2 (April 1993), www.mtosmt.org/issues/mto.93.0.2/mto.93.0.2.london.art.

Love, Harold. "How Music Created a Public." *Criticism* 46 (2004): 257–71.

Lowinsky, Edward. "On Mozart's Rhythm." *Musical Quarterly* 42 (1956): 162–86.

MacClintock, Carol, ed. *Readings in the History of Music in Performance*. Bloomington: Indiana University Press, 1979.

Mainka, Jürgen. "Haydns Streichquartette: 'Man hört vier vernünftige Leute sich untereinander unterhalten.'" *Musik und Gesellschaft* 32 (1982): 146–50.

Marpurg, Friedrich Wilhelm. *Abhandlung von der Fuge*. 2 vols. Berlin, 1753–54.

Marx, Adolf Bernhard. *Ludwig van Beethoven: Leben und Schaffen*. 2nd ed. 2 vols. Berlin, 1863.

Maus, Fred Everett. "Agency in Instrumental Music and Song." *College Music Symposium* 29 (1989): 31–43.

"Music as Drama." *Music Theory Spectrum* 10 (Spring 1988): 56–73.

McClelland, Ryan. "Extended Upbeats in the Classical Minuet: Interactions with Hypermeter and Phrase Structure." *Music Theory Spectrum* 28, no. 1 (2006): 23–56.

"Teaching Phrase Rhythm through Minuets from Haydn's String Quartets." *Journal of Music Theory Pedagogy* 20 (2006): 5–35.

McCreless, Patrick. "Analysis and Performance: A Counterexample?" *Dutch Journal of Music Theory* 14, no. 1 (2009): 1–16.

"Music and Rhetoric." In *Cambridge History of Western Music Theory*, edited by Thomas Christensen, 847–79. Cambridge University Press, 2002.

"The Pitch-Class Motive in Tonal Analysis: Some Critical Observations." *Res Musica* 3 (2011): 52–67.

McKee, Eric. "Extended Anacruces in Mozart's Instrumental Music." *Theory and Practice* 29 (2004): 1–37.

McLeod, John. "Rules of Games No. 5: Reversis." *Journal of the International Playing-Card Society* 5, no. 4 (May 1977): 23–30.

McVeigh, Simon. *Concert Life in London from Mozart to Haydn*. Cambridge University Press, 1993.

Merkle, Ludwig. *Bairische Grammatik*. Munich: Heimeran Verlag, 1975.

Mirka, Danuta. "Metre, Phrase Structure and Manipulations of Musical Beginnings." In *Communication in Eighteenth-Century Music*, edited by Danuta Mirka and Kofi Agawu, 83–111. Cambridge University Press, 2008.

    Metric Manipulations in Haydn and Mozart: Chamber Music for Strings, 1787–1791. Oxford University Press, 2009.

    "Topics and Meter." In *The Oxford Handbook of Topic Theory*, edited by Danuta Mirka, 357–80. Oxford University Press, 2014.

Momigny, Jérôme-Joseph de. *Cours complet d'harmonie et de composition*. 3 vols. Paris, 1806.

Monahan, Seth. "Action and Agency Revisited." *Journal of Music Theory* 57, no. 2 (Fall 2013): 321–71.

Monelle, Raymond. *The Sense of Music: Semiotic Essays*. Princeton University Press, 2000.

Morabito, Fabio. "Authorship, Performance and Musical Identity in Restoration Paris." Ph.D. diss., King's College, University of London, in progress.

Morellet, Abbé André. "De la conversation." In *Éloges de Madame Geoffrin . . . par MM. Morellet, Thomas, d'Alembert; suivis de lettres de Madame Geoffrin et à Madame Geoffrin et d'un essai sur la conversation . . . par M. Morellet*, 153–226. Paris, 1812.

Morrow, Mary Sue. *Concert Life in Haydn's Vienna: Aspects of a Developing Musical and Social Institution*. Stuyvesant, NY: Pendragon Press, 1989.

    German Music Criticism in the Late Eighteenth Century: Aesthetic Issues in Instrumental Music. Cambridge University Press, 1997.

Mozart, Konstanze. *Briefe, Aufzeichnungen, Dokumente, 1782–1842*. Edited by Arthur Schurig. Dresden: Opal-Verlag, 1922.

Mozart, Leopold. *Versuch einer gründlichen Violinschule*. Augsburg, 1756. Translated by Editha Knocker as *A Treatise on the Fundamental Principles of Violin Playing*. 2nd ed. Oxford University Press, 1951.

Mozart, Wolfgang Amadeus. *Briefe und Aufzeichnungen: Gesamtausgabe*. 7 vols. Edited by Wilhelm A. Bauer and Otto Erich Deutsch. Kassel: Bärenreiter, 1962–75.

    Mozarts Briefe. Edited by Ludwig Pohl. Salzburg, 1865.

    Mozart's Letters, Mozart's Life. Translated by Robert Spaethling. New York: W. W. Norton, 2000.

"Nachrichten. Wien." *Allgemeine musikalische Zeitung (Leipzig)* 3, no. 48 (August 26, 1801): cols. 797–800.

"Nachrichten. Wien, d. 27sten Febr." *Allgemeine musikalische Zeitung (Leipzig)* 9, no. 25 (March 18, 1807): cols. 398–400.

"Neuer Versuch einer Darstellung des gesammten Musikwesens in Wien." *Allgemeine musikalische Zeitung (Leipzig)* 3, no. 38 (June 17, 1801): cols. 638–43.

Neuwirth, Markus. "Joseph Haydn's 'Witty' Play on Hepokoski and Darcy's *Elements of Sonata Theory*." *Zeitschrift der Gesellschaft für Musiktheorie* 8, no. 1 (2011): 199–220.

Newcomb, Anthony. "Action and Agency in Mahler's Ninth Symphony, Second Movement." In *Music and Meaning*, edited by Jenefer Robinson, 131–53. Ithaca: Cornell University Press, 1997.

Nissen, Georg Nikolaus von. *Biographie W. A. Mozarts*. Leipzig, 1828.

Noguchi, Hideo. "Mozart: Musical Game in C, K. 516f." *Mitteilungen der Internationalen Stiftung Mozarteum* 38 (1990): 89–101.

Novello, Vincent, and Mary Novello. *A Mozart Pilgrimage: Being the Travel Diaries of Vincent & Mary Novello in the Year 1829*. Edited by Rosemary Hughes. 2nd ed. London: Eulenburg Books, 1975.

November, Nancy. *Beethoven's Theatrical Quartets: Opp. 59, 74, and 95*. Cambridge University Press, 2014.

"Haydn's Vocality and the Ideal of 'True' Quartets." Ph.D. diss., Cornell University, 2003.

"Theater Piece and *Cabinetstück*: Nineteenth-Century Visual Ideologies of the String Quartet." *Music in Art* 29, nos. 1–2 (Spring–Fall 2004): 134–50.

Ongley, Laurie H. "The Reconstruction of an 18th-Century Basso Group." *Early Music* 27, no. 2 (May 1999): 269–81.

Palm, Albert. *Jérôme-Joseph de Momigny: Leben und Werk*. Cologne: Arno Volk Verlag, 1969.

"Mozarts Streichquartett D-moll, KV 421, in der Interpretation Momignys." *Mozart-Jahrbuch* (1962/63): 256–79.

Panner, Daniel. "The Function of the Second Viola in the String Quintets of Wolfgang Amadeus Mozart." D.M.A. diss., City University of New York, 2003.

Parker, Mara. *The String Quartet, 1750–1797: Four Types of Conversation*. Burlington: Ashgate, 2002.

Parlett, David Sidney. *The Oxford Guide to Card Games*. Oxford University Press, 1990.

Pestelli, Giorgio. *L'età de Mozart e di Beethoven*. Revised ed. Torino: Edizioni di Torino, 1991.

P[etiscus, Johann Conrad Wilhelm]. "Ueber Quartettmusik." *Allgemeine musikalische Zeitung (Leipzig)* 12, no. 33 (May 16, 1810): cols. 513–23.

Pichler, Caroline. *Denkwürdigkeiten aus meinem Leben*. 4 vols. Vienna, 1844.

Piozzi, Hester Lynch. *Anecdotes of the Late Samuel Johnson*. Dublin, 1786.

Plantinga, Leon. "When Did Beethoven Compose His Third Piano Concerto?"
    Journal of Musicology 7, no. 3 (Summer 1989): 275–307.

Plath, Wolfgang, and Wolfgang Rehm. Preface to *Neue Mozart-Ausgabe* VIII/22/
    Abt. 2: *Klaviertrios*, vi–xv. Kassel: Bärenreiter, 1966.

Potter, Tully. "From Chamber to Concert Hall." In *The Cambridge Companion to
    the String Quartet*, edited by Robin Stowell, 41–59. Cambridge University
    Press, 2003.

Quantz, Joseph Joachim. *Versuch einer Anweisung die Flöte traversiere zu spielen.*
    Berlin, 1752. Translated by Edward R. Reilly as *On Playing the Flute.* London:
    Faber and Faber, 1985.

Ratner, Leonard G. "*Ars combinatoria*: Chance and Choice in Eighteenth-Century
    Music." In *Studies in 18th-Century Music: A Tribute to Karl Geiringer on His
    Seventieth Birthday*, edited by H. C. Robbins Landon and Roger E. Chapman,
    343–63. Oxford University Press, 1970.

    Classic Music: Expression, Form and Style. New York: Schirmer, 1980.

    "Harmonic Aspects of Classic Form." *Journal of the American Musicological
    Society* 11 (1949): 159–68.

Ratz, Erwin. *Einführung in die musikalische Formenlehre: Über Formprinzipien in
    den Inventionen und Fugen J. S. Bachs und ihre Bedeutung für die
    Kompositionstechnik Beethovens.* 3rd ed., enl. Vienna: Universal, 1973.

Reicha, Anton. *Traité de mélodie.* Paris, 1814. Translated by Peter M. Landey as
    Treatise on Melody. Hillsdale, NY: Pendragon Press, 2000.

Reichardt, Johann Friedrich. *Joh. Friedrich Reichardt: Sein Leben und seine Werke.*
    Edited by Hans Michel Schletterer. Augsburg, 1865.

    Vermischte Musikalien. Riga, 1773.

Review of Sonata in A Minor for Piano and Violin ("Kreutzer"), Op. 47, by Ludwig
    van Beethoven. *Allgemeine musikalische Zeitung (Leipzig)* 7, no. 48
    (August 28, 1805): cols. 769–72.

Richter, Joseph. *Bildergalerie weltlicher Misbräuche: ein Gegenstück zur
    Bildergalerie katholischer und klösterlicher.* Frankfurt and Leipzig, 1785.

Ridgewell, Rupert. "Artaria's Music Shop and Boccherini's Music in Viennese
    Musical Life." *Early Music* 33, no. 2 (May 2005): 179–89.

    "Biographical Myth and the Publication of Mozart's Piano Quartets." *Journal of
    the Royal Musical Association* 135, no. 1 (2010): 41–114.

Riepel, Joseph. *Anfangsgründe zur musicalischen Setzkunst.* Vol. 1, *De
    Rhythmopoeïa, oder von der Tactordnung.* Regensburg, 1752.

Riggs, Robert. "Mozart's Sonata for Piano and Violin, K. 379: Perspectives on the
    'One-Hour' Sonata." *Mozart-Jahrbuch* (1991): 708–15.

Riley, Maurice W. *The History of the Viola.* 2nd ed. 2 vols. Ann Arbor: Braun-
    Brumfield, 1980–91.

Rosen, Charles. *The Classical Style: Haydn, Mozart, Beethoven.* Expanded ed.
    New York: W. W. Norton, 1997.

    Sonata Forms. New York: W. W. Norton, 1980.

Rosenblum, Sandra P. *Performance Practices in Classic Piano Music*. Bloomington: Indiana University Press, 1988.

Rothstein, William. "Beethoven with and without 'Kunstgepräng': Metrical Ambiguity Reconsidered." In *Beethoven Forum 4*, edited by Lewis Lockwood, Christopher Reynolds, and James Webster, 165–93. Lincoln: University of Nebraska Press, 1995.

"Clash of the Titans: What to do when Tovey and Schnabel Disagree about Hypermeter in Beethoven's Piano Sonatas." Paper presented at the Music Theory Society of New York State and the New England Conference of Music Theorists, New Haven, CT, April 26, 2003.

"Hypermeter Reconsidered." Paper presented to the Society for Music Theory, New Orleans, LA, November 1, 2012.

"Metrical Theory and Verdi's Midcentury Operas." *Dutch Journal of Music Theory* 16, no. 2 (2010): 93–111.

"National Metrical Types in the Music of the Eighteenth and Early Nineteenth Centuries." In *Communication in Eighteenth-Century Music*, edited by Danuta Mirka and Kofi Agawu, 112–59. Cambridge University Press, 2008.

"On Implied Tones." *Music Analysis* 10, no. 3 (October 1991): 289–328.

Phrase Rhythm in Tonal Music. New York: Schirmer, 1989.

"Rhythm and the Theory of Structural Levels." Ph.D. diss., Yale University, 1981.

Rousseau, Jean-Jacques. *Dictionnaire de Musique*. Paris, 1768.

Sadie, Stanley. *Mozart: The Early Years, 1756–1781*. Oxford University Press, 2006.

Safire, William. "On Language: Sprezzatura." *New York Times Magazine*, October 27, 2002, www.nytimes.com/2002/10/27/magazine/27ONLANGUAGE.html (accessed May 1, 2015).

Saloman, Ora Frishberg. *Listening Well: On Beethoven, Berlioz, and Other Music Criticism in Paris, Boston, and New York, 1764–1890*. New York: Peter Lang, 2009.

Salzer, Felix, and Carl Schachter. *Counterpoint in Composition*. 2nd ed. New York: Columbia University Press, 1989.

Samarotto, Frank. "Strange Dimensions: Regularity and Irregularity in Deep Levels of Rhythmic Reduction." In *Schenker Studies 2*, edited by Carl Schachter and Hedi Siegel, 222–38. Cambridge University Press, 1999.

Sauzay, Eugène, and Brigitte François-Sappey. "La vie musicale a Paris a travers les *Mémoires* d'Eugène Sauzay (1809–1901)." *Revue de Musicologie* 60, nos. 1–2 (1974): 159–210.

Schachter, Carl. "The Adventures of an F-Sharp: Tonal Narration and Exhortation in Donna Anna's First-Act Recitative and Aria." *Theory and Practice* 16 (1991): 5–20.

"Rhythm and Linear Analysis: A Preliminary Study." *Music Forum* 4 (1976): 281–334.

"Rhythm and Linear Analysis: Aspects of Meter." *Music Forum* 6 (1987): 1–59.

"Rhythm and Linear Analysis: Durational Reduction." *Music Forum* 5 (1980): 197–232.

Unfoldings: Essays in Schenkerian Theory and Analysis. Edited by Joseph N. Straus. Oxford University Press, 1999.

Schenker, Heinrich. *Das Meisterwerk in der Musik.* 3 vols. Munich: Drei Masken Verlag, 1925–30. Translated by William Drabkin et al. as *The Masterwork in Music.* 3 vols. Cambridge University Press, 1994–97.

Der freie Satz. 2 vols. Vienna: Universal Edition, 1935. Translated by Ernst Oster as *Free Composition.* New York: Longman, 1979.

Schindler, Anton. *Biographie von Ludwig van Beethoven.* Münster, 1840. Translated by Ignaz Moscheles as *The Life of Beethoven.* 2 vols. London, 1841.

Schletterer, Hans Michel, ed. *Joh. Friedrich Reichardt: Sein Leben und seine Werke.* Augsburg, 1865.

Schmalfeldt, Janet. "Cadential Processes: The Evaded Cadence and the 'One More Time' Technique." *Journal of Musicological Research* 12 (1992): 1–52.

"Form as the Process of Becoming: The Beethoven-Hegelian Tradition and the Tempest Sonata." In *Beethoven Forum 4,* edited by Lewis Lockwood, Christopher Reynolds, and James Webster, 37–71. Lincoln: University of Nebraska Press, 1995.

In the Process of Becoming: Analytic and Philosophical Perspectives on Form in Early Nineteenth-Century Music. Oxford University Press, 2011.

Schmid, Ernst Fritz. "Mozart and Haydn." *Musical Quarterly* 42, no. 2 (April 1956): 145–61.

Schönfeld, Johann Ferdinand von. *Jahrbuch der Tonkunst von Wien und Prag.* Vienna, 1796. Partially translated by Kathrine Talbot as "A Yearbook of Music in Vienna and Prague, 1796." In *Haydn and His World,* edited by Elaine Sisman, 289–320. Princeton University Press, 1997.

Schroeder, David P. "The Art of Conversation: From Haydn to Beethoven's Early String Quartets." *Studies in Music from University of Western Ontario* 19–20 (2000–1): 377–8.

Haydn and the Enlightenment: The Late Symphonies and Their Audience. Oxford: Clarendon Press, 1990.

"Mozart and Late Eighteenth-Century Aesthetics." In *The Cambridge Companion to Mozart,* edited by Simon P. Keefe, 48–60. Cambridge University Press, 2003.

Mozart in Revolt: Strategies of Resistance, Mischief and Deception. Bath Press, 1999.

Schumann, Robert. *Gesammelte Schriften über Musik und Musiker.* 5th ed. 2 vols. Edited by Martin Kreisig. Leipzig: Breitkopf & Härtel, 1914.

Sisman, Elaine. *Haydn and His World.* Princeton University Press, 1997.

"Haydn's Career and the Multiple Audience." In *The Cambridge Companion to Haydn,* edited by Caryl Clark, 3–16. Cambridge University Press, 2005.

Mozart: The "Jupiter" Symphony, No. 41 in C Major, K. 551. Cambridge Music Handbooks. Cambridge University Press, 1993.

"Rhetorical Truth in Haydn's Chamber Music: Genre, Tertiary Rhetoric, and the Quartets." In *Haydn and the Performance of Rhetoric*, edited by Tom Beghin and Sander M. Goldberg, 281–326. University of Chicago Press, 2007.

Sivan, Noam. "Improvisation in Western Art Music: Its Relevance Today." D.M.A. diss., The Juilliard School, 2010.

Small, Christopher. *Musicking*. Middletown, CT: Wesleyan University Press, 1998.

Staël, Anne-Louise-Germaine de. *De l'Allemagne*. 3 vols. Paris, 1813. Translated by O. W. Wight as *Germany*. 2 vols. New York, 1861.

Steblin, Rita Katherine. *Key Characteristics in the Eighteenth and Early Nineteenth Centuries*. 2nd ed. University of Rochester Press, 2002.

Stendhal [Marie-Henri Beyle]. *Lettres écrites de Vienne en Autriche, sur le célèbre compositeur Jh. Haydn*. Paris, 1814. Translated by Richard N. Coe as *Lives of Haydn, Mozart and Metastasio*. London: Calder & Boyars, 1972.

Sterne, Laurence. *A Sentimental Journey through France and Italy by Mr. Yorick*. 2 vols. London, 1768.

Stowell, Robin. *Violin Technique and Performance Practice in the Late Eighteenth and Early Nineteenth Centuries*. Cambridge University Press, 1985.

Strebel, Harald. "Mozarts 'Kegelstatt'-Trio in Es-Dur KV 498 und seine Besetzung." *Mozart-Studien* 15 (2006): 165–78.

Sulzer, Johann Georg, ed. *Allgemeine Theorie der schönen Künste*. 4 vols. Leipzig, 1771–74.

Sulzer, Johann Georg, and Heinrich Christoph Koch. *Aesthetics and the Art of Musical Composition: Selected Writings of Johann Georg Sulzer and Heinrich Christoph Koch*. Edited by Nancy Baker and Thomas Christensen. Cambridge University Press, 1996.

Sutcliffe, W. Dean. "Haydn, Mozart and Their Contemporaries." In *The Cambridge Companion to the String Quartet*, edited by Robin Stowell, 185–209. Cambridge University Press, 2003.

Haydn String Quartets Op. 50. Cambridge Music Handbooks. Cambridge University Press, 1992.

"The Keyboard Music." In *The Cambridge Companion to Mozart*, edited by Simon P. Keefe, 61–77. Cambridge University Press, 2003.

"The Shapes of Sociability in the Instrumental Music of the Later Eighteenth Century." *Journal of the Royal Musical Association* 138, no. 1 (2013): 1–45.

Tarasti, Eero. *A Theory of Musical Semiotics*. Bloomington: Indiana University Press, 1994.

Taruskin, Richard. *Text and Act: Essays on Music and Performance*. Oxford University Press, 1995.

Tchaikovsky, Piotr Ilyich. *Letters to his Family: An Autobiography*. Translated by Galina von Meck. New York: Stein and Day, 1981.

Temperley, David. *The Cognition of Basic Musical Structures*. Cambridge, MA: MIT Press, 2001.

"End-Accented Phrases: An Analytical Exploration." *Journal of Music Theory* 47, no. 1 (2003): 125–54.

"Hypermetrical Transitions." *Music Theory Spectrum* 30, no. 2 (2008): 305–25.

Tetzel, Eugen. "Der Große Takt." *Zeitschrift für Musikwissenschaft* 3 (1920–21): 605–15.

Traeg, Johann. "Nachricht an die Musikliebhaber." *Wiener Zeitung* 16 (February 25, 1784): 395–96.

Treitler, Leo, ed. *Strunk's Source Readings in Music History*. Revised ed. New York: W. W. Norton, 1998.

Trimpert, Dieter Lutz. *Die Quatuors concertants von Giuseppe Cambini*. Tutzing: Hans Schneider, 1967.

Trotti de la Chétardie, Joachim. *Instructions pour un jeune seigneur*. 2 vols. Paris, 1684.

Tucker, Patrick. *Secrets of Acting Shakespeare: The Original Approach*. New York: Routledge, 2002.

Türk, Daniel Gottlob. *Klavierschule*. Leipzig, 1789. Translated by Raymond H. Haggh as *School of Clavier Playing*. Lincoln: University of Nebraska Press, 1982.

Tyson, Alan. *Mozart: Studies of the Autograph Scores*. Cambridge, MA: Harvard University Press, 1987.

"Über den jetzigen Musikzustand in Venedigs." *Allgemeine musikalische Zeitung (Vienna)* 1, no. 14 (April 3, 1817): cols. 105–9.

"Ueber die neueste Favorit-Musik in großen Concerten, sonderlich in Rücksicht auf Damen-Kunst, in Clavier-Liebhaberey." *Journal des Luxus und der Moden (Weimar)*, (June 1788): 230–35.

Vayer, François la Mothe. *Opuscules, ou petits traictez*. Paris, 1643–44.

Vial, Stephanie D. *The Art of Musical Phrasing in the Eighteenth Century*. University of Rochester Press, 2008.

Wakin, Daniel J. "Bytes and Beethoven: Borromeo String Quartet and the Digital Tide." *New York Times*, January 14, 2011, www.nytimes.com/2011/01/16/arts/music/16string.html (accessed May 1, 2015).

Walter, Horst. "Zum Wiener Streichquartett der Jahre 1780 bis 1800." *Haydn-Studien* 7, nos. 3–4 (February 1998): 289–314.

Walthew, Richard Henry. *The Development of Chamber Music*. London: Boosey and Hawkes, 1909.

Waterman, David. "Playing Quartets: A View from the Inside." In *The Cambridge Companion to the String Quartet*, edited by Robin Stowell, 97–126. Cambridge University Press, 2003.

Weber, William. "Did People Listen in the 18th Century?" *Early Music* 25, no. 4 (November 1997): 678–91.

Webster, James. "The Bass Part in Haydn's Early String Quartets." *Musical Quarterly* 63, no. 3 (July 1977): 390–424.

"The Eighteenth Century as a Music-Historical Period?" *Eighteenth-Century Music* 1, no. 1 (March 2004): 47–60.

"Haydn's Aesthetics." In *The Cambridge Companion to Haydn*, edited by Caryl Clark, 30–44. Cambridge University Press, 2005.

Haydn's "Farewell" Symphony and the Idea of Classical Style: Through-Composition and Cyclic Integration in His Instrumental Music. Cambridge University Press, 1991.

"The Rhetoric of Improvisation in Haydn's Keyboard Music." In *Haydn and the Performance of Rhetoric*, edited by Tom Beghin and Sander M. Goldberg, 172–212. University of Chicago Press, 2007.

"Towards a History of Viennese Chamber Music in the Early Classical Period." *Journal of the American Musicological Society* 27 (1974): 212–47.

"Violoncello and Double Bass in the Chamber Music of Haydn and His Viennese Contemporaries, 1750–1780." *Journal of the American Musicological Society* 29, no. 3 (Autumn 1976): 413–38.

Webster, James, and George Feder. *The New Grove Haydn.* New York: Macmillan, 2002.

Wegeler, Franz Gerhard, and Ferdinand Ries. *Biographische Notizen über Ludwig van Beethoven.* Edited by Alfred Christlieb Kalischer. Berlin: Schuster & Loeffler, 1906.

Weingust, Don. *Acting from Shakespeare's First Folio: Theory, Text and Performance.* New York: Routledge, 2006.

Weinmann, Alexander. *Johann Traeg: Die Musikalienverzeichnisse von 1799 und 1804.* Vienna: Universal Edition, 1973.

Wheelock, Gretchen A. *Haydn's Ingenious Jesting with Art: Contexts of Musical Wit and Humor.* New York: Schirmer, 1992.

"The 'Rhetorical Pause' and Metaphors of Conversation in Haydn's Quartets." In *Haydn und das Streichquartet. Eisenstädter Haydn-Berichte 2*, edited by Georg Feder and Walter Reicher, 67–88. Tutzing: Hans Schneider, 2003.

"*Schwarze Gredel* and the Engendered Minor Mode in Mozart's Operas." In *Musicology and Difference: Gender and Sexuality in Music Scholarship*, edited by Ruth A. Solie, 201–21. Berkeley: University of California Press, 1992.

White, Chappell, Jean Gribenski, and Amzie D. Parcell. "Cambini, Giuseppe Maria." In *The New Grove Dictionary*, edited by Stanley Sadie. Vol. 3, 639–41. 2nd ed. London: Macmillan, 1980.

"Wien, Anfang des Mays." *Allgemeine musikalische Zeitung (Leipzig)* 7, no. 33 (May 15, 1805): cols. 532–37.

Will, Richard. "When God Met the Sinner, and Other Dramatic Confrontations." *Music and Letters* 78, no. 2 (May 1997): 176–209.

Willner, Channan. "Sequential Expansion and Handelian Phrase Rhythm." In *Schenker Studies 2*, edited by Carl Schachter and Hedi Siegel, 192–221. Cambridge University Press, 1999.

Wilson, Andrew. "Meter in the Sarabande: Equal or Unequal, Consonant or Dissonant?" Paper presented at the Society for Music Theory, Milwaukee, WI, November; 7, 2014.

Wondrich, David. *Punch: The Delights (and Dangers) of the Flowing Bowl.* New York: Perigree Trade, 2010.

Woodfield, Ian. "Mozart's Compositional Methods: Writing for His Singers." In *The Cambridge Companion to Mozart*, edited by Simon P. Keefe, 35–47. Cambridge University Press, 2003.

Zaslaw, Neal. "The Breitkopf Firm's Relations with Leopold and Wolfgang Mozart." In *Bach Perspectives 2: J. S. Bach, the Breitkopfs, and the Eighteenth-Century Music Trade*, edited by George B. Stauffer, 85–103. Lincoln: University of Nebraska Press, 1996.

Zaslaw, Neal, and William Cowdery, eds. *The Compleat Mozart.* New York: W. W. Norton, 1990.

Z[elter, Carl Friedrich]. "Bescheidene Anfragen an die modernsten Komponisten und Virtuosen." *Allgemeine musikalische Zeitung (Leipzig)* 1, no. 10 (December 5, 1798): cols. 152–55.

Zuckerkandl, Victor. *The Sense of Music.* Princeton University Press, 1959.
Sound and Symbol. Translated by Willard R. Trask. New York: Pantheon Books, 1956.

Index

Aartman, Nicolaes, *Interior with a Musical Gathering*, 6–9
Abrams, M. H., 297
accompagnemens, 60–62, 69, 141. *See also* Momigny, Jérôme-Joseph de
actor. *See* theater (as metaphor for musical performance)
agency. *See* Cone, Edward T.; Monahan, Seth; multiple agency
Akademie, 87 n. 45. *See also* chamber music; string quartet
Albrechtsberger, Johann Georg, 12–13
Almén, Byron, 123 n. 22, 296 n. 18
analysis
  historicism and presentism in, 292–95
  inside vs. outside perspectives for, 135–36, 290
  in-time vs. end-state perspectives for, 133 n. 53, 156, 202–4, 220, 243
  and musical workhood, xvii–xviii, xxii–xxiii, 133, 156–57, 290
audience. *See* listeners

Bach, Carl Philipp Emanuel, *works*
  H. 537–39, Quartets for Keyboard, Flute, and Viola, 152 n. 73
  H. 579, Trio Sonata in C Minor ("Melancholicus and Sangiuneus"), 26–28
Bach, Johann Christian, 27 n. 20
Bach, Johann Sebastian, *works*
  B.W.V. 849, Fugue in C♯ Minor from *The Well-Tempered Clavier*, Book 1, 209–10
Bacon, Francis, 24
Baillot, Pierre, 48–52, 58, 59 n. 80, 76
Bakulina, Olga (Ellen), 72 n. 103, 296 n. 20
Bashford, Christina, 4, 9, 77
Beethoven, Ludwig van
  concert performances of his quartets, 50 n. 64, 51, 75–77
  critical reception of his chamber music, 76 n. 10, 77 n. 15, 85 n. 40

description of Mozart's keyboard playing, 236 n. 63
distribution of roles among parts, 50 n. 64, 152 n. 74
premiere of Piano Concerto No. 3, 104 n. 92
rehearsals of his chamber music, 73, 77 n. 15, 79, 85 n. 40
and the Schuppanzigh Quartet, 73, 75, 76 n. 13, 78–79
transformation of the string quartet, 76 n. 12, 78–80
Beethoven, Ludwig van, *works*
  op. 2, no. 1, Piano Sonata in F Minor, 250 n. 86
  op. 14, Piano Sonatas, 152 n. 74
  op. 18, no. 4, String Quartet in C Minor, 231
  op. 47, Sonata for Piano and Violin in A Minor ("Kreutzer"), 85 n. 40
  op. 95, String Quartet in F Minor ("Serioso"), 79
  WoO 10, no. 2, Minuet in G Major for Piano, 245 n. 79
Beghin, Tom, 106 n. 95, 292 n. 10
Berger, Karol, 167 n. 28
Berlioz, Hector, 46 n. 54, 50 n. 64
Boccherini, Luigi, 22, 51, 76, 81–84
Brahms, Johannes, 35 n. 38, 272 n. 16
Brahms, Johannes, *works*
  op. 120, no. 2, Sonata in E♭ Major for Piano and Clarinet, 215–20
Burke, Peter, 23 n. 8, 40 n. 48, 107 n. 99, 114–15, 122 n. 20, 126
Burney, Charles, 27 n. 20, 271 n. 14
Burney, Susan, 94–95
Busoni, Feruccio, 104

cadence
  abandoned, 187
  deceptive, 138–41, 144–48, 172–73, 283
  expanded cadential progression, 144 n. 69, 152, 164, 173, 175

CPSIA information can be obtained
at www.ICGtesting.com
Printed in the USA
LVHW04s1618120518
576992LV00008B/18/P